HOLMAN ILLUSTRATED POCKET BIBLE HANDBOOK

POCKET REFERENCE EDITION

HOLMAN
REFERENCE

NASHVILLE, TENNESSEE

Holman Illustrated Pocket Bible Handbook
© 2004 by Holman Bible Publishers
Nashville, Tennnessee
All rights reserved

Maps © 2000 by Holman Bible Publishers
Nashville, Tennessee
All rights reserved

ISBN 978-1-5864-0313-3

Dewey Decimal Classification: 220.02
Subject Heading: BIBLE—STUDY

The Holman Editorial Staff gratefully acknowledges the contribution of Dr. James McLemore and the staff of *Biblical Illustrator* for consultation on the *Holman Pocket Bible Handbook*. Many of the visual resources contained herein are from the archives of the *Biblical Illustrator*. For additional information about the *Biblical Illustrator* go to the following Web address: *www.lifeway.com* and then do a search on **Biblical Illustrator**.

Unless otherwise indicated, all Scripture passages are taken from the King James Version of the Bible.

Scripture passages marked HCSB are taken from the Holman Christian Standard Bible®, copyright © 1999, 2001, 2002, 2004 by Holman Bible Publishers. All rights reserved.

Scripture passages marked NLT are taken from the *Holy Bible*, New Living Translation, copyright © 1996. Used by permission of Tyndale House Publishers, Inc., Wheaton, Illinois 60189. All rights reserved.

Printed in China.
1 2 3 4 5 6 7 8 • 12 11 10 09 08 07
DBS

INTRODUCTION

The Bible is both a book—the world's best-selling book—and a library of sixty-six books. The impact of the Bible on Western civilization is enough to spark anyone's curiosity about its content.

Victor Hugo, author of *Les Miserables*, observed, "England has two books, the Bible and Shakespeare. England made Shakespeare, but the Bible made England."

Immanuel Kant, one of the world's most influential philosophers, said, "The Bible is the greatest benefit which the human race has ever experienced. . . . A single line in the Bible has consoled me more than all the books I ever read besides."

President John Quincy Adams treated the Bible as the key education resource in the lives of his children: "So great is my veneration for the Bible that the earlier my children begin to read it, the more confident will be my hope that they will prove useful citizens to their country and respectable members of society."

A number of years ago 1,200 university presidents and 1,000 CEOs were asked to name the book that had most affected their lives. The Bible was by far the most influential book in this survey of leaders. One in four listed the Bible as the most important book in their lives. The second book on the list— Charles Dickens' *A Tale of Two Cities*—was named as the most influential book by one in twenty-five.

In their classic, *How to Read a Book*, Mortimer Adler and Charles Van Doren noted, "It would be true to say that, in the European tradition at least, the Bible is the book in more sense than one. It has been not only the most widely read, but also the most carefully read, book of all."

The *Holman Illustrated Pocket Bible Handbook* is designed for those just beginning their study of this amazing book. The Bible is daunting just because of its size. More than that, it was written in times and cultures very different from our own. We are all like the Ethiopian treasurer, riding along in his chariot reading the prophet Isaiah. Philip approached him and asked, "Do you understand what you're reading?" He replied, "How can I . . . unless someone guides me?" (Acts 8:30-31 HCSB).

The *Handbook* walks with you through the Bible—book by book—and provides a concise overview of each book beginning with the following headings:

▶ **Key Bible Text:** a verse that gives a clue to the meaning of the book

▶ **Key Term:** summarizes the book in one word

▶ **One-Sentence Summary:** shows how this particular book relates to God's Story.

Fuller explanation of this summary is found in the section **GOD'S STORY.**

The *Handbook* then looks at how that particular book of the Bible contributes to and shapes a Christian's worldview. Twelve themes that make up a **Christian Worldview** are as follows: *God, creation, sovereignty and providence, faith and reason, revelation and authority, humanity, rebellion and sin, covenant and redemption, community and church, discipleship, ethics and morality,* and *time and eternity.*

For each book the *Handbook* indicates which of those themes are present in significant ways. It then addresses the questions of **Author and Date of Writing, First Audience and Destination**, and the **Occasion** that prompted its being written.

The sixty-six books of the Bible are made up of numerous genres. Knowing the type of literature of a particular text is an important step in interpreting the Bible. The *Handbook* addresses the **Literary Genres** of each book.

The great reformer, Martin Luther, found Christ in the Scriptures, first in Romans and then in the Psalms. As a result he came to the view that the center of all Scripture is Christ. "The Scriptures begin very gently, and lead us on to Christ as a man, and then to one who is Lord over all creatures, and after that to one who is God. So do I enter delightfully and learn to know God." Following Luther's cue, each chapter in the *Handbook* has a feature called:

CHRIST IN . . .

While the *Holman Illustrated Pocket Bible Handbook* is designed for those who are just beginning their journey with the Bible, it will serve well those who have considerable experience with this book. Pastors and experienced Bible teachers will be acquainted with much of the material in this book, but the way the material is configured may provide new perspectives as they teach and preach.

At the beginning of our journey with the Bible, it's helpful to summarize, to compress a lot of information into some bite-size statements. In fact, we can summarize the entire Bible in the following sentence:

The Lord God through his Christ
is graciously building a kingdom of redeemed people
for their joy and for his own glory.

Notice that there is one subject (*the Lord God*—it's his story) and one agent (*Christ*—the one actively bringing about God's story). There is one major activity (*building a kingdom*, the main theme of Scripture) and one object of that activity (*redeemed people*, the center of God's mighty acts in both Testaments). There are also specific goals for God's story (*their joy*—the human goal; *his own glory*—the ultimate divine end for everything). When we keep this central truth before us, everything in Scripture falls into place as a development of this single concept. This is not just a story that you read about and put the book down. It's a story in which you are a participant. That's exciting!

Think of the biblical narrative as something like a modern novel. There is a *prologue*, giving background information that helps make sense of the plot. Then there is the plot development in a number of chapters. In the biblical narrative the story develops in *six chapters* that take the account from beginning to culmination. Then finally at the end is an *epilogue*, telling what happens after the main story has ended.

PROLOGUE: THE NEED FOR REDEMPTION
(Genesis 1–11)
It all begins by explaining why the story must be told. God is building a kingdom of redeemed people because human beings are rebels who cannot save themselves. Other religions begin by assuming that people can do enough good works or perform enough religious deeds to earn a place in heaven. The Bible starts by telling the opposite story. Genesis 1–11 belongs to real human history, but the events are almost impossible to date. The main thing about the prologue is that it describes events involving the entire human race and shows that mankind has rebelled against God since the beginning.

CHAPTER 1: GOD BUILDS HIS NATION
Israel Chosen as the People of Promise, c. 2000–931 BC
(Genesis 12–1 Kings 11)
The first chapter in God's plan to build an everlasting kingdom was to build an earthly nation in a particular time and place. This chapter carries the plot from the first family he called to his covenant (Abraham and Sarah) to the full splendor of the Israelite nation at its grandest expression (under David and Solomon).

CHAPTER 2: GOD EDUCATES HIS NATION
Disobedient Israel Disciplined, c. 931–586 BC
(1 Kings 12–2 Kings 25; Some Prophets)
The second chapter in God's plan was to educate Israel about the consequences of sin.

The Israelites compromised by worshipping other gods during the entire time they were in the land. God raised his spokesmen the prophets to urge people to repent of idolatry and injustice, to warn of the coming "day of the LORD" in judgment. They also predicted the coming of the Messiah. Their message was largely ignored. This chapter carries the plot from the division of the nation (because of sin) to its destruction (because of sin).

CHAPTER 3: GOD KEEPS A FAITHFUL REMNANT

Messiah's Space and Time Prepared, c. 586–6 BC
(Ezra through Esther; Some Prophets)
Chapter 3 in God's story is the "quiet chapter." Outwardly, it appeared that God was doing nothing for more than five centuries. For those who read the story carefully, however, he was doing two important things. On one hand, God was keeping the Jews together as a nation. They had their own land, laws, and temple, even though the kingship and national independence had disappeared. God was preparing to send his Son "in the fullness of time." On the other hand, God scattered most Jews throughout the nations to be testimonies to his name. By building synagogues to preserve their religious and ethnic identity, these Jews were often the starting point for proclaiming the message that the promised Messiah had come. This chapter carries the plot from the Babylonian captivity until the birth of the Messiah.

CHAPTER 4: GOD PURCHASES REDEMPTION AND BEGINS THE KINGDOM

Jesus the Messiah, 6 BC–AD 30
(Matthew, Mark, Luke, and John)
The fourth chapter in God's plan to build an everlasting kingdom of redeemed people is the most important one of all—the four Gospels. It shows how God's unconditional covenant promises—first to Abraham, then to David—were fulfilled by the new covenant of Jesus. This chapter carries the plot from the birth of the Messiah to his resurrection and exaltation.

CHAPTER 5: GOD SPREADS THE KINGDOM THROUGH THE CHURCH

The Current Age, AD 30–?
(Acts and the Epistles)
With chapter 5 in God's story, we come to our own part of the story. We belong here. This is the period of the Great Commission, when God's plan no longer focuses on persons of one ethnic group in one place (Israel). He is now redeeming persons out of every ethnic group in every place. Wherever and whenever God's people are, they meet as churches, worshipping

communities of the new covenant. From Pentecost until the end-time scenario unfolds, God is about the business of spreading the message of the kingdom through the church.

CHAPTER 6: GOD CONSUMMATES REDEMPTION AND CONFIRMS HIS ETERNAL KINGDOM

(Revelation 1–20; Other Scriptures)

In chapter 6 God's plan to build an everlasting kingdom of redeemed people through his Christ for their joy and for his own glory is fully realized. Although students often disagree in interpreting the details of this chapter, the main points are clear. There will be violent hostility against God's people in the end times. Yet God will prevail through the personal, bodily, glorious return of Jesus. When he returns, the world's kingdoms will become the kingdom of Christ forever under his visible rule. This chapter carries the plot from the opening of "the day of the LORD" to the final judgment.

EPILOGUE: NEW HEAVEN AND NEW EARTH

(Revelation 21–22)

The kingdom of God will last forever. God's people will be filled with everlasting joy. God's glory will be magnified as his redeemed people fully enjoy him forever, without any taint of evil. This is visualized in the last two chapters of Revelation that describe a new heaven and a new earth. The people of God are compared to a great and glorious city, as well as to a wonderful bride. God's servants will reign with him forever and ever, and they will serve him gladly, fully beholding his face. The epilogue to God's story shows a brief glimpse of the glory that will be. The end of the story in time is only the beginning of the story in eternity, for *the Lord God through his Christ has graciously built a kingdom of redeemed people for their joy and for his own glory.*

May this book provide a growing understanding of the Bible and help you experience the abundant Life it reveals.

OVERALL CHRONOLOGY FOR "GOD'S KINGDOM THROUGH TIME"

2000 — Abraham

← 2091–931 BC
GOD BUILDS HIS NATION

1600

— Moses

1200

— David

← 931–586 BC
GOD EDUCATES HIS NATION

800

— Ezra

← 586–6 BC
GOD KEEPS A FAITHFUL REMNANT

400

B.C./A.D. — Jesus

← 6 BC–AD 30
GOD PURCHASES REDEMPTION AND BEGINS THE KINGDOM

400 — Augustine

AD 30–?
GOD SPREADS THE KINGDOM THROUGH THE CHURCH

800

— Medieval Period

?–?
GOD CONSUMMATES HIS ETERNAL KINGDOM

1200

1600 — Reformation

2000

2400

TABLE OF CONTENTS

GENESIS

THE FIRST BOOK OF MOSES

The English title is based on the name given by the Greek translators of this book in the second century BC. The name could be translated "source" or "generation." The original Hebrew title is simply the first word of the book, Bereshith, "In the Beginning."

▶ *Key Verses: 1:1 and 12:3*

"In the beginning God created the heaven and the earth."
"And I will bless them that bless thee, and curse him that curseth thee: and in thee shall all families of the earth be blessed."

▶ *Key Word: "Beginning"*

This book tells the beginning of many things: the creation of the world, the origin of the human race and marriage, the rise of sin and death. The book also shows the beginning of God's glorious plan to build a kingdom of redeemed people.

▶ *In Short*

The God who created mankind and punished disobedience with death began his great plan of redemption with his covenant to Abraham, whose descendants arrived in Egypt as God's cherished people.

◀ Haran, an important city of northern Mesopotamia. Abraham lived here before going to Canaan (Gen. 11:31).

11

GOD'S MESSAGE IN THE BOOK

Purpose

Genesis lays the historical and theological foundation for the rest of the Bible. If the Bible is the story of God's redemption of his people, Genesis 1–11 tells why redemption is necessary: humans are rebels, unable to redeem themselves. Further, Genesis 12–50 shows the steps God initiated to establish a redeemed people and to make a way for the Redeemer to come. He did this through his unconditional covenant with Abraham, Isaac, and Jacob, and with his providential care through Joseph's life. God's people who study Genesis today should view it with this original purpose in mind.

Christian Worldview Elements

Genesis deals particularly with the worldview categories of *God; creation; humanity; rebellion and sin;* and *covenant and redemption.* No Bible book more fully teaches God as Creator and humanity as sinners who cannot save themselves.

> ► **GOD**
> ► **CREATION**
> SOVEREIGNTY AND PROVIDENCE
> FAITH AND REASON
> REVELATION AND AUTHORITY
> ► **HUMANITY**
> ► **REBELLION AND SIN**
> ► **COVENANT AND REDEMPTION**
> COMMUNITY AND CHURCH
> DISCIPLESHIP
> ETHICS AND MORALITY
> TIME AND ETERNITY

Teachings about God

Genesis reveals God first as Creator. He is righteous in his commands, and he judges when mankind disobeys him. Genesis further reveals God as the one who makes his covenant with undeserving people (see Gen. 15). The first promise of Christ is given in Genesis 3:15; the Spirit of God is mentioned in Genesis 1:2 and 6:3.

Teachings about Humanity

Genesis shows the glory of humanity by emphasizing that mankind alone of all creation was made in "the image of God." On the other hand Genesis shows the shame of humanity by recounting three incidents involving the whole race: the fall, the flood, and Babel. All three events portray humans as sinners in need of a Savior.

Teachings about Salvation

Genesis introduces critical truths about salvation developed in later parts of Scripture. In particular, the incident of the death of a ram instead of Isaac points to a substitutionary understanding of sacrifice. Further, the New Testament makes much of Abraham as a pattern of salvation for all the redeemed: "And he believed in the LORD; and he counted it to him for righteousness" (Gen. 15:6). Genesis 12–50 shows the beginning of his covenant people.

CHRIST IN GENESIS

Creation is the first theme of Genesis, and Christ is the agent of creation. *"By Him everything was created"* (Col. 1:16 HCSB). Christ as Redeemer is first promised in Genesis 3:15. When God commanded Abraham to offer Isaac as a sacrifice, he provided a substitute for Isaac (Gen. 22:8) in the same way he provided Christ as our substitute through his sacrificial death. Through Abraham's seed, Jesus Christ, all families of the earth will be blessed.

GOD'S STORY

When the Events of This Book Happened
From creation until Joseph's death (about 1805 BC)

There is insufficient information to date the events of Genesis 1–11. Using the traditional early date for the exodus, Abraham's birth in Ur was around 2166 BC and Joseph's death in Egypt was about 1805 BC, an amazing total of some 360 years for four generations. (This was the time of the First Dynasty of Babylon in Mesopotamia and of the Middle Kingdom in Egypt. The Bronze Age had developed by the end of Genesis.)

2166 BC	2066	2006	1915	1805
Abraham born	Isaac born	Jacob & Esau born	Joseph born	Joseph dies

How Genesis Fits into God's "Story"

Genesis shows why redemption is needed and presents the first steps in God's bringing a people into right relationship with him. The beginning of God's plan is to bless all nations through the covenant he began with Abraham. Initially, that plan focused on Abraham's biological descendants, reaching its geographical zenith during the kingdom of David and Solomon. The greatest descendant of Abraham is Jesus, who inaugurated the kingdom of God at his first coming and will consummate it at his second coming.

ORIGINAL HISTORICAL SETTING

Author and Date of Writing
Moses, perhaps around 1445 BC

The book is technically anonymous. On the other hand, according to uniform Jewish and early Christian belief, the first five books of the Bible were written by Moses. Collectively these five books are called the Torah (Hebrew), the Pentateuch (Greek), or the Law (English). Both Jesus and Paul affirmed that Moses wrote the Law (John 7:19; Rom. 10:19). Scholars who accept the testimony of Scripture at face value continue to affirm that Moses wrote Genesis.

During the 1800s most critical scholars abandoned the belief that Moses wrote these books. The influential German scholar Julius Wellhausen presented evidence for a documentary theory (often called "JEDP") for the composition of the Law. This theory argued that the Torah evolved over several centuries and was finally compiled during the time of Israel's kings. Although Wellhausen's theory has been modified over the years, it still dominates scholarly discussions of the origin of the Pentateuch.

The time of Moses' life has been interpreted two ways. Because 1 Kings 6:1 notes the time between the exodus and Solomon, the exodus has been dated traditionally around 1446 BC. Others, however, date the exodus about 1290 BC, based on the word "Raamses" (or Rameses) in Exodus 1:11 and first known occurrence of that name applied to a pharaoh.

▶ THE MIGRATION OF ABRAHAM
Genesis 11:27–12:9

(See **EXODUS** for more information.) Assuming an early date for the exodus and that Moses wrote while Israel camped at Mount Sinai, Genesis was written in the middle of the fifteenth century BC.

First Audience and Destination
The Israelites at Mount Sinai

The original hearers and destination are not stated but are believed from tradition. The first audience was the Israelite nation in the wilderness on their way to Canaan.

Occasion

Genesis does not tell what prompted it to be written. Its events occurred centuries before the writer's birth. Although some historical records from the dawn of humanity may have survived for Moses to use as sources, this does not appear likely. If one believes that Moses received the Ten Commandments by divine revelation, then one can just as readily believe that God also revealed to Moses the content of Genesis.

 THE LIFE OF ABRAHAM

EVENT	OLD TESTAMENT PASSAGE	NEW TESTAMENT REFERENCE
The birth of Abram	Gen. 11:26	
God's call of Abram	Gen. 12:1-3	Heb. 11:8
The entry into Canaan	Gen. 12:4-9	
Abram in Egypt	Gen. 12:10-20	
Lot separates form Abram	Gen. 13:1-18	
Abram rescues Lot	Gen. 14:1-17	
Abram pays tithes to Melchizedek	Gen. 14:18-24	Heb. 7:1-10
God's covenant with Abraham	Gen. 15:1-21	Rom. 4:1-25; Gal. 3:6-25; Heb. 11:11-12
The birth of Ismael	Gen. 16:1-16	
Abraham and Sarah promised a son	Gen. 17:1-27	Rom. 4:18-25; Heb. 11:11-12
Abraham intercedes for Sodom	Gen. 18:16-33	
Lot saved and Sodom destroyed	Gen. 19:1-38	
The birth of Isaac	Gen. 21:1-7	
Hagar and Ismael sent away	Gen. 21:8-21	Gal. 4:21-31
Abraham challenged to offer	Gen. 22:1-19	Heb. 11:17-19
Isaac as sacrifice		James 2:20-24
The death of Sarah	Gen. 23:1-20	
The death of Abraham	Gen. 25:1-11	

LITERARY FEATURES

Genre and Literary Style
A historical narrative written in excellent Hebrew

Although Genesis was "The First Book of the Law," it recorded relatively few divine commands (but see 2:16-27; 9:6-7). Genesis has preserved two historical narratives. Chapters 1–11 contain a selective history of the entire human race. (Other religions have their stories about creation and beginnings, with which Genesis shares certain features. The Babylonian Gilgamesh Epic, for example, contains parallels to the flood narrative.) Chapters 12–50 tell the story of the direct ancestors of the Israelites. Genesis also contains a few passages of poetry (see 3:14-19) and important genealogies (see chap. 5). The Hebrew style of Genesis is like that of the rest of the Pentateuch. The writer composed his account carefully.

Themes
Creation, death, flood, covenant, providence

The account of the creation of the world and of mankind in God's image provides the theological basis for the Bible's insistence on human accountability to the Creator. The words "and he died," repeated with depressing regularity, show that the fall indeed had the effect God warned about. The flood narrative shows how God judged the race he had created. In God's covenants with Noah and then with Abraham, he reached out in mercy to his fallen human creatures. The last half of the book, notably the story of Joseph, emphasizes God's providential care over his covenant people (see Gen. 50:20).

Book Features and Structure

Genesis introduces themes that the rest of Scripture develops. Genesis is necessary to make sense of the rest of the Bible. The author organized chapters 1–11 around four great events: creation, fall, flood, and Babel. Genesis 12–50 has preserved the story of four great men: Abraham, Isaac, Jacob, and Joseph.

The geographical focus shifts from section to section. Chapters 1–11 happened generally in the Fertile Crescent. The action for Abraham, Isaac, and Jacob shifts between Haran and Canaan, while the Joseph story alternates between Canaan and Egypt. Ten times the author used the phrase "these are the generations." Many scholars use this as a clue to organize the book into sections.

EXODUS

THE SECOND BOOK OF MOSES

In the Hebrew text, the book's first two words are its title, *We'elleh Shemot*, "These Are the Names." The English title is the name first used by the book's Greek translators (second century B.C.). *Exodus* could be rendered "going out" or "departure."

▶ *Key Text: 14:30-31*

"Thus the LORD saved Israel that day out of the hand of the Egyptians; and Israel saw the Egyptians dead upon the sea shore. And Israel saw that great work which the LORD did upon the Egyptians: and the people feared the LORD, and believed the LORD, and his servant Moses."

▶ *Key Term: "Redeem"*

Exodus shows how the Lord for his name's sake redeemed his people Israel by buying them out of slavery through payment of a price, the death of the Passover lambs (see 6:6). Further, it records God's commands to those redeemed people.

▶ *One-Sentence Summary*

When God redeemed his chosen people Israel through his servant Moses, he entered a covenant relationship with them and instituted his dwelling with them, the tabernacle.

▼ Peaks of Jebel Musa, the traditional site of Mount Sinai, where God gave his law to Israel (Exod. 19).

GOD'S MESSAGE IN THE BOOK

Purpose

Exodus is double pronged. First, it narrates God's greatest redemptive act of the Old Testament, Israel's exodus from Egypt. Second, it recorded many of the laws by which those redeemed people were to live. If the overall Bible tells the story of God's kingdom, then Exodus tells how the first phase of that kingdom came into being by God's mighty power. Moses, of course, is the central human figure as God's agent of salvation. God's people who read and study Exodus today should also view it in light of the ultimate Redeemer who purchased people by his own death (John 1:17).

Christian Worldview Elements

Exodus provides insight on the worldview categories of *sovereignty and providence, revelation and authority, covenant and redemption,* and *ethics and morality.* No Old Testament book more fully portrays that humans cannot know God unless he reveals himself or that humans must depend wholly on God for their redemption.

> GOD
> CREATION
> ▶ **SOVEREIGNTY AND PROVIDENCE**
> FAITH AND REASON
> ▶ **REVELATION AND AUTHORITY**
> HUMANITY
> REBELLION AND SIN
> ▶ **COVENANT AND REDEMPTION**
> COMMUNITY AND CHURCH
> DISCIPLESHIP
> ▶ **ETHICS AND MORALITY**
> TIME AND ETERNITY

Teachings about God

Exodus reveals the Lord as Redeemer. Because of his love and for his name's sake he takes the initiative to save his people from bondage. Exodus further reveals him as the one who expects his redeemed people to live according to the provisions of the covenant made at Sinai. Christ is prefigured both by Moses and by the Passover lambs. Exodus 31:3; 35:31 mention the Spirit as empowering a person for special service.

Teachings about Humanity

Exodus highlights the universality of human evil by showing rebellion against God in a variety of ways. Pharaoh's wickedness (chaps. 4–14) and redeemed Israel's shameful idolatry in the golden calf incident (chap. 32) are perhaps the clearest examples. On the other hand, Exodus shows the great value God puts on humanity through the high price paid at the time of Israel's deliverance from Egypt.

Teachings about Salvation

Until Christ's coming and his death on the cross, the exodus was the greatest divine redemptive act. God taught explicitly the substitutionary meaning of the Passover lamb's death: "When I see the blood I will pass over you" (12:13). This, however, only prefigured the coming One, "the Lamb slain from the foundation of the world" (Rev. 13:8).

CHRIST IN EXODUS

Exodus is a book of redemption. God's freeing his people from Egyptian slavery is a picture of Christ's delivering sinners from their sin and its consequences. Christ was with Israel as the rock that followed them through their journey from slavery to the promised land (1 Cor. 10:4; Exod. 17:6). The Passover lambs are a picture of Christ's death for sinners (John 1:36; 19:36) and his providing access to God.

GOD'S STORY

When the Events of This Book Happened
From Joseph's death through the completion of the tabernacle (about 1805–1445 BC)

Based on the data in 1 Kings 6:1, the date of the exodus has been figured to the middle of the fifteenth century BC, around 1446. This is the traditional and early date for the exodus. Based on this view, the pharaoh who oppressed Israel was Thutmose I, and his son Amenhotep II was the one whom Moses challenged. (This was the time of the New Kingdom, the Eighteenth Dynasty in Egypt.)

Critical scholars understand the data differently, using the name "Raamses" (or Rameses) in Exodus 1:11 as a clue that the Israelites must have been building the new Egyptian capital of that title, named for Rameses I (ruled in the early 1300s). On this view, the pharaoh of the oppression was Sethos I, and Moses challenged his son Rameses II. In this view, the exodus occurred about 1290 BC. (This was the time of Egypt's Nineteenth Dynasty.) The critical view has been widely disseminated in popular culture through influential movies and television. The traditional date, however, remains credible and takes the wording of 1 Kings 6:1 (and Acts 13:20) to be reliable.

How Exodus Fits into God's "Story"

In bringing people into a right relationship with him, God determined to make the descendants of Abraham into a true nation. Exodus shows how this happened, beginning with a multitude of disheartened, enslaved Israelites. The book ends with a national identity established through a divinely called leader (Moses) and divinely given laws. The establishment of Israel as a nation prefigures God's great fulfillment of the eternal kingdom over which Jesus reigns forever.

1805 BC	1526	1486	1446	1446	1445
Joseph dies	Moses born	Moses flees Egypt	God calls Moses	The Exodus	Ten Commandments

19

ORIGINAL HISTORICAL SETTING

Author and Date of Writing

Moses, perhaps around 1445 BC

The book is anonymous. Because Moses is the central character, however, everything in the book is compatible with the traditional belief that he was its author. The book refers to Moses as physically writing down some of God's commands (24:4; see also 34:38). Scholars who accept the testimony of Scripture at face value continue to affirm that Moses wrote Exodus. (See **GENESIS** for comments about the critical theory that Exodus was written during the times of Israel's kings.) Assuming an early date for the exodus and that Moses wrote while Israel camped at Mount Sinai, this book was written in the middle of the fifteenth century BC.

First Audience and Destination

The Israelite people at Mount Sinai

The original hearers were the children of Israel living in the wilderness on their way to the promised land.

Occasion

Although the book does not say so, the need for Israel to have a permanent historical record of the events that brought it into existence as a nation surely is what prompted the composition. If one believes that Moses received the Ten Commandments by divine revelation, then one can just as readily believe that God also prompted him to write down everything recorded in Exodus.

▶ CHRONOLOGY FOR EXODUS

1900	1800	1700	1600	1500	1400	1300
Israel to Egypt			Slavery in Egypt		Exodus, conquest	

1876   1446

(430 years in Egypt, Exodus 12:41)

LEGEND

◀─── Northern route

◀── Central route

◀─ ─ Alternate central route

◀── Southern route

◀─ ─ Alternate route from Jebel Musa to Kadesh-barnea

● City

○ City (uncertain location)

▲ Mountain peak

▲ Possible locations for Mt. Sinai

─── Major roads

LITERARY FEATURES

Genre and Literary Style
Historical narrative, with some laws, composed in Hebrew

Although Exodus was "The Second Book of the Law," it preserved more historical narrative than law. Chapter 15, "The Song of Moses," is poetry rather than prose, and the first extensive poetry in Scripture. The Hebrew style of Exodus is like that of the rest of the Pentateuch.

Themes
The Lord, plagues, redemption, covenant, Ten Commandments, tabernacle

God's revelation of himself to Moses as Yahweh (rendered in English as "the Lord," using small capital letters for "ord") stands as one of the most profound passages in all Scripture. The famous account of the plagues demonstrates the power of the Lord over the gods of Egypt. The Ten Commandments remain unsurpassed as God's wise rules for living life to the fullest. The importance of the tabernacle is seen in God's solemn pledge about it: "I will dwell among the children of Israel, and will be their God. And they shall know that I am the Lord their God, that brought them forth out of the land of Egypt" (29:45-46).

Book Features and Structure

People of the ancient Near East understood the idea of a covenant agreement between a god and a king (or his people). They also grasped the related notion of a peace treaty between human parties. Many features of the covenant/treaty that God made with Israel at Sinai parallel ancient covenants/treaties discovered by archaeologists. The Sinaitic covenant began with the manifestation of God (chap. 19) and ended with confirmation by blood (chap. 24), with the "Book of the Covenant" stated in chapters 20–23. This was a "suzerain-vassal" covenant in which the master (suzerain) promised to protect and bless the subjects (vassals) as long as they obeyed and submitted to him. This contrasted with the "royal grant" unconditional covenant, such as the one in which God categorically promised to make Abraham into a worldwide blessing (Gen. 12; 15).

The life and travels of Moses provide the organizing principle for the book. The action occurs wherever Moses is present. The first half is mainly narrative, chapters 1–18 (Israel's deliverance from Egypt and journey to Sinai) as is the last fourth, chapters 32–40 (Israel's violation of the covenant, the restoration, and the building of the tabernacle). Sandwiched between the historical sections are law chapters 19–24 (the covenant at Sinai) and 25–31 (rules concerning the tabernacle and the priesthood).

LEVITICUS

THE THIRD BOOK OF MOSES

The English title is based on the name given by the Greek translators of this book in the second century BC. The name could be translated "pertaining to Levites." The original Hebrew title is the first word of the book, *Wayyiqra'*, "And He Called."

▶ *Key Text: 11:45*

"For I am the LORD that bringeth you up out of the land of Egypt, to be your God: ye shall therefore be holy, for I am holy."

▶ *Key Term: "Holiness"*

Holiness throughout Scripture, but especially in Leviticus, is first an attribute of God. It refers to his glorious moral perfections as the One who is the standard of ethical purity. Second, holiness is commanded by God to his redeemed people. This holiness includes both moral living (submitting gladly to God's laws) and being separated from common use (intentionally set apart to God and his service).

▶ *One-Sentence Summary*

God forgives sin and makes people holy through blood sacrifice; further, he then expects his people to live in fellowship with him by following his regulations concerning separated living.

A frieze of a priest making sacrifice. Priesthood and sacrifices are two major themes in Leviticus.

GOD'S MESSAGE IN THE BOOK

Purpose

Leviticus was God's word to Israel to teach two essential truths about how people may sustain a right relationship with God. First, people enter a relationship with God based on forgiveness of sins, obtained by offering the right sacrifices the right way by the right priest. Second, forgiven people maintain fellowship with God by living according to his regulations. This means that his people are separate (and therefore different) from others. The specific laws in Leviticus are both precise and peculiar.

Of all the books of the Old Testament, Leviticus is the most challenging for Christians to apply. First, the New Testament, especially Hebrews, teaches that the right sacrifice offered the right way by the right priest has been truly fulfilled in Jesus, thus rendering Leviticus 1–10 obsolete. Second, the entire thrust of the New Testament is that fellowship with God is no longer based on *external* matters such as circumcision, keeping dietary laws, or following Israel's holy days. Today fellowship with God and holy living are essentially *internal*. God's people who read and study Leviticus today should remember that its two essential principles are certainly still true, but that God intended its particular rules to be in effect only until Christ came (Gal. 4:24-25).

Christian Worldview Elements

Leviticus presents the worldview categories of *God; covenant and redemption, community,* and *ethics and morality.* This book proclaims that God is holy and that his people must live holy lives.

Teachings about God

Leviticus teaches that in his holiness God has the absolute right to instruct his people in what holiness demands, down to the minute details of life. Sinful people may approach him for forgiveness only through the

> **GOD**
> CREATION
> SOVEREIGNTY AND PROVIDENCE
> FAITH AND REASON
> REVELATION AND AUTHORITY
> HUMANITY
> REBELLION AND SIN
> **COVENANT AND REDEMPTION**
> **COMMUNITY** AND CHURCH
> DISCIPLESHIP
> **ETHICS AND MORALITY**
> TIME AND ETERNITY

sacrifices he has ordained. The specific sacrifices described suggest the multiple aspects of Christ's atoning sacrifice. The chapters on the priesthood foreshadow Christ's perfections as the ultimate high priest.

Teachings about Humanity

God has made complete provision for forgiving the sins and failures of people, if only they make use of his means. Further, humans can enjoy full fellowship with God, but only if they live according to the way he has revealed. Leviticus teaches that following the commands of a holy God is not only possible as a way of living, but the true way to lasting fulfillment: "Ye shall therefore keep my statutes, and my judgments: which if a man do, he shall live in them: I *am* the LORD" (18:5). Leviticus also shows how God expected his people to live in community with one another during that era.

Teachings about Salvation

"Blood" occurs more than sixty times in Leviticus. Readers are overwhelmed with the truth that in God's design, blood outpoured through ritual sacrifice is the key to atoning for sins (17:11). This is critical for understanding the necessity of Christ's violent death as the atoning sacrifice for the sins of people. The death of sacrificial animals in ancient Israel may be compared to the modern practice of using credit cards. When Israelites sacrificed an animal, they were truly forgiven—just as when persons today use a credit card, they truly receive the merchandise. Yet in both instances a future price is to be paid: on one hand the credit card bill comes due; on the other hand, the true cost of sin came due and was paid in full through the crucifixion of Jesus.

CHRIST IN LEVITICUS

The specific sacrifices (for example, chap. 16) described in Leviticus suggest the multiple aspects of Christ's atoning sacrifice. The chapters on the priesthood (21–22) foreshadow Christ's perfections as the ultimate high priest.

GOD'S STORY

When the Events of This Book Happened: *About 1445 BC*

The only historical events recorded in this book are the consecration of Aaron and his sons as priests and what happened to them next (chaps. 8–10). This all occurred while Israel was still camped at Mount Sinai in the year after their exodus from Egypt.

How Leviticus Fits into God's "Story"

Leviticus continues God's story that began in Exodus: God builds his nation (Israel chosen as the people of promise). It shows that God expected citizens of the earthly nation Israel to live holy lives. How much more does he desire citizens of his heavenly kingdom today to live in holiness. Sanctification is not optional for God's people. The New Testament equivalent is to "walk worthy of the calling you have received" (Eph. 4:1).

ORIGINAL HISTORICAL SETTING

Author and Date of Writing

Moses, around 1445 BC

The book is anonymous. But the exact words, "the Lord spake unto Moses, saying," occur twenty-seven times in the KJV text. This is one basis for the belief that Moses wrote Leviticus. (See **GENESIS** for comments about the critical theory that Exodus was written during the times of Israel's kings.) Assuming an early date for the exodus and that Moses wrote while Israel camped at Mount Sinai, this book was written in the middle of the fifteenth century BC. (See **EXODUS** for comments about a later possible date for the life of Moses.)

First Audience and Destination

The Israelite people at Mount Sinai

The first hearers were the Israelites camped around Mount Sinai.

Occasion

Apparently what prompted Leviticus to be written was the need to preserve permanently for Israel the oral commands God gave Moses. Even the brief narrative sections deal with the application of God's laws concerning the priesthood.

▶ JEWISH FEASTS AND FESTIVALS

Name	Month: Date	Reference	Significance
Passover	Nisan (Mar./April) 14-21	Exod. 12:2-20 Lev. 23:5	Commemorates God's deliverance of Israel out of Egypt.
Feast of Unleavened Bread	Nisan (Mar./April) 15-21	Lev. 23:6-8	Commemorates God's deliverance of Israel out of Egypt. Includes a Day of Firstfruits for barley harvest.
Feast of Weeks or Harvest (Pentecost)	Sivan (May/June) 6 (7 weeks after Passover)	Exod. 23:16; 34:22 Lev. 23:15-21	Commemorates the giving of the Law at Mount Sinai. Includes a Day of Firstfruits for the wheat harvest.
Feast of Trumpets (Rosh Hashanah)	Tishri (Sept./Oct.) 1	Lev. 23:23-25 Num. 29:1-6	Day of the blowing of the trumpets to signal the beginning of the civil new year.
Day of Atonement (Yom Kippur)	Tishri (Sept./Oct.) 10	Lev. 23:26-33 Exod. 30:10	The high priest makes atonement for the nation's sin. Also a day of fasting.
Feast of Booths or Tabernacles (Sukkot)	Tishri (Sept./Oct.) 15-21	Lev. 23:33-43, Num. 29:12-39 Deut. 16:139	Commemorates the forty years of wilderness wandering.
Feast of Dedication or Festival of Lights (Hanukkah)	Kislev (Nov./Dec.) 25-30; and Tebeth (Dec./Jan.) 1-2	John 10:22	Commemorates the purification of the temple by Judas Maccabeus in 164 BC.
Feast of Purim or Esther	Adar (Feb./Mar.) 14	Esther 9	Commemorates the deliverance of the Jewish people in the days of Esther.

Leviticus makes a distinction between animals that are ceremonially clean and unclean. "The animals you may use for food include those that have completely divided hooves and chew the cud. You may not, however, eat the animals named here because they either have split hooves or chew the cud, but not both. The camel may not be eaten, for though it chews the cud, it does not have split hooves" (Lev. 11:2-4).

LITERARY FEATURES

Genre and Literary Style
Ancient laws, with a little narrative, composed in Hebrew

The laws in Leviticus were stated in two forms. First was "command law" (or "apodictic law"), often introduced with the formula "thou shalt . . ." (positive) or "thou shalt not . . ." (negative). This parallels modern constitutional law or legislative acts. Second was "case law" (or "casuistic law"), often using the formula "if a man . . ." These introduced examples or situations are parallel to modern verdicts of judges that then become the basis for later judicial rulings. The Hebrew is like that of the rest of the Pentateuch.

Themes
Holiness, blood, atonement, priesthood, uncleanness, feasts, rules

This chapter has already discussed the first four themes. The issue of "clean or unclean" was not a matter of "healthful or unhealthful" but rather "fit for God's presence or unfit for God's presence." Because God is holy, he has the absolute right to declare what pleases him. The same was true concerning the feasts, whether weekly (such as the Sabbath) or yearly (such as the Feast of Tabernacles). Many rules in Leviticus had a social dimension, telling how to live in fellowship with fellow human beings. According to Jesus, Leviticus contained the second greatest commandment, "Thou shalt love thy neighbour as thyself" (19:18; see Mark 12:31).

Book Features and Structure
Many scholars designate Leviticus 17–26 "The Holiness Code" based on the words, "I the LORD, which sanctify you, am holy" (21:8). In Christian theology, some scholars have attempted to divide the laws of Leviticus (and other commands in the Pentateuch) into the categories moral, civil, and ceremonial. Evidence does not support that the people of Israel made these distinctions. The law was a complete entity that stood together, and Leviticus makes the best sense when read in this way.

Leviticus 1–10 recorded laws concerning sacrifices and the priesthood.

Leviticus 11–16 focused on "uncleanness" in a variety of ways.

Leviticus 17–26 presented laws concerning holy living for the Israelites, ending with a magnificent chapter (26) proclaiming blessings for obedience.

Leviticus 27 originated as an appendix dealing with paying vows and tithes.

NUMBERS

THE FOURTH BOOK OF MOSES

The English title is based on the lists of numbers in the book and is the name given by its Greek translators in the second century BC. The Hebrew title is more apt, *Bemidbar*, "In the Wilderness," a word taken from the opening verse.

▶ *Key Text: 9:17*

"And when the cloud was taken up from the tabernacle, then after that the children of Israel journeyed: and in the place where the cloud abode, there the children of Israel pitched their tents."

▶ *Key Term: "Wilderness"*

This book explains what happened to the Israelites during the thirty-eight years they traveled through the wilderness from Mount Sinai to the border of Canaan. The term "wilderness" appears more than forty times.

▶ *One-Sentence Summary*

God used Moses to lead Israel from Sinai to Kadesh, but even after they rejected him there, resulting in the wilderness years, he remained faithful to them and led a new generation to the edge of the promised land.

Jebel Harun with Aaron's tomb on top of the mountain (Num. 20:22-29).

29

GOD'S MESSAGE IN THE BOOK

Purpose

Numbers mainly answers the questions, How did Israel get from Mount Sinai to the border of Canaan? and Why did the journey take so long? The book contrasts God's faithfulness with Israel's disobedience. Ultimately, however, Numbers shows the progress of God's people in moving toward the goals he had promised. Because God accomplished this despite his people's waywardness, he received all the glory. Those studying Numbers today should view it with this original purpose in mind.

Christian Worldview Elements

Numbers deals particularly with the worldview categories of *sovereignty and providence, rebellion and sin,* and *covenant and redemption.* This book clearly demonstrates God's sovereign power to accomplish his purposes. He even used a talking donkey.

GOD
CREATION
► **SOVEREIGNTY AND PROVIDENCE**
FAITH AND REASON
REVELATION AND AUTHORITY
HUMANITY
► **REBELLION AND SIN**
► **COVENANT AND REDEMPTION**
COMMUNITY AND CHURCH
DISCIPLESHIP
ETHICS AND MORALITY
TIME AND ETERNITY

Teachings about God

Numbers emphasizes two attributes of God: his sovereign power and his covenant faithfulness. He is faithful to Israel on account of the covenant he made with Abraham (32:11). God's Spirit is present as the One enabling service and inspiring true prophecy (11:25-26; 24:2).

Teachings about Humanity

This book shows how painfully sinful and flawed all humans are. The rebellion at Kadesh led by Korah and the story of Balaam demonstrate this. Moreover, even Moses the lawgiver, to whom God spoke directly, sinned and was not allowed to enter Canaan. Without divine mercy all perish.

Teachings about Salvation

Exodus (redemption through the death of the Passover lambs) and Leviticus (forgiveness provided through many blood sacrifices) teach more extensively about salvation than Numbers. The incident concerning the brass serpent on the pole, however, shows the centrality of faith in receiving God's provision: "And the Lord said unto Moses, Make thee a fiery serpent, and set it upon a pole: and it shall come to pass, that every one that is bitten, when he looketh upon it, shall live. And Moses made a serpent of brass, and put it upon a pole, and it came to pass, that if a serpent had bitten any man, when he beheld the serpent of brass, he lived" (21:8-9).

CHRIST IN NUMBERS

Christ is foreseen both as the water-giving Rock (1 Cor. 10:4) and as the raised serpent that gives life to those who look (John 3:14-15). He is foretold as a star that will come out of Jacob and a scepter out of Israel. The first fulfillment of this prophecy is in David who brought down a wicked nation (Moab). The perfect fulfillment of this prophecy is in David's Son, Jesus Christ, who will subdue all the enemies of God.

GOD'S STORY

When the Events of This Book Happened
From Israel's encampment at Sinai to its encampment by the Jordan River near Jericho (about 1445–1407 BC)

The events covered by Numbers took almost thirty-nine years, from the second month of the second year after the exodus to the eleventh month of the fortieth year (Num. 10:11; Deut. 1:3). The years noted above assume the early date for the exodus.

How Numbers Fits into God's "Story"
Numbers continues God's story: God builds his nation (Israel chosen as the people of promise). God's plan to bless his people despite their unworthiness magnifies his mercy. Numbers shows that the progress of God's kingdom depends on him and not on sinful people. The odd story of Balaam and his prophecies shows that no force can stop God's kingdom purposes. In fact, Balaam even predicted the coming of Jesus, the true King over God's kingdom (24:19).

The Plains of Moab at the northern end of the Dead Sea. Here Moses delivered his final address to Israel. The flanks of Mount Nebo are on the left. From Mount Nebo God allowed Moses to view the promised land. Moses died on Mount Nebo.

ORIGINAL HISTORICAL SETTING

Author and Date of Writing
Moses, circa 1407 BC

The book is anonymous, but like Exodus and Leviticus, Moses is the central human character. Further, 33:2 notes that Moses kept a journal of the Israelite travels. The exact words, "the Lord spake unto Moses, saying," occur thirty-five times in the KJV text. There are many good reasons to affirm that Moses wrote Numbers.

The book may have been slightly edited after Moses' death. For example, 21:14-15 seems to insert a citation from an otherwise unknown "Book of the Wars of the Lord." Further, many Bible students believe that if Moses himself penned comment about his meekness (12:3), it would disprove the point. Under divine inspiration the end product of Numbers is entirely true and exactly what God intended it to be. See **GENESIS** for the critical view of authorship of the Pentateuch, and see **EXODUS** for the view of a later date for Moses' life.

First Audience and Destination
The Israelite people, camped at the Jordan River

The original hearers and destination are stated directly but were apparently the Israelite nation camped on the plains of Moab shortly before they crossed the Jordan River into the promised land.

Occasion

Although the book does not say so, Israel needed a permanent historical record of the events that continued their national existence from the time of the covenant ratification at Sinai to the edge of the promised land. If one believes that Moses received the divine commands recorded in this book, then one can just as readily believe that God also prompted him to write down everything recorded in Numbers.

JOURNEY OF THE SPIES
Numbers 13:25-33; 34:1-12

LEGEND
- City
- City (uncertain location)
- Oasis
- ▲ Mountain peak
- ← Journey of the twelve spies
- The promised land

36 E

Zedad

Ziphron
Hazar-enan

Lebo-hamath

Byblos

34 N

Sidon

Damascus

Mt. Hermon

Pharpar River

Tyre

Laish (Dan)

Acco

Hazor

Mt. Carmel ▲

Ain

Ashtaroth

Kenath

N

*Mt. Hauran
(Jebel Druze)* ▲

Megiddo

Mt. Tabor ▲

Yarmuk River

Riblah

Shepham

Salecah

Beth-shan

Yarkon River

Jabbok River

Joppa

N

Shechem

32 N

32 N

Jericho

GILEAD

Jerusalem

Mt. Nebo ▲

Hebron

Valley of Eshcol

N. Besor

Gerar

Arad

Arnon River

Beersheba

Hormah

DEAD SEA

MEDITERRANEAN SEA

C

A

N

A

A

N

Negev

MOAB

AMALEK

Zoar

Mt. Hor ? ▲

Tamar

Zered River

Karka

Azmon

Hazar-addar

Wilderness of Zin

Ain el-Qudeirat

Ain Qedeis

Ascent of Akrabbim

Arabah

Punon

EDOM

36 E

| 0 | 20 | 40 Miles |
| 0 | 20 | 40 Kilometers |

33

LITERARY FEATURES

Genre and Literary Style
Narrative and laws (written in Hebrew prose) with some prophecies (written in Hebrew poetry)

The narrative portions of Numbers continue along the lines of the narrative of Exodus and Leviticus. As "The Fourth Book of the Law," its laws are also similar to those previously recorded. One new feature is the prophetic oracle, given by Balaam (chaps. 23–24), written in the poetic parallelism so familiar in such books as Isaiah and Jeremiah. The Hebrew style of Numbers is like that of the rest of the Pentateuch.

Themes
God's faithfulness, human waywardness, wilderness sojourn, numbering the people

The contrast between God's covenant faithfulness and the waywardness of his people has already been noted. Numbers develops this historically by telling why Israel had to sojourn in the wilderness for so long and what happened to them there. The censuses at the beginning (chaps. 1–4) and the end (chap. 26) of the wilderness era figure prominently in the book.

Book Features and Structure
One feature that challenges Bible interpreters is the record of huge numbers of Israelite adult men (those of military age). An army of 600,000 suggests an overall population of at least two million (2:32; 26:51). This raises many questions: How could the seventy that went with Joseph into Egypt multiply to such a host in a few generations? How could so many be managed? Is an organized camp of two million really possible? How could the massive herds and flocks of so many survive in the desert? Why aren't there archaeological remains if such a great migration actually occurred?

There have been several "solutions" to account for these large numbers. Many scholars dismiss them as simply wrong. Others have argued that the Hebrew words translated "thousand" and "hundred" may mean something else (such as "clan"). Some see the numbers as symbolic rather than literal. The problem of the large numbers has not been satisfactorily resolved, yet the numbers in Numbers demonstrate the greatness of God's providence and his miraculous supply during his people's time in the wilderness.

DEUTERONOMY

THE FIFTH BOOK OF MOSES

The Hebrew title is 'Elleh Haddebarim, "These Are the Words," or more succinctly Debarim, "Words," from the opening of the book. The English title reflects the Greek word Deuteronomion, meaning "Second Law."

▶ Key Text: 6:4-5

"Hear, O Israel: The LORD our God is one LORD: And thou shalt love the LORD thy God with all thine heart, and with all thy soul, and with all thy might."

▶ Key Term: "Commandments"

Keeping the commandments of God (out of love for him) lies at the heart of his covenant with Israel, seen especially by the repetition of the Ten Commandments. Forms of the noun or verb command occur almost one hundred times in the book.

▶ One-Sentence Summary

Through Moses' great speeches near the end of his life, God reminded Israel on the verge of entering the promised land about his mighty acts, his covenant, and his many commands.

▼ Jewish boy receives his first phylactery (Deut. 6:4-8).

GOD'S MESSAGE IN THE BOOK

Purpose

According to its own testimony, Deuteronomy originated as farewell messages from Moses to a new generation of Israelites. He pleaded passionately for them to keep God at the center of their national life once they settled in the land. The book is essentially a covenant-renewal document. The large central section largely repeats laws found earlier in the Pentateuch. So important was Deuteronomy to early Christians that the New Testament writers cited it more than fifty times.

Christian Worldview Elements

Deuteronomy deals especially with the worldview categories of *revelation and authority, covenant and redemption,* and *ethics and morality.* No Old Testament book more clearly teaches that God's love for his people means that he asks for their love in return, which gladly expresses itself in obeying his commands.

> GOD
> CREATION
> SOVEREIGNTY AND PROVIDENCE
> FAITH AND REASON
> ▶**REVELATION AND AUTHORITY**
> HUMANITY
> REBELLION AND SIN
> ▶**COVENANT AND REDEMPTION**
> COMMUNITY AND CHURCH
> DISCIPLESHIP
> ▶**ETHICS AND MORALITY**
> TIME AND ETERNITY

Teachings about God

Deuteronomy emphasizes the unity of God in the famous Shema, "Hear!" (see **Key Text** on page 35). God's love as the basis for his covenant, his acts on Israel's behalf, and his commands are also prominent. On the other hand, idolatry or apostasy is so serious an affront to God's glory that the book commands the most severe penalties against those who insult God by turning away from him.

Teachings about Humanity

Deuteronomy faithfully records Israel's failures and gives solemn warnings of divine curse on disobedient and rebellious people. Yet the tenor of the book is that living according God's commands is a true delight and that obedience is no drudgery but the response of love and faith—an easy yoke. "But the word is very nigh unto thee, in thy mouth, and in thy heart, that thou mayest do it" (30:14; see Matt. 11:29).

Teachings about Salvation

Deuteronomy emphasizes that salvation is entirely God's provision. He sets his covenant love on people sheerly out of his love. The remarkable text in Deuteronomy 7:1-10 denies that God's redemption of Israel from Egypt was based on any quality in Israel but only "because the LORD loved you" (7:8)—his sovereign choice. This book also shows that redeemed people demonstrate their love and faith by their obedience.

CHRIST IN DEUTERONOMY

Moses tells of a prophet like him whom God will raise up from among Israel (18:15-22). Christ is seen as a fulfillment of that prophecy (Acts 3:22; 7:37). The Law states that whoever is hung on a tree is under God's curse (Deut. 21:23). Christ has redeemed us from the curse of the Law by himself becoming a curse for us (Gal. 3:13).

GOD'S STORY

When the Events of This Book Happened
In the last days of Moses (about 1406 BC)

Using the traditional early date for the exodus, Israel crossed the Jordan River and began the conquest of the promised land about 1406 BC. The events recorded in Deuteronomy occurred just before this. (Critical scholars who date the exodus much later put Israel's entrance into Canaan around 1250 BC.)

How Deuteronomy Fits into God's "Story"

Deuteronomy continues God's story: God builds his nation (Israel chosen as the people of promise). Deuteronomy looks forward to the time Israel will be settled in the land, at peace with her enemies, under the rule of a righteous king (17:14-20). The king must "write him a copy of this law in a book out of that which is before the priests the Levites: And it shall be with him, and he shall read therein all the days of his life: that he may learn to fear the LORD his God, to keep all the words of this law and these statutes, to do them" (17:18-19).

Shema

Hear, O Israel: The LORD our God is one LORD.
And thou shalt love the LORD thy God with all thine heart,
and with all thy soul, and with all thy might.

—Deuteronomy 6:45

 The Shema became for Israel a confession of faith by which they acknowledged the one true God and his commandments for them. When Jesus was asked about the "greatest commandment," he answered by quoting the Shema (Mark 12:29).

ORIGINAL HISTORICAL SETTING

Author and Date of Writing
Moses, about 1406 BC

The book refers to Moses' involvement in writing it (1:5; 31:9,22,24). Later Scripture refers to Mosaic authorship (1 Kings 2:3; 8:53; 2 Kings 14:6; 18:12). Both Jesus and Paul believed Moses wrote Deuteronomy (Mark 10:3-5; John 5:46-47; Rom. 10:19). The book's formal prologue (1:1-5) and the epilogue about Moses' death (chap. 34) were perhaps added by Joshua to round out the book.

Many modern critical scholars believe that Deuteronomy (or at least chaps. 12–26) first came into being as a pious fraud composed by scribes during the 600s BC at the time of King Josiah. These scribes subsequently "discovered" the book and claimed it came from the time of Moses (2 Kings 22–23). This belief became the keystone of the famous Documentary Hypothesis, sometimes called "JEDP." Two centuries of modern critical study, however, have not proven that anything in the book could not have occurred from the time of Moses.

First Audience and Destination
The Israelite people on the plains of Moab

Of all the books of the Pentateuch, Deuteronomy is the one that most clearly began as oral communication by a human speaker. Later he put it in written permanent form. The first audience was the new generation of Israelites listening to their beloved leader of forty years as they faced the prospect of entering Canaan without him. (Without doubt the religious reforms instituted during the time of King Josiah were an application of the teachings of Deuteronomy for a new audience in another situation.)

Occasion

Deuteronomy alone of the books of Moses states its precise occasion: "And it came to pass, when Moses had made an end of writing the words of this law in a book, until they were finished, That Moses commanded the Levites, which bare the ark of the covenant of the LORD, saying, Take this book of the law, and put it in the side of the ark of the covenant of the LORD your God, that it may be there for a witness against thee" (31:24-26).

JOURNEY FROM KADESH-BARNEA TO THE PLAINS OF MOAB
Deuteronomy 1–2

LEGEND
- City
- ○ City (uncertain location)
- ▲ Mountain peak
- ← Possible routes from Kadesh-barnea to the Plains of Moab
- ← Possible alternate route I
- ← Possible alternate route II
- ◄- Israelite battle missions
- ← Sihon attacks
- ◄- Og attacks
- ⚔ Battle
- — King's Highway
- ---- Other routes

Megiddo

Beth-shan

Ramoth-gilead

Edrei

Defeat of Og

GILEAD

Shechem

T. Deir Alla

Jazer

Plains of Moab

Rabbah

32 N

Jericho

Jerusalem

Beth-jeshimoth

Abel-shittim

Heshbon

Beth-peor

Medeba

Death and burial of Moses

Mt. Nebo (Pisgah)

Almon-diblathaim

Defeat of Sihon

Jahaz

MISHOR

Hebron

Balaam blessed Israel

Dibon

Kedemoth

Wilderness of Kedemoth

Mattanah

PHILISTIA

DEAD SEA

Arnon River

Gerar

Arad

Ar

Beersheba

Kir-haresheth

Hormah

MOAB

Negev

Zered River

Zoar

Iye-abarim

AMALEK

Wilderness of Zin

Tamar

Zalmonah

Tophel

Bozrah

Mt. Seir (Jebel Esh-Shera)

Mt. Hor ?

Punon

Kadesh-barnea

EDOM

Teman

The way to the Red Sea

The way to the Arabah

The way to the Wilderness of Moab

30 N

30 N

Timna

0   10   20   30   40 Miles

0 10 20 30 40 Kilometers

36 E

Ezion-geber

LITERARY FEATURES

Genre and Literary Style
A record of Moses' final speeches, composed in Hebrew

Many scholars have noted the sermonic style of Deuteronomy, which sets it apart from the other books of Moses. The three speeches are a combination of narrative (reminders of God's acts) and repetition of God's laws. Together they serve to renew the covenant for a new generation. At the end of the book, the extraordinary "Song of Moses" (chap. 32) and his "Final Blessing on Israel" (chap. 33) show Moses to be a poet of considerable skill. The Hebrew of Deuteronomy is similar to that of the rest of the Pentateuch.

Themes
Commandments, covenant, God's mighty acts, transition

The first eleven chapters of Deuteronomy look back at the past concerning what God had already accomplished for his people. Beginning in chapter 12 the focus is on the future. Thus, Deuteronomy serves as a transition book from the time of Israel's national founding (with a charismatic leader and laws) to the time of its settlement (with a land and a royal dynasty). In both the past and the future, Israel must remember its status as God's chosen, covenant people who owe him supreme allegiance.

Book Features and Structure

There is general agreement that three sermons of Moses form the essential structure of the book. Scholars disagree whether chapters 12–26 were originally the astonishingly long conclusion of the second speech or whether Moses inserted the catalogue of laws at this point when he converted his speeches into writing. The topic changes from speech to speech.

Deuteronomy 1:1–4:43—Speech one reviews the mighty acts of the Lord.

Deuteronomy 4:44–28:68—Speech two presents the wonderful laws of the Lord.

Deuteronomy 27:1–30:20—Speech three proposes covenant renewal with the Lord.

Deuteronomy 31–34—These chapters describe the change of leadership from Moses to Joshua.

JOSHUA

The English (and Hebrew) title is based on the name of the central character. Moses changed his original name *Hoshea* ("Salvation") to *Yehoshua* ("The LORD Is Salvation"), traditionally spelled "Joshua" in English. The Greek equivalent is "Jesus."

▶ *Key Text: 21:44-45*

"And the LORD gave them rest round about, according to all that he sware unto their fathers: and there stood not a man of all their enemies before them; the LORD delivered all their enemies into their hand. There failed not ought of any good thing which the LORD had spoken unto the house of Israel; all came to pass."

▶ *Key Term: "Conquest"*

This is a book of victory and conquest. It shows God's people on the march throughout Canaan, subduing their enemies and claiming their promised possession.

▶ *One-Sentence Summary*

God fulfilled his promises to Israel to give them a land through the conquest of Canaan and through the allocation of the land among the tribes, all under the leadership of Joshua.

▼ Defense walls of Old Testament Jericho (Josh. 6).

GOD'S MESSAGE IN THE BOOK

Purpose

The covenant God made with Abraham included a promise that his descendents would take possession of Canaan (Gen. 12:7). For long ages the promise lay unfulfilled. The book of Joshua shows how God—in his time and way—fulfilled the land aspect of the Abrahamic Covenant. Yet the new Testament book of Hebrews speaks of a greater Joshua who gives his people ultimate rest (Heb. 4:8-9). God's people who read and study the book today should view it with both Joshuas in mind: the Israelite general and the King of kings.

Christian Worldview Elements

Joshua draws attention to the following worldview categories: *sovereignty and providence, covenant and redemption, ethics and morality,* and *community.* This book shows God as the righteous Judge who will not forever tolerate those who insult him, such as the Canaanites.

GOD
CREATION
► **SOVEREIGNTY AND PROVIDENCE**
FAITH AND REASON
REVELATION AND AUTHORITY
HUMANITY
REBELLION AND SIN
► **COVENANT AND REDEMPTION**
► **COMMUNITY** AND CHURCH
DISCIPLESHIP
► **ETHICS AND MORALITY**
TIME AND ETERNITY

Teachings about God

The two attributes of God most on display in Joshua are his faithfulness to fulfill his promises and his ultimate judgment on evil. If the promise made to Abraham concerning land for Israel was kept only after many centuries, then today's believers should not be surprised if the promise he made concerning the return of Christ is kept after many centuries.

Teachings about Humanity

Although the book is careful to report Israel's occasional failures during the conquest, it is optimistic in its view that God's people can "live in victory" as they trust in him. For this reason, Joshua has been popular in Christian pulpits with the positive principles it contains.

Teachings about Salvation

The account of Rahab the harlot (chaps. 2 and 6) profoundly illustrates salvation by "grace through faith." So thoroughly was she converted that she was considered an Israelite and became a biological ancestor of Jesus (Josh. 6:25; Matt. 1:5; Heb. 11:31). Although most of the victories in Joshua are military, the entire tenor of the book is that salvation—of whatever kind—comes only from God's hand.

CHRIST IN JOSHUA

The very name *Joshua* is a variation of *Jesus*. Joshua's leadership of God's people in taking possession of the promised land foreshadows Christ's leading the people of God to their eternal inheritance. Joshua is only one of a few Old Testament heroes pictured without major character flaws or sins. The "captain of the LORD's host" (5:15) was doubtless Christ in preincarnate form.

GOD'S STORY

When the Events of This Book Happened
From Israel's entry into Canaan until Joshua's death (about 1406–1380 BC)

Archeologists of the ancient Near East call the period of 1550–1200 BC the Late Bronze Age. Many Canaanite ruins from this era have been excavated, revealing an advanced but idolatrous civilization. The archaeological data support either an early date for the destruction of Jericho (about 1406 BC) or a late date (about 1250 BC). The late date, however, does not allow the pre-monarchy period to last at least three hundred years (Judg. 11:26). The earlier, more traditional date, is preferred (see also 1 Kings 6:1 and **EXODUS**).

How Joshua Fits into God's "Story"

Joshua continues God's story: God builds his nation (Israel chosen as the people of promise). Joshua describes how God's kingdom triumphed at a time when nations were viewed as the creation of local deities and the proof of their power. The Lord's victories over the Canaanites demonstrated that Israel's God is the one true God. It looks forward to the climax of all human history when God will triumph over all the world's kingdoms through his anointed King.

▶ JOSHUA'S CENTRAL AND SOUTHERN CAMPAIGNS

Amorites flee into the Valley of Aijalon, where sun stands still. Hail kills many Amorites.

Initial attack occurs near Ai and fails. However, clever ambush defeats defenders.

Camp is established at Gilgal

Main Force

Joshua sends spies ahead to Jericho

Battle begins as Joshua attacks Amorites on behalf of Gibeonites

Ambush Force

Jericho falls, opening the way into Canaan and attack on Ai

All five Amorite kings perish. Joshua seizes opportunity and captures several cities in the Shephelah.

Joshua continues and takes several cities in the Negev as well.

Ashdod, Gezer, Lod, Beth-horon, Bethel, Ai, Gibeon, Michmash, Naaran, Jericho, Gilgal, Abel-shittim, Ashkelon?, Ekron, Aijalon, Chephirah, Jerusalem, Shephelah, Gath, Azekah, Beth-shemesh, Eglon?, Libnah, Lachish, Mareshah, Beth-zur, Hebron, Debir, Baal-peor, Beth-jeshimoth, SALT SEA, Arabah, Plains of Moab

ORIGINAL HISTORICAL SETTING

Author and Date of Writing
Possibly Joshua, around 1380 BC, or Samuel, around 1050 BC

The book is anonymous. Because Joshua is the central character, Jewish tradition held him to be the author. Joshua's writing activity is mentioned twice in the book (18:8; 24:26). Everything in the book could have been written by Joshua, except for the last few verses that tell of his death. On the other hand, many students believe that several instances of the phrase "unto this day" (for example, 4:9; 5:9) point to a time after Joshua's lifetime. The reference to the "Book of Jasher" (10:13; see also 2 Sam. 1:18) may also suggest a later date. If the book was not written by Joshua, then the next likely candidate is Samuel, who would have used sources that were passed on to him from the time of Joshua.

First Audience and Destination
Israelite people after they settled in Canaan, before kingship was established

The first audience was the Israelite nation living in its own land. No doubt the book—which first existed in scroll form, as did all the biblical books—was deposited with the five books of Moses at the tabernacle (24:26).

Occasion
The book does not tell what prompted it to be written. If Joshua was the primary author, then he was continuing the pattern established by Moses. He put into written form the mighty acts God accomplished through his leadership. If the author was Samuel or some writer living shortly before kingship was established, the need was to give Israel a permanent account of its early days of triumph in the land.

▶ JOSHUA'S NORTHERN CAMPAIGNS
Joshua 11:1-15

THE TRIBAL ALLOTMENTS OF ISRAEL
Joshua 13:8–19:49

LEGEND
- • City
- ○ City (uncertain location)
- ▲ Mountain peak

ASHER
NAPHTALI
ZEBULUN
ISSACHAR
WEST MANASSEH
EAST MANASSEH
EPHRAIM
DAN
BENJAMIN
JUDAH
SIMEON
GAD
REUBEN
AMMON
MOAB

MEDITERRANEAN SEA
Lake Hulleh
Sea of Galilee
Jordan River
Yarkon River
DEAD SEA

Kedesh
Yiron
Hazor
Merom
Acco
Cabul
Aphek
Nahalal
Mishal
Hannathon
Achshaph
Rimmon
Capernaum
Rakkath
Hammath
Golan
Ashtaroth
Mt. Carmel
Helkath
Chesulloth
Daberath
Jabneel
En-haddah
Yokneam
Sarid
Tabor
Mt. Tabor
Endor
Lo-debar
Edrei
Dor
Megiddo
Shunem
Jarmuth
Ramoth-gilead
Jezreel
Beth-shan
Taanach
En-gannim
Ibleam
Jabesh-gilead
Dothan
Socoh
Tirzah
Gerasa
Zaphon
Penuel
Mahanaim
Mt. Ebal
Shechem
Pirathon
Mt. Gerizim
Janoah
Succoth
Aphek
Tappuah
Shiloh
Joppa
Gath-rimmon
Ophrah
Jazer
Jehud
Bethel
Lod
Gittaim
Upper Beth-horon
Mizpah
Naaran
Gilgal
Beth-nimrah
Amman
Shaalbim
Chephirah
Gibeon
Jabneel
Gezer
Ramah
Jericho
Abel-shittim
Heshbon
Baalath
Gibbethon
Aijalon
Chesalon
Kiriath-jearim
Adummim
Beth-hoglah
Bezer
Ashdod
Ekron
Zorah
Eshtaol
Jerusalem
Mt. Nebo
Medeba
Timnah
Beth-shemesh
Bethlehem
Kedemoth
Gath
Tekoa
Ashkelon
Beth-zur
Lachish
Mareshah
Hebron
Dibon
Aroer
Eglon
Juttah
En-gedi
Jahaz
Gerar
Ziklag
Eshtemoa
Arad
Bethul
Jattir
Ashan
Kir-haresheth
Simeon
Kabzeel
Beersheba
Hormah
Hazar-shual
Baalah
Eltolad

45

LITERARY FEATURES

Genre and Literary Style
A historical narrative composed in Hebrew

Joshua is mainly a report of the military conquest and settling of Canaan, recounted with a great deal of skill. The dialogues and the farewell speech of Joshua add vividness and excitement. In the Hebrew Scriptures, this book is positioned as the first of the four "Former Prophets." (The others are Judges, Samuel, and Kings.) Together these books describe the 800-year period from Israel's entry into Canaan (about 1406 BC) through the destruction of the temple and Jerusalem and the exile to Babylon (about 586 BC). See comments on **Genre and Literary Style** in **2 KINGS** for further material about the possible literary relationship of the "Former Prophets."

Themes
Conquest, God's promises, "holy war"

The notions of conquest and fulfillment of God's long-standing promises are cherished by all devout students of Scripture. However, the idea of "holy war" is more challenging. The destruction of all remnants of the pagan culture of Canaan must be understood as the sovereign God's judgment on human sin in his time and manner. It was strictly limited to that time and place, so the book cannot be used today to justify military or civil violence for the purpose of advancing God's kingdom. (The notion of a "just war" is a different matter.) The book does show, however, that those who oppose God will not stand forever. During the present (Christian) era the only weapon Christians are to wield as Christians is "the sword of the Spirit, which is the word of God" (Eph. 6:17). One day, the "second Joshua" will smite all evil with his powerful sword (Rev. 19:15).

Book Features and Structure

Perhaps the most interesting feature of the book is its realistic presentation of Joshua's military strategy, a "divide and conquer" approach. After the victory over Jericho, the Israelite army drove west to take Ai and then neutralized Gibeon, breaking the backbone of opposition. Then they conquered the southern cities (chap. 10) and later the northern cities (chap. 11).

The Hebrew term *cherem*, translated "accursed" in the KJV (6:17-18; 7:11-15), deserves mention. It carried the idea of "religious taboo" or "ban." *Cherem* referred to people or things that were so consecrated to God that they were totally given up to him, even to the extent of destroying them (so that they could not be used in ordinary life).

JUDGES

The name translates the Hebrew title, *Shofetim*, which could also be rendered "Leaders" or "Chieftains." It refers to the style of government in Israel from Joshua's death to Saul's kingship. The judges did not preside over courts as the English term might suggest.

▶ *Key Text: 21:25*

"In those days there was no king in Israel: every man did that which was right in his own eyes."

▶ *Key Term: "Delivered"*

Judges tells the repeated cycle of how the Israelites fell into apostasy, so God *delivered* them to their political enemies. Then after they cried out to God, he raised up a leader who *delivered* them from their oppressors. In both situations, God was the one who *delivered* his people because he is the ultimate Judge (11:27).

▶ *One-Sentence Summary*

Israel experienced the repeated cycle of apostasy, oppression, repentance, and restoration by divinely appointed judges throughout the long period following Joshua's death.

The Harod Spring at Ainharod at the foot of the Gilboa Mountain Range. This is where Gideon's men were tested on how they drank water to see if they were qualified to fight against the Midianites (Judg. 7:4-8).

GOD'S MESSAGE IN THE BOOK

Purpose

Judges serves two main purposes. Historically, it sketches the dark period in Israel's history from the exciting days of Moses and Joshua to the promising time of Samuel and Saul. Sadly, there were only fleeting times when Israel truly fulfilled its role as God's people. Theologically, it tells with tedious repetition that when God's people sin, he punishes them, but that when they repent, he forgives and restores. With its negative understanding of how easily God's people may turn away from him, Judges balances the positive picture of inevitable conquest shown in the book of Joshua. God's people who interpret Judges today should view it with its original purposes in mind.

Christian Worldview Elements

Judges emphasizes two complementary pairs of world-view elements: *rebellion and sin* (the people's readiness to forsake God) and *covenant and redemption* (God's gracious restoration of the people because of his cov-enant). As clearly as any book in Scripture, Judges shows the close connection between people's commitment to God and his dealings with them.

GOD
CREATION
SOVEREIGNTY AND PROVIDENCE
FAITH AND REASON
REVELATION AND AUTHORITY
HUMANITY
▶**REBELLION AND SIN**
▶**COVENANT AND REDEMPTION**
COMMUNITY AND CHURCH
DISCIPLESHIP
ETHICS AND MORALITY
TIME AND ETERNITY

Teachings about God

Judges shows the severity of God, who does not lightly ignore it when people claiming his name forsake his ways (2:11-15). It also shows the mercy of God, who is moved with pity when his children cry out to him, even when their troubles are caused by their own sins (2:16-18). The Spirit's power in enabling certain judges to perform mighty works is noteworthy in the book.

Teachings about Humanity

This book paints an embarrassing picture of human fickleness. Israel was seemingly ready to turn away from God to serve idols at the drop of a hat. The shameful incident of the Levite's concubine (chapter 19) demonstrates how degraded the times of the judges could be. Even the three most memorable judges (Gideon, Jephthah, and Samson) were seriously flawed heroes.

Teachings about Salvation

Judges teaches that salvation involves more than just an individual's forgiveness from sin. Sin has consequences that are social and can affect an entire society. Therefore, when God brings salvation, he may dramatically change societies and nations as well as individuals. Further, this book teaches that salvation—deliverance—is always from the Lord and never because someone (or some group) deserves it.

CHRIST IN JUDGES

The judges were God's agents for delivering his people from a variety of enemies. In a much greater way, Christ confronts and defeats Satan and his forces, thereby delivering the people of God from their enemies. This theme is seen in Matthew, Mark, and Luke, in Paul's letter to the Ephesians, and in the Revelation.

GOD'S STORY

When the Events of This Book Happened
From Joshua's death until Samson's death, almost three centuries (about 1380–1060 BC)

While archaeologists debate the date of Israel's conquest of Canaan (see **JOSHUA**), there is general agreement that Saul's kingship began around 1050. Jephthah's reference to three hundred years (11:26) is evidence for a very long period for the judges. Archaeologists consider this period remarkable for two reasons. First, the ancient Near East advanced technologically from the Bronze Age to the Iron Age. According to Judges 1:19 the Israelites lagged behind in this development. Second was the increasing Philistine challenge. Mentioned in the record of the patriarchs and the exodus, they were evidently a serious military threat to Israel only in the days of Samson and later (at the end of the period of judges and the beginning of the monarchy). The Philistines were probably "Sea Peoples" who arrived at the southern coast of Canaan in boats from their original homeland in Caphtor (Crete).

How Judges Fits into God's "Story"

Judges continues God's story: God builds his nation (Israel chosen as the people of promise). Judges functions negatively in the story of God's kingdom. After the exhilarating days of victory under Joshua, it stands to warn God's people not to be careless in their relationship with him. After three centuries of judges, Israel was worse off at the end of the period than at the beginning. Their darkest hour, however, was just before a wonderful new day. David's birth (about 1040 BC) came only a few years after the tragic death of Samson and the seeming triumph of the Philistines (about 1060 BC).

ORIGINAL HISTORICAL SETTING

Author and Date of Writing
Unknown, perhaps Samuel, about 1050 BC

The book is anonymous. It could hardly have been completed until after all its events, and the repeated refrain "in those days there was no king in Israel" (17:6; 18:1; 19:1; 21:25) suggests the author wrote at a time when there was a king. Jewish tradition identified Samuel as the author. There is no reason Samuel could not have written from the early days of Saul's kingship, in which case this is his companion to the book of Joshua. The author used ancient sources, such as "The Song of Deborah" (chap. 5).

First Audience and Destination
Israelite people after they settled in Canaan, after kingship was established

The first audience was the Israelite nation living in its own land. No doubt the book—which first existed in a scroll form, as did all the biblical books—was deposited with the growing canon of Hebrew Scripture at the tabernacle in Shiloh.

Occasion

Judges captured for a later generation the story of earlier national failure. It was perhaps prompted by the need to give a long historical explanation to the question first asked by Gideon: "If the Lord be with us, why then is all this befallen us?" (6:13). Some scholars believe Judges originated as a long prophetic sermon.

 # THE JUDGES OF ISRAEL

Judge	Oppressor	Years of Oppression/Peace	Reference in Judges	Province or Tribal Affiliation
Othniel	Cushan-rishathaim (Aramean King)	8/40	3:8-11	Judah
Ehud	Eglon, King of Moab	18/80	3:12-30	Benjamin
Shamgar	Philistines	-/-	3:31	Son of Anath; possibly a non-Israelite
Deborah with Barak	Canaanites led by Jaban and Sisera	20/-	4:1–5:31	Issachar? Ephraim? Barak came from Napthali
Gideon	Midianites & Amelekites	7/40	6:1–8:27	Manasseh
Tola			10:1-2	Issachar
Jair		-/22	10:3-5	Gileadite; East Manasseh?
Jephthah	Amonites & Philistines	18/-	10:6–12:7	Gileadite; East Manasseh?
Ibzan			12:8-10	from Bethlehem: most likely Judah or Zebulum
Elon			12:11-12	Zebulum
Abdon			12:13-15	Pirathonite (Ephraim)
Samson	Philistines	40/-	13–16	Dan

THE JUDGES OF ISRAEL

LEGEND

GIDEON	Major judges
TOLA	Other judges
●	City
○	City (uncertain location)
▲	Mountain peak

Ijon

Tyre

Dan (Laish)

SHAMGAR (Judges 3:31)

Beth-anath

Kedesh

Achzib

Kedesh

Hazor

ASHER

NAPHTALI

EAST MANASSEH

Acco

Lake Huleh

ELON (Judges 12:11–12)

Golan

Ashta

Rimmon

Sea of Galilee

Mt. Carmel ▲

ZEBULUN

Kedesh-naphtali

Dor

Megiddo

ISSACHAR

Mt. Tabor ▲

GIDEON
(Judges 6:1–8:27)

Ophrah

Kamon

Mt. Gilboa ▲

JAIR (Judges 10:3–5)

Beth-shan

R

WEST MANASSEH

JEPHTHAH
(Judges 10:6–12:7)

TOLA (Judges 10:1–2)

Tirzah

Shamir

Mt. Ebal ▲

ABDON (Judges 12:13–15)

Zaphon

Shechem

Succoth

Pirathon

Mt. Gerizim ▲

Arumah

MEDITERRANEAN SEA

Yarkon River

EPHRAIM

Shiloh

Adam

GAD

DEBORAH
(Judges 4:1–5:31)

EHUD
(Judges 3:12–30)

Jazer

Bethel

Upper Beth-horon

Mizpah

DAN

Lower Beth-horon

Gibeon

Gilgal

Rabbah (Amman)

Gezer

Ramah

Michmash

Jericho

Heshbon

Kiriath-jearim

Gibeah

Bezer

Ashdod

Ekron

Timnah

Eshtaol

Jerusalem

Gath

Zorah

BENJAMIN

Mt. Nebo ▲

SAMSON
(Judges 13:1–16:31)

Bethlehem

IBZAN (Judges 12:8–10)

Ashkelon

REUBEN

Hebron

JUDAH

DEAD SEA

Dibon

Gaza

N. Besor

Debir

Ziklag

OTHNIEL
(Judges 3:7–11)

Arad

SIMEON

Arnon River

Beersheba

Kir-hareseth

LITERARY FEATURES

Genre and Literary Style
A narrative with a long prologue and epilogue, composed in Hebrew

Judges is essentially narrative, but "The Song of Deborah" (chap. 5) is a superb example of early Hebrew poetry. In the Hebrew Scriptures, this book is positioned as the second of the four "Former Prophets." (The others are Joshua, Samuel, and Kings.) Judges (like Kings) tells the story of several centuries with only a few episodes given any detail. (Joshua and Samuel lavish attention on central characters: Joshua, Samuel, Saul, and David). See comments on *Genre and Literary Style* in **2 KINGS** for further material about the possible literary relationship of the "Former Prophets." The book of Judges is composed in good Hebrew style, with chapters 3–16 noted for the repetitive language describing the cycles of oppression and deliverance.

Themes
Apostasy, oppression, repentance, and restoration

These four theme words make up the cycle described six times in the book. The following exact phrases are repeated often: (1) "The children of Israel did evil in the sight of the Lord;" (2) "[God] delivered [or sold] them into the hand of ____;" (3) "The children of Israel cried unto the Lord;" (4) "He judged Israel ____ years."

The oppressor kingdom and the divine deliverer associated with restoration are as follows: (1) Mesopotamia defeated by Othniel; (2) Moab defeated by Ehud; (3) Canaan defeated by Deborah; (4) Midian defeated by Gideon; (5) Ammon defeated by Jephthah; (6) Philistia defeated by Samson.

Book Features and Structure
The cyclical nature of the book is its most unusual literary feature. Judges is also noted for its long explanatory prologue, which lays the foundation for the repeated cycles that follow. Also of note is the long epilogue, which gives two horrible examples of how morally degenerate life was in the days of the judges.

When the six major judges are added with the six minor judges, the total of twelve matches the total number of tribes. That one of these judges was female (Deborah) is striking confirmation of God's sovereignty in raising up leaders that he chooses in any era. The structure of the book is clear:

Judges 1:1–3:6—Prologue
Judges 3:7–16:3—Cycles of oppression and deliverance
Judges 17:1–21:25—Epilogue

RUTH

The English title is the name of the heroine of the story. The title carries over from the Hebrew Bible.

▶ *Key Text: 4:14*

"And the women said unto Naomi, Blessed be the Lord, which hath not left thee this day without a kinsman, that his name may be famous in Israel."

▶ *Key Term: "Kinsman"*

Boaz willingly fulfilled the responsibility of the *go'el*, "kinsman" or "redeemer" for Ruth (as well as for Naomi). As such he beautifully illustrates God, who gladly redeems his people. Ruth and Boaz became ancestors of Jesus, the ultimate Redeemer.

▶ *One-Sentence Summary*

Ruth, a Moabite widow, found love and fulfillment through Boaz, a rich Israelite bachelor who redeemed the land and the name of Ruth's deceased husband, thereby restoring Naomi, Ruth's mother-in-law, from emptiness to fullness.

▼ Woman gathering grain at the foot of Herodium (Ruth 2).

GOD'S MESSAGE IN THE BOOK

Purpose

Biblical scholars have debated the original purpose of this book, for there are a number of lessons the author may have been teaching, for example, the need for a society to take care of its childless widows or the importance of racial tolerance. More obvious than these, however, is its portrayal of God's providential care of people committed to him in the midst of overwhelming challenges to their faith. This charming account of faith in God contrasts sharply with the faithlessness displayed in Judges, the other Bible book that tells of the same time period. God's people who read and study Ruth today should enjoy it for its own sake in its Old Testament setting.

Christian Worldview Elements

The book of Ruth focuses attention on the worldview category of God's *sovereignty and providence* like few other passages in the Scriptures. Further, Ruth the foreigner came to Israel and to Israel's God and then became an ancestor of King David. This reflects the worldview category *community*.

> GOD
> CREATION
> ▶ **SOVEREIGNTY AND PROVIDENCE**
> FAITH AND REASON
> REVELATION AND AUTHORITY
> HUMANITY
> REBELLION AND SIN
> COVENANT AND REDEMPTION
> ▶ **COMMUNITY** AND CHURCH
> DISCIPLESHIP
> ETHICS AND MORALITY
> TIME AND ETERNITY

Teachings about God

The sovereign hand of God in all circumstances is prominent throughout Ruth. The famine and the deaths of three husbands at the beginning of the book were not random acts that "just happened." They were the divinely arranged circumstances for Ruth's incorporation into God's family and to bring her to joy. God's bringing about Naomi's journey from emptiness to fullness parallels the way he brings all his people in the end to eternal fullness of joy. Many scholars recognize Boaz's role of kinsman-redeemer as a prefiguring of Jesus Christ.

Teachings about Humanity

One of the virtues held up throughout the Old Testament is *chesed*, "loving-kindness" or "act of loyal friendship." Ruth, Boaz, and Naomi all did memorable deeds based on *chesed*. Further, although human life inevitably includes pain and loss, it becomes purposeful when people see themselves living under God's protective care. Also, people find great blessing when they live according to God's commands, illustrated by Boaz's blessing because he followed both the law of gleaning and the law concerning levirate marriage (see **Book Features** on p. 51).

Teachings about Salvation

In this story, the most unlikely person was reached by God's grace and gained full membership in the community of God's people. This shows that, even in the Old Testament, God's grace was not limited only to the descendants of Jacob. Further, Ruth's famous declaration of loyalty to Naomi (1:16-17) includes the concept that conversion and commitment to the LORD is a way of life, not just a point of decision.

CHRIST IN RUTH

Boaz' role as kinsman-redeemer is fulfilled in greater measure by Christ who is both our Brother and our Redeemer. Ruth is in the genealogy of Christ. She is the great-grandmother of Israel's Messiah figure, King David.

GOD'S STORY

When the Events of This Book Happened
Late during the period of the judges (about 1140 BC)

This love story is about King David's great-grandparents. David's birth is dated around 1040, but there is no data for the length of each generation. A reasonable opinion is that about a century passed from the time of Ruth's marriage to Boaz until David—youngest son of their grandson Jesse—was born. For more information about this era in general, see **JUDGES**.

How Ruth Fits into God's "Story"

Ruth tells part of "chapter 1" of God's story: God builds his nation (Israel chosen as the people of promise). This book shows that even in the Old Testament era the family of God was not limited only to persons of one ethnic group. God chose people from nations other than Israel as well. Second, Ruth tells the beautiful story of some of King David's ancestors—in fact, the ancestors of Jesus Christ, even though they could not have known this.

ORIGINAL HISTORICAL SETTING

Author and Date of Writing
Unknown, any time from 1000–500 BC

The book does not leave any personal traces of the author. It was written after David's rise to power, but beyond that little is certain. The author's skill in writing is matchless in the Old Testament, but who this was cannot be established.

First Audience and Destination
Israelites living sometime after David came to power

The golden age of Israelite culture during the days of Solomon would serve admirably as the original setting for the book's composition. It is, however, strikingly different from the Song of Songs, the other Old Testament book that tells an individual love story.

Occasion

The beauty of a story told well is sufficient reason to bring it into being. Because nothing is known about its original author or audience, no one knows what first prompted it to be written.

 View overlooking Bethlehem, Ruth's adopted home. It was here that Ruth's great-grandson, David, was born. A thousand years later, Bethlehem was the birthplace of Jesus.

LITERARY FEATURES

Genre and Literary Style
A compact narrative written in excellent Hebrew

Many call Ruth a short story, and it may be called this with the understanding that its events really happened. In the Hebrew Scriptures it was placed in the third section, the Writings or *Kethuvim* (the other two sections are the Law and the Prophets). Among the Writings it was one of the Five Scrolls. Each of these Five Scrolls became associated with one of the Israelite festivals and was read publicly during that festival. Ruth was identified with *Shavuoth*, "Weeks" or "Pentecost," which celebrated the end of the barley harvest and the beginning of the wheat harvest. Its Hebrew is so carefully polished that Ruth has been likened to a precious jewel.

Themes
Loyalty, redeemer, contrast

The concepts of loyalty (*chesed*) and redeemer (*go'el*) have already been noted in this chapter. The contrasts in the book are part of its literary attractiveness: pleasant versus bitter; full versus empty; living versus dead. The greatest contrast is between Ruth (the poor foreigner) and Boaz (the rich Israelite), who come together in delightful resolution. Both of these central characters acted according to loyalty (*chesed*), but were related to minor characters who did not show loyalty.

Book Features and Structure

The book is noteworthy because it includes four cultural expressions that appear exceptionally odd to modern readers. First, "gleaning" was a kind of early welfare provision that allowed the poor to reap the edges of grain fields (2:2). Second was the symbolism of Ruth's claiming Boaz's protection by urging him to cover her with his cloak (3:9). Third is the real estate transaction made legal by exchanging sandals, which had to be explained even for the first readers (4:7). Most important of all, however, the entire story makes sense only in light of the law of levirate marriage, stated in Deuteronomy 25:5-6. The law guaranteed ongoing family lines and decentralized the control of farmland. It required that when a married man died childless, his brother or next of kin had to marry the widow. Their firstborn would then receive the name and inheritance of the deceased.

The story is framed by a historical prologue of Naomi's emptying (1:1-5) and a forward-looking epilogue of Naomi's filling (4:13-22). Between these are four deftly drawn scenes: Naomi's journey home (chap. 1); Ruth's gleaning (chap. 2); Ruth's visit to Boaz (chap. 3); and Boaz's redemption of Ruth (chap. 4).

THE KINGDOM OF SAUL AND HIS WARS
1 Samuel 11; 13; 14:47-48

LEGEND

ATTACK ROUTES
- Ammonites' route
- Saul's routes
- Jonathan's (Saul's son) routes
- Israel's routes
- Philistines' routes
- Saul's pressure

- ★ Capital city
- • City
- ○ City (uncertain location)
- ▲ Mountain peak
- ⤸ Pass
- ⚔ Battle
- Saul's kingdom
- Aramean lands
- Moab
- Ammon
- Amalekites
- Edom
- Philistine heartland
- Philistine encroachments
- Phoenicia

Tyre, Dan, ARAM, Achzib, Kedesh, Lake Huleh, Hazor, Acco, GESHUR, Aphek, Hannathon, Sea of Galilee, Golan, Ashtaroth, Mt. Carmel, Mt. Tabor, Mt. Moreh, Edrei, Megiddo, Jezreel, Shunem, Taanach, Mt. Gilboa, Ramoth-gilead, Dothan, Ibleam, Beth-shan, Saul defeats Nahash, Socoh, Tirzah, Jabesh-gilead, GILEAD, Mt. Ebal, Zaphon, Mahanaim, Mt. Gerizim, Shechem, Succoth, Aphek, Adam, Jogbehah, Ophrah, Beth-horon, Mizpah, Bethel, Gilgal, Rabbah (Amman), AMMON, Gezer, Aijalon, Michmash, Jericho, Heshbon, Ekron, Ramah, Geba, Area enlarged at right, Gibeon, Gibeah, Mt. Nebo, Medeba, Beth-shemesh, Jebus (Jerusalem), ASHDOD, Gath, Azekah, Bethlehem, Ashkelon, PHILISTIA, Lachish, Hebron, DEAD SEA, En-gedi, Dibon, Aroer, Gaza, Gerar, Ziklag, Sharuhen, Beersheba, Arad, Hormah, MOAB, Kir-hareseth, Zoar, AMALEK

32 N

31 N

1 SAMUEL

THE FIRST BOOK OF KINGDOMS

The book is named for Samuel, the judge who anointed Saul and David, the first two kings of Israel, of whom 1 and 2 Samuel tell the story. In the Hebrew Bible, 1 and 2 Samuel were originally one book. The Greek translators (second century BC), who divided the book, used the titles 1 and 2 Kingdoms.

▶ Key Text: 18:7

"And the women answered one another as they played, and said, Saul hath slain his thousands, and David his ten thousands."

▶ Key Term: "Monarchy"

This book describes the beginning of the monarchy in Israel. The first king, Saul, was a failure; the second king, David, succeeded, even though he struggled to survive Saul's bitter jealousy.

▶ One-Sentence Summary

After Samuel's leadership as judge, the people of Israel turned to Saul as their first king, whom God rejected and instead chose David, who had many adventures as a renegade from Saul's court.

▼ Gibeah, the site of King Saul's palace where David played his harp for the king (1 Sam. 18:10-11).

GOD'S MESSAGE IN THE BOOK

Purpose

Since this book was originally the first half of a single composition, the purpose for the books now called 1 and 2 Samuel must be considered together. This work answered important questions for Israelites (probably living in the days of Solomon) about the true nature of the Davidic dynasty. If the people had been wrong to ask for a king and if God had rejected Saul as king, then why should they now suppose that the monarchs of the Davidic line would continue? The work is filled with narrative tension between the dangers of a king (1 Sam. 8) and the hope for an enduring dynasty (2 Sam. 7). The answer is that despite human evil God worked to bring about his plan for an everlasting kingdom with an everlasting King (2 Sam. 7:16). God's people who study the books of Samuel today should view it with this original purpose in mind.

GOD
CREATION
SOVEREIGNTY AND PROVIDENCE
FAITH AND REASON
REVELATION AND AUTHORITY
HUMANITY
▶**REBELLION AND SIN**
COVENANT AND REDEMPTION
COMMUNITY AND CHURCH
DISCIPLESHIP
▶**ETHICS AND MORALITY**
TIME AND ETERNITY

Christian Worldview Elements

First Samuel brings into sharp focus the worldview categories of *rebellion and sin* (demonstrated in the life of Saul especially) and *ethics and morality* (demonstrated especially in the life of David, who was treated unfairly and had to respond righteously).

Teachings about God

God of Israel was responsible for shaping Israel's destiny. He allowed Israel's choice of Saul to stand, but he judged Saul for his disobedience. He chose David, who by the end of 1 Samuel was not yet secure in his position as king. The Spirit of God is seen as the divine enabler: he came upon both Saul and David to empower their service.

Teachings about Humanity

This book teaches about mankind through telling the stories of three heroes: Samuel, Saul, and David. Samuel was a dedicated servant of God who nevertheless failed as a parent. Saul was a handsome, talented leader who failed in his primary task: glad obedience to God's revealed will. David's life (in 1 Samuel) demonstrates that those whom God chooses may come as a surprise (to other humans), and that they may face great difficulties and yet serve him wholeheartedly.

Teachings about Salvation

This book shows that a right relationship with God inevitably brings with it obedience from the heart and that God values heart obedience much more than external conformity to religious rituals: "And Samuel said, Hath the L<small>ORD</small> *as great* delight in burnt offerings and sacrifices, as in obeying the voice of the L<small>ORD</small>? Behold, to obey *is* better than sacrifice, *and* to hearken than the fat of rams" (15:22).

☧ *CHRIST IN 1 SAMUEL*

First Samuel presents Israel's first two kings, Saul and David. These kings of Israel foreshadow Israel's true King, Jesus Christ. Jesus is in the lineage of David and is called Son of David, a term that is equivalent to Messiah. Samuel's model of priest, prophet, and political leader foreshadows Jesus' role as prophet, priest, and king. First Samuel includes the first mention of a person being called the anointed of Yahweh. This is significant because the word *Messiah* means "anointed one."

GOD'S STORY

When the Events of This Book Happened
From Samuel's birth until Saul's death (about 1105–1010 BC)

This is the first Bible book for which scholars generally agree concerning the dates. Although not all the events for 1 Samuel can be dated with certainty, there is a general consensus that David's reign over Judah began around 1010 BC. This dates the beginning of Saul's kingship around 1050 BC and the birth of David about ten years later. (The Iron Age had fully developed in Israel by the time of David.)

How 1 Samuel Fits into God's "Story"

First Samuel continues God's story: God builds his nation (Israel chosen as the people of promise). Throughout the period of the judges, the people of Israel had stagnated. In 1 Samuel the story of God's kingdom leaps ahead dramatically. Just as Moses came as a powerful God-sent leader to bring change after centuries of little progress, so now Samuel came as a powerful God-sent leader. Just as Moses led Israel to receive the law, so Samuel led the people of his day to receive the king of God's choice. This book tells the rise of that king: "The Lord hath sought him a man after his own heart" (13:14).

ORIGINAL HISTORICAL SETTING

Author and Date of Writing
Unknown, perhaps around 950 BC (during Solomon's reign)

The book (1 and 2 Samuel together) was composed by someone who used sources, for none of the characters in it could have been an eyewitness to all the events mentioned. Some scholars think a clue to authorship is found in 1 Chronicles 29:29: "Now the acts of David the king, first and last, behold, they are written in the book of Samuel the seer, and in the book of Nathan the prophet, and in the book of Gad the seer." The author's repeated use of the phrase "unto this day" (see 1 Sam. 30:25) suggests a time of composition somewhat removed from when the events occurred. If the purpose of the composition was to answer questions about the legitimacy of Israel's kingship (see **Purpose** above), then a date during Solomon's reign but before the divided monarchy fits. Other scholars suggest that the historical note in 1 Samuel 27:6 requires a date after the monarchy divided, but this could be an editorial comment added later.

First Audience and Destination
Israelites living in their land during the monarchy

The book does not state its original audience or destination. The deduction noted above is surely true. Perhaps the original "Scroll of Samuel" was deposited in a book depository in Solomon's temple when it was first completed. There it would have joined the growing collection of Israel's sacred Scriptures.

Occasion

Since the authorship and date of composition are unknown, the occasion cannot be surmised. Because of its ultimate position in the Hebrew canon of Scripture as the third of the "Former Prophets," 1 and 2 Samuel may have been prompted by the author's desire to continue the story of God's people Israel that the books of Joshua and Judges began. Some scholars believe that the author was propelled by discovering long passages originally composed by someone else and which stood on their own. These include the "Ark Narrative" (1 Sam. 4:1–7:1), "David's Rise to Power" (1 Sam. 16:14–2 Sam. 5:10), and "Absalom's Revolt" (2 Sam. 13–20).

LEGEND
- • City
- ○ City (uncertain location)
- ▪ Stronghold at Masada
- ← David's odyssey
- ◄--- Possible route to Moab
- ◄ Philistine attacks
- ◄ Amalekite pressure
- ▨ Saul's kingdom

35 E

Shechem

Jordan River

Jabbok River

Aphek

Samuel provides temporary shelter

Ahimelech provides David with food and arms

Slaying of Goliath

Ramah
Gibeah (of Saul)
Nob
Jebus (Jerusalem)
Bethlehem

David returns to Gath after stealing Saul's spear in the Wilderness of Maon

Ashdod
Ekron
Gath
Azekah
Socoh
Adullam
Keilah

Forest of Hereth

Wilderness of Judah

DEAD SEA

David rescues Keilah from attack

Hebron

Wilderness of Ziph

David spares Saul's life

Ashkelon

Ziph

En-gedi

Horesh

After second incident at Keilah, Saul pursues David through wilderness, to En-gedi

Gaza

PHILISTIA

Shephelah

David marries Abigail

Carmel

Wilderness of Maon

Maon
Arad

MOAB

Achish, king of Gath, gives city of Ziklag to David

Ziklag
Bethul
Ashan
Kabzeel

Beersheba

Wilderness of Kenites

Hormah

Baalah

Negeb of Jeraheelmites

Ezem

Mizpah of Moab (Kir-hareseth)

AMALEK

Negeb

Safe refuge is sought for parents in Moab

Zered River

David pursues the Amalekites

Amalekites apply pressure against villages of Judah

Arabah

EDOM

| 0 | 15 | 30 Miles |
| 0 | 15 | 30 Kilometers |

35 E

63

LITERARY FEATURES

Genre and Literary Style
A historical account written in Hebrew

First Samuel tells the story of the rise of monarchy in Israel by giving the biographies of three men: Samuel, Saul, and David. When secondary characters such as Hannah and Jonathan enter the story, they are important only as they relate to the major characters. Although the Hebrew writing style is acceptable, the hand-copied Hebrew manuscripts of 1 and 2 Samuel have occasional defects in which words are missing, for example Saul's age and length of reign in 1 Samuel 13:1. (Compare a contemporary translation with the KJV at this point.) In these cases, scholars rely on other ancient versions of the book. In the Hebrew canon this was included in the "Former Prophets." See comments on *Genre and Literary Style* in **2 KINGS** for further material about the possible literary relationship of the "Former Prophets."

Themes
Kingship and covenant, the ark of the covenant, David's adventures

These three concepts dominate the book. Explaining the relationship between Israel's desire for a king and the national covenant with the LORD was the central concern of the writer. The writer's focus on the ark of the covenant is significant for two reasons. First, it looked back to the time of the ark's origin (Exodus). Second, it looked forward to the permanent home for the ark that David longed to build but which Solomon finally constructed (1 Kings). The ark theme is thus one of continuity. The writer's pleasure in preserving David's adventures has given us some of the most memorable stories in Scripture, for example his encounters with Goliath, Jonathan, and Abigail.

Book Features and Structure

David's career anticipates what his descendant Jesus later experienced. Both were identified by a prophet (Samuel and John the Baptist); empowered by the Spirit (16:13); and found refuge in a foreign land (Egypt and Philistia). Other parallels could be found.

Everything in this book happened in Israel or Philistia. Hannah's song (chap. 2) is a devotional high point of the Old Testament. The book is organized around three great men and tells their stories successively: Samuel and his ministry (1–7); Saul's selection and rejection (8–15); David's selection and adventures while Saul falls (16–31).

2 SAMUEL

THE SECOND BOOK OF KINGDOMS

The book is named for Samuel, the judge who anointed Saul and David, the first two kings of Israel, of whom 1 and 2 Samuel tell the story. In the Hebrew Bible, 1 and 2 Samuel were originally one book. The Greek translators (second century BC), who divided the book, used the titles 1 and 2 Kingdoms.

▶ Key Text: 7:16

"And thine house and thy kingdom shall be established for ever before thee: thy throne shall be established for ever."

▶ Key Term: "David"

The name "David" appears more than two hundred times in this book. It focuses entirely on the time that he was king of Israel.

▶ One-Sentence Summary

David's reign over Israel included times of elation, such as his conquest of Jerusalem and the LORD's promise of an everlasting dynasty, as well as times of failure, such as his adultery with Bathsheba and the treason of his son Absalom.

▼ Late afternoon in Bethlehem, city of David.

GOD'S MESSAGE IN THE BOOK

Purpose

Because 1 and 2 Samuel first existed as a single composition, see the discussion in the **Purpose** section for **1 SAMUEL**.

Christian Worldview Elements

Second Samuel touches on a number of worldview elements. However, above all it draws attention to the category *covenant and redemption*. God's covenant promise to David that he was the first king of an everlasting dynasty marked a major advance in the progress of divine revelation.

Teachings about God

God is sovereign in carrying out his kingdom plans. His unconditional covenant with undeserving David (chap. 7) is as magnificent as his covenant with Abraham. This book also says a great deal about approaching God in worship. He desires the worship of his people, but only in the ways he has revealed, as the material about the ark of the covenant emphasizes.

> GOD
> CREATION
> SOVEREIGNTY AND PROVIDENCE
> FAITH AND REASON
> REVELATION AND AUTHORITY
> HUMANITY
> REBELLION AND SIN
> **COVENANT AND REDEMPTION**
> COMMUNITY AND CHURCH
> DISCIPLESHIP
> ETHICS AND MORALITY
> TIME AND ETERNITY

Teachings about Humanity

Second Samuel throws the spotlight on one individual, David, who modeled magnificently that humans can accomplish great tasks for God when their heart is passionately turned to pleasing him. On the other hand, David's sins and failures show that redeemed humans still must deal with the effects of the fall in their lives.

Teachings about Salvation

The account of David's adultery, Nathan's confrontation with the king, and David's subsequent repentance and restoration stand as a profound paradigm of salvation. The following exchange distills the message of redemption even today: "And David said unto Nathan, I have sinned against the LORD. And Nathan said unto David, The LORD also hath put away thy sin; thou shalt not die" (12:13). David's reflection on this experience, Psalm 51, stands unsurpassed in Scripture on the relationship between confession of sin and divine forgiveness.

CHRIST IN 2 SAMUEL

As founder of the dynasty of which Jesus ("Son of David") is the eternal King, David illustrates Christ's kingship in many ways. His compassion and loyalty to Mephibosheth was one example of the undeserved love we receive from God.

GOD'S STORY

When the Events of This Book Happened
From Saul's death to David's death (about 1110–970 BC)

The forty-year reign of David saw the beginning of the flowering of Israelite culture. Although schol-ars have a general consensus about the years of David's rule, there is insufficient evidence to date some of the prominent events of his reign, such as the birth of Solomon or the rebellion of Absalom.

How 2 Samuel Fits into God's "Story"

The book of 2 Samuel brings almost to a climax the beginning of God's story: God builds his nation (Israel chosen as the people of promise). This book tells, in more detail than for any other Israelite king, the story of the dynastic founder. It was critical to show that David, the man after God's heart (1 Sam. 13:14), had valued wholehearted obedience to God above all else in the way he went about establishing his kingship. Despite his flaws, David was the model king to whom the later kings looked for inspiration. Jesus, the greatest descendant of David, established the kingdom of God at his first coming and will consummate it at his second coming.

▼ The Citadel was built by King David on the highest point at Arad in Israel.

ORIGINAL HISTORICAL SETTING

Because 1 and 2 Samuel first existed as a single composition, see the discussion in the **Original Historical Setting** section in **1 SAMUEL**.

Author and Date of Writing
Unknown, perhaps around 950 BC (during Solomon's reign)

First Audience and Destination
Israelites living in the land of Israel during the monarchy

Occasion: *Unknown*

 # LITERARY FEATURES

Genre and Literary Style
A historical narrative written in Hebrew, with a few passages of poetry

The narrative of 2 Samuel focuses on David's exploits as king. His relationship to God, Israel's true King, also receives attention. The writer portrayed him realistically and was careful not to gloss over David's faults. The memorable poetic sections were David's compositions: "The Song of the Bow" (1:19-27); "Psalm of Praise" (22:1-51, which is also Psalm 18); and "David's Last Words" (23:1-7). Second Samuel in the Hebrew canon was part of the "Former Prophets." See comments on **Genre and Literary Style** in **2 KINGS** for further material about the possible literary relationship of the "Former Prophets."

Themes
Kingship and covenant, the ark of the covenant, David's adventures

Because 1 and 2 Samuel first existed as a single composition, see the discussion in the **Themes** section of **1 SAMUEL**.

Book Features and Structure

The central theological feature of 2 Samuel is the unconditional promise of an unending dynasty that God made to David. In the overall understanding of God's redemptive purposes, it stands with and is an extension of the "royal grant" covenant that God initiated with Abraham (Gen. 12; 15). God promised that Abraham would be the father of nations; he promised that David would be the first king of an unending dynasty of kings that would rule forever. Jesus Christ fulfills these promises: "The kingdoms of this world are become the kingdoms of our LORD, and of his Christ; and he shall reign for ever and ever" (Rev. 11:15).

The narrative of David's rule is developed in three stages: David's kingdom secured (1–4); David's capital, covenant, and conquests (5–10); David's faults (11–20). Chapters 21–24 are an epilogue, perhaps complied from a variety of materials about David's reign.

DAVID'S WARS OF CONQUEST
2 Samuel 11:1-12, 31

LEGEND

- • City
- ○ City (uncertain location)
- ▲ Mountain peak
- ⟵ David's routes of conquest
- ⟵ Edomite threat and retreat
- ⟵ Philistine threat
- ⟵ Aramean forces
- ▨ Saul's (now deceased) kingdom
- ▨ Territory of David's conquest

10. David took quantities of bronze from Tibhath, Cun, and Berothai to make the Bronze Sea in Solomom's temple

3. David strikes Hadadezer, king of Zobah

6. Hadadezer assembles large Aramean army

7. David pursues Hadadezer a second time, and inflicts serious defeat at Helam

9. David defeats the Ammonites (2 Sam. 8:3–12; 10:1–13; 12:26–31)

8. David sends Joab in retaliation of public humiliation

1. David defeats Philistine advance, gains control of the Shephelah (2 Sam. 5:17–22)

HAMATH
Tibhath
Byblos
Cun
Berothai
ZOBAH
DAMASCUS
PHOENICIA
BETH-REHOB
Damascus
Abana River
Sidon
Mt. Hermon
Pharpar River
ARAM
Litani River
Tyre
Dan
MAACAH
Hazor
Lake Huleh
Acco
Sea of Galilee
GESHUR
Mt. Carmel
Ashtaroth
Helam
LAND OF TOB
Mt. Tabor
Mt. Moreh
Megiddo
Mt. Gilboa
Ramoth-gilead
Beth-shan
Jordan River
Yarmuk River
MEDITERRANEAN SEA
Yarkon River
Mt. Gerizim
Shechem
Mahanaim
AMMON
Aphek
Bethel
Beth-horon
Rabbah (Amman)
Gezer
Kiriath-jearim
Gibeon
Jericho
Aijalon
Sorek River
Valley of Rephaim
Jerusalem
Medeba
Gath
Baal-perazim
PHILISTIA
Shephelah
Hebron
DEAD SEA
Aroer

KINGDOM OF DAVID AND SOLOMON

UNQI
T. Tayinat
Arpad

Aleppo
BIT-AGUSI

BETH-EDEN
BETH-EDEN
(BIT ADINI)

Tiphsah

Euphrates R.

Orontes R.

HAMATH

ARAM-ZOBAH
Hamath
Qatna

Arvad

MEDITERRANEAN
SEA

PHOENICIA

Kadesh
(on the
Orontes)

Tadmor

Byblos

BETH-REHOB

Abana R.

Sidon

Damascus

Pharpar R.

Tyre

Dan

MAACAH

Acco

Hazor

GESHUR

Chinnereth

Ashtaroth

Megiddo

Beth-shan

Ramoth-gilead

*International
Coastal Highway*

Shechem

King's Highway

Joppa

AMMON

PHILISTIA
Gezer
Ashdod
Gath
Gibeah
Jerusalem

Rabbah
(Amman)

Gaza

Raphia

Beersheba

MOAB
Kir-
hareseth

**Eastern
Desert**

Tamar

EDOM

Kadesh-
barnea

W. el-Arish

MEDITERRANEAN SEA

EGYPT

Ezion-
geber

Gulf of

LEGEND

- • City
- ⎯ Boundary of Solomon's kingdom
- Saul's kingdom
- Territory conquered by David
- Solomon's area of influence
- Non-conquered territory
- ⎯ Major highway

0 20 40 60 80 100 Miles
0 20 40 60 80 100 Kilometers

1 KINGS

THE THIRD BOOK OF KINGDOMS

Melakim, the Hebrew title, means "Kings." Originally a single work, 1 and 2 Kings was first divided into two books by the Greek translators (second century BC), and English Bibles follow this pattern. The Greek version used the titles 3 and 4 Kingdoms.

▶ *Key Text: 11:35-36*

"But I will take the kingdom out of his son's hand, and will give it unto thee, even ten tribes. And unto his son will I give one tribe, that David my servant may have a light alway before me in Jerusalem, the city which I have chosen me to put my name there."

▶ *Key Term: "Division"*

This book describes the division of the Israelites into two competing kingdoms. The kings of Israel, the Northern Kingdom, were invariably idolatrous, while the kings of Judah, the Southern Kingdom, were sometimes good and sometimes evil.

▶ *One-Sentence Summary*

After Solomon's splendid rule, culminating in the dedication of the temple in Jerusalem, the kingdom divided, and God raised up prophets to confront idolatry, notably Elijah, who opposed the evil Ahab.

▼ Ahab's palace in Samaria (1 Kings 21).

GOD'S MESSAGE IN THE BOOK

Purpose

Since this book was originally the first half of a single composition, the purpose for the books now called 1 and 2 Kings must be considered together. This work answered important questions for Israelites (probably living in the years of exile in Babylon) about the period of the kings from God's perspective. If they were now in exile, why had this happened, especially since Solomon's rule had been so splendid? Had the later kings failed militarily? politically? economically? The answer was that the kings (and the people under them) had all in all failed religiously. They had abandoned the Lord, their true King, and he had sent three painful lessons to teach them the importance of staying true to him. First, he divided Israel into two kingdoms (1 Kings 12, about 931 BC); second, he sent the idolatrous Northern Kingdom into permanent captivity through the Assyrians (2 Kings 17, about 722 BC); third, he sent the idolatrous Southern Kingdom into (temporary) exile through the Babylonians (2 Kings 25, about 586 BC).

Thus, the author wrote a highly selective account of the kings, evaluating each one as to whether he did right or evil in the eyes of the LORD. The author's religious perspective is also seen in that about a third of the narrative focuses on the prophetic ministries of Elijah and Elisha. God's people who study the books of Kings today should do so with this original purpose in mind.

Christian Worldview Elements

Because 1 Kings covers more than 120 years in so brief a narrative, it brings into sharp focus the worldview category of *time and eternity* (that history moves forward according to God's plan). It also adds insight into the categories of *covenant and redemption* (demonstrated in the wonderful achievements of Solomon, especially the temple) and *rebellion and sin* (shown particularly in the conflict between Ahab and Elijah).

> GOD
> CREATION
> SOVEREIGNTY AND PROVIDENCE
> FAITH AND REASON
> REVELATION AND AUTHORITY
> HUMANITY
> ► **REBELLION AND SIN**
> ► **COVENANT AND REDEMPTION**
> COMMUNITY AND CHURCH
> DISCIPLESHIP
> ETHICS AND MORALITY
> ► **TIME AND ETERNITY**

Teachings about God

First Kings emphasizes "one God, one temple." Because Israel's God is the one true LORD of all, then he can be worshipped properly at the one place that he has designated: the temple in Jerusalem. He will not tolerate the worship of rival deities (such as Baal). He will not long endure being worshipped in rival sites (such as at the shrines of the golden calves in Dan and Bethel, or on the "high places"). The Spirit is present to inspire God's prophets.

Teachings about Humanity

This book looks at humanity by evaluating the kings' lives. The only thing that really mattered was whether a king did "right in the eyes of the LORD" (15:5,11; 22:43) or whether he did "evil in the sight of the LORD" (11:6; the exact phrase occurs eight times in the KJV text).

Teachings about Salvation

On one hand, 1 Kings emphasizes that salvation is entirely due to God's sovereign work. Solomon's temple dedication prayer emphasized this: "For thou didst separate them from among all the people of the earth, to *be* thine inheritance" (8:53). On the other hand his people were expected to live in loyalty to the covenant, and both kings and people are evaluated according to the terms of the covenant established at Mount Sinai.

CHRIST IN 1 KINGS

Solomon, David's son and Israel's third king, is prominent in 1 Kings. Solomon's wisdom and splendor were known far beyond Israel. This shining hour in Israel's history points to the wisdom and glory of Christ. Jesus reminded one of his audiences that the Queen of Sheba made a long journey to hear Solomon and One greater than Solomon is now among them (Luke 11:31).

GOD'S STORY

When the Events of This Book Happened
From David's death through Jehoshaphat's death (about 970–848 BC)

During the first forty years covered by this book, the Israelite nation reached its splendid apex. After Solomon's death about 931 BC, the Davidic dynasty was restricted to the Southern Kingdom of Judah. First Kings describes the rule of the next four Davidic monarchs. In the Northern Kingdom during the same era, political instability was the norm, with dynasties coming and going. The most important Northern kings politically were Jeroboam I (who established the Northern Kingdom and set up golden calves); Omri (who established Samaria as his capital); and Ahab (who forged a foreign alliance by marrying a pagan princess, Jezebel, daughter of Ethbaal, king of Tyre and Sidon).

How 1 Kings Fits into God's "Story"

First Kings completes "chapter 1" of God's story: God builds his nation (Israel chosen as the people of promise). It begins "chapter 2" of the story: God educates his nation (disobedient Israel disciplined). It depicts the earthly nation of Israel at its grandest and most glorious during the rule of Solomon. Jerusalem was truly splendid as a wealthy, walled capital city whose king was legendary for his wisdom and to whom other nations brought tribute. Although this was a blip in the history of the ancient Near East, it stood forever in the hearts of Israelites as a time that could be regained. Strikingly, the portrait of the eternal state in Revelation 21–22 is like Solomon's Jerusalem, but infinitely more glorious.

ORIGINAL HISTORICAL SETTING

Author and Date of Writing
Unknown, perhaps Jeremiah about 560 BC

First and Second Kings are anonymous, but Jewish tradition named Jeremiah, who was also credited with the books of Jeremiah and Lamentations. Most modern scholars discount the traditional view. Whoever the author was cannot now be known. The perspective is that of the exile in Babylon. The writer, however, used sources from an earlier time, incorporating their phrase "unto this day" (for example, 1 Kings 8:8; 2 Kings 8:22) for matters that did not exist during the exile.

First Audience and Destination
Probably the Israelites living in Babylonian exile

The original audience is not stated but is judged from reading the book. See the discussion above on ***Purpose*** for an explanation of how 1 and 2 Kings met the needs of Israelites living after the destruction of Jerusalem and the temple.

Occasion

Some official court records from the monarchy were evidently preserved and transported to Babylon. These included "The Book of the Acts of Solomon" (1 Kings 11:41); "The Book of the Chronicles of the Kings of Israel" (1 Kings 14:19 and seventeen other references); and "The Book of the Chronicles of the Kings of Judah" (1 Kings 14:29 and fourteen other references). The writer selected materials from these records to interpret the era of Solomon and the divided monarchy for people of his day.

JERUSALEM IN THE TIME OF DAVID AND SOLOMON
1 Kings 5–7; 9:15

LEGEND
- ▲ Mountain peak
- ⑁ Gate
- ┅┅┅ City walls
- "City of David" The Old Jebusite/Canaanite City
- Possible addition by David
- Temple Mount
- x Spot elevation
- ~2400~ Contour interval = 33ft. (10m)

MEDITERRANEAN SEA

PRESENT-DAY ISRAEL

Area enlarged below

30 N

30 E   40 E

E   35 E   36 E

33 N

MEDITERRANEAN SEA

Jordan R.

Jerusalem

Area enlarged at right

32 N

DEAD SEA

31 N

0   1/8 Mile

Transversal Valley

Mount Moriah
Temple ⛪

Temple Mount

Tyropoeon Valley

Ophel

Stepped stone structure
Warren's Shaft

Millo ?
City of David
Gihon Spring

Kidron Valley

x2486

2600

2500

2400

2300

2200

2100

2000

King's Pool ?

En-rogel

2437 x

2400

2300

Valley

LITERARY FEATURES

Genre and Literary Style
An extremely selective account written in Hebrew

First Kings lingers on the days of Solomon and then tells of the reigns of most other kings with broad strokes. Then when he comes to Ahab, the author provides a number of details once again, in particular describing the role of Elijah as the prophet of the Lord. First Kings in the Hebrew Scriptures was one of the "Former Prophets." See comments on **Genre and Literary Style** in **2 KINGS** for further material about the possible literary relationship of the "Former Prophets."

Themes
The temple, kingship and covenant, the rise of the prophets

The completion of the temple brought the Israelite people to their finest hour. After Solomon's death, the unending challenge was to keep Israel and its kings true to the Lord and true to worshipping him only at the temple. Thus, monarchs are evaluated as righteous or evil in this light. God raised up the prophet Elijah (and his successors) to call Israel back to God.

Book Features and Structure

The author was interested in chronological data. He noted that the temple was built 480 years after the exodus (6:1). For the period of the divided monarchy, he maintained a cross reference system between the kings of Israel and Judah, which has the effect of showing that both kingdoms were still God's people. The typical formula the author used was, "in the ___ year of ___ son of ____, ____ began to rule over Judah [or Israel], and he ruled ___ years" (see 15:1 for an example).

Everything in this book happened in either Israel or Judah, with the exception of Elijah's travels outside the land. The book has three sections: Solomon and his splendid reign (1–11); the early period of the divided monarchy (12–16); and Elijah and the events surrounding his ministry (17–22).

2 KINGS

THE FOURTH BOOK OF KINGDOMS

Melakim, the Hebrew title, means "Kings." Originally a single work, 1 and 2 Kings was first divided into two books by the Greek translators (second century BC), and English Bibles follow this pattern. The Greek version used the titles 3 and 4 Kingdoms.

▶ *Key Text: 17:22-23*

"For the children of Israel walked in all the sins of Jeroboam which he did; they departed not from them; until the Lord removed Israel out of his sight, as he had said by all his servants the prophets. So was Israel carried away out of their own land to Assyria unto this day."

▶ *Key Term: "Dispersion"*

This book tells the ongoing story of the Israelites in two competing kingdoms with its sad conclusion. The Northern Kingdom fell to Assyria and was dispersed forever. Then the Southern Kingdom fell to the Babylonians and likewise went into dispersion.

▶ *One-Sentence Summary*

Even after Elisha's ministry, Israel persisted in idolatry and so went into permanent captivity; yet Judah, despite the prophets and a few righteous kings, continued to be so wicked that God sent Babylon to remove the people into exile.

Six-sided clay prism on which Sennacherib, King of Assyria, tells of the siege of Jerusalem during his third campaign (c. 701 BC): ". . . I then besieged Hezekiah of Judah who had not submitted to my rule, and I captured forty-six of his large towns and fortresses with innumerable small villages round about them . . . I took 200,150 people prisoner. . . . Hezekiah himself, like a caged bird, I besieged in Jerusalem, his royal city."

GOD'S MESSAGE IN THE BOOK

Purpose

Because 1 and 2 Kings first existed as a single composition, see the discussion in the **Purpose** section of **1 KINGS**.

Christian Worldview Elements

Second Kings covers nearly three centuries, so it brings into sharp focus the worldview category of *time and eternity* (that history moves forward according to God's plan). It also adds insight into the category of *rebellion and sin*, demonstrated in the ongoing idolatry of Israel and Judah culminating in their destruction.

GOD
CREATION
SOVEREIGNTY AND PROVIDENCE
FAITH AND REASON
REVELATION AND AUTHORITY
HUMANITY
▶ **REBELLION AND SIN**
COVENANT AND REDEMPTION
COMMUNITY AND CHURCH
DISCIPLESHIP
ETHICS AND MORALITY
▶ **TIME AND ETERNITY**

Teachings about God

Like Judges and 2 Chronicles, 2 Kings shows the severity of God in judging those who rebel against him. Deuteronomy had promised divine condemnation on those who were unfaithful to the Lord. The story of 2 Kings is largely one of disloyalty, and God's "educational program" meant teaching his people that he values faithfulness to him above all else, even if that means exiling them. The book ends with a ray of hope: God's promises about an everlasting Davidic dynasty are intact, for the king is still alive.

Teachings about Humanity

Like 1 Kings, this book evaluates people by just one criterion: did they do "right in the sight of the Lord" or not? Tragically, for the most part both kings and people did not (see **Key Text**). The author reached the following verdict about the last king of Judah: "And he did that which was evil in the sight of the Lord, according to all that Jehoiakim had done. For through the anger of the Lord it came to pass in Jerusalem and Judah, until he had cast them out from his presence" (24:19-20).

Teachings about Salvation

God's prophets in 2 Kings (Elijah, Elisha, Jonah, Huldah, and Isaiah are named) called people to repent for their religious apostasy and to worship the Lord alone. Hezekiah is the model of trust in the Lord for salvation (18:5-6). Turning from the sin of idolatry, when accompanied by a desire for God's glory to be displayed, may even bring salvation from military threats (see Hezekiah's prayer and God's response in 19:15-37).

CHRIST IN 2 KINGS

Second Kings presents the ministries of Elijah and Elisha, prophets through whom God performed mighty acts. Jesus is described as "a Prophet powerful in action and speech before God and all the people" (Luke 24:19 HCSB). God preserved Israel's monarch as long as he did because of his promises to David (8:19). Israel may even count on God to preserve a lamp for David forever (Rev. 21:23).

GOD'S STORY

When the Events of This Book Happened

From Ahab's death through the thirty-seventh year of King Jehoiachin's exile in Babylon (about 853–561 BC)

During the early years of the divided kingdom, the enemies of Israel and Judah were the surrounding petty kingdoms, for example Aram to the north (called "Syria" in the KJV), with its capital in Damascus. About 900 BC the Mesopotamian power Assyria, with Nineveh as its capital, entered a period of aggressive expansion. In the 730s under Tiglath-Pileser III (also called "Pul"), most of the eastern Mediterranean came under Assyrian domination. Shalmaneser V laid siege to Samaria, and his successor, Sargon II took Samaria and the Northern Kingdom captive in 722 BC. His successor, Sennacherib, invaded Judah about 701, but God protected King Hezekiah and the temple.

The ancient Babylonian Empire experienced new power and came to dominate the ancient Near East 626–536 BC, conquering Nineveh in 612. Scholars refer to this as the "neo-Babylonian" or the "Chaldean" period. Their most important king was Nebuchadnezzar, who invaded Judah more than once. He was responsible for burning the temple and Jerusalem in 586 BC and for carrying the people of Judah into captivity.

How 2 Kings Fits into God's "Story"

Second Kings completes "chapter 2" of the story: God educates his nation (disobedient Israel disciplined). It depicts Israel in spiritual disgrace and shame. Despite the ministry of Elisha, the Northern Kingdom never had a righteous king—all worshiped idols—and true to his word, God sent them into permanent dispersion. The Southern Kingdom had a few righteous moments, particularly in the reigns of Hezekiah and Josiah. Ultimately, however, God sent the Southern Kingdom to exile. Yet God's kingdom plan was never in jeopardy. The royal Davidic line lived on, even though a temporal kingdom and temple were not the goal.

ORIGINAL HISTORICAL SETTING

Because 1 and 2 Kings first existed as a single composition, see the discussion in the **Original Historical Setting** section in **1 KINGS**.

Author and Date of Writing
Unknown, perhaps Jeremiah about 560 BC

First Audience and Destination
Probably the Israelites living in Babylonian exile

Occasion
Unknown, but see **1 KINGS**

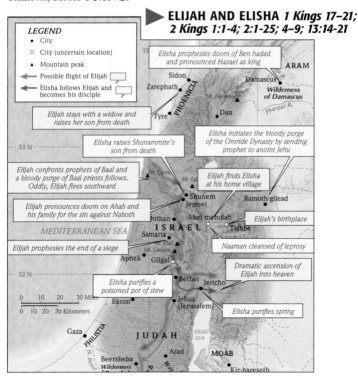

► **ELIJAH AND ELISHA** *1 Kings 17–21;*
2 Kings 1:1-4; 2:1-25; 4–9; 13:14-21

LEGEND
- • City
- ○ City (uncertain location)
- ▲ Mountain peak
- ← Possible flight of Elijah
- ← Elisha follows Elijah and becomes his disciple

Elisha prophesies doom of Ben-hadad and pronounced Hazael as king

ARAM

Sidon

Damascus

Zarephath

Wilderness of Damascus

Mt. Hermon ▲

PHOENICIA

Tyre

Dan

Pharpar R.

Elijah stays with a widow and raises her son from death

Elisha initiates the bloody purge of the Omride Dynasty by sending prophet to anoint Jehu

Elisha raises Shunammite's son from death

Elijah confronts prophets of Baal and a bloody purge of Baal priests follows. Oddly, Elijah flees southward

Mt. Carmel ▲ Mt. Tabor ▲

Elijah finds Elisha at his home village

Shunem

Jezreel

Ramoth-gilead

Elijah pronounces doom on Ahab and his family for the sin against Naboth

Dothan • Abel-meholah ○

Elijah's birthplace

MEDITERRANEAN SEA

I S R A E L

Tishbe

Elijah prophesies the end of a siege

Samaria •

Mt. Ebal ▲ Mt. Gerizim ▲

Naaman cleansed of leprosy

Aphek •

Gilgal ○

32 N

Bethel • Jericho

Dramatic ascension of Elijah into heaven

0   10   20   30 Miles
0 10 20 30 Kilometers

Elisha purifies a poisoned pot of stew

Ekron •

Jebus (Jerusalem) •

Elisha purifies spring

Gaza •

PHILISTIA

JUDAH

DEAD SEA

Beersheba •

Arad •

MOAB

Wilderness

Kir-hareseth

LITERARY FEATURES

Genre and Literary Style
An extremely selective account written in Hebrew

In describing the period of the divided monarchy, the writer alternated between the kings of Israel and the kings of Judah. He gave attention only to Jehu, the founder of yet another dynasty in Israel, and Joash the boy king of Judah. After describing the fall of the Northern Kingdom, the author lingered only on two righteous kings, Hezekiah and Josiah. His interpretation of the reason Israel fell (chap. 17) and then Judah (chap. 25) was entirely theological, rather than military, political, or economic.

In the Hebrew Scriptures, the single composition 1 and 2 Kings was placed as the last of the four "Former Prophets." Beginning with Joshua and Judges, and then moving on to Samuel (collectively) and Kings (collectively), these books described the 800-year period from Israel's entry into Canaan (about 1406 BC) through the destruction of the temple and Jerusalem and the exile to Babylon (about 586 BC). Their common theme is that sin brings divine punishment, but obedience brings blessing and peace (in line with the teachings of Deuteronomy, especially chaps. 27–28).

This interpretation is commonly called "Deuteronomic History." Critical scholars have argued that this view arose late in the Israelite monarchy, perhaps at the time of Josiah, yet it is much more believable that Moses himself by divine revelation originated this perspective, as Deuteronomy plainly claims. Then the later historians more or less uniformly used the interpretive lens of Deuteronomy to write their respective parts of Israel's history. Finally, the books reflecting this perspective were gathered into Israel's canon as the first section of "The Prophets."

Themes
The temple, kingship and covenant, the rise of the prophets

Because 1 and 2 Kings first existed as a single composition, see the discussion in the **Themes** section in **1 KINGS**.

Book Features and Structure

The writer was especially interested in the ministry of Elisha (chaps. 2–8), for which he may have borrowed from an existing source. He also emphasized two major sieges of Jerusalem. The first by Sennacherib of Assyria, around 701 BC, was thwarted by divine intervention (chap. 19). The second by Nebuchadnezzar of Babylon, about 586 BC, destroyed the city and Solomon's temple (chap. 25).

Second Kings has three sections: Elisha's ministry (1–8); the later period of the divided monarchy (9–17); and the period of Judah alone (18–25).

LEGEND
- • City
- ★ Capital city
- ○ City (uncertain location)
- ▲ Mountain peak
- Israel
- Judah
- International roads
- Local roads

Jeroboam built a sanctuary

Political capital of Israel from Omri onward

Jeroboam built a sanctuary

MEDITERRANEAN SEA

ISRAEL

JUDAH

Negeb

DEAD SEA

PHILISTIA

AMMON

MOAB

EDOM

ARAM

GESHUR

Eastern Desert

Damascus

1 CHRONICLES

First divided by the Greek translators (second century BC), 1 and 2 Chronicles were original-ly one book, *Dibre Hayyamin*, "Events of the Days," in the Hebrew Bible. The English title comes from *Chronicon*, the name given by the Latin translator Jerome.

▶ Key Text: 28:4

"Howbeit the Lord God of Israel chose me before all the house of my father to be king over Israel for ever: for he hath chosen Judah to be the ruler; and of the house of Judah, the house of my father; and among the sons of my father he liked me to make me king over all Israel."

▶ Key Term: "Dynasty"

First Chronicles focuses on how God established the everlasting dynasty of David, describing David's positive achievements, both religiously and militarily.

▶ One-Sentence Summary

After extensive introductory genealogies, the author tells how David ruled for forty years under the blessing of God, particularly as he lavished attention on Jerusalem, the priesthood, and preparation for building the temple.

Ark of the Covenant ▶
1 Chron. 13:7-14).

GOD'S MESSAGE IN THE BOOK

Purpose

Since this book was originally the first half of a single composition, the purpose for the book now called 1 and 2 Chronicles must be considered together. This work answered important questions for Israelites who had returned after years of exile in Babylon. Their times were difficult and disappointing. Did they still fit into God's plan? Were the promises of God still applicable to them? Further, what religious and political institutions were important? Finally, what lessons from the past could they learn to keep from making the same mistakes?

The author answered these questions by compiling a highly selective religious history. The covenant God made with David concerning an eternal dynasty was still in effect. Even with no Davidic king on the throne, they were still God's people and could still wait in hope for restoration of the monarchy. While waiting, they could do the things God required, such as offer the right sacrifices with the right priests at the right place. Finally, although David and Solomon are presented as ideal kings, the apostasy of later kings is noted as the cause of Babylonian exile (2 Chron. 36:16). God's people who study the books of Chronicles today should do so with the author's original purposes in mind.

Christian Worldview Elements

First Chronicles touches on a number of worldview elements. However, above all it draws attention to the category *covenant and redemption*. God's covenant promise to David that he was the first king of an everlasting dynasty marked a major advance in the progress of divine revelation.

GOD
CREATION
SOVEREIGNTY AND PROVIDENCE
FAITH AND REASON
REVELATION AND AUTHORITY
HUMANITY
REBELLION AND SIN
▶ **COVENANT AND REDEMPTION**
COMMUNITY AND CHURCH
DISCIPLESHIP
ETHICS AND MORALITY
TIME AND ETERNITY

Teachings about God

God is sovereign in carrying out his kingdom plans. His unconditional covenant with undeserving David (chap. 17) is as magnificent as his covenant with Abraham. He desires the worship of his people in the ways he has revealed. (See 1 Chron. 28:1 for the Holy Spirit's work in revealing the plans for temple construction.) David's concern for the ark, his preparation for building the temple, and the elaborate material on organizing the priests and Levites properly all shows this.

Teachings about Humanity

The long genealogies at the beginning of 1 Chronicles show that God cares for persons as individuals. Each one has worth as created in the image of God. If a historian took the trouble to discover and preserve these lists that may seem tedious, how much more does God care for the "little people" that can appear to be insignificant? Moreover David modeled magnificently that humans can accomplish great tasks for God when their heart is passionately turned to pleasing him.

Teachings about Salvation

The book's clearest teaching on salvation as the gift of God is David's psalm of thanksgiving when the ark of the covenant was finally moved into a tent (chap. 16). The conclusion especially demonstrates that the purpose of salvation is to bring glory to God: "O give thanks unto the LORD; for *he* is good; for his mercy *endureth* for ever. And say ye, Save us, O God of our salvation, and gather us together, and deliver us from the heathen, that we may give thanks to thy holy name, *and* glory in thy praise. Blessed *be* the LORD God of Israel for ever and ever" (16:34-36).

CHRIST IN 1 CHRONICLES

The Messianic promise of a son of David to rule over Israel occupies the center of 1 Chronicles (chap. 17). The family lines of Israel's kings are traced (chap. 3), showing God has been faithful to maintain a son of David to lead Israel even in the face of exile. This son of David is described as the eternally loved son of God (17:13; Luke 1:32-33; Heb. 1:5). David's prayer of praise (29:10-13) is applied to Jesus (Rev. 5:12-13).

GOD'S STORY

When the Events of This Book Happened
During David's reign (about 1010–970 BC)

The genealogies at the beginning of 1 Chronicles cover the generations from Adam until sometime after the return from Babylonian exile, perhaps around 450 BC. The forty-year reign of David saw the beginning of the flowering of Israelite culture. Although scholars have a general consensus about the years of David's rule, there is insufficient evidence to date some of the prominent events of his reign, such as the conquest of Jerusalem or the purchase of the land on which to build the temple.

How 1 Chronicles Fits into God's "Story"

First Chronicles tells part of "chapter 1" of God's story: God builds his nation (Israel chosen as the people of promise). David desired to build a house (temple) for God. God promised instead to build an everlasting house (dynasty) for David (17:1-15). Although temple and kingship go together throughout Chronicles, neither existed by the end of the book. This was, however, only temporary. God intended for his people to become his temple (1 Cor. 3:16; Eph. 2:21). Further, Jesus, the greatest descendant of David, fulfills the promise of everlasting kingship. Thus Chronicles tells the initial space-and-time fulfillment of a reality that will come to joyful fruition throughout eternity.

ORIGINAL HISTORICAL SETTING

Author and Date of Writing
Unknown, possibly Ezra around 450 BC

Scholars refer to the anonymous author of 1 and 2 Chronicles as "the Chronicler." According to Jewish tradition, Ezra was the composer, but this can neither be proved nor disproved. The work was written after the return of the exiles from Babylon. Some scholars date the book in the 300s, but on the whole an earlier date seems more likely.

First Audience and Destination
Israelites in Jerusalem after they returned from exile

The book does not state its original audience or destination, but see the earlier discussion on the book's purpose. Perhaps the original manuscript was placed in a book depository in the rebuilt temple. There it would have joined the growing collection of Israel's sacred Scriptures.

Occasion
Because the authorship and date are uncertain, no one knows what prompted Chronicles to be written. The author used many sources, including the biblical books of Samuel and Kings. The author mentioned official court documents, called "The Book of the Kings of Israel and Judah" (1 Chron. 9:1; 2 Chron. 16:11). He also had access to material written by certain prophets, such as "The Books of Samuel the Seer, Nathan the Prophet, and Gad the Seer" (1 Chron. 29:29); "The Book of Jehu the Son of Hanani" (2 Chron. 20:34); and "The Vision of Isaiah the Prophet" (2 Chron. 32:32). Other sources, such as old genealogies and temple lists, appear likely.

SOLOMON'S ECONOMIC ENTERPRISES
1 Kings 5–10

SPAIN

Massalia (Marseilles)

Lead

ITALY

Sardinia TYRRHENIAN SEA

ADRIATIC SEA

MACEDONIA

BLACK SEA

AEGEAN SEA

ASIA

Opium, copper

Horses

KUE

Tarsus

Haran

Silver, tin, copper, iron

Gold

Crete

MEDITERRANEAN SEA

Malta

Cyprus

Arvad

Hamath

Tadmor

Mesopotamia

Sidon

ARAM

Tyre

Damascus

Babylon

T. Qasile

Joppa

Jerusalem

Memphis

NORTH AFRICA

War chariots

EGYPT

Ezion-geber

Gulf of Aqaba

Arabia

Ur

Thebes

Dedan

Nile R.

RED SEA

ETHIOPIA

Gold, gems, perfumes, precious woods, ivory

Yathrib (Medina)

Mecca

Gold, exotic animals, woods, silver, precious stones

Ophir

SOLOMON'S ECONOMIC ENTERPRISES

- ● City
- ○ City (uncertain location)
- ● City (modern name)
- Red Sea trade
- Arabian spice trade
- Phoenician connection
- Other import routes
- *Gold* Commodity
- Solomon's kingdom

| 0 | 500 | 1,000 | 1,500 Miles |
| 0 | 500 | 1,000 | 1,500 Kilometers |

LITERARY FEATURES

Genre and Literary Style
Genealogical tables, narrative history, and some poetry, all composed in Hebrew

The genealogical material is the most extensive found in Scripture. The account of David's kingship is focused differently from the account in 2 Samuel. Neither his adultery with Bathsheba nor the treason of Absalom is considered. David is almost perfect in 1 Chronicles; even his taking a census of Israel is attributed to Satan and resulted in the royal discovery of the proper site for the temple (chap. 21). The brief poetic sections preserve prayers of David (chaps. 16; 29). See comments on *Genre and Literary Style* in **NEHEMIAH** for further material about the possible literary relationship of Chronicles, Ezra, and Nehemiah.

Themes
Davidic dynasty, temple, blessing of obedience and punishment of disobedience

The author focused only on the Davidic kings. The rising and falling fortunes of Solomon's temple are another great theme. In 1 Chronicles (unlike 2 Samuel) David is shown making grand preparations to build the temple. In 2 Chronicles, the temple is built and dedicated—and restored more than once—before being destroyed. The Chronicler also demonstrated that obeying the laws of Moses and proper worship in the temple resulted in divine blessing, while unfaithfulness brought disaster.

Book Features and Structure
By repeating often the phrase "all Israel," especially in reference to the exiles (1 Chron. 9:1), the author emphasized to his initial audience that they were God's people. Perhaps the most striking feature of 1 Chronicles is the variety of name lists. Chapters 1–9 are genealogical lists. Other lists include "David's Mighty Men" (11); "Divisions of the Levites" (23); "Divisions of the Priests" (24); "The Musicians" (25); "The Gatekeepers" (26); and "Military Divisions and Other Leaders" (27). First Chronicles has two major sections: genealogies (1–9) and David's reign (10–29).

2 CHRONICLES

First divided by the Greek translators (second century BC), 1 and 2 Chronicles were originally one book, *Dibre Hayyamin*, "Events of the Days," in the Hebrew Bible. The English title comes from *Chronicon*, the name given by the Latin translator Jerome.

▶ Key Texts: 7:1 and 36:19

"Now when Solomon had made an end of praying, the fire came down from heaven, and consumed the burnt offering and the sacrifices; and the glory of the Lord filled the house."

"And they burnt the house of God, and brake down the wall of Jerusalem, and burnt all the palaces thereof with fire, and destroyed all the goodly vessels thereof."

▶ Key Term: "Temple"

The book begins with Solomon's plans to build the temple in Jerusalem and ends with its destruction. Between dedication and destruction (about 384 years, from 959 to 586 BC), the temple was sometimes neglected and sometimes refurbished, but it was always the most important building in Israel.

▶ One-Sentence Summary

After Solomon's glorious reign, which culminated in the dedication of the temple, kings of the Davidic dynasty—some righteous and some evil—continued ruling in Jerusalem, ending in the destruction of the temple and the exile.

▲ Model of Solomon's Temple.

GOD'S MESSAGE IN THE BOOK

Purpose

Because 1 and 2 Chronicles first existed as a single composition, see the discussion in the *Purpose* section of **1 CHRONICLES**.

Christian Worldview Elements

Second Chronicles covers more than four centuries, so it brings into sharp focus the worldview category of *time and eternity* (that history moves forward according to God's plan). The category of *community* is also important, demonstrated in the ongoing use of the phrase "all Israel."

Teachings about God

Second Chronicles shows that God blesses faithfulness to him and punishes his people when they turn away from him. God's "educational program" meant teaching his people that he values allegiance to him above all else. The book ends with a note of hope: the Israelite exiles have been permitted to return home in order to rebuild their temple. God's Spirit is noted as inspiring certain priests and prophets.

GOD
CREATION
SOVEREIGNTY AND PROVIDENCE
FAITH AND REASON
REVELATION AND AUTHORITY
HUMANITY
REBELLION AND SIN
COVENANT AND REDEMPTION
▶ **COMMUNITY** AND CHURCH
DISCIPLESHIP
ETHICS AND MORALITY
▶ **TIME AND ETERNITY**

Teachings about Humanity

Second Chronicles focuses at length on Solomon, whose splendid rule in Jerusalem was a preview of Christ's everlasting reign in the New Jerusalem (Matt. 12:42; Rev. 21–22). As in 2 Kings, the worth of the kings is determined only by whether they did right or evil in the sight of the Lord. (This terminology occurs eighteen times in the KJV text of 2 Chronicles.)

Teachings about Salvation

As in 2 Kings, God's prophets in 2 Chronicles called both king and people to repent for religious apostasy and to worship the Lord alone. (Shemaiah, Oded, Micaiah, Eliezer, and Huldah are less familiar; Isaiah and Jeremiah are known from their writings.) Four kings led Israel to turn from sin, repair the temple, and recommit to wholehearted worship of the Lord (Asa, Joash, Hezekiah, and Josiah).

⬭ *CHRIST IN 2 CHRONICLES*

Solomon's glorious reign as third king of Israel is a picture of Christ's eternal reign in the New Jerusalem (Rev. 21-22).

GOD'S STORY

When the Events of This Book Happened

From the beginning of Solomon's reign until the first year that Cyrus, king of Persia, ruled over Babylon (more than 430 years, about 970–538 BC)

The military superpowers of the ancient Near East were weak and not aggressive during the time of Solomon, allowing his kingdom to expand to Israel's greatest geographical size. Later, three successive Mesopotamian superpowers took their turn at world dominion. First was Assyria, which fell in 612 BC (after conquering the Northern Kingdom of Israel in 722). Next was Babylon (or Chaldea), which fell in 538 BC (after conquering the Southern Kingdom of Judah in 586). Third was Persia, which allowed the Israelite exiles to return and which endured throughout the rest of the Old Testament period, falling to Alexander the Great and the Greeks in 331 BC.

How 2 Chronicles Fits into God's "Story"

Second Chronicles concludes "chapter 1" of God's story: God builds his nation (Israel chosen as the people of promise). It also describes the entire period of "chapter 2" of the story: God educates his nation (disobedient Israel disciplined).

Second Chronicles tells the story of David's royal successors that ruled from Jerusalem. They succeeded when they honored God and worshipped at his temple. By the book's end, there was neither reigning king nor temple. Yet God's long-term kingdom plans were never in jeopardy. A temporal kingdom and temple were not the goal. God was preparing the way for the birth of the eternal King who will rule as Son of David forever. The everlasting temple is the people of God, indwelt by his Spirit (Eph. 2:20-21).

► SOLOMON'S BUILDING ACTIVITIES
1 Kings 6–7; 9:1-22; 2 Chronicles 2–4; 8:1-12

LEGEND
- • City
- ○ City (uncertain location)
- ● City (modern name)
- Hazor City built or rebuilt by Solomon
- ○ Cities and towns showing building/rebuilding in the 10th century B.C.
- ▣ Fortified by Solomon
- ■ Fortified enclosures
- —— Major routes
- —— Other routes
- ▨ Territory ceded to Hiram of Tyre

Source of timbers used in construction of Temple of Yahweh

Damascus

PHOENICIA

Tyre • Dan

ARAM

LAND OF CABUL   Hazor

Shiqmona   T. Kinrot   Sea of Galilee

Tell Abu Hawam

Yokneam   Yarmuk R.

Tell Mevorak   Megiddo

Taanach   Beth-shan

Tirzah   Zarethan   Casting of bronze vessels

Succoth   Jabbok R.

Tell el Mazar

Joppa   Adam   AMMON

Lower Beth-horon   Upper Beth-horon   32 N

Gezer   Jerusalem   Rabbah (Amman)

Baalah   Timnah

Beth-shemesh   Construction of the temple of Yahweh, palace and city

Gaza   Lachish   Hebron

PHILISTIA   T. Beit Mirsim   DEAD SEA   Aroer

Arad   Amon R.

T. Beersheba   Tel Mahalta   Kir-hareseth

Built fortress and agricultural settlements   Tel Masos

Rogem   Baalath-beer   MOAB

AMALEK   Ma-ro'am

Tamar   Zered R.

Ramat Matred

Punon

MEDITERRANEAN SEA

30 N

Built fortress, port and ships

Ezion-geber

Gulf of Aqaba

Kadesh-barnea

EDOM

34 E   36 E

0   20   40   60 Miles
0   20   40   60 Kilometers

92

ORIGINAL HISTORICAL SETTING

Because 1 and 2 Chronicles first existed as a single composition, see the discussion in the *Original Historical Setting* section for **1 CHRONICLES**.

Author and Date of Writing
Unknown, possibly Ezra around 450 BC

First Audience and Destination
Israelites in Jerusalem after they returned from exile

Occasion
Unknown, but see *Occasion* for **1 CHRONICLES**.

HEZEKIAH'S PREPARATION FOR REVOLT
2 Kings 18:1-8; 20:12-20; 1 Chronicles 4:39-42; 2 Chronicles 32:1-8, 27-31

LITERARY FEATURES

Genre and Literary Style
An extremely selective account written in Hebrew

Although 2 Chronicles describes the same time period as 1 and 2 Kings, its approach is distinctive, concentrating only on the kings of Judah. The author's perspective on the Northern Kingdom is plain: "And Israel rebelled against the house of David unto this day" (10:19). Thus King Hezekiah (who ruled in Judah both before and after the fall of the Northern Kingdom) invited people from "all Israel and Judah" to his great Passover, and many people came (30:1,6,10). Consequently, from Hezekiah's time until the final destruction of Jerusalem, the Davidic king in Jerusalem ruled "all Israel" (31:1; 35:3). The Chronicler was concerned mainly with the state of the temple and whether the Davidic king was devoutly following the LORD.

In the Hebrew Bible, Chronicles was placed in the third section, the Writings (*Kethubim*), rather than in the Law or the Prophets. In fact it was the last book of the Hebrew Scriptures. Thus, just as modern Christians use the phrase "Genesis to Revelation" to mean the entire canon, Christians living in the first century thought in terms of "Genesis to Chronicles." See comments on **Genre and Literary Style** in **NEHEMIAH** for further material about the possible literary relationship of Chronicles, Ezra, and Nehemiah.

Themes
Davidic dynasty, temple, blessing of obedience and punishment of disobedience

Because 1 and 2 Chronicles first existed as a single composition, see the discussion in the **Themes** section for **1 CHRONICLES**.

Book Features and Structure
The most striking feature of 2 Chronicles is the way the author connected the temple and the kingship by noting the kings who initiated repairs to the temple and thus initiated religious reform and renewal. The history of Solomon's temple can thus be outlined as follows:

Event	King	Text	
Approx. Year			
Temple dedication	Solomon	5:1	959
First repair and reform	Asa	15:8	895
Second repair and reform	Joash	24:13	830
Third repair and reform	Hezekiah	29:3	715
Fourth repair and reform	Josiah	34:8	622
Temple destruction	Zedekiah	36:19	586

Second Chronicles has three major sections: Solomon's reign (1–9); the divided kingdom (10–28); and the reunited kingdom (29–36).

EZRA

THE FIRST BOOK OF EZRA

The book is named for Ezra, the leading character. In the Hebrew Bible, Ezra and Nehemiah were initially one book. English Bibles follow the Latin translator Jerome, who named the two parts Ezra and Nehemiah. Others have used the titles 1 and 2 Ezra.

▶ *Key Text: 6:16*

"And the children of Israel, the priests, and the Levites, and the rest of the children of the captivity, kept the dedication of this house of God with joy."

▶ *Key Term: "Restoration"*

The book describes two restorations from Babylonian captivity. First, more than 40,000 Israelites returned under Sheshbazzar (530s BC). Second, a smaller group accompanied Ezra, whose goal was to teach the people the law of Moses (about 458 BC).

▶ *One-Sentence Summary*

The first group of returning exiles restored worship of the Lord, culminating in a rebuilt temple, but Ezra, who led the second group, reestablished Israelite community under Mosaic law, culminating in putting away mixed marriages.

▼ Tomb of Cyrus the Great, whom God used in restoring his people to Judea from Babylon.

GOD'S MESSAGE IN THE BOOK

Purpose

Since this book was originally the first half of a single composition, the purpose for the book now called Ezra and Nehemiah must be considered together. This work continued the history of Israel at the point that 2 Chronicles ended. It showed Israelites who had come back to their land that they were still God's people, despite the years of exile and the difficulties they had experienced since their return. God was at work through pagan kings such as Cyrus and Artaxerxes (Ezra 1:1; 7:27) to bring about the return from exile and the rebuilding of the temple. God had worked to bring devout teachers (Ezra 7:9) and strong governors (Neh. 2:12) to help the people of God. From an even broader perspective, the second temple, the Jewish community, and a stable Jerusalem were important circumstances for the coming of Jesus more than four centuries later. God's people who read and study Ezra and Nehemiah today should keep the author's purpose in mind.

Christian Worldview Elements

Ezra deals particularly with the worldview categories of *sovereignty and providence, community,* and *ethics and morality.* The notion of the people of God working together to accomplish his objectives is especially prominent.

GOD
CREATION
▶ **SOVEREIGNTY AND PROVIDENCE**
FAITH AND REASON
REVELATION AND AUTHORITY
HUMANITY
REBELLION AND SIN
▶ **COVENANT AND REDEMPTION**
▶ **COMMUNITY** AND CHURCH
DISCIPLESHIP
▶ **ETHICS AND MORALITY**
TIME AND ETERNITY

Teachings about God

Because God is righteous, he acts on behalf of his people. This includes working through pagan kings (who issue decrees) and godly teachers (who teach his word to his people). Further, as the last two chapters show, God may require his people to forsake family ties for the sake of following his will.

Teachings about Humanity

As with 1 Chronicles, Ezra has many name lists. Although such lists may seem tedious today, they show the importance of each individual in God's purposes. If the author made the effort to preserve all these names and numbers, then how much more does God care about individuals! This perspective is strengthened by observing that the work of restoring worship (altar and temple) was a community task. The work accomplished for God was done by people working together more than by a great leader.

Teachings about Salvation

The people who returned from exile were cured of the idolatry that had taken their ancestors into captivity. Ezra revives an emphasis found in Mosaic law: without the shedding of blood, there is no forgiveness (Lev. 17:11). Thus, the first concern of the returning Israelites was to reinstate an altar on which to offer the appointed sacrifices (3:1-6). Only secondarily were they concerned with the temple (6:13-18). As throughout the Old Testament era, personal trust in God is expressed through participation in the right sacrifices and through obeying God's law.

⊙ CHRIST IN EZRA

Ezra was a priest who played an important role in leading God's people from captivity in Babylon back to Judea. In a sermon at the synagogue in Nazareth, Jesus announced his agenda, part of which was "to proclaim freedom to the captives" (Luke 4:18 HCSB).

⊙ GOD'S STORY

When the Events of This Book Happened
(From Cyrus's decree permitting the return through Ezra's initial ministry — more than eighty years, about 538–457 BC)

The emperor Cyrus the Great ruled Persia from about 559. The Persians defeated the Chaldean Empire and the city of Babylon in 539, then initiated the policy of allowing exiles of all ethnic groups to return to their homeland. The first Israelite return under Sheshbazzar occurred during Cyrus's rule. The second temple was dedicated in 516, exactly seventy years after Solomon's temple was destroyed (2 Chron. 36:21). The next return of exiles (with Ezra the priest) occurred in 458, during the time of Artaxerxes I, some eighty years later than the first return.

How Ezra Fits into God's "Story"

Ezra begins "chapter 3" of God's story: God keeps a faithful remnant (Messiah's space and time prepared). It is an important historical link in the story of God's rule. Although there was no Davidic king, that did not keep God's people from worshipping properly or doing what they were able to do. Although the second temple was only a pale replica of Solomon's temple, it would prove to be more important. Jesus, the Son of God and Son of David, was presented in this temple and ended his public ministry by teaching there. The book of Ezra shows how such a temple came into being.

ORIGINAL HISTORICAL SETTING

Author and Date of Writing
Unknown, perhaps Ezra around 430 BC

Jewish tradition held that Ezra the priest composed the single work Ezra-Nehemiah. There is no reason he could not have done so, particularly since he was a "ready scribe" (7:6). In 7:28–9:15, Ezra is referred to in the first person ("I," "me," "my"). If Ezra was not the composer, then a later composer directly copied his memoirs. (The book of Nehemiah includes similar first-person memoirs of Nehemiah.)

First Audience and Destination
Israelites in Jerusalem after they returned from exile

The book was a permanent record of the events that reestablished Israel's national identity. Perhaps the original "Scroll of Ezra-Nehemiah" was placed in a book depository in the rebuilt temple when it was first completed. There it would have joined the growing collection of Israel's sacred Scriptures.

Occasion

What originally prompted the writing of this book is not clear. The author could not have been an eyewitness to all the events of Ezra-Nehemiah since they cover about a century. He could, however, have seen all events of both Ezra's and Nehemiah's ministries. The author skillfully knitted his sources into a powerful account of God's provision and protection of his people.

THE PROVINCE OF JUDAH AND NEHEMIAH'S ENEMIES IN THE FIFTH CENTURY BC
Nehemiah 4–6; 13:4-9

LEGEND
- City
- ○ City (uncertain location)
- ★ Possible district capitals
- ▬ Major trade route

Given to Sidon about 450 B.C.

Nehemiah's enemy Sanballat, governor of Samaria, constantly interferes with Judean efforts to rebuild their homeland.

The wealthy Tobiads meddle in the affairs of Judah for centuries

Geshem the Arab, one of Nehemiah's enemies, controls trade routes vital to Persian interest.

DOR

Samaria

Mt. Ebal

Shechem

SAMARIA

GILEAD

Jabbok River

Jordan River

Yarkon River

Aphek

Shiloh

TOBIADS

Joppa
Apollonia

Jamnia

Lod

Gittaim ○   Beth-horon   Bethel ▲ Ai

Gezer ★   Mizpah   Michmash   Gilgal ○

Emmaus   Ramah ● Geba   Jericho

Zorah   Kiriath-   Beeroth

A S H D O D

Ekron   jearim ● Nob

Ashdod   Jerusalem   AMMON   Heshbon

Jarmuth   Beth-haccherem

YEHUD   Mt.
(JUDAH)   Bethlehem   Nebo   Medeba

Azekah   Gedor

Keilah ★ Adullam ● Tekoa

Ashkelon   Mareshah   ★ Beth-zur

Lachish ●   Hebron ●

Gaza

DEAD
SEA

En-gedi   Arnon River

N. Besor

Ziklag ●

K E D A R I T E   A R A B S

IDUMEA
(EDOMITES)

Eshtemoa

MOAB

Beth-pelet ●   Arad ●

Beersheba ●   Kir-hareseth ●

Negev

0   5   10   15   20 Miles
0   5   10   15   20 Kilometers

Arabah   EDOM

35 E

LITERARY FEATURES

Genre and Literary Style
Court documents, lists, and narratives written in Hebrew, with some Aramaic sections

The author had access to many sources, including official Persian documents, lists, and memoirs. The lists are similar to the lists in Chronicles and may indicate the same historian at work (Ezra?). The Hebrew vocabulary and style are considered "late Hebrew," as is fitting for a postexilic composition.

One striking element of Ezra is the presence of documents untranslated from their original Aramaic form. (Aramaic was the international trade language of the ancient Near East under the Persians.) The Aramaic parts of Ezra are 4:8–6:18; 7:12-26.

In the Hebrew Bible, Ezra-Nehemiah was placed in the third section, the Writings (*Kethubim*), rather than in the Law or the Prophets. See comments on **Genre and Literary Style** in **NEHEMIAH** for further material about the possible literary relationship of Chronicles, Ezra, and Nehemiah.

Themes
Return from exile, rebuilding the temple, reestablishing life under Mosaic law

These three themes are specific displays of the overall motif "restoration" (see **Key Term**). A secondary theme is the relationship between Ezra as a qualified interpreter of Scripture and the response of his hearers. The italicized verbs in the following verses show the connection between devout teachers and a heartfelt response by the students: "Ezra had prepared his heart to *seek* the law of the Lord, and to *do* it, and to *teach* in Israel statutes and judgments" (7:10). "There were *assembled* unto me every one that *trembled* at the words of the God of Israel" (9:4).

Book Features and Structure
Ezra has preserved seven official documents and letters similar to nonbiblical Persian records that have survived. These are "Cyrus's Decree" (1:2-4); "Letter of Rehum to Artaxerxes" (4:8-16); "Artaxerxes' Reply to Rehum" (4:17-22); "Letter of Tattenai to Darius" (5:6-17); "Memorandum Concerning Cyrus's Decree" (6:1-5); "Darius's Letter to Tattenai" (6:6-12); "Letter of Artaxerxes to Ezra" (7:11-26). All are preserved in Aramaic except for the first, which was copied from the end of 2 Chronicles.

The book of Ezra has two sections. The first describes the first return of exiles and the rebuilding of the temple (1–6); the second describes the return of Ezra and his ministry (7–10).

NEHEMIAH

THE SECOND BOOK OF EZRA

The book is named for Nehemiah, the leading character. In the Hebrew Bible, Ezra and Nehemiah were initially one book. English Bibles follow the Latin translator Jerome, who named the two parts Ezra and Nehemiah. Others have used the titles 1 and 2 Ezra.

▶ *Key Text: 6:15*

"So the wall was finished in the twenty and fifth day of the month Elul, in fifty and two days."

▶ *Key Term: "Walls"*

In the ancient world, a city without walls was helpless before its enemies. For Jerusalem once more to have its walls complete was evidence of divine favor and meant that the inhabitants could carry on life with a measure of security.

▶ *One-Sentence Summary*

Through Nehemiah's leadership God enabled the Israelites to rebuild and dedicate Jerusalem's walls as well as to renew their commitment to God as his covenant people.

▼ Golden drinking cup. Nehemiah was cupbearer for Artaxerxes I, king of Persia (Neh. 2:1-9).

101

GOD'S MESSAGE IN THE BOOK

Purpose

Because Nehemiah and Ezra first existed as a single composition, see the discussion in the **Purpose** section for **EZRA**.

Christian Worldview Elements

Nehemiah focuses on the worldview categories of *sovereignty and providence, community,* and *covenant and redemption.* The notion of God's people working together to accomplish his objectives is particularly noticeable.

Teachings about God

God works on behalf of his people to enable them to accomplish his purposes. He works through kings; he sends good leaders (such as Ezra and Nehemiah). Further, God does not change, even though the circumstances of his people change. The same God who had graciously revealed himself at Mount Sinai as the covenant-making God a thousand years before (about 1446 BC) still wanted Israel to be in a covenant relationship with him (10:29).

> GOD
> CREATION
> ▶ **SOVEREIGNTY AND PROVIDENCE**
> FAITH AND REASON
> REVELATION AND AUTHORITY
> HUMANITY
> REBELLION AND SIN
> ▶ **COVENANT AND REDEMPTION**
> ▶ **COMMUNITY** AND CHURCH
> DISCIPLESHIP
> ETHICS AND MORALITY
> TIME AND ETERNITY

Teachings about Humanity

Nehemiah shows that there are really only two kinds of people: those who oppose God and his purposes and those who identify with God and his purposes. Equally evident in this book (as in Leviticus) is the concept that God's holiness requires his redeemed people to live different from the pagans that surround them. Although Ezra and Nehemiah fulfilled different personal roles, each illustrates someone who was wholly committed to God and whom God used to accomplish kingdom purposes.

Teachings about Salvation

Nehemiah teaches the doctrine of salvation as clearly as any Old Testament book. It contains no more profound confession of sin at the community level than Nehemiah 9: salvation means acknowledging and turning away from wrongdoing and then clinging steadfastly to God.

CHRIST IN NEHEMIAH

Nehemiah was a key leader in the restoration of God's people from Babylon to Jerusalem. He called for undivided loyalty to the work at hand in the same way that Jesus did when he said, "Anyone who is not with Me is against Me, and anyone who does not gather with Me scatters" (Luke 11:23 HCSB).

GOD'S STORY

When the Events of This Book Happened
From Nehemiah's prayer for Israel until his second term as governor (about 446–430 BC)

Artaxerxes I ruled Persia 465–424 BC. The events of the book of Nehemiah occurred during his reign. Nehemiah's first term as governor of Judah lasted twelve years (the 20th to the 32nd year of Artaxerxes, 445–433 BC, Neh. 5:14). There is insufficient information to date the length of Nehemiah's absence from Judah (when he returned to Artaxerxes' service, Neh. 13:6). His second term as governor possibly began around 431 ("after certain days," 13:6) and lasted an unknown length of time.

How Nehemiah Fits into God's "Story"
Nehemiah continues God's story: God keeps a faithful remnant (Messiah's space and time prepared). It continues the historical link in the story of God's kingdom that Ezra began. With the second temple complete, the people were able to turn their attention to making Jerusalem secure and to functioning as a covenant community. In God's plan, Jesus came to this community centuries later and presented himself to Jerusalem as both "Son of David" and "King of Israel" (Matt. 21:9; John 12:13). The book of Nehemiah tells how this city and this covenant community were reestablished.

ORIGINAL HISTORICAL SETTING

Because Ezra-Nehemiah first existed as a single composition, see the discussion in the *Original Historical Setting* section for **EZRA**.

Author and Date of Writing
Unknown, probably Ezra around 430 BC

First Audience and Destination
Israelites in Jerusalem after they returned from exile

Occasion
Unknown, but see *Occasion* for **EZRA**.

LITERARY FEATURES

Genre and Literary Style
Mainly Nehemiah's first person memoirs and official lists, written in Hebrew

The book of Nehemiah has the longest first-person sections (where the writer uses "I," "my," and "me") of any narrative book in Scripture. Chapters 1–7 and 12:27–13:30 appear to be copied from "The Memoirs of Nehemiah" (except for the lists noted in ***Book Features and Structure*** below). The material in chapters 8–10 tells about Ezra's preaching, which is further eyewitness material if Ezra in fact wrote this work.

In the Hebrew Bible, Ezra-Nehemiah was placed in the third section, the Writings (*Kethubim*), rather than in the Law or the Prophets. Many Bible scholars believe that 1 and 2 Chronicles (originally one book) and Ezra-Nehemiah were composed by a single author, designated "the Chronicler," perhaps Ezra himself. The books all have a common postexilic perspective, share a fondness for lists, like to describe Israelite feasts, and focus extensively on the temple and the temple workers (priests and Levites). They also share unusual vocabulary features, such as calling the temple "the house of God" (more than sixty times in these books) and the reference to "porters" (or "gatekeepers," more than thirty times). Further, the end of Chronicles is the same as the beginning of Ezra.

Themes
Rebuilding the walls of Jerusalem, reestablishing life under Mosaic law

Because Ezra-Nehemiah first existed as a single composition, see the discussion in the ***Themes*** section for **EZRA**. In Nehemiah, the focus is on rebuilding the walls instead of rebuilding the temple.

Book Features and Structure

Ezra-Nehemiah includes striking lists: "Temple Articles Returned" (Ezra 1:9-11); "Exiles Who Returned" (Ezra 2 and Neh. 7); "Ezra's Genealogy" (Ezra 7:1-5); "Heads of Families Returning with Ezra" (Ezra 8:1-14); "Men Guilty of Mixed Marriages" (Ezra 10:18-43); "Wall Builders" (Neh. 3); "Covenant Signers" (Neh. 10:1-27); "Citizens of Jerusalem and Other Towns" (Neh. 11); and "Priests and Levites" (Neh. 12:1-26).

The book of Nehemiah has three sections. The first describes the first return of Nehemiah and the rebuilding of the walls (1–7); the second describes the ministry of Ezra and the covenant renewal (8–10); the third describes the dedication of the walls and then Nehemiah's second term as governor (11–13).

ESTHER

The English title is the name of the heroine of the story. The title carries over from the Hebrew Bible.

▶ Key Text: 4:14b

"Who knoweth whether thou art come to the kingdom for such a time as this?"

▶ Key Term: "Providence"

This book is famous because it does not directly mention God. Yet one cannot understand the story apart from God's remarkable presence and providence with his people—however invisible he may seem to be at times.

▶ One-Sentence Summary

Esther, a Jewish beauty selected by Persian king Ahasuerus to become his new queen, saved the Jews from Haman's wicked plot, so her relative Mordecai established the yearly Jewish Feast of Purim.

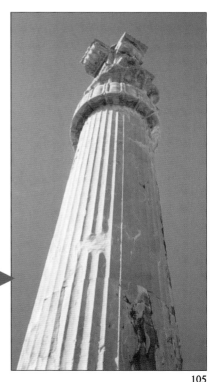

From Persepolis, the Persian royal retreat, a column with a lotus flower. The events recorded in Esther took place in Persia.

GOD'S MESSAGE IN THE BOOK

Purpose

Esther primarily preserves the historical origins of the Jewish festival of Purim. Secondarily it por trays God's providential care of people committed to him in the midst of overwhelming cha lenges to their faith. In this sense, Esther functions similarly to Ruth, the only other biblical boo named for a woman. The characters Esther and Ruth, however, are a study in contrasts: th one was a powerful and wealthy Jew who always lived outside the promised land and became the bride of a pagan king; the other was a humble and impoverished Gentile who moved to th promised land and became an ancestor of Israelite kings. People who read and study Esthe today should enjoy it for its own sake in its Old Testament setting.

Christian Worldview Elements

The book of Esther presents the worldview category of God's *sovereignty and providence* in a tangential way, for God is not directly mentioned or visible. Further, Esther's risky work in preserving the Jewish people reflects the worldview category *ethics and morality.*

GOD
CREATION
▶ **SOVEREIGNTY AND PROVIDENCE**
FAITH AND REASON
REVELATION AND AUTHORITY
HUMANITY
REBELLION AND SIN
COVENANT AND REDEMPTION
COMMUNITY AND CHURCH
DISCIPLESHIP
▶ **ETHICS AND MORALITY**
TIME AND ETERNITY

Teachings about God

The book reveals the providence of God in caring for his covenant people. Although many evils—including satan- ic opposition—may come against God's people, nothing ever happens beyond God's ability to work all things "together for good to them that love God, to them who are the called according to his purpose" (Rom. 8:28).

Teachings about Humanity

The villainy of Haman demonstrates human depravity at its worst; the integrity of Mordeca shows the enormous good that one person can do. Esther's story (like Joseph's in Genesis demonstrates that when God's people face difficult circumstances they are to act courageous ly and risk themselves for a righteous cause rather than give in to "fate" or "being unlucky."

Teachings about Salvation

God will accomplish his redemptive purposes. If Haman's edict to destroy the Jews had suc ceeded, the coming of the Jews' ultimate deliverer, Jesus the Messiah-King, would have beer imperiled. God's plan to save cannot be thwarted, and he has always taken the initiative to bring about salvation.

CHRIST IN ESTHER

Although the name of God is not mentioned in Esther, nowhere in Scripture is the care of God for his people more evident. Prior to his arrest, Jesus prayed, "While I was with them I was protecting them by Your name that You have given Me. I guarded them and not one of them is lost, except the son of destruction, that the Scripture may be fulfilled" (John 17:12 HCSB).

GOD'S STORY

When the Events of This Book Happened
During the reign of Xerxes I of Persia (ruled 486–465 BC)

Bible scholars have generally agreed that the king called "Ahasuerus" in Esther was known to the Persians as Xerxes I, who ruled a huge empire at the height of its powers. Esther became queen in Xerxes' seventh year (Esther 2:16; around 478 BC). The events of Esther are not preserved in any other ancient source. Xerxes I reigned just prior to Artaxerxes I, who ruled during the time that Ezra and Nehemiah were leaders among the exiles that had returned to the land of Israel.

How Esther Fits into God's "Story"

Esther continues God's story: God keeps a faithful remnant (Messiah's space and time prepared). First, it shows how God preserved the Jewish people from annihilation, thus keeping alive the promise and hope of a future everlasting King to come from the Davidic dynasty. Second, Esther illustrates that many Israelites that had been scattered in the exile remained faithful to the one true God. These Jews later came to preserve their identity through the synagogue. The synagogues became the beginning point for spreading the good news of Jesus Christ throughout the Roman Empire in the first century (as the book of Acts shows).

ORIGINAL HISTORICAL SETTING

Author and Date of Writing
Unknown, perhaps Mordecai around 465 BC

The book is anonymous, but according to Jewish tradition the author was Mordecai. There i
no reason he could not have composed the book, since he was an eyewitness to everythin;
that occurred (or had direct access to eyewitnesses). As Xerxes' prime minister, he is a likel
candidate for adding this incident to the official Persian archives (9:32; 10:2). The writer wa
gifted in developing plot and narrative tension and wrote with considerable literary skill.

First Audience and Destination
Jewish exiles living in Persia

The first ones to hear Esther were Jews in Persia, sometime after the feast of Purim hac
become an established custom. By this time, the postexilic people of Israel had adopted th
name "Jew," for the term Jew(s) occurs more often in the book of Esther than in the rest c
the Old Testament combined.

Occasion
The book of Esther was prompted in general by the desire to preserve the origins of the feas
of Purim. Since the author is not known, the specific occasion is unclear.

The traditional site of the tombs of Esther and Mordecai in the modern country of Iran.

HEART OF THE PERSIAN EMPIRE DURING THE TIME OF ESTHER

BLACK SEA

Danube

MACEDONIA

THRACE • Byzantium *Pontus Mts.* • Phasis Caucasus Mts. CASPIAN SEA

• Sinope

Dascylium • *Plateau of Anatolia* MOSCHI Trapezus (MESHECH) ARMENIA • Mt. Ararat

Troas Pergamum *Halys River* Malatya

LYDIA Gordion CAPPADOCIA Tyana

IONIA PHRYGIA Iconium • Mt. Van

Athens • Sardis • Derbe MTS. Carchemish Nineveh MEDIA Elburz M

amis • Ephesus CARIA PAMPHYLIA *Taurus* COMMAGENE Haran ATHURA Arbela Ecbatana

Marathon Miletus *Taurus Mts.* Tarsus Issus Asshur *Tigris River*

> The Persian advance is
> stopped in 480 B.C.
> by Greek warriors.
> Darius retreats in defeat.

Xanthus CILICIA Aleppo

Rhodes Salamis Hamath Thapsakos Behistun

Gortyna • Crete Cyprus Tripolis Tadmor SUSIANA

Byblos • Susa

RANEAN SEA Sidon • Damascus Cunaxa • Sippar

Tyre *BEYOND THE RIVER* Eshnunna Opis

> Darius builds a canal
> which helps to exploit
> the Red Sea trade.

Borsippa • Der

Joppa • Shechem Nippur

Daphne Gaza Rabbah (Amman) BABYLONIA ELAM

Sais Jerusalem Uruk • Ur

Naucratis Pelusium ARABIA

> Xerxes sacks
> Babylon in 480 B.C.

Memphis • Heliopolis Ezion-geber

Saqqarah Sinai ▲

EGYPT Mt. Sinai

> Southern Palestine is valuable due
> to its control of the major routes
> leading to Egypt.

• Tema Syro-
Arabian
Desert

Nile River RED • Dedan

El Kharga

THE PERSIAN EMPIRE

- **•** City
- **◦** Major Persian administrative center
- **⌂** Royal citadel of Persian kings
- **▲** Mountain peak
- **✗** Battle
- **RSIS** Satrapy or regional name
- **—** Royal road

▼ The gate building of Xerxes (Ahasuerus) at Persepolis which led to a mammoth terrace built by his father, Darius the Great.

LITERARY FEATURES

Genre and Literary Style
A historical narrative written in excellent Hebrew

Esther is a carefully crafted short story, but its events really happened. In English Bibles it is positioned as the last of the historical books of the Old Testament. In the Hebrew Scriptures it was placed in the third section, the Writings or Kethuvim (the other two sections are the Law and the Prophets). Among the Writings it was one of the Five Scrolls. Each of these Five Scrolls became associated with one of the Israelite festivals and was read publicly during that festival. Esther was, of course, identified with Purim, a late winter festival that originated in the fifth century BC and which is still celebrated annually by Jewish people as a minor holiday.

The Hebrew of Esther is carefully polished, but the Greek translators (second century BC) were apparently troubled by the lack of reference to God. Therefore, when they translated Esther from Hebrew to Greek, they inserted more than a hundred verses that frequently refer to God. Protestants, however, have accepted as Old Testament Scripture only texts that had Hebrew original.

Themes
Providence, accomplishments of a woman of integrity, rest from enemies

God's providential care has already been discussed in this introduction. The narrative of Esther highlights what one woman did for good more than any other Old Testament book. The importance of God's people finding rest from their enemies is noted in several Old Testament books: Joshua 21:44; 1 Chronicles 23:25; 2 Chronicles 14:6; Esther 9:22 are important examples. Ultimately rest for God's people is found only in Jesus Christ (Heb. 4:8-11).

Book Features and Structure
Particularly interesting is the author's use of paired elements. There are twin banquets of Ahasuerus (1:3-4,5-8), twin banquets of Esther (5:4-8; 7:1-10), and twin festivals of Purim (9:17-19). There are also two lists of royal servants (1:10,14), two references to Esther's hiding her ethnic identity (2:10,20), two fasts (4:3,16), two royal decrees (3:12-15; 8:9-13), and two letters establishing Purim (9:20-32). Other repeated elements add a certain stylized feel to the book: the size of Ahasuerus's kingdom (1:1; 8:9; 9:30), the king's promise to give up to half his kingdom to Esther (5:3,6; 7:2), and Esther's repeated reception of the king's favor (2:9,17; 5:2,8; 7:3; 8:5). The chamberlains (eunuchs) always come on the scene at just the right time to move the story along (1:10,15; 2:3,14-15; 4:4-5; 6:14; 7:9). Another striking literary element may be called "reversal of fortune." Vashti and Esther, as well as Haman and Mordecai, dramatically exchange positions by the end of the story.

JOB

The English title is the name of the central character in the narrative and the chief speaker in the poetic dialogues. The title carries over from the Hebrew Bible.

► *Key Text: 1:21*

"Naked came I out of my mother's womb, and naked shall I return thither: the Lord gave, and the Lord hath taken away; blessed be the name of the Lord."

► *Key Term: "Suffering"*

The book of Job explores the issue of human suffering despite God's goodness and power. The question of why people suffer and why evil continues has been the focus of intense thought throughout the ages. Job is the main biblical treatment of this issue.

► *One-Sentence Summary*

After the upright Job suddenly lost family, health, and possessions, he and his friends dialogued at length about the reasons for his sufferings, but God alone had the final word and ultimately restored Job's losses.

▼ Shepherd with sheep. Job, a wealthy man, owned 7,000 sheep (Job 1:3).

GOD'S MESSAGE IN THE BOOK

Purpose

Job is the fullest development in Scripture of the issue referred to by theologians and philosophers as "the problem of evil" or "theodicy." Simply put, the matter is this: since humans, especially the seemingly innocent, suffer pain and evil, then what kind of God must there be? Logic suggests one of three answers: (1) God is righteous, but he is not powerful enough to prevent suffering; (2) God is all-powerful, but he is not truly good and has elements of evil in his nature; or (3) all pain and evil is in fact deserved by the sufferer and sent by God (in other words, the truly innocent do not suffer).

The biblical view finds these answers unacceptable, and the book of Job wrestles with the alternative. Job reveals a wider arena than humanity can observe. The conflict of the ages between God and Satan must in the end demonstrate both the righteousness and supremacy of God. He lets the innocent suffer to demonstrate that in his sovereignty he receives glory even when his people suffer and persevere in faith without understanding why. From a merely human point of view, the answer is that there is no answer given to the problem of evil. From a divine perspective, the answer is that God's glory is served even when evil is permitted. (Christ's death is God's ultimate answer to the problem of evil.) Those who study Job today should interpret it in view of its original purpose.

Christian Worldview Elements

Job focuses attention particularly with the worldview categories of *God, sovereignty and providence,* and *ethics and morality.* No Bible book more fully teaches that human beings who live uprightly before God may experience suffering that they will never understand in this life.

▶GOD
CREATION
▶SOVEREIGNTY AND PROVIDENCE
FAITH AND REASON
REVELATION AND AUTHORITY
HUMANITY
REBELLION AND SIN
COVENANT AND REDEMPTION
COMMUNITY AND CHURCH
DISCIPLESHIP
▶ETHICS AND MORALITY
TIME AND ETERNITY

Teachings about God

Job reveals God in his heavenly court (Isa. 6 and Ezek. 1 may be compared). The book shows that God permits an adversary (Satan) to challenge his sovereign righteousness, but that God's glory is served in the end. Job's expectation of a coming Redeemer (19:25) was fulfilled in Jesus Christ. The creative work of God's Spirit is evident in such texts as Job 33:4.

Teachings about Humanity

The prose sections of Job (chapters 1–2 and 42) show that human behavior is on display before supernatural powers. The poetic sections (chapters 3–41) show that, however logical it appears, human reasoning alone can never penetrate to the mind of God. Job and his counselors reached

nly partial truth about suffering, and only when God revealed himself did the inadequacy of
uman wisdom became evident.

Teachings about Salvation

ob 1 is consistent with Genesis in showing a family head offering sacrifices for the sins of his
wn family members. Job's personal confession of faith anticipated both the coming of Christ
nd the resurrection (19:25-26).

CHRIST IN JOB

In his great losses and suffering, Job cries out for a mediator to stand between him
nd God. Christ is the answer to that heart cry. "For there is one God and one mediator
etween God and man, a man, Christ Jesus" (1 Tim. 2:5 HCSB).

GOD'S STORY

When the Events of This Book Happened
*Unknown, but probably in the time of the patriarchs (sometime between
2000 and 1500 BC)*

here is insufficient information to date the events of Job. Job's long life (42:16), the meas-
urement of wealth in livestock, and the fact that Job acted as personal priest for his family
oints to the time of Abraham, Isaac, and Jacob. Further, Job and his friends prefer to refer to
he Creator as "God" (*Elohim*) or "the Almighty" (*Shaddai*) instead of by the Israelite
ovenant name, the Lord (*Yahweh*), suggesting a time before the exodus.

How Job Fits into God's "Story"

ob does not fit into the narrative of the story of the kingdom. Rather, it offers timeless insights
or those already committed to the King of the kingdom of God. The wisdom teachings of this
ook are directly applicable to kingdom citizens, whether Israelites living in premodern tenth
entury BC or North Americans living in a postmodern twenty-first century AD. It shows how
o live in submission to what God sends onto his people, even when his purposes are
unknown and when suffering and evil appear to fall unfairly. Job does not tell how to get into
he kingdom of God; rather it tells those already in the kingdom one important aspect of living in
ight relationship to God in this lifetime. If Job (and later Jesus) suffered evil triumphantly and
hereby served the purposes of God, then God's people today can do the same. (The only New
estament reference to Job commends his perseverance or endurance; he wasn't really all that
atient; see James 5:11 in contemporary translations.)

ORIGINAL HISTORICAL SETTING

Author and Date of Writing
Unknown, perhaps during Solomon's rule (about 950 BC)

The book is anonymous. The author's frequent use of "the LORD" (Yahweh) in the prose sections suggests that he wrote from an Israelite national perspective. It may have been penned anytime in the millennium between Moses and the end of the Old Testament period (1400–400 BC). The flowering of Hebrew culture under Solomon, particularly in light of Solomon's association with wisdom literature, suggests a date during or shortly after Solomon.

First Audience and Destination
The Israelite people

The original hearers are not stated and can only be generally suggested.

Occasion

The book does not tell what prompted it to be written. Its events evidently occurred centuries before the writer's birth. Although some records of the various speeches may have survived for the author to use as sources, the material in chapters 1–2 could only be known by divine revelation.

 A modern variety of the ancient papyrus plant from whose stalks writing material was made. Bildad referred to papyrus in his argument to Job (Job 8:11).

Sunrise ("eyelids of the morning" in Job 3:9) over the Mediterranean coast of Israel.

LITERARY FEATURES

Genre and Literary Style
Wisdom literature, emphasizing dialogues in poetry, framed by a narrative prologue and epilogue, written in difficult Hebrew

The book of Job belongs to the literary type called "speculative wisdom," which explored the great questions of human existence. A number of other ancient Near Eastern texts have parallels to Job, for example the Egyptian "Admonitions of Ipuwer" or the Mesopotamian "I Will Praise the Lord of Wisdom." Israelite wisdom, however, based on the fear of the Lord, surpassed that of other nations. Job was placed in the third section, "The Writings" (*Kethubim*) of the Hebrew canon.

The narrative prologue (1–2) and epilogue (42) are necessary frames for the extended body of the book. The poetic dialogues and monologues (3–41) were composed entirely in the form of Hebrew parallelism found in the other wisdom books and the Psalms (as well as elsewhere in the Old Testament). See *Genre and Literary Style* for **PROVERBS** for more information on Hebrew parallelism.

The Hebrew vocabulary and style was so challenging to the Greek translators of Job (second century BC) that they skipped translating a number of lines, further suggesting an earlier date for the composition of Job.

Themes
The character of God; the character of humanity; the problem of evil

The long central section of dialogues and monologues shows the futility of supposing that humans can understand the purposes of God apart from divine revelation. Job's "friends" were heartless and arrogant. Job sank into despair and complained bitterly to God. Only when God revealed himself to Job (38–41) did Job return to a confident trust that the Creator—supreme in power and goodness—was his true Friend.

Book Features and Structure
Chapters 3–26 contain three cycles of dialogues between Job and his counselors, Eliphaz, Bildad, and Zophar. Chapter 28 is noted as Job's beautiful poem on "wisdom." In chapters 32–37 a previously unmentioned fourth friend, Elihu, gave a masterful monologue. God's speeches (chapters 38–41) provide the spiritual climax to the book.

The entire book may be organized into five sections, each with either a God-centered or a human-centered perspective: Job's suffering (1–2, God-centered); Job's disputes with his counselors (3–26, human-centered); Job's and Elihu's monologues (27–37, human-centered); God's answer (38–41, God-centered); Job's restoration (42, God-centered).

PSALMS

THE BOOK OF PSALMS or THE PSALTER

The English title is based on the name given by the Greek translators of this book in the second century BC. The name could be translated "Songs." The original Hebrew title is *Tehillim*, "Hymns" or "Praises."

► *Key Text: 150:6*

"Let every thing that hath breath praise the LORD. Praise ye the LORD."

► *Key Term: "Hallelujah"*

The Psalter became Israel's hymnal. Not all psalms were hymns (songs honoring or about God), but praise to God was their dominant theme. The well-known *hallelujah*, "praise Yah(weh)," was rendered "praise ye the LORD" by the KJV translators.

► *One-Sentence Summary*

God, the true and glorious King, is worthy of all praise and prayer, thanksgiving and confidence—whatever the occasion in personal or community life.

▼ Olive trees in the valley leading to Jericho from Jerusalem (Ps. 1:3).

GOD'S MESSAGE IN THE BOOK

Purpose

The purpose of the individual poems as well as the entire collection process for the Psalter was to preserve the inspired words of Israelite songwriters as they expressed the heights (and depths) of their relationship with God. Their poems were preserved to guide God's people in later times in how to approach him no matter what experiences they were undergoing. Thus, there are songs of exultation and high worship, songs of respect for God's Word, songs of trust when evil prevails, songs of confession, and other expressions of true religion. Although the Psalms contain doctrine, prophecy, and instruction, above all they were meant to be sung to God as expressions of delight in him. God's people today should use the Psalms in light of their original purpose.

Christian Worldview Elements

Every worldview element is taught in the Psalms! Psalms focuses, however, on the worldview categories of *community* (God's people worshipping and serving him together with others) and *discipleship* (living a personal life of worship and devotion to God).

GOD
CREATION
SOVEREIGNTY AND PROVIDENCE
FAITH AND REASON
REVELATION AND AUTHORITY
HUMANITY
REBELLION AND SIN
COVENANT AND REDEMPTION
▶ **COMMUNITY** AND CHURCH
▶ **DISCIPLESHIP**
ETHICS AND MORALITY
TIME AND ETERNITY

Teachings about God

The Psalms display God as Creator. He is also Redeemer and Covenant-maker. Many attributes of God are praised throughout the Psalms. The Spirit is God's active agent in accomplishing his purposes (Ps. 51:11 and Isa. 63:10-11 are the only Old Testament passages referring to the Holy Spirit by name).

Teachings about Humanity

The essential teaching of Psalms about the human race is that God desires (and enables) people to praise and thank him. Humans reach their highest potential only when they seek joy and fulfillment in the Creator rather than in the creation. The Psalms note the extremes of human existence. Psalm 8 shows the glory of humanity as made by God. On the other hand, the many Psalms that mention enemies of God and of God's people show the shameful sinfulness to which humans may fall.

Teachings about Salvation

The quotation of Psalm 32:1-2 by Paul in Romans 4:7-8 demonstrates that justification by faith was the same in Old Testament times as in New Testament times. Other passages, such as Psalm 51, confirm that the perspective of the psalmists was that salvation was initiated by the

God of the covenant and was his gift to those who trusted in his *chesed* (usually translated "mercy" or "loving-kindness" in the KJV).

⊙ *CHRIST IN PSALMS*

Both Christ's first and second comings are prophesied. For example, Psalm 22 looks ahead to the crucifixion and Psalm 2 looks forward to the time that his kingdom is universally acknowledged.

⊙ GOD'S STORY

When the Events of This Book Happened
Timeless, although historical events are mentioned

A few psalms refer to events in Israel's history, such as Psalm 105. Others refer to a historical event in the inscription, such as Psalm 3. Because God's people throughout the ages have seen the Psalms as the songs that they too are to sing, it is best to recognize the timeless quality of this part of Scripture.

How Psalms Fits into God's "Story"

Psalms does not fit into the narrative of the story of the kingdom. On one hand, it preserves songs of worship for those already committed to the King of the kingdom of God. On the other hand it looks forward to the time that "all nations whom thou hast made shall come and worship before thee" (86:9). The book was compiled for those who were already in God's kingdom and were seeking to express themselves to the Lord, their King. The book of Psalms shows kingdom citizens how to worship God in this life, both as the gathered community and the individual. Even the seven penitential psalms (6; 32; 38; 51; 102; 130; 143) express how those already numbered among God's people may repent and be restored to fellowship with him. The royal psalms (such as 2; 18; 20; 45; 72; 89; 110) in honor of Israel's earthly kings will find their greatest fulfillment when the unending King reigns unopposed forever and ever Rev. 11:15). The New Testament commends the singing of Psalms for Christians (Eph. 5:19; Col. 3:16), showing their ongoing value.

ORIGINAL HISTORICAL SETTING

Author and Date of Writing
Many authors, perhaps finally compiled around 400 BC

The titles of more than seventy psalms mention David, a noted musician and poet (1 Sam. 16:23; 2 Sam. 1:17). Both Asaph and "the sons of Korah" wrote several. Other named authors are Moses, Solomon, Heman, and Ethan. Of these, Moses was the earliest (1400s BC). Some psalms may have been composed after Israel returned from exile.

The collection grew gradually over time. For example "Book One" (1–41) could have been completed early in Solomon's time. The "Asaph Collection" (73–83) and the "Songs of Ascents" (120–134) were perhaps added as a group. The final compilation probably did not occur until after the second temple had been completed.

First Audience and Destination
The Israelite people living in their land

Each of the 150 psalms was first intended for a particular audience. Sometimes the psalm title is suggestive, for example the "Songs of Ascents" (120–134; "Songs of Degrees," KJV) were evidently composed as songs for Israelite travelers to sing as they were going up (literally) to Jerusalem. The Psalter in its final form was designed as "The Hymnal of Second-Temple Judaism."

Occasion

Only fourteen psalms provide a historical occasion in the title (3; 7; 18; 30; 34; 51; 52; 54; 56; 57; 59; 60; 63; 142). For others, the content is suggestive but not conclusive. The final editors of the collection were prompted by the need to preserve the psalms they had. Many scholars believe that the final editors composed Psalms 1, 2, and 150 as the formal introduction and conclusion to the Psalter.

A view of the beautiful snow-capped peaks of Mount Hermon, mentioned in several psalms (Pss. 42:6; 89:12; 133:3).

LITERARY FEATURES

Genre and Literary Style
An anthology of poetry in honor of Israel's God and Israel's faith, written in Hebrew

The poetic style of the Psalms has much in common with the poetry of every culture: the rich use of figurative language and hyperbole that comes from thoughtful use of the imagination. Who can forget the metaphor, "The LORD is my shepherd" (23:1) or the hyperbole, "Let the floods clap their hands" (98:8)? See **Genre and Literary Style** for **PROVERBS** for more information on Hebrew parallelism. Psalms was the first book in "The Writings" (*Kethubim*), the third section of the Hebrew canon. Jesus referred to this threefold organization in Luke 24:44: "All things must be fulfilled, which were written in the law of Moses, and in the prophets, and in the psalms, concerning me."

Themes
Praise and thanksgiving, lament and trust, wisdom, kingship

By careful observation, most psalms may be assigned to one of the themes or "psalm types" listed above. Many psalms exalt God for who he is (praise) and what he has done (thanksgiving). Some psalms are laments or calls to God for help, either because of personal or national distress. These are prayers of petition more than psalms of praise, but they express confident trust in God. A few psalms exhort the righteous to live in wisdom along the lines of the book of Proverbs. The royal psalms have already been noted.

Book Features and Structure

Of the 150 psalms, 116 have a title of some sort. (The other 34 are called "orphan psalms.") These provide information about authorship, historical context, musical notations, or original usage. For the most part, the meaning of the musical terms (*shiggaion, maskil, miktam,* and *selah,* for example) is lost.

The present five-section organization of the Psalms was possibly meant to echo the five books of Moses. Each section ends on a note of praise to the LORD.

Book One (mainly by David):   Psalms 1–41

Book Two (mainly by David):   Psalms 42–72

Book Three (mainly by Asaph):   Psalms 73–89

Book Four (mainly anonymous):   Psalms 90–106

Book Five (Davidic and anonymous): Psalms 107–150

PROVERBS

THE BOOK OF PROVERBS

he longer title translates the name found in Latin Bibles (*Liber Proverbiorum*). In Hebrew he title was "Proverbs of Solomon." Solomon was named as the main contributor. Proverb *mashal* in Hebrew) may be rendered "maxim" or "wise saying."

▶ *Key Text: 3:5-6*

'Trust in the Lord with all thine heart; and lean not unto thine own understanding. n all thy ways acknowledge him, and he shall direct thy paths."

▶ *Key Term: "Wisdom"*

his book shows God's people how to live life skillfully: "The fear of the LORD is the beginning f knowledge" (1:7). These principles for everyday life combine common sense as well as roper reverence for God, resulting in true wisdom. Wisdom (Hebrew *hokmah*) goes beyond heoretical knowledge into practical guidelines for facing life's challenging issues successfully.

▶ *One-Sentence Summary*

hose who follow God's wise design for living—particularly in areas of sexual purity and ntegrity of speech—avoid the perils that others fall into and enjoy life on earth as God meant to be lived.

▼ A gold necklace (Prov. 1:8-9).

GOD'S MESSAGE IN THE BOOK

Purpose

Proverbs gives positive and negative principles for successful living, no matter the situation. The book applies to everyday life the great commandments to love God supremely and to love one's neighbors as oneself (Lev. 19:18; Deut. 6:5). Because proverbial teachings, by their nature, tell what works in human relationships, they cannot be treated as absolutes or as prophecies. The book assumes (but does not explicitly mention) covenant and redemption of Israel's history. Living well means enjoying successful relationships now, whatever happened in history or whatever the future brings.

Christian Worldview Elements

Proverbs presents two worldview categories extremely well. First, *sovereignty and providence* are taught by the laws of cause and effect in the moral realm. Second, the book provides practical insight on *ethics and morality*. No Bible book more fully teaches that God's people are to have a different quality of life than the ungodly.

GOD
CREATION
▶ **SOVEREIGNTY AND PROVIDENCE**
FAITH AND REASON
REVELATION AND AUTHORITY
HUMANITY
REBELLION AND SIN
COVENANT AND REDEMPTION
COMMUNITY AND CHURCH
DISCIPLESHIP
▶ **ETHICS AND MORALITY**
TIME AND ETERNITY

Teachings about God

In Proverbs, God is the one who has set up the world so that those who live by his principles will find blessing and success. The highest virtue is "the fear of the LORD."

Teachings about Humanity

Proverbs shows that humans may live by a right way or a wrong way, a wise way or a foolish way. The right way is not the easy way, but those who live by it find great reward. All of life's relationships may be governed by the wise teachings of this book.

Teachings about Salvation

Proverbs assumes God's covenant but does not teach about it directly. This surely serves to demonstrate that the wisdom coming from the people of God is superior to and results in greater blessing than the wisdom coming from others—even without explicitly referring to the mighty acts of God on behalf of his people.

CHRIST IN PROVERBS

Wisdom as an attribute of God is pictured as a person in Proverbs. In light of the New Testament, we know that Wisdom as Jesus Christ, the Word by whom the worlds were created and are sustained (John 1:1; Heb. 1:3).

GOD'S STORY

When the Events of This Book Happened

Timeless

These principles are operative in human relationships without reference to time.

How Proverbs Fits into God's "Story"

Proverbs does not fit into the narrative of the story of the kingdom. Rather, it offers timeless principles for those already committed to the King of the kingdom of God. Although Jesus is "greater than Solomon" (Matt. 12:42), the wisdom teachings of this book apply directly to all kingdom citizens, whether ancient Israelites or contemporary believers. The book of Proverbs shows how to live with love for God foremost and love for others second. Proverbs does not tell how to get into the kingdom of God; rather it tells those already in the kingdom how to live in right relationship to others. This is essentially the same approach that Jesus took in the Sermon on the Mount (Matt. 5–7) and the approach taught in the letter from James.

Cuneiform tablet and its envelope dealing with the sale of some land. Proverbs 31 describes a virtuous woman: "She considereth a field, and buyeth it"(Prov. 31:16).

ORIGINAL HISTORICAL SETTING

Author and Date of Writing
Primarily Solomon, but also others, about 950–700 BC

Solomon ruled Israel about 970–931 BC. He "spake three thousand proverbs: and his songs were a thousand and five" (1 Kings 4:32). Many of these were preserved in this book. Solomon wrote the first section (1:8–9:18) and the second section (10:1–22:16). More than two centuries later, more of Solomon's proverbs were compiled by scholars working for King Hezekiah (25:1–29:27). Unnamed wise men wrote the proverbs collected in 22:17–24:22. Two others, unknown outside this book, contributed short sections: Agur (30:1-33) and King Lemuel (31:1-9). The final compiler of Proverbs evidently wrote the prologue, stating the book's purpose (1:1-7) and the epilogue about the virtuous woman (31:10-31).

Solomon may have collected his own proverbs and put them into written form. The later contributions could have been completed by 700 BC. Some scholars believe that the book of Proverbs was not edited into its final form until after the Jews returned from their Babylonian exile, perhaps the fifth century BC.

First Audience and Destination
The Israelite people living in their own land

The first hearers were the Israelite people who came to admire the wisdom of their great king, Solomon (1 Kings 3:28). According to 1 Kings 4:29-34, representatives of "all people" of the surrounding nations came to Jerusalem to hear Solomon's divinely inspired wisdom.

Occasion

When God asked Solomon at the beginning of his reign to name a gift, he asked for "wisdom and knowledge" to rule the Israelite people well (2 Chron. 1:10). God granted this, and over the course of years Solomon's wisdom became legendary so that it "excelled the wisdom of all the children of the east country, and all the wisdom of Egypt" (1 Kings 4:30). Perhaps most of Solomon's proverbs were written during his early years as king, before he was led astray by "many strange women" (1 Kings 11:1).

FORMS OF WISDOM TEACHING IN PROVERBS

1. Proverb
A proverb is a short, carefully constructed ethical observation (13:7) or teaching (14:1).

2. Admonition
An admonition is a command written either as a short proverb or as part of a long discourse.

3. Numerical Saying
The numerical pattern lists items that have something in common after an introduction like, "Six things the Lord hates; in fact, seven are detestable to Him" (6:16 HCSB).

4. Better Saying
A better saying follows the pattern "A is better than B" (21:19).

5. Rhetorical Question
A rhetorical question is a question with an obvious answer that still draws the reader into deeper reflection (30:4).

6. Wisdom Poem
Wisdom poems or songs teach a series of moral lessons (31:10-31). These poems are often acrostic which means that the first letter of the first line begins with the first letter in the Hebrew alphabet. The first letter of the second line is the second letter of the Hebrew alphabet, and so on.

7. Example Story
An example story is an anecdote meant to drive home a moral lesson (7:6-27).

LITERARY FEATURES

Genre and Literary Style
Wisdom literature emphasizing short maxims, written entirely in Hebrew poetry

People of the ancient Near East greatly admired the wise men who collected and publishe[d] guidelines for successful living. Wisdom literature was of two types: proverbial (such as the pre[s]ent book, stating principles for living well) and speculative (such as Job or Ecclesiastes, pon[-]dering deep issues of human existence). Both the Mesopotamians and the Egyptians deve[l]oped wisdom traditions. Israelite wisdom, however, based on the fear of the Lord, surpasse[d] that of other nations. Proverbs was placed in the third section, "The Writings" (*Kethubim*[)] of the Hebrew canon.

Hebrew poetry characteristically had two (sometimes three) lines that are parallel i[n] thought (rather than in rhyme). In *synonymous* parallelism, the second line repeated th[e] essence of the first in different words (see 5:7). In *antithetic* parallelism, the second line sta[t]ed the opposite of the first (see 10:3). When the later line built on the first without eithe[r] repeating or contrasting, it is referred to as *synthetic* parallelism (see 31:15).

Themes
Fear of the Lord; cause and effect in the moral realm; wisdom and folly (each personified as a woman)

Although common sense does not take God into account, true wisdom is based on reverenc[e] and trust in the God who has revealed himself. He has built into the moral world the rele[nt]less law of sowing and reaping, cause and effect. Good choices result in good ends; evil choic[-]es result in evil ends. One way to understand these is contrast those who follow "Dam[e] Wisdom" and those who follow "Dame Folly."

Book Features and Structure

Beyond the parallelism of Hebrew poetry, this book has a number of noteworthy literary fea[-]tures. Vivid comparisons abound: "A word fitly spoken is like apples of gold in pictures of si[l]ver" (25:11). Another device is to use numbers; especially striking is the "x plus 1" pattern[.] "There are three things that are never satisfied, yea, four things say not, It is enough" (30:15[).] Chapters 1–9 feature several long wisdom poems that use striking female imagery. Not onl[y] are wisdom and folly portrayed as attractive women, but there are also warnings against th[e] immoral woman. These chapters were crafted as instructions to youth. Chapters 10–30 con[-]tain a string of two-line sayings unrelated to their immediate context. The epilogue (31:10–3[1]) was written as an acrostic, with each verse beginning with successive letters of the Hebre[w] alphabet.

ECCLESIASTES

The Greek translators used this name when they titled it in the second century BC. It was their rendering of the Hebrew title, *Qoheleth*, "Preacher" or "Teacher." "Ecclesiastes" means "One Who Assembles People," akin to *ekklesia*, "assembly."

▶ *Key Text: 1:2 (which is the same as 12:8)*

"Vanity of vanities, saith the Preacher, vanity of vanities; all is vanity."

▶ *Key Term: "Vanity" (uselessness or absurdity)*

The Hebrew term *hebel* literally meant "breath" or "vapor." It referred to something without meaning or something absurd or useless (rather than conceit or self-admiration, as "vanity" implies today). The term occurs more than thirty times in the book but only once elsewhere in the Bible.

▶ *One-Sentence Summary*

Although human beings can accumulate many things, accomplish much, and achieve great wisdom, these are without profit and ultimately pointless unless one has lived in fear and obedience to God.

▼ A Jewish lad receiving instruction from a rabbi at his Bar Mitzvah ceremony by the Western Wall in Jerusalem.

GOD'S MESSAGE IN THE BOOK

Purpose

Ecclesiastes answers the question, What is the meaning of life? The way Qoheleth ("the Preacher") argued was to show at length the failure of the answers offered by those who live life "under the sun," that is, apart from revealed religion. *Materialists* find life's object in the abundance of possessions or achievements. *Sensualists* discover meaning in physical pleasure (food, sex, excitement, adventure). *Scholars* seek purpose through intellectual inquiry (wisdom). All these answers are "vanity of vanities" or "utterly meaningless." Life's meaning cannot be *discovered;* it is only *revealed* by God. Life is brief; judgment is coming; God is sovereign. Qoheleth's answer is that of divine revelation: "Let us hear the conclusion of the whole matter: Fear God, and keep his commandments: for this *is* the whole *duty* of man. For God shall bring every work into judgment, with every secret thing, whether *it be* good, or whether *it be* evil" (12:13-14).

Christian Worldview Elements

Ecclesiastes focuses attention on the worldview categories of *God* first and *humanity* second. When the order is reversed, the result is "vanity of vanities." No other Bible book does a better job of teaching that the meaning of life is found only outside oneself and only in right relationship to God.

▶ **GOD**
CREATION
SOVEREIGNTY AND PROVIDENCE
FAITH AND REASON
REVELATION AND AUTHORITY
▶ **HUMANITY**
REBELLION AND SIN
COVENANT AND REDEMPTION
COMMUNITY AND CHURCH
DISCIPLESHIP
ETHICS AND MORALITY
TIME AND ETERNITY

Teachings about God

In Ecclesiastes God is referred to simply as "God" (*Elohim*) or "Creator." He is not called "the Lord" or "the LORD." This emphasizes God in relationship to all humanity—their Creator and the One to whom they are ultimately accountable—as opposed to God in relationship to Israel as the covenant people.

Teachings about Humanity

Ecclesiastes has an optimistic view of human capacity apart from God. Materialists, sensualists, and scholars alike can reach worthwhile goals that bring temporary satisfaction and the appearance of meaning. Yet the book is pessimistic about the ability of persons to understand their true purpose unaided by divine revelation. Left to themselves, humans never reach right answers to the question, "Why am I here?"

Teachings about Salvation

Salvation in Ecclesiastes is spoken of in terms of proper fear (reverence, awe, respect) of God (see 3:14; 5:7; 8:12; 12:13). Ultimately, only those who "fear God and keep his commandments" (12:13) give evidence of experiencing salvation, which like existence itself comes from the Creator. The meaning of human life is displayed when redeemed people magnify the glory of God by joyfully fearing and obeying him.

CHRIST IN ECCLESIASTES

Ecclesiastes gives a graphic picture of life's emptiness and futility apart from God. Jesus uses the image of a vine with branches to underscore this truth: "The one who remains in Me and I in him produces much fruit, because you can do nothing without Me" (John 15:5 HCSB).

GOD'S STORY

When the Events of This Book Happened: *Timeless*

The questions and answers about life's purpose discussed in Ecclesiastes are valid in all times and places.

How Ecclesiastes Fits into God's "Story"

Ecclesiastes does not fit into the narrative of the story of the kingdom. Rather, people already in the kingdom need to know that he gladly gives them exuberant human experiences to savor when their priority is fearing and obeying him.

Ecclesiastes must be considered from two different perspectives. Much of the book focuses on the emptiness of everything done apart from God. "For what shall it profit a man, if he shall gain the whole world, and lose his own soul?" (Mark 8:36).

But are human accomplishments inherently evil? Not at all. For those already in the kingdom—who fear God and obey his commands—human life is a wondrous and good gift from God to be enjoyed to the fullest (9:7-10). This is true despite the harsh realities of life. Thus, those in the kingdom may delight in the material possessions, sensual experience, and wisdom that this present life offers: "Whatsoever thy hand findeth to do, do it with thy might" (9:10). Ecclesiastes serves kingdom purposes by reminding God's people that they are to enjoy this present existence fully.

ORIGINAL HISTORICAL SETTING

Author and Date of Writing
Probably Solomon, perhaps near the end of his reign (about 935 BC)

The author called himself Qoheleth, "Preacher" or "Teacher" in the sense of one who assembles people for instruction. He was also "the son of David, king in Jerusalem" (1:1). Jewish and Christian tradition alike have identified him as Solomon, and the perspective of an experienced old man is certain (see 12:1-7).

On the other hand, several features of the book point to a writer other than and later than Solomon. The Hebrew style is unusual and considered late; the reference to "all that were in Jerusalem before me" (2:9) seems odd for Solomon, Jerusalem's second Israelite king; and the writer expressed negative views about rulers (see 4:13; 5:8-9; 7:19; 8:2-3) that are hard to imagine coming from Solomon.

It may be, as is clear in the case of Proverbs, that the material was mainly written by Solomon but that it was expanded and revised by an unknown editor at a later time, perhaps as late as the 400s BC. There is nothing in the book that Solomon could not have written, and he certainly is the best Old Testament character to fit the description of one who "taught the people knowledge . . . and sought out, *and* set in order many proverbs" (12:9; see 1 Kings 4:32).

First Audience and Destination
The Israelite people living in their own land

The first hearers were the Israelite people who came to admire the wisdom of Solomon (1 Kings 3:28). According to 1 Kings 4:29-34, representatives of "all people" of the surrounding nations came to hear Solomon's divinely inspired wisdom.

Occasion

Solomon reigned about 970–931 BC. The precise occasion for Ecclesiastes is unknown. The teachings of Ecclesiastes come from late in Solomon's reign—after he had experienced everything life had to offer and was contemplating once again "what's it all about?" (The book of Proverbs was evidently his wisdom from early in his reign.)

"A time to dance" (Eccles. 3:4). Jewish men dancing during a private ceremony in the Court of the Men at the Wailing Wall in Jerusalem.

LITERARY FEATURES

Genre and Literary Style
Wisdom literature composed in a mixture of prose and poetry, written in unusual Hebrew

Ancient wisdom literature was of two types: proverbial (such as the book of Proverbs, stating principles for living well) and speculative (such as Job or the present book, pondering deep issues of human existence). In the Hebrew canon, Ecclesiastes was placed in the third section, the Writings or *Kethubim* (the other two sections are the Law and the Prophets). Among the Writings it was one of the Five Scrolls. Each of these Five Scrolls became associated with one of the Israelite festivals and was read publicly during that festival. Ecclesiastes was identified with *Sukkoth*, "Tabernacles" or "Booths," a happy time that celebrated the completion of all agricultural labors. The Hebrew style is markedly different from anything else in the Old Testament.

Themes
Vanity (uselessness), under the sun, profit

The theme of the uselessness of humanity's work apart from God has already been considered. The phrase "under the sun" occurs 27 times in the KJV text and seems to refer to life lived independently of God. The theme of "profit" sometimes occurs in rhetorical questions in the modern sense of "What's the use of that?" with the expected answer, "No use at all."

Book Features and Structure

Ecclesiastes is easy to read, but it is almost impossible to give a satisfactory outline of how the topics develop. The prose and poetry sections shift without warning. Many of the statements, taken by themselves, are enigmas. Memorable passages include "To Every Thing There Is a Season" (3:1-18) and "Wise Sayings" (7:1-14). Because Qoheleth referred to himself in the third person only at the beginning and end of the book, a three-part structure—which admittedly does not show the inner development of the book—may be suggested: introduction and theme (1:1-11); discourses on the meaning of life—with and without God (1:12–12:8); "conclusion of the whole matter" (12:9-14).

SONG OF SONGS

SONG OF SOLOMON or CANTICLES

The Hebrew title is *Shir Hashirim*, "Song of Songs," meaning "The Best Song." Because 1:1 mentions Solomon, English Bibles have often included his name in the title. *Canticles* is Latin for "Songs."

▶ *Key Text: 6:3*

"*I* am *my beloved's, and my beloved* is *mine: he feedeth among the lilies.*"

▶ *Key Term: "Beloved"*

Song of Songs is a book of romantic love poetry. The lovers—bride and groom—refer to each other passionately. The bride calls him "beloved," a term found more than twenty times; the groom calls her "my love."

▶ *One-Sentence Summary*

A bride and groom (or wife and husband) celebrate with exuberant passion God's wonderful gift of the love they share by describing the intimate dimensions of their love—physical, emotional, and spiritual.

Pomegranate blossoms taken at Sabaste, Israel. ". . . your brow is like a slice of pomegranate" (Song 4:3 HCSB).

GOD'S MESSAGE IN THE BOOK

Purpose

Many parts of Scripture address human sexuality, and a number of divine commands regulate marriage, adultery, divorce, and sexual immorality. Other than this book, however, little is noted in Scripture about whether a man and woman should enjoy or merely endure romance. In the tradition of ancient Near Eastern wisdom literature, Song of Songs explores one of the "big issues" of life. It definitively answers the question, Should a husband and wife enjoy the amorous dimension of their relationship? The answer is, Yes indeed! Although people often abuse or distort erotic love, it is a wondrous and normal part of marriage to be savored as God's gift. Strikingly, the dominant speaker is the wife, whose delight in the intimacies she enjoys demonstrates that the biblical view of sex is neither negative nor repressed. It is not claiming too much to call this book "The Bible's Romance Manual for Marriage." God's people should enjoy the Song of Songs today in light of its original purpose.

Christian Worldview Elements

This book deals with the worldview categories of *humanity* and *ethics and morality*. No other Bible book more fully teaches that human beings may enjoy rich and sensual love. On the other hand, this love is suitably expressed only within the marriage of a man and a woman, according to the standards God revealed elsewhere in Scripture.

GOD
CREATION
SOVEREIGNTY AND PROVIDENCE
FAITH AND REASON
REVELATION AND AUTHORITY
▶HUMANITY
REBELLION AND SIN
COVENANT AND REDEMPTION
COMMUNITY AND CHURCH
DISCIPLESHIP
▶ETHICS AND MORALITY
TIME AND ETERNITY

Teachings about God

God is not directly named in this book. None of his usual names are found, such as God, Lord, the LORD, or the Almighty. God is affirmed indirectly as the Creator who conceived of romantic love between husband and wife, as in the account of the first man and woman coming together as one flesh (Gen. 2:18-25).

Teachings about Humanity

Song of Songs celebrates the glory of wedded bliss possible for human beings, despite the many obstacles to true love. The climax of the book shows how strong and wonderful romantic love is: "Many waters cannot quench love, neither can the floods drown it: if a man would give all the substance of his house for love, it would utterly be contemned" (8:7).

Teachings about Salvation

The book does not teach directly about redemption. If the love of a husband for his wife can be as rich and satisfying as the book describes, however, how much greater is the love of God for his beloved people? (see Rev. 21:9).

CHRIST IN SONG OF SONGS

Love between a husband and wife is taken by Paul as a picture of the love Christ has for his bride, the church (Eph. 5:32).

GOD'S STORY

When the Events of This Book Happened
Timeless

The romantic love celebrated by this book is authentic for all times and places.

How Song of Songs Fits into God's "Story"

Song of Solomon does not fit into the narrative of the story of the kingdom. However, for those already part of God's kingdom, when true love is aroused, it is to be enjoyed (see 2:7; 3:5; 8:4 in contemporary versions). It says nothing about how to get into God's kingdom, but it shows one important aspect of earthly life to those already in the kingdom. This wisdom book serves kingdom purposes by reminding God's people that they are to savor the bliss of married love while they look forward to the consummation of God's redemptive purposes in eternity.

ORIGINAL HISTORICAL SETTING

Author and Date of Writing
Probably Solomon, perhaps near the beginning of his reign (about 965 BC)

The author wrote the most exquisite romantic poetry in the Bible, and the perspective of a young couple captivated with each other is transparent. The inscription (1:1) as well as Jewish and Christian tradition identified the author as Solomon. According to 1 Kings 4:32 Solomon's "songs were a thousand and five." Many believe that the pure and passionate words of love described in this book were necessarily written early in his life—before he was married to so many women (1 Kings 11:1-8).

Some scholars have argued that the title is a dedication to Solomon (rather than a statement of authorship) and find it hard to imagine that a polygamous king wrote such beautiful celebration of monogamous love. Although their arguments for later anonymous authorship have merit, there is no reason that a young Solomon could not have written the song in its entirety.

First Audience and Destination
Israelites living in their own land

The first hearers were the Israelite people who admired both the proverbs and the songs of their great King Solomon (1 Kings 4:32).

Occasion

Scholars have a variety of opinions about what prompted the composition of this book. Two major suggestions follow. Some believe that the book describes an ideal romance composed for a royal occasion, such as a state wedding. In this view, the bride and groom were not individuals but "Every-Bride" and "Every-Groom," depicting the possibilities of human romance with all its challenges and glories. Others have argued that this is Solomon's poem about an actual, historical romance and marriage between an unnamed girl (called the "Shulamite," 6:13) and her beloved (either Solomon himself or an unnamed lover). The former view of the occasion appears preferable.

One of the "cedars of Lebanon." From these Solomon made a chariot (Song 3:9).

LITERARY FEATURES

Genre and Literary Style
Wisdom literature emphasizing the value of romantic love, written entirely in Hebrew poetry

Although some scholars have questioned whether this book is properly "wisdom literature," it answers one of the grand questions of life: Should a husband and wife enjoy the erotic dimension of their relationship? (See earlier discussion under **Purpose**.) As such, it belongs to the literary category "speculative wisdom." The poetic imagery is exquisite, lavish, and delicate, even if modern lovers do not fully appreciate the vivid metaphors from the ancient Near East (see 4:1-7; 5:10-16; 6:4-10; 7:1-10). The lines of poetry are short, and the Hebrew style is appropriate to the subject matter.

In the Hebrew canon this book was placed in the third section, the Writings or *Kethubim* (the other two sections are the Law and the Prophets). Among the Writings it was the first of the Five Scrolls, each of which became associated with one of the Israelite festivals and was read publicly during that festival. Song of Songs was associated with *Pesach*, "Passover." Although this connection seems strange, this can be understood in light of the Jewish allegorical interpretation of the book. Its deeper (and truer) meaning was said to be its declaration of God's love for Israel, of which the greatest historical evidence was the exodus at the first Passover. This view was also taken up by Christians in the medieval period but revised and seen as an allegory of Christ's love for the church. Bible scholars today generally reject such allegorical readings as a misunderstanding of the book's purpose by theologians unwilling to admire as literally true the frankly erotic elements of the book.

Themes
Desire, commitment, giving of self to one's lover despite obstacles

The passionate desire of the woman for her husband and of the husband for his wife is the major theme of the book. This passion, however, lies in the mutual commitment of one to the other (see **Key Text**). True love is so strong that it overcomes all obstacles (see 5:6-8), yet it should not be wakened until due season (2:7; 3:5; 8:4).

Book Features and Structure

Although it was originally a song, no clues about the original musical notation have survived. The Hebrew text distinguishes the characters by changing gender and number in certain verbs and pronouns. On this basis many translations have added subheadings to clarify changes in speaker from "Bride" to "Groom" (with their "Friends" also talking in places, probably the "daughters of Jerusalem," 1:5; 2:7; 3:5,10; 5:8,16; 8:4).

ISAIAH

aiah, the eighth-century Israelite prophet from Judah, has given his name to this book as its omposer. His name means "The LORD Saves" in Hebrew.

▶ Key Text: 1:19-20

"If ye be willing and obedient, ye shall eat the good of the land: But if ye refuse and ebel, ye shall be devoured with the sword: for the mouth of the Lord hath spoken it."

▶ Key Term: "Judgment"

aiah's vision of the heavenly throne compelled him to proclaim God's case against his people efore their earthly throne in Jerusalem. Although divine judgment was inevitable, Isaiah ffered hope, comfort, and a glorious future for God's kingdom.

▶ One-Sentence Summary

aiah prophesied that because of continued idolatry God would send Judah into Babylonian aptivity, yet he would graciously restore them (through the work of his Servant, who would ear away their sins by his death), so that his kingdom would be unending in the new heavens id the new earth.

Young grapes growing near Tel Lakhish (Isa. 5:1-7).

GOD'S MESSAGE IN THE BOOK

Purpose

This book preserves the divinely inspired prophecies Isaiah made during his ministry of mo*r*e than forty years. These prophecies were originally for the people of Judah facing Assyrian inv*a*sions. Because of rebellion and idolatry, their kingdom would be destroyed—even though ind*i*viduals could still repent and seek the Lord.

The last part of Isaiah (40–66) was really addressed to later generations. On the one han*d* it would comfort exiles returning to the land after Babylonian captivity (late sixth century BC*).* on the other hand it speaks to every later generation of God's people who long for God's kin*g*dom to be revealed to all in its holiness and righteousness.

Christian Worldview Elements

Isaiah deals with the worldview categories of *rebellion and sin, covenant and redemption,* and *time and eternity.* Judah's sin—like all sin—had tragic consequences. Yet judgment was not the final word, only the means of bringing God's people to ultimate salvation. Isaiah gives the big picture of redemption from his own day until the consummation of all things.

GOD
CREATION
SOVEREIGNTY AND PROVIDENCE
FAITH AND REASON
REVELATION AND AUTHORITY
HUMANITY
▶ **REBELLION AND SIN**
▶ **COVENANT AND REDEMPTION**
COMMUNITY AND CHURCH
DISCIPLESHIP
ETHICS AND MORALITY
▶ **TIME AND ETERNITY**

Teachings about God

God expects his people to fulfill his requirements. He is outraged by sin and will judge it. Yet he is also the God of help and hope. Isaiah's portrait *of* God is thus one of tension between judgment and comfort. The book is famous for its detaile*d* prophecies about Christ, especially his birth (7:14; 9:6-7) and his death (53). The Spirit w*ill* empower both the Servant and the servants of the Lord (11:2; 32:15; 42:1; 44:3; 61:1).

Teachings about Humanity

Aside from its general teachings that humans are fallen sinners whom God must redeem, th*e* book provides personal glimpses into the lives of two persons whom God used. Isaiah show*s* that God may call and use someone who is well educated. The section on Hezekiah (36–3*9)* shows a ruler who valued trust in God more than military or economic success.

eachings about Salvation

Isaiah, salvation is based on God's forgiveness of sins (1:18; 6:5-6). The passage on the uffering Servant (52:13–53:12) is the most detailed biblical prophecy about Jesus' death as a ubstitute, and the New Testament writers quoted it often. Ultimately, however, salvation cludes the restoration of Zion (62) as well as the nations (60). The goal is for the nations to how forth the praises of the Lord" (60:6). This will be brought to completion in the eternal ate (Isa. 65:17; compare Rev. 21:1).

CHRIST IN ISAIAH

Isaiah is the only Old Testament book to prophesy the virgin birth of Christ (7:14). hrist as Suffering Servant is foretold in Isaiah (52:13–53:12).

GOD'S STORY

When the Events of This Book Happened

aiah prophesied during the reigns of four kings of Judah: Uzziah, Jotham, haz, and Hezekiah (mainly about 740–700 BC)

econd Kings 15–20 and 2 Chronicles 26–32 provide the historical narrative for the four kings entioned in Isaiah 1:1. The kingdom of Judah was isolated, with powerful enemies especially the north. From Samaria, idolatrous kings ruled over the kingdom of Israel. North of there, ie power of Aram (Syria, KJV) with its capital in Damascus, was a constant threat. Beyond I these was the terrible world superpower, the Assyrians, with their capital in Nineveh.

Now Isaiah Fits into God's "Story"

he events of Isaiah's time belong to "chapter 2" of the story: God educates his nation (dis-bedient Israel disciplined). Judah was weak and impotent because it had become like the sur-ounding nations: self-sufficient and selfish. There was little sense that it was part of God's king-om of righteousness and holiness. Yet Isaiah prophesied the coming of a righteous King—a escendant of David—who would one day rule God's kingdom forever (9:7).

ORIGINAL HISTORICAL SETTING

Author and Date of Writing
Isaiah, perhaps finally compiled around 680 BC

Because of the message of good news in the last section of his book, the author has been called "The Evangelist of the Old Covenant." Isaiah the son of Amoz was evidently from Jerusalem. According to Jewish tradition, he was from a noble family. He had a wife and at least two sons with symbolic names, "A Remnant Will Return" and "Speed the Spoil; Hasten the Plunder" (Shear-jashub and Maher-shalal-hash-baz, 7:3; 8:3). He was possibly martyred by being sawed in half (see Heb. 11:37). The kings Isaiah mentioned ruled almost a century, from 792 to 686 BC. His years of influence were about 740–700 BC.

For the past two centuries, critical scholars have argued that chapters 40–66 were necessarily written later than Isaiah's lifetime. These chapters focus on return from Babylonian exile (which did not happen until centuries after Isaiah) and name Cyrus (44:28; 45:1), the Persian king who allowed the Jewish exiles to return (Ezra 1:1-2). Isaiah 40–55 are thus assigned to "Deutero-Isaiah" (an unknown prophet with an exilic perspective) and Isaiah 56–66 are assigned to "Trito-Isaiah" (an unknown postexilic prophet). The basic assumption of this critical view appears to be that Scripture does not contain true predictive prophecy. For Bible students who accept that God gave specific revelations of the distant future to his prophets, there is no reason to doubt that Isaiah wrote all the book that bears his name.

First Audience and Destination
The people of Judah living during Isaiah's lifetime

The first hearers were people living in Judah near the end of the 700s BC.

Occasion

The specific occasion of a few parts of Isaiah are clear, for example chapter 7 was prompted by the Syrian-Israelite coalition against Judah (734–732 BC), and chapters 36–39 were prompted by Sennacherib's invasion of Judah (701 BC). The last event that may be dated in Isaiah's lifetime is the murder of Sennacherib (681 BC). By this time Isaiah was an old man, for he had been commissioned around 740 BC, the year of King Uzziah's death. Isaiah did not tell what prompted his compilation of the entire book.

▶ THE "SYRO-EPHRAIMITE WAR" *Isaiah 7*

LEGEND
- City
- ▲ Mountain peak
- ⟡ Siege
- Israel
- Judah
- Aram-Damascus
- ← Routes of the anti-Assyrian coalition
- ← Pressure from Edom
- ← Philistine advances

Rezin, king of Aram

Pekah, son of Remaliah, king of Israel

Damascus and Israel besiege Jerusalem

Isaiah urges Ahaz to remain steadfast

Philistines raid towns in Judah

The Edomites attack Judah and take prisoners

Rezin, king of Aram, drives out the men of Judah and recovers Elath for Aram

LITERARY FEATURES

Genre and Literary Style
Prophecies and a few historical narratives written in excellent Hebrew poetry and prose

The genius of Hebrew prophecy was that it both "forth tells" and "foretells." The essence of the prophetic message was its clear "thus saith the Lord." Isaiah includes the three classic elements of prophecy: (1) call to people to turn from their sins in the face of divine judgment, (2) predictions of near events (such as the fall of Damascus), and (3) predictions of remote events (such as the coming of the Servant of the Lord).

The book is mainly Hebrew poetry. The main prose section, the narrative about King Hezekiah (36–39), skillfully makes the transition from the challenges Judah faced from the Assyrians to those they would later face from the Babylonians. Isaiah was a master of Hebrew vocabulary and style. His book has a larger vocabulary than any other Old Testament book. He particularly used the literary technique of personification, such as the sun being ashamed or the mountains singing (24:23; 44:23). In the Hebrew Scriptures, the book of Isaiah was the first of the four "Latter Prophets."

Themes
The Holy One of Israel, judgment, comfort, the Servant of the Lord

Isaiah's special name for God was "the Holy One of Israel" (26 occurrences), found only six times elsewhere in Scripture. The first section of the book describes the coming of divine judgment. The last section emphasizes comfort and hope, looking forward to Zion's restoration. Isaiah is noted for four "Servant Songs" in which the Messiah representatively fulfills the responsibilities of Israel as the Lord's Son.

Book Features and Structure
Isaiah predicted important details of the first coming of the Messiah. Especially noteworthy are his prophecies of the virgin birth (7:14); the child born to be Prince of Peace (9:6-7); God's Spirit on the Branch (11:1-2); the gentleness of the Servant (42:1-4); and the suffering of the Servant (52:13–53:12).

In addition to Isaiah's oracles against Judah, chapters 13–23 are noted as prophecies of coming judgment against the surrounding nations, especially the taunt against Babylon in chapter 14. Isaiah is readily divided into two major sections, "The Book of Judgment" (chaps. 1–39) and "The Book of Comfort" (chaps. 40–66).

JEREMIAH

Jeremiah, the sixth- and seventh-century Israelite prophet from Judah, has given his name to his book as its composer. His name probably means either "The LORD Exalts" or "The LORD Throws Down" in Hebrew.

► Key Texts: 30:15 and 31:31

"Why criest thou for thine affliction? thy sorrow is incurable for the multitude of thine iniquity: because thy sins were increased, I have done these things unto thee."

"Behold, the days come, saith the LORD, that I will make a new covenant with the house of Israel, and with the house of Judah."

► Key Term: "Curse"

Jeremiah was the original "doomsday prophet." He called people to repent, but his main message was that Judah had fallen under the curse of God and was doomed to Babylonian exile because of its refusal to turn from sin.

► One-Sentence Summary

Anguished by the burden of his prophetic call and the rejection of his message, Jeremiah witnessed what he warned about, the Babylonian captivity, yet he prophesied God's gracious restoration through the new covenant.

▼ Cooking pot. "I see a seething pot; and the face thereof is toward the north (Jer. 1:13)."

GOD'S MESSAGE IN THE BOOK

Purpose

This book preserves both the divinely inspired prophecies Jeremiah made during his long ministry and a great many of his personal experiences. These prophecies were originally for people of Judah facing invasions and then Babylonian captivity. They were facing the curse that Deuteronomy 27 had predicted for rejecting the covenant. Although he prophesied doom, Jeremiah foretold that the exile would be limited, that Babylon would fall, and that salvation lay on the other side of divine wrath.

Christian Worldview Elements

Jeremiah deals especially with the worldview categories of *rebellion and sin*, *covenant and redemption*, and *humanity*. The consequences of rebelling against God cannot be postponed indefinitely. Although the covenant people would be judged, yet God would provide a new covenant. Because there is so much biographical material on the prophet, the book shows the importance of individuals coming to terms with their personal significance.

GOD
CREATION
SOVEREIGNTY AND PROVIDENCE
FAITH AND REASON
REVELATION AND AUTHORITY
▶**HUMANITY**
▶**REBELLION AND SIN**
▶**COVENANT AND REDEMPTION**
COMMUNITY AND CHURCH
DISCIPLESHIP
ETHICS AND MORALITY
TIME AND ETERNITY

Teachings about God

Jeremiah's understanding of God explicitly included such attributes as his omnipresence (he is everywhere) and his omnipotence (he is all powerful). The classic text is 23:24: "Can any hide himself in secret places that I shall not see him? saith the LORD. Do not I fill heaven and earth? saith the LORD." Neither Christ nor the Spirit is explicitly present in the book. Jesus, however, liked to quote Jeremiah and taught that his crucifixion established the "new covenant" that Jeremiah had predicted (31:31-34).

Teachings about Humanity

The book manifests both the wickedness and the greatness possible in human beings. King Jehoiakim's destruction of the scroll and King Zedekiah's mistreatment of Jeremiah (36–38) show the great evil that political leaders can fall into. On the other hand, more is known about the godly Jeremiah than any other writing prophet.

Teachings about Salvation

Individuals in Jeremiah's own time, at least early in his ministry, could still turn from sin and avoid destruction (7:5-7; 18:7-8). Later on he announced that doom was inevitable. The overall perspective of the book is that redemption will happen only after judgment (29:10-14). The passage on the new covenant (31:31-34), the longest text quoted in the New Testament (Heb. 8:8-12), looked forward to what Christ would accomplish by his coming and death, as the argument of Hebrews makes clear.

CHRIST IN JEREMIAH

Jeremiah's own sufferings anticipate the sufferings of Jesus, Israel's Messiah. There are numerous parallels between Jeremiah and Jesus. Both wept over Jerusalem (Jer. 9:1; Luke 19:41) and both foretold the imminent destruction of the temple (Jer. 7:11-15; Matt. 24:1,2).

GOD'S STORY

When the Events of This Book Happened

Jeremiah prophesied during the reigns of the last five kings of Judah and during the early days of Judah's exile (about 626–585 BC)

Second Kings 22–25 and 2 Chronicles 34–36 provide the historical narrative for the kings of the Davidic dynasty of Jeremiah's ministry (Josiah, Jehoahaz, Jehoiakim, Jehoiachin, and Zedekiah). At the time of Jeremiah's call, the great empires of Egypt, Assyria, and Babylon were vying for dominion. Judah was an insignificant player, but the geography of the ancient Near East meant that Judah could not be ignored. Jeremiah lived to see Babylon defeat its rivals: Assyria (fall of Nineveh, 612 BC); Egypt (battle of Carchemesh, 605 BC); and Judah (fall of Jerusalem, 586 BC). By the end of Jeremiah's ministry Babylon had become the single world superpower.

How Jeremiah Fits into God's "Story"

Jeremiah tells about the end of "chapter 2" of the story: God educates his nation (disobedient Israel disciplined). He understood God's sovereignty in determining the rise and fall of all earthly nations. Mighty Babylon would fall (25:11-12; 29:10). God's plans to establish a new covenant form a magnificent vision for the future of God's people and kingdom. Through Jeremiah God pledged, "I will give them an heart to know me, that I am the LORD: and they shall be my people, and I will be their God: for they shall return unto me with their whole heart" (24:7). The last two chapters of the Bible describe the final fulfillment of this promise.

ORIGINAL HISTORICAL SETTING

Author and Date of Writing
Jeremiah, perhaps finally compiled around 585 BC

Because of his personal anguish over the coming captivity, Jeremiah has often been called "The Weeping Prophet." Jeremiah, son of Hilkiah the priest, was from Anathoth, a town near Jerusalem in the territory of Benjamin. God required him to remain unmarried and childless (16:2). His prophetic call came around 626 BC, when he was still young (1:6). His message of coming doom isolated him and exposed him to danger time and again. For forty years he proclaimed God's word in Judah and stayed there even after Jerusalem fell. According to chapter 43, finally he was forcibly taken to Egypt and probably died there. Although many critical scholars believe that portions were written by other anonymous prophets, there is no good reason to doubt that Jeremiah authored the entire book.

First Audience and Destination
The people of Judah living during Jeremiah's lifetime

The first hearers were the kings and people living in Judah during the forty years before the Babylonian captivity. A few parts were originally for Jews living just after the fall of Jerusalem.

Occasion

This book records its origins as a piece of literature more than any other prophetic work. That Jeremiah caused his prophecies to be put in scroll form is explicitly told in several passages, for example, 25:13; 30:2; 36:2; 45:1; 51:60. Of special interest is the bitter story of Jehoakim's contempt for the word of God by burning one of Jeremiah's scrolls (36). "Baruch son of Neriah" was Jeremiah's personal assistant, who physically wrote down at least some of the words of the book (45:1). Since he accompanied Jeremiah to Egypt (43:6), the two may have worked together on the final compilation of the book of Jeremiah, the longest book in the Bible composed by a single author.

DOR

Samaria Mt. Ebal
Shechem
Mt. Gerizim ▲

SAMARIA

Shiloh

GILEAD

Baalis, king of Ammon, supports Ishmael against Gedaliah

Joppa

Ono

Gedaliah establishes his court at Mizpah where he is eventually killed by Ishmael in 582 B.C.

Bethel

Ai

AMMON

Rabbah (Amman)

Lod

Gittaim

Beth-horon

Gezer

Timnah

Emmaus

Zorah

Mizpah

Gibeon

Michmash

Geba

Jericho

Ramah

Kiriath-jearim

Jerusalem

Beth-haccherem

Mt. Nebo

Jeremiah released from prison by Nebuzardan

Ashdod

Ekron

Jarmuth

JUDAH

Bethlehem

Azekah

Adullam

Keilah

Beth-zur

Tekoa

Mareshah

Lachish

DEAD SEA

En-gedi

Aroer

Johanan and Jewish leaders left for Egypt, taking Jeremiah against his wishes

Gerar

Ziklag

IDUMEA
(EDOMITES)

Arad

MOAB

Beersheba

Kir-hareseth

ARABS

Negev

LEGEND

●	City
○	City (uncertain location)
🏚	Sites of great destruction
▲	Mountain peak
←	Jeremiah's flight to Egypt
←	Possible route of Ishmael to Ammon
JUDAH	Provinces of Babylonian administration

LITERARY FEATURES

Genre and Literary Style
Prophecies and historical narratives written in a mixture of Hebrew poetry and prose

Jeremiah's prophecies both "forth tell" and "foretell." Jeremiah includes the three classic elements of Hebrew prophecy: (1) call to people to turn from their sins in the face of divine judgment, (2) predictions of near events (such as the fall of Jerusalem), and (3) predictions o remote events (such as the coming of the new covenant).

The majority of the book is poetic. The prose sections are mainly found in chapters 7; 11 16; 19; 21; 24–29; 32–45; 52. The biographical sections were written in the third person, perhaps evidence of Baruch's input. Jeremiah's style included repetition, such as "sword . . . famine . . . pestilence" (fifteen times), and the use of cryptograms ("Sheshach" for Babylon in 25:26) Memorable phrases abound, for example, "Can the Ethiopian change his skin, or the leopard his spots?" (13:23). In the Hebrew canon, Jeremiah was the second of the four "Latter Prophets."

Themes
God's judgment and salvation; Jerusalem's fall; Jeremiah's personal life

The tension between judgment on sin and salvation yet to come make Jeremiah a book o hope, especially when God's people live in difficult times. The material on Jerusalem's last days is agonizing. Even apart from studying the content of his prophecies, believers today can benefit from tracing the course of Jeremiah's life as one filled with self-doubt and misgivings ye faithful to his calling from God.

Book Features and Structure

One of the striking features of the book is its inclusion of symbols to which Jeremiah supplied an interpretation. Of note are the linen belt ("girdle," KJV) that was ruined (13); the potter and clay (18); and the hiding of stones (43).

The organization of the book is challenging to determine. It is not at all chronological, but seems to be topical. Between chapter 1 (the prophet's call) and chapter 52 (an appendix parallel to 2 Kings 24–25), there are three major sections: prophetic warnings to Judah (2–35) Jeremiah's suffering and Jerusalem's fall (36–45); prophetic warnings to the nations (46–51).

LAMENTATIONS

The English title renders the name given by the Greek translators of this book in the second century B.C., *Thrénoi*. The original Hebrew title is simply the first word of the book, *'Ekah*, "How!"

► Key Text: 1:1

"How doth the city sit solitary, that was full of people! how is she become as a widow! she that was great among the nations, and princess among the provinces, how is she become tributary!"

► Key Term: "Lament"

A "lament" or "lamentation" is a formal expression of grief in the face of loss or death. This book expresses the anguish the author felt over the fall of Jerusalem.

► One-Sentence Summary

A skillful and emotional poet described the devastation of the city of Jerusalem —brought by the Babylonians but ultimately caused by the Lord's anger against his people—and poured out his own personal expressions of sorrow.

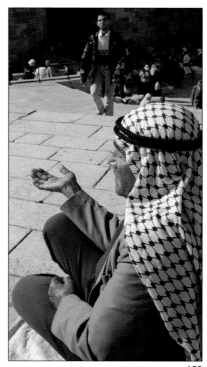

Beggar at the Damascus gate in Jerusalem. The Babylonians' third assault on Jerusalem was devastating. Lamentations gives expression to this devastation: "All her people groan as they search for bread; they barter their treasures for food to keep themselves alive" (Lam. 1:11).

GOD'S MESSAGE IN THE BOOK

Purpose

This book comes to grips with the destruction of Jerusalem on several levels, especially the emotional and the theological. On one hand, Lamentations shows that bitter grief is a fitting response to loss and death. On the other hand, it shows that the prophets who had warned "repent or be destroyed" had given a true message from God after all. God's people who study Lamentations today should view it with its original purpose in mind, but it can also help them to express their own grief in times of sorrow.

Christian Worldview Elements

Lamentation deals particularly with the worldview categories of *sovereignty and providence* and *rebellion and sin*. This Bible book, like the book of Job, explores the relationship of human sin to God's sovereignty.

GOD
CREATION
▶**SOVEREIGNTY AND PROVIDENCE**
FAITH AND REASON
REVELATION AND AUTHORITY
HUMANITY
▶**REBELLION AND SIN**
COVENANT AND REDEMPTION
COMMUNITY AND CHURCH
DISCIPLESHIP
ETHICS AND MORALITY
TIME AND ETERNITY

Teachings about God

God's holiness resulted in his destroying Jerusalem for her many sins. Yet at the very center of the book, the author emphasized God's mercy and faithfulness (3:22-26). The most often quoted text is 3:22-23: "*It is of* the LORD's mercies that we are not consumed, because his compassions fail not. *They are* new every morning: great *is* thy faithfulness." There is no specific reference to Christ or to the Holy Spirit.

Teachings about Humanity

Because human beings are moral agents responsible to God, their sins will be punished. The destruction of Jerusalem and the temple is the chief Old Testament event showing that rebellion against God cannot go on indefinitely. Yet because God made mankind in his image, they are capable of emotion, including sorrow and despair. Even when the loss is deserved, intense expressions of grief are a normal part of human experience.

Teachings about Salvation

Despite the grief he expressed, the author did not waver in his faith in God (see 3:26). The author's steadfast trust in God in the presence of national catastrophe and personal disaster makes him one of the greatest heroes of faith found in Scripture.

CHRIST IN LAMENTATIONS

Lamentations shows God's wrath poured out on the city he loves just as his wrath was later poured out on his beloved Son. Lamentations 1:12 has often been used of Christ as he suffered on the cross: "Is it nothing to all you who pass this way? Look and see if there is any pain like my pain which was severely dealt out to me, which the LORD inflicted on the day of his fierce anger" (NASB).

GOD'S STORY

When the Events of This Book Happened
Jerusalem was destroyed in 586 BC

The Chaldean (Babylonian) army under Nebuchadnezzar came against Jerusalem three times before the city was finally destroyed. The first siege (605 BC), at which King Jehoiakim surrendered, resulted in his becoming a vassal of Babylon. Nebuchanezzar looted the temple and deported a number of the nobility such as Daniel and his friends (Dan. 1:1-7). The second seige (597 BC), at which King Jehoiachin surrendered, resulted in his deportation to Babylon along with 10,000 others, including Ezekiel (2 Kings 24:8-17; Ezek. 1:1-3). The third siege (586 BC), at which Zedekiah, the last king, surrendered, resulted in his deportation to Babylon, along with many others (Jer. 52). The temple and city were plundered and burned on August 14, 586 BC.

How Lamentations Fits into God's "Story"

Lamentations was written in response to the end of "chapter 2" of the story: God educates his nation (disobedient Israel disciplined). It shows how to live in submission to the discipline that God sends his people, even when suffering and evil fall on them deservedly. The book does not tell how to get into the kingdom of God; rather it expresses for those already in the kingdom important aspects of living in right relationship to God. If the author of Lamentations could hope in God, then God's people today can do the same no matter what happens to them.

ORIGINAL HISTORICAL SETTING

Author and Date of Writing
Unknown, perhaps Jeremiah, written soon after 586 BC

The book is anonymous. Jewish and Christian tradition alike affirmed that Jeremiah the prophet wrote this book. According to 2 Chronicles 35:25, Jeremiah was a writer of laments. For more information, see ***Author and Date of Writing*** for **JEREMIAH**.

On the other hand, both the literary style and some of the content of Lamentations is unlike the book of Jeremiah. In particular, it is hard to imagine that the composer of the longest prophetic book would also write, "The law *is* no *more*; her prophets also find no vision from the LORD" (2:9). If Jeremiah did not write the book, then one of his contemporaries, now unknown, wrote it. Ultimately, there is no reason Jeremiah could not have written the book. If so, this confirms his reputation as "The Weeping Prophet."

Because the book expresses such raw emotions, it was almost certainly composed shortly after Jerusalem's demise. It was necessarily written before the Jews returned from exile in 516 BC.

First Audience and Destination
Jewish witnesses to Jerusalem's fall

If an unknown author wrote the book, then his audience could have been exiles newly arrived in Babylon. If Jeremiah wrote the book, he composed it for those who had remained in the ruined Jerusalem or else for those who fled Jerusalem for Egypt after Gedaliah's assassination (Jer. 40–42).

Occasion
The book does not tell what prompted it to be written other than the fall of Jerusalem. It is possible that Lamentations was originally composed in order to be read on "The Ninth of Ab," the annual commemoration of the temple's destruction.

JEWISH REFUGEES IN EGYPT
Jeremiah 41–42

MEDITERRANEAN SEA

JUDAH

The group that brought Jeremiah to Egypt settled in Tahpanhes

Mizpah
Jericho
Jerusalem
Beth-zur
Bethlehem
Lachish
Pelusium
Gaza
Arad
Tahpanhes (Daphne)
Beersheba
Migdol
Punon
Kadesh-barnea

DEAD SEA

Eastern Desert

Noph (Memphis)
On (Heliopolis)
Al-Faiyum
Ezion-geber

Sinai
Mt. Sinai ▲

EGYPT

Nile R.

Sahara Desert

RED SEA

Thebes (No-amon)
PATHROS

LEGEND
● City
■ City of refuge
▲ Mountain peak
→ Refugees' route into Egypt

Syene (Aswan)
Yeb (Elephantine)
Location of Jewish military colony and Jewish temple

0   50   100   150   200 Miles
0 50 100 150 200 Kilometers

30 E
30 N

157

LITERARY FEATURES

Genre and Literary Style
A lament written in Hebrew poetry with acrostic features

People of the ancient Near East often composed laments in the face of tragedy. "Lamentatio over the Destruction of Ur" (Sumerian) is an early example. The Old Testament has man examples: David's "Lament of the Bow" (2 Sam. 1:19-27); psalms of lament (for example Ps 44; 60; 88); and expressions by the prophets (Isa. 63–64; Ezek. 19; Amos 5; Mic. 1).

The entire book is Hebrew poetry, and more than in any other book, the poetry seems t have a definite rhythm or meter. Many of the lines follow the *qinah* (lament) meter: lines c five beats, divided into three beats and then two. An example is 5:14:

> The elders have ceased from the gate,   (3 beats)
>
> the young men from their music.   (2 beats)

In English Bibles, Lamentations follows the Greek translators by placing it after Jeremiah In Hebrew Scripture it was placed in the third section, the Writings or *Kethubim*. Among th Writings it was one of the Five Scrolls (*Megilloth*). Lamentations became the scroll read pub licly on "The Ninth of Ab," the solemn annual Jewish remembrance of both the destructio of Solomon's temple (586 BC) and of the second temple (AD 70). The month of Ab corre sponds to July-August.

Themes
Descriptions of devastation, the writer's emotions, God's justice and mercy

Nothing is more horrible than destruction that results in mothers cannibalizing their own chi dren (2:20; 4:10). Other descriptions are equally vivid. The writer's weeping (1:16; 2:11 comes to full expression in chapter 3. Although God's justice in punishing his people is in th foreground, the background note is one of his mercy, so that the book ends with an appeal fc God to restore his people.

Book Features and Structure

Each of the five chapters is dominated by alphabetical considerations. The Hebrew alphabet ha twenty-two letters—and chapters 1, 2, 3, and 5 all have twenty-two verses. Further, chapte 1–4 are acrostic. (Chapter 5 is not.) In chapters 1–3, the first verse begins with the letter *'aleph* the second verse begins with *beth* and so on alphabetically to the end. (See Ps. 119 and Pro 31:10-31 for other 22-part Hebrew acrostic poems.) In Lamentations 4, with 66 verses, th acrostic is triple. Verses 1-3 begin with *'aleph*; verses 4-6 begin with *beth*, and so on. By th means, the author has said everything "from A to Z" (or *'aleph* to *taw*) on his subject.

EZEKIEL

Ezekiel, the sixth-century Israelite prophet exiled to Babylon, has given his name to this book its composer. His name means "God Strengthens" in Hebrew.

▶ Key Text: 38:23

Thus will I magnify myself, and sanctify myself; and I will be known in the eyes of many nations, and they shall know that I am the LORD."

▶ Key Term: "Visions"

This book is built around the three "visions of God" (1:1; 8:3; 40:2) that Ezekiel received. The first vision revealed God's glory (1–3); the second God's judgment (8–11); the third God's people and temple idealized (40–48).

▶ One-Sentence Summary

From exile in Babylon, Ezekiel's stunning visions and startling symbolic acts were prophecies for the Israelites to teach God's sovereign plan over them in the history of his kingdom, so that "they shall know that I am the LORD."

▼ Tile dragons. Relief from sixth-century Babylon, where Ezekiel had the visions recorded in the prophecies that bear his name.

159

GOD'S MESSAGE IN THE BOOK

Purpose

This book preserves the divinely inspired prophecies that Ezekiel made during his ministry of more than twenty years. These prophecies were originally for Israelites that had been exiled to Babylon shortly before the final fall of Judah. Ezekiel warned that God's destruction of Jerusalem was looming but that God responded to individuals based on their relationship to him. Ezekiel also foresaw the distant time that God would act decisively so that Israel and all the nations would know that the Lord alone is God.

Christian Worldview Elements

Ezekiel deals with a number of worldview categories. Especially prominent are *God, covenant and redemption,* and *time and eternity.* The book begins with Ezekiel's remarkable vision of the glory of God, unequalled in the Old Testament. The entire book makes sense only in the context of God's covenant with his people and his great redeeming purpose. Ezekiel's final vision looks down through time to portray the ideal temple and people of God.

> **GOD**
> CREATION
> SOVEREIGNTY AND PROVIDENCE
> FAITH AND REASON
> REVELATION AND AUTHORITY
> HUMANITY
> REBELLION AND SIN
> **COVENANT AND REDEMPTION**
> COMMUNITY AND CHURCH
> DISCIPLESHIP
> ETHICS AND MORALITY
> **TIME AND ETERNITY**

Teachings about God

All that God does on behalf of people is ultimately for the sake of his name or glory (39:7). He is absolutely sovereign in the affairs of all people and all nations. Prophecies of a coming Davidic king, fulfilled by Christ, are scattered throughout the book (17:22-24; 37:24-28). In the future the Spirit will enable God's people to obey his laws from their heart (36:27; 39:29).

Teachings about Humanity

One of the clearest biblical passages about the responsibility of each individual before God is Ezekiel 18. This is famously stated in 18:4: "The soul that sinneth, it shall die." Ezekiel illustrates one whom God used in a time of crisis, and whose intimate family life became a symbol of God's dealing with his people (24:15-18).

Teachings about Salvation

Ezekiel teaches both the individual and the corporate dimensions of salvation. Chapter 18 teaches that the wicked child of a righteous parent will die (18:10-13). A person showing the fruit of righteousness—even if the parents are wicked—will live (18:14-17). Corporately, salvation is the sovereign act of God's Spirit, who breathes on people ("dry bones"), giving them spiritual life and enabling them to follow God's ways.

CHRIST IN EZEKIEL

The expression "Son of man" is used more than 90 times in Ezekiel. God uses the term to address Ezekiel. "Son of Man" is the expression Jesus uses most frequently to refer to himself. The phrase has two different meanings. First, it simply designates a human being. Second, it refers to a divine being. When used of Jesus, it carries both of these meanings.

GOD'S STORY

When the Events of This Book Happened

Ezekiel prophesied during the first part of the Jews' Babylonian captivity (about 593–571 BC)

This was the time that the Chaldean Empire (Babylonians) dominated the world under Nebuchadnezzar (ruled 605–562). Twelve times Ezekiel listed the exact day that he received messages from God, and all of these can be transferred into dates using modern calendar equivalents. Called to minister at age thirty, Ezekiel prophesied for seven years before the temple was destroyed (593–586) and for fifteen years after (586–571). See **When the Events of This Book Happened** for **LAMENTATIONS** for more details.

How Ezekiel Fits into God's "Story"

The events of Ezekiel's time belong to the first part of "chapter 3" of God's story: God keeps a faithful remnant (Messiah's space and time prepared). Ezekiel saw God's glory depart from Israel (10). After Jerusalem was destroyed, with no temple, no king, and no capital, the people had no hope. Had the covenant failed? Was God's promise of an everlasting dynasty for David a cruel joke? Through Ezekiel, God promised that he would be merciful to a remnant. In a wonderful new era of the kingdom of God, God's people would be indwelt by the Spirit and would have new hearts of obedience (36:24-27). God would live in their midst (48:35) and a Davidic king (37:24-28) would rule in righteousness (34:23-24).

ORIGINAL HISTORICAL SETTING

Author and Date of Writing
Ezekiel, perhaps finally compiled around 570 BC

Ezekiel, the son of Buzi, was born into a priestly family and grew up in Judah. As a your
adult, he was taken captive by the Babylonians in 597 and deported, along with Kir
Jehoiachin and 10,000 others (2 Kings 24:14-17). He settled in Tel-Abib by the Kebar Can
(Chebar River, KJV). At age thirty Ezekiel was called as a prophet (1:1-3). He was married, b
his wife died suddenly just before Jerusalem's final fall (24:15-18). God called Ezekiel "son (
man" ("human being") more than ninety times.

Ezekiel's strange visions and symbolic actions marked him as strange both in his own da
and by modern people. His message was not well received (3:25; 33:31-32). Some rece
scholars have even suggested he suffered from mental illness. Other scholars accept th
Ezekiel wrote parts of the book, but that many editorial insertions were made at a later dat
The only prophetic work written entirely in the first person, the book claims to be Ezekie
work. Scholars who accept the testimony of Scripture at face value continue to affirm th
Ezekiel, under divine inspiration, composed the entire book. He perhaps compiled the wo
shortly after the last dated prophecy (571 BC; 29:17-21).

First Audience and Destination
Israelite exiles living in Babylon

The first hearers were Israelites who had been taken into exile along with Ezekiel. By the time
Ezekiel's first vision, five years had elapsed, so the people had begun to establish themselves in
foreign land. After the final fall of Jerusalem, recently arriving exiles also heard Ezekiel's messag

Occasion

The messages God sent to Ezekiel were at God's initiative, not the prophet's. God sometim
told him, "Set thy face against" someone. His references to specific dates on which he receive
messages are 1:1-2; 8:1; 20:1-2; 24:1; 26:1; 29:1,17; 30:20; 31:1; 32:1,17; 40:1. Ezekiel d
not tell what prompted his compilation of the entire book.

JEWISH EXILES IN BABYLONIA
Ezekiel 3:15

The site of the ancient city of Babylon in modern Iraq—a general overview of the ruins.

📖 LITERARY FEATURES

Genre and Literary Style
Prophecies, including visions and symbolic actions, written mainly in Hebrew prose but with some poetry

Ezekiel's prophecies both "forth tell" and "foretell." Ezekiel includes the classic elements of Hebrew prophecy: (1) call to people to turn from their sins, (2) predictions of near events (such as the destruction of the temple, 24), and (3) predictions of remote events (such as the coming of the new temple, 40–48).

Ezekiel's three visions (1–3; 8–11; 40–48) are a special kind of prophecy. The first "forth tells" God's glory; the second "foretells" a near disaster; the third "foretells" a remote blessing. More than any other prophet, Ezekiel performed actions with symbolic meaning, which he then interpreted. The best known of these include his lying on one side (4), shaving his head with a sword (5), and the death of his wife (24). Ezekiel also told a number of parables. Chapters 7; 17; 19; 21; 24; 26–32 are the main poetic sections; the rest are in Hebrew prose.

Themes
God's glory; the temple; present judgment; future blessings

God's concern for his name is central in the book. More than sixty times God declares his intention for people to "know that I *am* the LORD." Perhaps because he was a priest, Ezekiel emphasized both the destruction of the temple as well as the ideal temple of the future. His book begins with a message of judgment and ends with hope.

Book Features and Structure
The most challenging feature is the vision of a future temple (40–48), which has had no literal fulfillment. Interpretations have generally fallen along one of three lines, each of which faces certain difficulties. The *millennial* view anticipates a literal fulfillment, with a physical temple and a real earthly King in Jerusalem for an intermediate era before the final consummation. The *spiritual* view applies the prophecy to the Christian age, with the church seen as the new temple and Christ as the church's Lord. The *eternal* view sees the prophecy as fulfilled in the eternal state, understood along the same lines as Revelation 21–22. No matter what interpretation is taken, the important truth is that "the LORD *is* there" (48:35).

The book follows a topical order rather than a chronological sequence. There are three main sections: prophecies against Israel (1–24); prophecies against the nations (25–32); future blessings for God's people (33–48).

DANIEL

Daniel, the sixth-century Israelite prophet exiled to Babylon, has given his name to this book as its composer. His name means "God Judges" or "God's Judge" in Hebrew.

▶ *Key Text: 4:3*

"How great are his signs! and how mighty are his wonders! his kingdom is an everlasting kingdom, and his dominion is from generation to generation."

▶ *Key Term: "Kingdoms"*

This book contrasts all earthly kingdoms, both in Daniel's day and those of the future, with God's glorious everlasting kingdom. Of all the Old Testament books, this one has a more sharply defined kingdom perspective than any other.

▶ *One-Sentence Summary*

Daniel demonstrated remarkable trust in God and revealed God's plans for the future, not only for his own day but also for the Maccabean period and on through the time that God's kingdom is fully established by the Son of Man.

 Sarcophagus lid showing Hebrews in fiery furnace (Dan. 3).

GOD'S MESSAGE IN THE BOOK

Purpose

This book preserves the divinely inspired prophecies Daniel made during his long ministry o
more than sixty years. These prophecies were originally for the assurance of Israelites that had
been exiled to Babylon at the fall of Judah. The book looks at God's kingdom through three
lenses: the lens of the present; the lens of the second century BC (the Maccabean period); and
the remote lens of the completion of God's kingdom.

Christian Worldview Elements

Daniel deals with the worldview categories of *sovereignty and providence, ethics and morality,* and *time and eternity.* This book shows God's sovereignty in all things, perhaps like no other. Daniel's obedience to God shows godly behavior when it would have been easier to follow the crowd. The panorama of the future broadly reveals the direction of history.

> GOD
> CREATION
> ► **SOVEREIGNTY AND PROVIDENCE**
> FAITH AND REASON
> REVELATION AND AUTHORITY
> HUMANITY
> REBELLION AND SIN
> COVENANT AND REDEMPTION
> COMMUNITY AND CHURCH
> DISCIPLESHIP
> ► **ETHICS AND MORALITY**
> ► **TIME AND ETERNITY**

Teachings about God

God is both the revealer of secrets and the sovereign of
the universe. His ultimate purpose is to give dominion to the Son of Man (7:13-14), fulfillec
by Jesus, who deliberately called himself "Son of Man." Daniel was recognized as having "the
spirit of the holy gods," but this appears to fall short of a clear reference to the Holy Spirit.

Teachings about Humanity

Daniel and his friends modeled living as God's people in a pagan world. The kings in the
book—Nebuchadnezzar, Belshazzar, and Darius—are all seen to be agents of God. Truly evi
characters are predicted, yet they too are unwittingly God's agents. The clearest Old Testamen
statement about a future bodily resurrection is Daniel 12:2-3.

Teachings about Salvation

Daniel 9:26 ("after threescore and two weeks shall Messiah be cut off, but not for himself"
refers to Christ's crucifixion on behalf of his people. Some scholars believe that Daniel 9:27 pre
dicts Christ's first coming, when he established the new covenant, resulting in the end of ani
mal sacrifices. (Other scholars believe that the covenant referred to will be made not by Chris
but by the antichrist shortly before Jesus' second coming.) In any event, Daniel 9:24 anticipate
"everlasting righteousness."

CHRIST IN DANIEL

Daniel has a vision of "One like the Son of Man coming with the clouds of heaven!" This is a prophesy of Christ's second coming at which time he will be given glory and dominion over all people.

GOD'S STORY

When the Events of This Book Happened
Daniel prophesied during the reigns of Babylonian kings and one Persian king (about 605–530 BC)

Daniel was taken to Babylon as part of the first deportation from Jerusalem (605 BC). In exile he influenced Nebuchadnezzar and later Belshazzar (son and viceroy of the emperor Nabonidus). After Babylon fell to the Medo-Persians in 539 BC, Daniel served "Darius the Mede," perhaps an alternate name for Cyrus the Great.

Daniel 8 details wars between a "ram" (the Persians) and a "he goat" (the Greeks, led by Alexander the Great, who would defeat the Persians in 330 BC). Daniel 11 gives particulars about the Hellenistic (Greek) kingdoms that succeeded Alexander. The "king of the south" (the Ptolomies in Egypt) would war against "the king of the north" (the Seleucids in Syria), with Palestine caught between them. The "vile person" (11:21) who would arise in the north was Antiochus IV (Epiphanes). His hatred of the Jews would lead to the infamous sacrilege at the second temple, December 15, 168 BC, which led to the Maccabean Revolt of the Jews.

How Daniel Fits into God's "Story"
The events in Daniel belong to "chapter 3" of God's story: God keeps a faithful remnant (Messiah's space and time prepared). Daniel predicted the progress of the kingdoms of the world from his own time until the arrival of God's kingdom. This is seen chiefly in the visions of chapters 2 and 7.

ORIGINAL HISTORICAL SETTING

Author and Date of Writing
Daniel, perhaps finally compiled around 530 BC

The book is technically anonymous, although much of it is recorded as the first-person memoirs of Daniel. According to uniform Jewish and early Christian belief, Daniel wrote the book. In Matthew 24:15 Jesus affirmed this view.

Critical scholarship for the past two centuries has uniformly rejected that a sixth-century author could possibly have written detailed accounts of events centuries in the future. Therefore an unknown prophet living in the Maccabean era (second century B.C.) necessarily composed large parts of the book. The basic assumption of this critical view appears to be that Scripture does not contain true predictive prophecy. For Bible students who accept that God gave specific revelations of the distant future to his prophets, there is no reason to doubt that Daniel wrote all the book that bears his name.

First Audience and Destination
Israelite exiles living in Babylon

The first hearers were Israelites who had been taken into exile along with Daniel. After the final fall of Jerusalem, recently arriving exiles would also have heard Daniel's message. By the time of Daniel's last prophecies, Babylon was no more, and the time had come for the exiles to be permitted to return to their homeland (9:2).

Occasion

Daniel's early ministry as a young man was initiated by Nebuchanezzar (1–4). During the last years of Babylon, God initiated visions of the future (7–8), and then Daniel was called to interpret the handwriting on the wall (5). Daniel's encounter with the lions (6) and his final visions of the future (9–12) came when he was a very old man, shortly after the time the Persians defeated Babylon.

▼ Relief of Darius I giving an audience. Darius the Mede conquered Babylon and was ruler when Daniel was thrown into the lion's den.

LITERARY FEATURES

Genre and Literary Style
Prophecies, including visions and interpretations, written partly in Hebrew and partly Aramaic

Daniel included little "forth telling," emphasizing instead "foretelling" prophecies. He predict ed near events (such as the destruction of Babylon) and remote events (such as the coming of the Son of Man). The book was written in two languages. Chapters 1 and 8–12, written in Hebrew, deal with God's people and their future. Chapters 2–7, written in Aramaic, the international trade language of the day, deal with the kingdoms of the world as they carry on apart from acknowledging the true God.

In English Bibles, Daniel comes after Ezekiel as one of the "Major Prophets," following the order of the Greek translators. In Hebrew Scripture it was placed in the third section, the Writings or *Kethubim*. The Greek translation added sections with no Hebrew original. These "Additions to Daniel" are considered scriptural by Roman Catholics, but Protestants believe them to be merely interesting parts of the Apocrypha.

Themes
Sovereignty, kingdoms of the world, God's kingdom

God's sovereignty in individual lives is seen by the personal history of Daniel. In the case of Nebuchadnezzar, God took the most powerful man in the world and sent him through a period of insanity. The prophecies of four world kingdoms (2; 7) is the most extensive "philosophy of history" in the Old Testament. The message of God's kingdom triumphing through the Son of Man became a dominant feature of Jesus' preaching.

Book Features and Structure
Daniel's famous prophecies of "the abomination that maketh desolate" (11:31; 12:11) and of the "seventy weeks" (9:24) are two of the most difficult elements of the book. The original abomination occurred in 168 BC when swine were sacrificed at the Jerusalem temple. Jesus predicted a second abomination (Matt. 24:15) that occurred in AD 70 when the second temple was burned. Both Daniel and Jesus may also point to a third abomination to be perpetrated by the future antichrist. The "seventy weeks" (490 years) may have been completely fulfilled in the first century AD, but some believe the "seventieth week" (seven years) will happen only in the days before Christ's return.

The content of Daniel neatly divides into halves. The first half (1–6) collects stories about Daniel while the second half (7–12) collects four visions of Daniel.

HOSEA

Hosea, the eighth-century prophet to the Northern Kingdom of Israel, has given his name to this book as its composer. His name means "Salvation" in Hebrew.

▶ *Key Text: 1:10*

"Yet the number of the children of Israel shall be as the sand of the sea, which cannot be measured nor numbered; and it shall come to pass, that in the place where it was said unto them, Ye are not my people, there it shall be said unto them, Ye are the sons of the living God."

▶ *Key Term: "Unfaithfulness"*

The marital unfaithfulness of Gomer, Hosea's wife, became a symbol that Hosea used to proclaim his message. The people of the Northern Kingdom had become unfaithful to the Lord by aligning with Baal, yet God longed to take them back.

▶ *One-Sentence Summary*

Hosea's marriage to an adulterous wife and the children she bore graphically demonstrated God's "marriage" to his spiritually adulterous people Israel, who must respond to his covenant love and repent or face severe judgment.

Baal, the Canaanite weather god (Hos. 2:13). ▶

GOD'S MESSAGE IN THE BOOK

Purpose

This book preserves the divinely inspired prophecies that Hosea made during his ministry of more than thirty-five years. (He and Amos were the only writing prophets to target the Northern Kingdom of Israel.) Hosea warned Israel that because of rebellion and idolatry, the kingdom faced destruction, yet God still loved his covenant people.

Christian Worldview Elements

Hosea deals particularly with the worldview categories of *rebellion and sin* and *covenant and redemption*. God's case against Israel was put in terms of a woman's unfaithfulness to her husband ("the LORD") and seeking liaison with another (Baal). Yet no Bible book more fully teaches God's love in reaching out to people who cannot save themselves.

GOD
CREATION
SOVEREIGNTY AND PROVIDENCE
FAITH AND REASON
REVELATION AND AUTHORITY
HUMANITY
► **REBELLION AND SIN**
► **COVENANT AND REDEMPTION**
COMMUNITY AND CHURCH
DISCIPLESHIP
ETHICS AND MORALITY
TIME AND ETERNITY

Teachings about God

Hosea's doctrine of God is based mainly on the analogy of a husband-wife relationship. The Lord is jealous and will not forever tolerate his people "lusting" after other deities. He must judge unfaithfulness. At the same time, his love for his covenant people endures forever, and one day Ephraim (the Northern Kingdom of Israel) will be healed of rebelliousness (14). Matthew recognizes Hosea's historical note about Israel's exodus from Egypt as a picture foreshadowing Jesus' coming from Egypt (Hos. 11:1; Matt. 2:15). The Spirit is not directly present in the book.

Teachings about Humanity

The adultery of Gomer and the idolatry of Israel both paint rather dark portraits of human shame and sinfulness. Hosea's exceptional love for Gomer provides a stark contrast and shows something of what it means to experience the love of God.

Teachings about Salvation

The clearest text in this book on the nature of salvation is 6:6: "For I desired mercy, and not sacrifice; and the knowledge of God more than burnt offerings." Offering sacrificial animals without an inner heart of love for God and one's neighbors was never a part of the biblical understanding of salvation. The word translated "mercy" (Hebrew, *chesed*) included loyalty to God as well as compassionate actions toward others.

CHRIST IN HOSEA

Matthew tells of Joseph and Mary taking the child Jesus to Egypt to escape the wrath of Herod. Following Herod's death, Jesus' family returned to Nazareth. Matthew quoted Hosea 11:1 to show the parallel being God's calling Israel and his calling Jesus: "Out of Egypt have I called my son" (Matt. 2:15).

GOD'S STORY

When the Events of This Book Happened

Hosea prophesied during the last decades of the Northern Kingdom of Israel (at least 753–715 BC; mainly about 750–722 BC)

Second Kings 14–17 provide the historical background for the times of Hosea. In general, it was the time that Assyria was asserting itself as the world superpower. Hosea's earliest prophecies and marital woes came from the end of the rule of Jeroboam II of Israel (593–753 BC). He continued to minister in Israel during the reigns of the last kings there and on through the conquest of Israel by the Assyrians in 722. Afterward, he evidently ministered in the Southern Kingdom of Judah, judging from his reference to Hezekiah (1:1), who became king in Jerusalem in 715.

How Hosea Fits into God's "Story"

The events of Hosea's time belong to "chapter two" of the story: God educates his nation (disobedient Israel disciplined). Israel had forgotten that the Lord had called them into existence and blessed them. They were offering bounty sent by God to Baal (2:8). In order to break them, for a time God would call them Lo-ammi ("not my people," 1:9). Yet his purposes were settled. One of the great statements of God's everlasting kingdom plan is Hosea 2:19: "And I will betroth thee unto me for ever; yea, I will betroth thee unto me in righteousness, and in judgment, and in lovingkindness, and in mercies." Both Peter and Paul applied Hosea's message to God's including Gentiles among his people (1 Pet. 2:10; Rom. 9:26).

ORIGINAL HISTORICAL SETTING

Author and Date of Writing
Hosea, perhaps around 715 BC

Hosea was a contemporary of Isaiah and Micah. The son of Beeri, he was evidently from the Northern Kingdom of Israel. See **Occasion** below for information about Hosea's marriage. The book does not mention the fulfillment of Hosea's prophecies against Israel, but he witnessed the fall of Samaria and the Northern Kingdom. Since his prophecies also include calls for Judah to repent, it is believed that his last ministry was to people of Judah after the Northern Kingdom fell. He probably compiled his book during that time.

First Audience and Destination
Israelites living in the Northern Kingdom

Hosea's first audience was people living in the Northern Kingdom—also called Ephraim or Samaria—in the mid-700s BC.

Occasion

Hosea's tragic marriage to Gomer—who left the prophet and became a slave, only to be bought back by her own husband—is one of the great love stories (but hardly a romance) in Scripture. Gomer bore three children: Jezreel (a son); Lo-ruhamah (No Mercy, a daughter); and finally Lo-ammi (Not My People, a son). The last two children may have been fathered by one of Gomer's lovers; if so, it makes Hosea's personal story that much more poignant.

Hosea's marriage experiences and the names of his children were at the Lord's command. Other than this, no precise occasion can be offered for his prophecies, but clearly he spoke in the name of the Lord. No one knows exactly what prompted Hosea to compile his writings at the end of his long ministry.

THE FALL OF SAMARIA AND DEPORTATION OF ISRAELITES
Hosea 7:11; 12:1

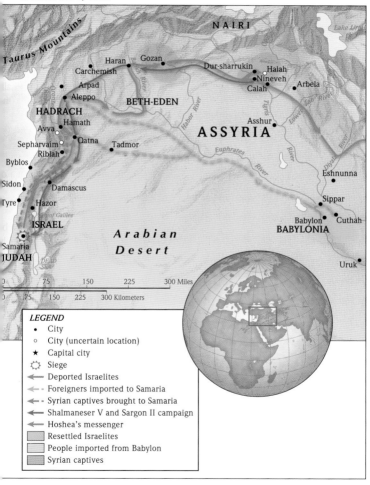

LEGEND
- • City
- ○ City (uncertain location)
- ★ Capital city
- ✧ Siege
- ← Deported Israelites
- ←- Foreigners imported to Samaria
- ←-· Syrian captives brought to Samaria
- ← Shalmaneser V and Sargon II campaign
- ← Hoshea's messenger
- ▢ Resettled Israelites
- ▢ People imported from Babylon
- ▢ Syrian captives

LITERARY FEATURES

Genre and Literary Style
Prophecies and a few historical narratives, written mainly in Hebrew poetry

Hosea's prophecies both "forth tell" and "foretell." He includes the three classic elements of Hebrew prophecy: (1) call to people to turn from their sins in the face of divine judgment, (2) predictions of near events (such as the fall of Samaria), and (3) predictions of remote events (such as the coming of ideal peacetime conditions).

The majority of the book is Hebrew poetry. The prose sections are limited to chapters 1 and 3, the narrative about Hosea's marriage and children. The Hebrew style reveals an author with rhetorical skill. In English Bibles, Hosea is the first of the twelve Minor Prophets, "minor" in the sense that they are shorter than Isaiah, Jeremiah, or Ezekiel. In the Hebrew canon the Minor Prophets were compiled as a composite book called "The Twelve." Thus "The Twelve" was the last book of the Latter Prophets (following Isaiah, Jeremiah, and Ezekiel). These four Latter Prophets balanced the four Former Prophets in the Hebrew Bible (Joshua, Judges, Samuel, and Kings).

Themes
Faithfulness vs. unfaithfulness, the Lord vs. Baal; judgment vs. restoration

Hosea is a book of contrasts. God was faithful to Israel; Israel was unfaithful. In terms of the marriage analogy, one of the Hebrew words for husband (*baal*) was the same as the name of the deity the Israelites found so attractive. God longed for Israel to call him *Ishi* (My Husband) instead of *Baali* (My Husband); see 2:16-17. Like many other prophetic books, Hosea contrasts present judgment with the promise of future restoration.

Book Features and Structure
The most challenging feature of the book is the nature of Hosea's relationship to Gomer. As a "wife of whoredoms" (1:2), was she already a prostitute when Hosea married her, or was he simply told by God in advance that his bride would betray him bitterly? The evidence is not clear, and Bible scholars have argued for both interpretations. Another question concerns chapter 3, in which Hosea was told to "love a woman . . . yet an adulteress" (3:1). Does this (1) retell the story of chapter 1 from a first-person perspective, or (2) tell a later episode in the story of Hosea and Gomer, or (3) describe Hosea's second marriage to an unnamed slave woman after Gomer's death? In this instance the most reasonable answer seems to be number 2. Hosea is readily divided into two major sections. The first is narrative about an unfaithful wife (chaps. 1–3); the second contains prophecies against an unfaithful nation (chaps. 4–14).

JOEL

Joel, an otherwise unknown Israelite prophet to Judah, has given his name to this book as its composer. His name means "The LORD Is God" in Hebrew.

► *Key Text: 1:4*

"That which the palmerworm hath left hath the locust eaten; and that which the locust hath left hath the cankerworm eaten; and that which the cankerworm hath left hath the caterpillar eaten."

► *Key Term: "Locusts"*

Joel described a locust swarm that devoured the crops of Judah. He understood them to be an army sent by God to judge his people for their sins.

► *One-Sentence Summary*

Joel proclaimed that the people of Judah should interpret a severe locust plague as a forerunner of "the great and terrible day of the LORD," which would consume the pagan nations but also unfaithful Judah unless the people repented.

Flowers at Ashkelon, one of the five cities of Philistia (Joel 3:4).

GOD'S MESSAGE IN THE BOOK

Purpose

This book preserves the divinely inspired prophecies that Joel made during his ministry Judah. Although the era in which he ministered is not clear, the people were evidently assum ing that the coming "day of the LORD" would involve God's judgment on the pagan nation and not on God's people. Joel proclaimed that this view was wrong. The people of Juda would be restored only after they had been judged and repented of their sins.

Christian Worldview Elements

Joel deals with the worldview categories of *rebellion and sin* and *covenant and redemption*. Judah's sin was not trivial. Yet judgment was to be the means of bringing God's people to ultimate salvation. Joel gives a long-term picture of redemption from his own time until the day that God poured out his Spirit on all people.

GOD
CREATION
SOVEREIGNTY AND PROVIDENCE
FAITH AND REASON
REVELATION AND AUTHORITY
HUMANITY
▶**REBELLION AND SIN**
▶**COVENANT AND REDEMPTION**
COMMUNITY AND CHURCH
DISCIPLESHIP
ETHICS AND MORALITY
TIME AND ETERNITY

Teachings about God

God is a righteous judge, and in the coming "day of the LORD" he will bring sure and swift devastation on all who have opposed him. Yet he also "will pity his people" (2:18).

Teachings about Humanity

Joel explicitly denied the (usual) tendencies of God's people to presume that the Lord is lenien with them concerning their lifestyles and that they are therefore immune from the times h comes in judgment. Although God's judgment will utterly destroy the pagan nations (3:1-13 it will also be a decisive turning point that his people must also go through—on the way ultimate blessing.

Teachings about Salvation

This short book contains two profound passages on salvation. First, "whosoever shall call c the name of the LORD shall be delivered" (2:32; compare Rom. 10:13). Second, Joel describe repentance as a tearing ("rending," KJV) of one's heart rather than external actions such as tea ing clothes (2:12-14).

CHRIST IN JOEL

Peter and Paul taught that prophecies about the "day of the LORD" applied to the second coming of Jesus (1 Thess. 5:2; 2 Pet. 3:10). Joel also prophesied the coming of God's Spirit in all flesh: "Your sons and your daughters shall prophesy, your old men shall dream dreams, your young men shall see visions" (2:28). According to Peter, this prediction began to be fulfilled on the day of Pentecost when the Holy Spirit filled the followers of Jesus (Acts 2:16-21).

GOD'S STORY

When the Events of This Book Happened
Unknown, perhaps either the ninth century or the fifth century BC

This prophet is not mentioned in any other Old Testament book, and there is insufficient information in the book to date the locust plague or the ministry of Joel. Traditionally, he has been thought of as the earliest writing prophet. Evidence for an early date includes references to Tyre, Sidon, and Philistia (see 3:4 in contemporary translations), Judah's military enemies during the ninth century. There are no references to Assyria or Babylon, Judah's enemies later on. Evidence for a later date is found in Joel's call to the elders and priests, who led the nation after the return from exile, to repent (1:9,13; 2:17). There is no mention of a king, which also fits the postexile situation. Ultimately the message of the book does not depend on when the locust plague occurred, but there is no reason to reject the traditional early date for the book.

How Joel Fits into God's "Story"

Depending on the date of its composition, Joel belongs either to "chapter 2" of God's story: God educates his nation (disobedient Israel disciplined) or "chapter 3" of God's story: God keeps a faithful remnant (Messiah's space and time prepared).

The people of Joel's day supposed that religiously they were all right. Joel's book is a reminder that sin always threatens God's people. Although the iniquities were not specified, all the people, not just the leaders, were to acknowledge their sins, repent with fasting and broken hearts, and turn to God. Such a kingdom message is ongoing until "the day of the LORD." Joel's long-term prophetic lens looks forward to the time that all God's people will have his Spirit, a kingdom reality since the day of Pentecost (Rom. 8:9). Like other prophets, Joel anticipated a glorious future for the kingdom: "But Judah shall dwell for ever, and Jerusalem from generation to generation" (3:20).

Author and Date of Writing
Joel, perhaps either ninth or fifth century BC

Although there are numerous Joels in the Old Testament, the prophet bearing this name known only from this book. He only identified himself as "the son of Pethuel" and did n name his hometown or the kings of his ministry. Because of his frequent references Jerusalem (6 times in 73 verses), he may have lived there. No other personal details of his li are known. See **When the Events of This Book Happened** for information on the e in which Joel prophesied.

First Audience and Destination
The people of Judah living in Jerusalem

The first hearers were people and priests living in Judah, perhaps about 800 BC or abo 500 BC.

Occasion
Swarms of locusts were a constant threat to farmers of the ancient Near East. Hoards consis ing of millions of the creatures could strip everything green in a short period of time. The su cessive stages of locust life span (or else four varieties of locusts) that he mentioned in 1:4 an 2:25 show that this was a long-lasting scourge. Locusts easily symbolized an invading huma army that could wreak utter destruction. As early as Exodus 10, locusts were a divinely se plague, as was the swarm of Joel's day (see also Rev. 9). God used the locust plague of Joel day as the occasion to warn of a coming day of even greater disaster.

In the Middle East the locust periodically multiplies t astronomical numbers. As the swarm moves across the land, it devours all vegetation. The locust plague used in the Bible of what God's judgment will be like "That which the palmerworm hath left hath the locu eaten" (Joel 1:4).

The lush green fronds of a date palm tree in Haifa, Israel. "The vine is dried up, and the fig tree languisheth; the pomegranate tree, the palm tree also, and the apple tree, even all the trees of the field are withered: because joy is withered away from the sons of men" (Joel 1:12).

LITERARY FEATURES

Genre and Literary Style
Prophecy written entirely in Hebrew poetry

Even as one of the shortest prophetic works, the book includes two of the classic elements of Hebrew prophecy: (1) call to people to turn from their sins, and (2) predictions of remote events (the coming day of the Lord).

Joel's poetry is vivid and visual. He also uses sarcasm, for example when God summons the nations to assemble for their own destruction (3:9-11). In 3:10 his call to arms uses the opposite of Isaiah's and Micah's peaceful images: "Beat your plowshares into swords, and your pruning hooks into spears."

In English Bibles, Joel is the second of the twelve Minor Prophets. In the Hebrew canon it belonged to the composite book called "The Twelve" (see **Genre and Literary Style** for **HOSEA** for more information).

Themes:
Locusts, the day of the Lord

The matter of the locusts has already been mentioned. Joel's prophecy is really more about "the day of the LORD" than about locusts. See the section that follows.

Book Features and Structure

If Joel is early, he was the first prophet to use the phrase "the day of the LORD." The exact phrase occurs more often (five times) than in any other book of the Bible. (In the Old Testament, only the major or minor prophets use the phrase; they may also use the equivalent phrase "that day.") In general, the term points to events that take place at history's decisive turning points, in which God intervenes to accomplish specific aspects of his kingdom plan. In Joel, as well as in the other prophets, "the day of the LORD" usually refers to the final times (just before and including Christ's return). It will involve the nations as well as God's people, but afterward there will be unending blessing.

The book, consisting of only 73 verses, has two sections. The first interprets the locust plague as a preview of the day of the Lord (1:1–2:17); the second focuses on the day of the Lord as a time of judgment for the nations but restoration for God's people (2:18–3:21).

AMOS

Amos, the eighth-century prophet from Judah to the Northern Kingdom of Israel, has given his name to this book as its composer. His name means "Burden Bearer" in Hebrew.

► Key Text: 5:24

"But let judgment [justice] run down as waters, and righteousness as a mighty stream."

► Key Term: "Injustice"

Amos proclaimed God's disgust with both the pagan nations and the people of Israel because of their many acts of injustice. God holds all people everywhere, even those who do not recognize him, responsible for practicing social justice.

► One-Sentence Summary

Although Amos prophesied against the nations surrounding Israel including Judah, his main message was against Israel, who must repent of injustice and idolatry or else go into exile—but then be restored to divine favor.

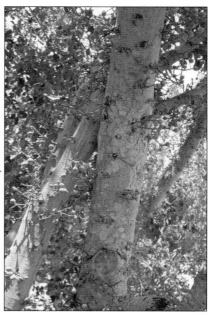

Sycamore fig on the shore of the Sea of Galilee. Amos took care of sycamore fig trees (Amos 7:14).

GOD'S MESSAGE IN THE BOOK

Purpose

This book preserves the divinely inspired prophecies that Amos made during his ministry of undetermined length. (He and Hosea were the only writing prophets to the Northern Kingdom of Israel.) During Amos's day the people of the Northern Kingdom felt politically, economically, and religiously secure. Amos announced that these were false securities. Politically Assyria would soon assert itself as the major threat to Israel; economically the good times had led to social corruption, violence, and injustice; religiously the worship of the Lord had been compromised by idolatry. Amos warned that injustice, immorality, and idolatry would bring divine judgment in the form of exile.

Christian Worldview Elements

Amos deals especially with the worldview categories of *rebellion and sin* and *ethics and morality*. Disloyalty to God is sin, but so is the selfish lack of concern for the needs of others. In other words, failure to live by either of the Great Commandments (Matt. 22:37-39) offends God. Amos's emphasis on personal ethics and morality should be seen in this light.

GOD
CREATION
SOVEREIGNTY AND PROVIDENCE
FAITH AND REASON
REVELATION AND AUTHORITY
HUMANITY
▶ **REBELLION AND SIN**
COVENANT AND REDEMPTION
COMMUNITY AND CHURCH
DISCIPLESHIP
▶ **ETHICS AND MORALITY**
TIME AND ETERNITY

Teachings about God

God is absolutely sovereign. He raises up and puts down nations. He is also a God who reveals himself and his plans to "his servants the prophets" (3:7). Therefore, he has revealed himself to be the judge of all, pagan and people of God alike. He is also—and not least—a God who has a wonderful future for his people when they are restored at last (9:11-15).

Teachings about Humanity

The people of Amos's day showed the universal human tendency to do the wrong thing rather than the right thing. In particular, this often evidences itself in religious compromise and complacency (4:4-5). On the other hand, humanity will be salvaged! Both Israel and "all the heathen which are called by my name" (9:12) will one day experience unmeasured blessings. (James declared that this prophecy began to be fulfilled by Gentiles turning to Jesus, Acts 15:5-18.)

Teachings about Salvation

In Amos, redemption is based entirely on God's initiative. God reminded them that they were "the whole family which I brought up from the land of Egypt" and that "you only have I known of all the families of the earth" (3:1-2). What God desires from redeemed people is righteous living and obedience. Religious rituals and festivals, even those that God commanded, cannot substitute for a right relationship with him (5:21-24).

CHRIST IN AMOS

Amos proclaimed the righteousness of God and called on God's people to turn from their unrighteousness and return to God. The high standards of God's righteousness were a passion with Jesus who told his followers he had not come to put aside the Law as an expression of God's righteousness. Rather he had come to fulfill God's righteous requirements.

GOD'S STORY

When the Events of This Book Happened
Amos prophesied during the reign of Jeroboam II of Israel (793–753 BC) while Uzziah king of Judah ruled (792–740 BC)

Second Kings 14:23–15:6 and 2 Chronicles 26 provide the historical narrative for the two kings mentioned in Amos. Under Jeroboam II, the Northern Kingdom of Israel experienced its golden age of peace and prosperity. Jeroboam ruled a kingdom from the city of Samaria that extended to Damascus in the north and to the Dead Sea in the south. (Both Aram [Syria, KJV] and Assyria, which would later threaten Israel, were politically weak during Amos's time.)

How Amos Fits into God's "Story"
The events of Amos's time belong to "chapter 2" of the story: God educates his nation (disobedient Israel disciplined). It reminds God's people that peace and prosperity can be threats to their behaving like God's people. Whenever plenty leads God's people to religious complacency or lack of concern for others, they should read the book of Amos. This book claims that "the day of the LORD" will take such people into judgment (5:18-20). On the other hand the book looks forward to the ultimate time of the kingdom's fullness when the earth will be restored to an Eden-like bounty (5:13-15).

ORIGINAL HISTORICAL SETTING

Author and Date of Writing
Amos, perhaps around 750 BC

Amos was a contemporary of Jonah. He was from Tekoa, a small town about ten miles south of Jerusalem. He was a rural person, by profession a shepherd and a gatherer of sycamore figs. He was not especially trained for religious work: "I *was* no prophet, neither *was* I a prophet's son" (7:14). Nothing is known of his family life. He evidently preached to the northern cities of Samaria (Israel's capital, 3:12; 4:1) and Beth-el (a center for idolatry, 7:13). Amos's message was perhaps as startling and as well received as would be a farm boy from Nebraska preaching in Manhattan. His ministry was probably short, limited to the period "two years before the earthquake" (1:1), an event otherwise unknown. The year 750 is a "best-guess estimate."

First Audience and Destination
Israelites living in the Northern Kingdom

Amos's first audience was people living in the Northern Kingdom of Israel in the mid-700s BC.

Occasion

Amos's only explanation of what prompted his prophetic ministry was, "Thus hath the Lord GOD shewed unto me" (7:1,4; 8:1) and "I saw the Lord" (9:1). Thirteen times he declared "thus saith the LORD." The only personal incident of his ministry that he recorded was his confrontation with Amaziah, the priest of Beth-el (7:10-17). Amos did not explain what prompted him to commit his prophecies to writing.

ISRAEL AND JUDAH IN THE DAYS OF JEROBOAM II AND UZZIAH

LEGEND
- • City
- ○ City (uncertain location)
- • City captured by Uzziah
- ▲ Mountain peak
- ← Jeroboam II's route
- ← Uzziah's route
- Israel
- Judah
- Reclaimed by Jeroboam II

Amos's Oracles
against the nations
- A. Damascus
- B. Gaza
- C. Tyre
- D. Edom
- E. Ammon
- F. Moab

A. Amos 1:2–5

C. Amos 1:9–10

E. Amos 1:13–15

Uzziah attacked Philistia and built towns among the Philistines

Uzziah built towers in Jerusalem

B. Amos 1:6–8

F. Amos 2:1–3

D. Amos 1:11–12

Uzziah attacked Arabs in Gurbaal

Uzziah restored Elath to Judah

To Hamath

SEA

PHOENICIA

Sidon

Tyre

Mt. Hermon

Damascus

Pharpar R.

Dan

A R A M

Kedesh

Hazor

Gath-hepher

Aphek

Karnaim

Mt. Carmel

Mt. Tabor

Lo-debar

Ramoth-gilead

Samaria

Mt. Ebal

I S R A E L

Rabbah
(Amman)

AMMON

Jabneh

Bethel

Ashdod

Ekron

Anathoth

Jerusalem

Gath

Moresheth-gath

Tekoa

Hebron

En-gedi

DEAD
SEA

Amnon R.

Kir-hareseth

Gaza

PHILISTIA

Beersheba

Arad

MOAB

Tamar

Negeb

J U D A H

Arabah

Kadesh-barnea

EDOM

Kuntillet 'Ajrud

Gurbaal

MEUNIM

Elath

MEDITERRANEAN

0   10   20   30   40   50 Miles

34 N

32 N

LITERARY FEATURES

Genre and Literary Style
Prophecies and one short narrative, written mainly in Hebrew poetry

Amos may be the earliest writing prophet to complete his ministry. (Joel might have preceded him.) He includes all the elements of prophecy: a clear "thus saith the LORD," which includes "forth telling" and "foretelling." Amos's announcement that God despised the people's deeds implicitly included a call to repentance. Further, he predicted both near events (such as the fall of Samaria) and remote events (such as the coming restoration of "the tabernacle of David that is fallen," 9:11).

Except for 7:10-16, the book is written in vigorous Hebrew poetry. Amos created startling word pictures, from his opening salvo ("the LORD will roar from Zion," 1:2) to his bold reference to the women of Samaria ("kine [cows] of Bashan," 4:1). His opening chapters are memorable for repeated use of the formula, "For three transgressions of ___, and for four, I will not turn away" (1:3,6,9,11,13; 2:1,4,6).

In English Bibles, Amos is the third of the twelve Minor Prophets. In the Hebrew canon it belonged to the composite book called "The Twelve" (see **Genre and Literary Style** for **HOSEA** for more information).

Themes
Social justice, true religion, "the day of the LORD"

With his attacks on the violent and those who oppressed the poor, Amos spoke not only for his own era, but for all eras to come. He understood the enduring truth that genuine religion is not based on ritual but a heart desiring to please God. If Amos preceded Joel, his references to "the day of the LORD" (5:18,20) are the earliest in Scripture (see **Book Features and Structure** for **JOEL** for further information).

Book Features and Structure

One of the striking features of Amos is the last section, which records five brief visions, along with the divine interpretation of each. Collectively they add to the striking nature of the book: the locusts (grasshoppers, KJV, 7:1-3), the fire (7:4-6), the plumb line (7:7-9), the basket of summer fruit (8:1-14), and the Lord by the altar (9:1).

The book has three major sections. First, there are eight brief announcements of judgment on individual nations (1–2). Second, there are oracles of judgment against Israel (3–6). Third, there are five visions of coming wrath (7–9).

OBADIAH

Obadiah, the sixth-century Israelite prophet against Edom, has given his name to this book as its composer. His name means "Servant of the Lord" in Hebrew.

▶ Key Text: verse 15

"For the day of the LORD is near upon all the heathen: as thou hast done, it shall be done unto thee: thy reward shall return upon thine own head."

▶ Key Term: "Edom"

The people of Edom were descendants of Esau who lived southeast of Israel. God's wrath against Edom for its sins is the single concern of this book.

▶ One-Sentence Summary

Obadiah prophesied that God would destroy the nation of Edom because of its pride and violence, particularly in looking down on Judah's misfortune, and ultimately "the kingdom shall be the LORD's."

▼ Vista of Edomite territory. Obadiah's prophecy concerns Edom.

GOD'S MESSAGE IN THE BOOK

Purpose

This book preserves the divinely inspired prophecies Obadiah made during his (perhaps) brief ministry. These prophecies served a twofold purpose. First, they were meant to warn the people of Edom of their coming doom. Second they were an encouragement to the people of Judah to believe that God would punish one of their enemies for their sins against God's people.

Christian Worldview Elements

Obadiah deals particularly with the worldview categories of *sovereignty and providence* and *community.* God's sovereignty in the rise and fall of nations is clearly addressed here. The matter of the covenant community's identity as God's people under his protection is also in view.

GOD
CREATION
▶ **SOVEREIGNTY AND PROVIDENCE**
FAITH AND REASON
REVELATION AND AUTHORITY
HUMANITY
REBELLION AND SIN
COVENANT AND REDEMPTION
▶ **COMMUNITY** AND CHURCH
DISCIPLESHIP
ETHICS AND MORALITY
TIME AND ETERNITY

Teachings about God

God's justice in dealing with human sin is displayed in Obadiah. His promised destruction of Edom will be based on the criterion noted in the **Key Text** on the previous page.

Teachings about Humanity

On one hand Obadiah continues the biblical emphasis that there are only two kinds of people: those who belong to "Mount Zion" (God's covenant people) and all the rest. On the other hand, the book shows that when God judges people and nations, he will have enough evidence to condemn based on their (mis)treatment of others.

Teachings about Salvation

In Obadiah, salvation is thought of in terms of God's ultimate deliverance of his people based on his sovereign care: "But upon mount Zion shall be deliverance" (v. 17). Nothing is said about personal conversion.

⊙ CHRIST IN OBADIAH

Obadiah prophesied that Edom would be judged and destroyed for its pride against God and its treachery against God's people. Herod the Great who ruled Judea during the time of Jesus' birth had Edomite ancestry. The old treachery of Edom against Israel is seen in Herod's attempt to kill Jesus when he was less than two years old.

GOD'S STORY

When the Events of This Book Happened
Probably about 605–586 BC

The context is one in which the people of Edom, relatives of the people of Judah, had gloated about a military disaster that had befallen Jerusalem. They had even helped ransack the city (v. 13). The reference is probably to the successive Babylonian attacks on Jerusalem (in 605, 597, and 586). According to Psalm 137:7 and Ezekiel 35:1-15, Edom joined with Babylon in Judah's downfall. See **When the Events of This Book Happened** for **LAMENTATIONS** for more details.

How Obadiah Fits into God's "Story"

The events of Obadiah's time belong to "chapter 2" of the story: God educates his nation (disobedient Israel disciplined). Sometimes God judges his own people because of their sins. Sometimes they are persecuted not because of sin but because it suits God's kingdom purposes. In such situations, evil people may gloat in satisfaction at the humiliation of God's people. In either case, however, such people have become God's enemies. Sooner or later God's sovereign justice will prevail. His kingdom purposes for human history will succeed, not the purposes of evil. Obadiah's last word is, "The kingdom shall be the LORD's" (v. 21).

ORIGINAL HISTORICAL SETTING

Author and Date of Writing
Obadiah, perhaps around 590 BC

Obadiah did not name his father or any king, and he left no personal traces in his prophecy. If the Babylonian invasions of Judah are indeed the context for Obadiah's ministry, he was a contemporary of Jeremiah. Scholars can only make a reasonable judgment about the date of composition. The year 590 would fit the evidence. This was the period after the first two Babylonian invasions, but before the final disaster of 586.

First Audience and Destination
The Edomite people of "Mount Seir" and the Judahite people of "Mount Zion"

The first hearers of Obadiah were evidently the descendants of Esau. Ultimately, however, this was a message for the descendants of Jacob (that is, the people living in and around Jerusalem). This book was preserved by the Israelites as part of their canon of Scripture at least partly because it contained a message relevant to them.

Occasion

There was an ancient and bitter hatred between the Israelites and the Edomites, going all the way back to the rivalry between their respective patriarchs, Jacob and Esau (Gen. 27; 32–33). The descendants of Esau had settled southeast of the Dead Sea. From there, they had caused grief to the Israelites both in the last days of Moses and in the days of King Saul (Num. 20; 1 Sam. 22). Now they had once again demonstrated their hostility against a nation whose ethnic identity was not so different from their own (see **When the Events of This Book Happened** above).

The book of Obadiah was prompted by divine revelation. It explicitly claimed to originate as a divinely sent "vision." The prophet had no doubt that his words were simply relaying "Thus saith the Lord GOD" (v. 1).

NEBUCHADNEZZAR'S CAMPAIGNS AGAINST JUDAH
Obadiah 10-14

LEGEND
- • City
- ▲ Mountain peak
- ✿ Siege
- ← Nebuchadnezzar's first campaign (604)
- ← Nebuchadnezzar's second campaign (598-597)
- ← Nebuchadnezzar's third campaign (587-586)
- ← Egyptian campaign of 604-601
- ← Zedekiah's escape route
- ← Edomite's attack on Jerusalem
- ▨ Area of Babylonian dominance

Byblos

Sidon

PHOENICIA

Litani R.

Tyre

Kedesh

Hazor

Acco

Mt. Carmel

Mt. Tabor

Megiddo

MEDITERRANEAN SEA

Aphek

Joppa

32 N

Ashdod

Ashkelon

Azekah

Gaza

Lachish

N. Besor

Beth-shemesh

Beersheba

Negeb

PHILISTIA

Beth-zur

Hebron

Mizpah

Bethel

Jerusalem

Bethlehem

Arad

JUDAH

Mt. Hermon

Abana R.

Damascus

Pharpar R.

ARAM

Dan

Sea of Galilee

Yarmuk R.

Ramoth-gilead

Mt. Ebal

Mt. Gerizim

AMMON

Jabbok R.

Jordan R.

Jericho

Rabbah (Amman)

Mt. Nebo

En-gedi

DEAD SEA

Arnon R.

Kir-hareseth

MOAB

Zoar

Zered R.

Arabah

EDOM

36 E

After Jerusalem fell, the Babylonians destroyed its fortifications and burnt down the temple

Zedekiah tries to escape, but is caught in the plains of Jericho. He then is taken to the king of Babylon at Riblah where he receives his sentence.

Letters from Babylonian siege found in debris

As Judah weakens, the Edomite kingdom takes advantage of the situation and sends troops

| 0 | 10 | 20 | 30 | 40 Miles |
| 0 | 10 | 20 | 30 | 40 Kilometers |

LITERARY FEATURES

Genre and Literary Style
A brief prophecy written in Hebrew poetry

Obadiah is one of three prophetic books whose initial audience was outside of God's people. (The other two are Jonah and Nahum, both directed against the Assyrian capital of Nineveh.) His book "forth tells" the sins of Edom and God's displeasure. Then it "foretells" the coming ruin of Edom and the ultimate greatness of God's kingdom. Interpreters disagree about whether the prediction of Edom's destruction was fulfilled in the inter-testamental period or whether it still waits for an end-time fulfillment.

The entire book is written in Hebrew poetry. In English Bibles, Obadiah is the fourth of the twelve Minor Prophets. In the Hebrew canon it belonged to the composite book called "The Twelve." (See *Genre and Literary Style* for **HOSEA** for more information.)

Themes
Judgment on Edom; triumph of God's kingdom

Obadiah was the only prophet whose message focused extensively on Edom's coming judgment. Others, however, pronounced God's judgment against Edom as a secondary theme (see Jer. 49:7-22; Ezek. 35:1-15; Joel 3:19; Amos 1:11-12). Ultimately God will judge all his enemies and his kingdom will triumph. Thus, this book has an ongoing message for God's people when their enemies seem to be in control. In the end, "there shall be holiness" (v. 17).

Book Features and Structure

There is great similarity between verses 1-9 and Jeremiah 49:7-22. Since the two men were probably contemporaries, it may be that they collaborated, although Obadiah wrote the shortest prophetic book while Jeremiah wrote the longest.

The book has two sections. The first (vv. 1-16) describes Edom's sins and coming destruction. The second (vv. 17-21) describes ultimate deliverance for "mount Zion."

JONAH

Jonah, the eighth-century Israelite prophet against Nineveh, has given his name to this book as its central character and composer. His name means "Dove" in Hebrew.

▶ Key Text: 4:11

"And should not I spare Nineveh, that great city, wherein are more than sixscore thousand persons that cannot discern between their right hand and their left hand; and also much cattle?"

▶ Key Term: "Fish"

Although this book is not about the fish, clearly Jonah's being swallowed by the fish is the most exciting and memorable incident in the book. This is what keeps interest in the book alive and makes it the best known of all the minor prophets.

▶ One-Sentence Summary

After Jonah's disobedience to God's command for him to preach in Nineveh resulted in his being swallowed by a fish, he then obeyed God and preached in Nineveh, with the result that the entire city repented and turned to God.

Reconstructed site of ancient Joppa, the port where Jonah sailed as he attempted to flee from the Lord (Jon. 1:3).

195

GOD'S MESSAGE IN THE BOOK

Purpose

Jonah was the "missionary prophet." This book preserves the experiences of a reluctant preach-er who, of all the prophets, had the most visibly positive results. The people of Israel had forgotten that God is concerned for all people. God meant for Israel to "declare his glory among the heathen; his marvellous works among all nations" (1 Chron. 16:24). Even though the people of Nineveh were the enemy (and would destroy the Northern Kingdom within a century), they were not beyond God's mercy. This book teaches that the most unlikely, most evil people in the world may respond favorably when they are given an opportunity to know the one true God. It also teaches that salvation is a matter of undeserved forgiveness, a truth that God's people have sometimes forgotten.

Christian Worldview Elements

Jonah deals principally with the worldview categories of *God* and *sovereignty and providence*. No Bible book more fully demonstrates God's mercy on the undeserving.

> **GOD**
> CREATION
> **SOVEREIGNTY AND PROVIDENCE**
> FAITH AND REASON
> REVELATION AND AUTHORITY
> HUMANITY
> REBELLION AND SIN
> COVENANT AND REDEMPTION
> COMMUNITY AND CHURCH
> DISCIPLESHIP
> ETHICS AND MORALITY
> TIME AND ETERNITY

Teachings about God

Jonah reveals God as Creator. He is sovereign over the storms and fish of the sea, as well as the plants and worms of the land. The book also shows God as loving and compassionate. God's unanswered question that ends the book (see **Key Text**) is meant to provoke readers to think about how his mercy relates to "the heathen."

Teachings about Humanity

God's enumeration of the vast city of Nineveh shows that each human life is valuable in the eyes of God. Jonah was personally a mass of contradictions—a prophet known mainly for disobeying God; a preacher angry at the success of his ministry; a believer more concerned about "creature comforts" than about people dying without knowing God. As such, he certainly demonstrates that God may use imperfect and reluctant persons to accomplish his plans.

Teachings about Salvation

Jonah demonstrates the principle that those whom God saves do so in response to hearing the word of God. No salvation occurs apart from the proclamation—whether willingly or reluctantly, partially or completely of a word from God. The Apostle Paul (who also knew about storms on the Mediterranean Sea) would later ask, "How then shall they call on him in whom they have not believed? and how shall they believe in him of whom they have not heard? and how shall they hear without a preacher?" (Rom. 10:14).

CHRIST IN JONAH

Some crowds who heard Jesus clamored for a sign. Jesus told them that the only sign they would be given is the sign of Jonah. As Jonah was in the belly of the fish for three days, so Jesus was in the earth for three days and then was resurrected (Luke 11:29-32).

GOD'S STORY

When the Events of This Book Happened
Sometime during the reign of Jeroboam II of Israel (ruled 793–753 BC)

According to 2 Kings 14:25, Jonah was a prophet during the days of Jeroboam II. (See 2 Kings 14:23-29 for the biblical narrative of his reign.) This was a time of unprecedented peace and prosperity in the Northern Kingdom of Israel. Aram (Syria in the KJV) to the north was so weak that Israel was able to expand, even taking control of Damascus. The Assyrians, with their capital in Nineveh, were in a period of retrenchment and inner turmoil. At the same time, they were well known throughout the ancient Near East as a potent military threat. (Shortly after Jeroboam's death and the ministry of Jonah, Assyria entered a period of aggression and expansion under Tiglath-Pileser III. It would conquer Samaria and exile the people of the Northern Kingdom in 722.)

How Jonah Fits into God's "Story"

The events of Jonah's time belong to "chapter 2" of the story: God educates his nation (disobedient Israel disciplined). Jonah shows that God's kingdom purposes were never meant to be limited only to one ethnic entity. God's mercy in sending his prophet to the Assyrians foreshadowed his plan to send the good news of the gospel "unto the uttermost part of the earth" (Acts 1:8).

ORIGINAL HISTORICAL SETTING

Author and Date of Writing
Jonah, perhaps around 780 BC

The book is anonymous. On the other hand, according to uniform Jewish and early Christian belief, Jonah wrote this narrative of which he was the central human figure. If so, he likely wrote down the account of his ministry shortly after completing it.

Jonah was a contemporary of Amos. The only information known of his background is that his father was Amittai and he was from Gath-hepher, an Israelite town originally in the tribal allotment of Zebulun (Josh. 19:13). Because critical scholars dismiss the narrative as nonhistorical, they suppose the book was composed by some unknown writer, probably after the Jews returned from exile.

First Audience and Destination
The people of the Northern Kingdom living in and around Samaria

Although the people of Nineveh heard and responded to Jonah's message, the book was written for the benefit of the people of Israel. According to 2 Kings 14:25, Jonah was involved in a prophetic ministry to Jeroboam II, presumably early in his reign.

Occasion

The book did not tell what prompted it to be written. Unlike all the other major and minor prophets, it is essentially a narrative. The only prophecy as such in the book is Jonah's warning, "Yet forty days, and Nineveh shall be overthrown" (3:4).

 The ancient seaport of Joppa (Jaffa).

A relief from the palace of Ashurbanipal at Nineveh showing Assyrian soldiers subjecting captives to a series of tortures. In spite of the ruthlessness of the Assyrians, God sent his servant Jonah to offer them mercy. Jonah attempted to run in the opposite direction.

LITERARY FEATURES

Genre and Literary Style
A compact narrative written in Hebrew

Although this book contains almost none of the elements of Hebrew prophecy (see, for example, **Genre and Literary Style** for **ISAIAH**), this book is listed among the prophetic books for two reasons. First, its central character was a prophet (2 Kings 14:25); second, it issued a call to repentance. It contains no predictions at all. As a compact, well-written narrative, it has literary parallels with the book of Ruth or the stories about Elijah or Elisha (see 1 Kings 17–2 Kings 8).

Because taking the story as history requires believing the astonishing miracle of Jonah's survival in the fish and the otherwise unreported repentance of Nineveh, most critical scholars have suggested that the book belongs to a different genre. It has variously been called a parable or an allegory of God's love, that is, it is fictional in one way or another. Jesus himself, however, affirmed both Jonah's being swallowed by the fish and the repentance of Nineveh (Matt 12:39-41), so there can be no doubt that the events reported in this book happened in history. If one believes in God's sovereignty over nature and history, then he can intervene supernaturally whenever it pleases him.

The entire book is written in Hebrew prose except for Jonah's prayer. In English Bibles, Jonah is the fifth of the twelve Minor Prophets. In the Hebrew canon it belonged to the composite book called "The Twelve." (See **Genre and Literary Style** for **HOSEA** for more information.)

Themes
God's mercy; God's sovereignty over nature

The mercy of God to those who do not deserve it is one of the great themes of the Bible. In this book it is cast in a new light. God's sovereignty is seen explicitly in four things "God prepared" in the book: a great fish (1:17); a gourd (4:6); a worm (4:7); and a vehement east wind (4:8).

Book Features and Structure

Jonah's prayer of thanksgiving from inside the fish (2:1-9) is a remarkable statement of trust in God. From that uncomfortable place he affirmed, "Salvation *is* of the LORD" 2:9). It should also be noted that the text does *not* identify the kind of fish that swallowed Jonah, though it may have been a whale, as has been popularly imagined.

The book reflects a very wide geographical spread, from Tarshish (probably in southern Spain) in the far west to Nineveh on the Tigris River in Mesopotamia. In fact, the four chapters can be organized on the basis of Jonah's movements: (1) Jonah travels west (away from God); (2) Jonah sinks down (inside the fish); (3) Jonah travels east (to Nineveh to preach); (4) Jonah sits down (outside Nineveh to wait for its destruction).

MICAH

Micah, the eighth-century Israelite prophet from Judah, has given his name to this book as its composer. His name is a short form of Micaiah, meaning "Who Is Like the LORD" in Hebrew.

▶ *Key Text: 3:8*

"But truly I am full of power by the spirit of the LORD, and of judgment, and of might, to declare unto Jacob his transgression, and to Israel his sin."

▶ *Key Term: "Idolatry"*

The essential sin of Judah was idolatry, a rejection of the "First Table" of the Ten Commandments (the first four commandments). This brought about corruption, violence, and many other sins, a rejection of the "Second Table" (the last six commandments).

▶ *One-Sentence Summary*

Although Micah also prophesied against Israel, his main message was against Judah, who must repent of idolatry and injustice or else go into exile—but then be restored to divine blessing under the Ruler from Bethlehem.

▼ Palace of Ahab in Samaria, a place where idolatry flourished (Mic. 1:3-7).

GOD'S MESSAGE IN THE BOOK

Purpose

This book preserves the divinely inspired prophecies that Micah made during his ministry of at least twenty years. These prophecies were originally for the people of Judah facing Assyrian invasions. Micah warned that because of idolatry and injustice, God's case against Judah (and Israel) was severe. Their kingdoms would be destroyed—even though individuals could still repent and seek the Lord. Like Isaiah his colleague, Micah looked beyond the Assyrian captivity of Israel and the Babylonian captivity of Judah to the time that they would be forgiven and restored in righteousness, living under the Davidic Ruler that God would send.

Christian Worldview Elements

Micah deals with the worldview categories of *rebellion and sin, covenant and redemption,* and *time and eternity.* Judah's sin was about to have catastrophic consequences. Yet exile was not the final word. Micah offered a broad understanding of redemption from his own day until the time that "their king shall pass before them, and the Lord on [= at] the head of them" (2:13).

GOD
CREATION
SOVEREIGNTY AND PROVIDENCE
FAITH AND REASON
REVELATION AND AUTHORITY
HUMANITY
► **REBELLION AND SIN**
► **COVENANT AND REDEMPTION**
COMMUNITY AND CHURCH
DISCIPLESHIP
ETHICS AND MORALITY
► **TIME AND ETERNITY**

Teachings about God

God's wrath against idolatry and all forms of human sin against others (violence, corruption, exploitation) is manifest in this book. The Assyrian and Babylonian captivities were the result of God's justice. Yet he is also a merciful God who does not retain anger forever. He will ultimately "cast all their sins into the depths of the sea" (7:19). Christ's birth in Bethlehem is specifically prophesied (5:2). The Spirit of God was present to empower the prophet (3:8).

Teachings about Humanity

Micah painted a dark picture of humanity as all too prone to wickedness. People from small to great were lying awake at night planning evil (2:1). The only hope was divine interference, which will happen when God personally takes responsibility for shepherding his flock (2:12).

Teachings about Salvation

In Micah, salvation is mainly corporate. It is based on God's forgiveness of sins (7:18-20) and restoring his people under the coming King. There is, however, an individual dimension. Those in a right relationship with God in this lifetime show it in the way they live now, reflected in perhaps the most beloved text from this book: "He hath shewed thee, O man, what *is* good,

nd what doth the LORD require of thee, but to do justly, and to love mercy, and to walk
umbly with thy God?" (6:8).

CHRIST IN MICAH

Micah repeats (4:1-5) Israel's Messianic promise (2:2-4) centering in the exalta-
on of God's temple as a worship place for all nations and the end of war. Israel will walk in
he name of the Lord (4:5). This is possible because God will once again visit David's birth-
lace in Bethlehem and bring forth a new, everlasting king (5:2-5a; compare Matt. 2:6).

GOD'S STORY

When the Events of This Book Happened
Micah prophesied during the reigns of three kings of Judah: Jotham, Ahaz,
nd Hezekiah (mainly about 740–700 BC)

econd Kings 15:32–20:21 and 2 Chronicles 27–32 provide the historical narrative for the
ree kings mentioned in Micah 1:1. In the city of Samaria, idolatrous kings ruled the
Iorthern Kingdom of Israel. The power of Aram (Syria, KJV) with its capital in Damascus was
constant threat. Then there were the Assyrians, with their capital in Nineveh. Judah was iso-
ted, with many powerful enemies.

During the rule of King Ahaz (735–715 BC), the Assyrians conquered Samaria, fulfilling
Iicah's word. Ahaz's son Hezekiah (715–686 BC) paid attention to the prophets Isaiah and
Iicah and instituted religious reform.

How Micah Fits into God's "Story"

he events of Micah's time belong to "chapter 2" of the story: God educates his nation (dis-
bedient Israel disciplined). Judah was weak and impotent. It had become like the surround-
g nations, idolatrous and corrupt to the core. There was little sense that it was part of God's
ingdom of righteousness and holiness. They were a disobedient and sinful people who would
e judged. Yet Micah prophesied the coming of a Ruler—a descendant of David to be born in
ethlehem—who would one day rule the kingdom in righteousness (5:2).

ORIGINAL HISTORICAL SETTING

Author and Date of Writing
Micah, perhaps around 700 BC

Micah was a contemporary of Isaiah and Hosea. He was from the small town of Moresheth, probably Moresheth-gath in southern Judah (1:14). Almost nothing is known of his personal life. He saw the fulfillment of his predictions about the fall of Samaria to the Assyrians. Micah also witnessed the great religious revival intitiated by Hezekiah, which delayed by a century the fulfillment of his prophecies about the coming fall of Jerusalem. Thus, he was one of the few prophets whose warnings of judgment were heeded. He probably wrote down his prophecies during the last years of Hezekiah.

First Audience and Destination
The people of Judah living during Micah's lifetime

The first hearers were people living in Judah near the end of the 700s BC.

Occasion

The specific occasion for Micah's prophecies is not known. They do, however, fit the period of religious and social corruption present during the rule of Ahaz (see 2 Kings 16). According to Jeremiah 26:18, Hezekiah repented in response to hearing Micah 3:12, a prophecy of the coming fall of Jerusalem. The religious revival Hezekiah instituted marked a genuine return to worship of the Lord. (Later on, Isaiah worked with Hezekiah when the Assyrian army under Sennacherib laid siege against Jerusalem in 701 BC, and God miraculously spared the city, Isa 36–37.) Micah did not tell what prompted the collection of his writings.

PROPHETS OF THE EIGHTH CENTURY

LEGEND
- • City
- ○ City (uncertain location)
- ▲ Mountain peak

| 0 | 10 | 20 | 30 Miles |
| 0 | 10 | 20 | 30 Kilometers |

MEDITERRANEAN
SEA

Sidon

PHOENICIA

Tyre

ARAM

Damascus

Abana R.

Mt. Hermon

Litani R.

Pharpar R.

Dan

Kedesh

Hazor

Acco

Sea of Galilee

Ashtaroth

Mt. Carmel

Gath-hepher

Dor

Mt. Tabor

Yarmuk R.

Megiddo

Beth-shan

Abel-meholah

ISRAEL

Jordan R.

Tishbe

Hosea's marriage portrays Israel's faithlessness to Yahweh; predicts Assyria will destroy Israel

Samaria

Mt. Ebal

Mt. Gerizim

Jabbok R.

AMMON

Joppa

Hosea's homeland?

Shiloh

Amos denounces the social sins of Israel and warns of God's impending judgement

Bethel

Micah condemns corrupt leaders in Jerusalem

Mizpah

Gilgal

Rabbah (Amman)

Ramah

Anathoth

Elkosh

Medeba

Ashdod

Azekah

Jerusalem

Ashkelon

Moresheth-gath

Tekoa

Amos's homeland

Isaiah advises Ahaz and Hezekiah in attack against Jerusalem

PHILISTIA

Shephelah

Lachish

Hebron

DEAD SEA

Dibon

Gaza

Gerar

JUDAH

En-gedi

Arnon R.

Eastern Desert

Raphia

N. Besor

Beersheba

Arad

MOAB

Negeb

Kir-hareseth

W. el-Arish

Tamar

Arabah

Zered R.

EDOM

LITERARY FEATURES

Genre and Literary Style
Prophecies written entirely in Hebrew poetry

Micah's prophecies both "forth tell" and "foretell." He includes the three classic elements of Hebrew prophecy: (1) call to people to turn from their sins in the face of divine judgment (which in fact happened), (2) predictions of near events (such as the fall of Samaria), and (3) predictions of remote events (such as the birth in Bethlehem of the coming Ruler).

Micah's poetic style alternates between a hard charging attack against sins and the promise of a coming restoration. Sometimes he uses "I" to voice God's own words (chap. 6); sometimes the "I" is his own voice (chap. 7). He is also known for quoting both false prophets (2:6, 7) as well as the nations that will be converted (4:2).

Themes
True religion, social justice, future restoration

Micah's message to Judah included basically the same themes as the message Amos had delivered to the Northern Kingdom half a century earlier. With his attacks on the violent and those who oppressed the poor, Micah spoke not only for his own era but for all eras to come. He understood also the enduring truth that genuine religion is based on a heart desiring to please God, not ritual. Along with his contemporary, Isaiah, Micah foresaw an age of blessedness under a great Davidic Ruler who would wisely lead God's people in righteousness.

Book Features and Structure

Micah 4:1-3 is almost exactly like Isaiah 2:2-4, which demonstrates that these contemporaries indeed knew each other. Scholars disagree as to whether the time he referred to as the "latter days" began with the first coming of Christ or yet awaits his return. These verses reverse the imagery of Joel 3:10.

One of the striking features of the book is the way it alternates between prophecies of judgment and prophecies of future blessing. This pattern occurs three times and provides a clue for organizing the book.

First cycle	Judgment (1:1–2:11)	Blessing (2:12-13)
Second cycle	Judgment (3:1-12)	Blessing (4:1–5:15)
Third cycle	Judgment (6:1–7:7)	Blessing (7:8-20)

NAHUM

Nahum, the seventh-century Israelite prophet against Nineveh, has given his name to this book as its composer. His name means "Comfort" in Hebrew.

▶ *Key Text: 1:2*

"God is jealous, and the LORD revengeth; the LORD revengeth, and is furious; the LORD will take vengeance on his adversaries, and he reserveth wrath for his enemies."

▶ *Key Term: "Nineveh"*

Nineveh was the capital of Assyria, the world superpower of the 600s BC. God's wrath against Nineveh for its sins is the concern of this book. Nahum, the prophet of God's judgment, followed Jonah, the prophet of God's mercy, to Nineveh.

▶ *One-Sentence Summary*

Nahum prophesied that God would destroy Nineveh because of its wickedness and violence, never to rise again.

▼ Hills of Gilead (Bashan) (Nah. 1:4).

GOD'S MESSAGE IN THE BOOK

Purpose

This book preserves the divinely inspired prophecies that Nahum made during his (perhaps) brief ministry. These prophecies served a twofold purpose. First, they were meant to warn the people of Nineveh of their coming doom. Second, they were an encouragement to people living in the kingdom of Judah to believe that God would punish their great enemy for their sin against God's people.

Christian Worldview Elements

Nahum focuses attention on the worldview categories of *sovereignty and providence* and *community*. God is supreme in the rise and fall of nations, as this book clearly addresses. The importance of God's people recognizing themselves as his people under his ultimate protection is also in view.

GOD
CREATION
▶ **SOVEREIGNTY AND PROVIDENCE**
FAITH AND REASON
REVELATION AND AUTHORITY
HUMANITY
REBELLION AND SIN
COVENANT AND REDEMPTION
▶ **COMMUNITY** AND CHURCH
DISCIPLESHIP
ETHICS AND MORALITY
TIME AND ETERNITY

Teachings about God

God's wrath against every affront to his holiness is on full display in Nahum. He is patient, but this should not be misunderstood as weakness. His promised destruction of Nineveh was necessary because of the divine attributes noted in the **Key Text** above.

Teachings about Humanity

On one hand this book shows that human beings can achieve a great deal apart from God. The Assyrian civilization was highly advanced economically and militarily. On the other hand, the Assyrians were cruel and evil, an abomination to God. The book shows that God does not recognize as great (or good) any person or nation that measures success apart from obedience to him.

Teachings about Salvation

In Nahum, salvation is presented as God's final rescue of his people based on his sovereign care: "The LORD is good, a strong hold in the day of trouble; and he knoweth them that trust in him" (1:7).

CHRIST IN NAHUM

Nahum told Judah to look for a messenger who would bring the good news of Assyria's downfall, thus proclaiming peace for the world (1:15). The New Testament sees Jesus Christ as God's ultimate messenger, preaching God's peace for the world (Acts 10:36). As God is the one who rebukes seas and dries up rivers (1:4), so Jesus rebukes the sea and calms the storm (Matt. 8:26).

GOD'S STORY

When the Events of This Book Happened
Sometime between 663 and 612 BC

During this time Assyria dominated the ancient Near East. Samaria and the Northern Kingdom of Israel fell to Assyria in 722. In 663 Assyria had conquered the magnificent Egyptian stronghold of Thebes, located on the Nile River some four hundred miles south of the Nile Delta. In Nahum 3:8 the prophet reminded the Assyrians of their great triumph. ("No" in the KJV is an alternate name for Thebes.) His argument was, If mighty Thebes fell, who are you to think you will stand forever? Nineveh did fall in 612 to the Babylonians, just as Nahum predicted. Second Kings 21–23 and 2 Chronicles 33–35 describe the three kings who ruled Judah between the fall of Thebes and the fall of Nineveh: Manasseh, Amon, and Josiah. It is unclear which one was reigning when Nahum prophesied.

How Nahum Fits into God's "Story"

The events of Nahum's time belong to "chapter 2" of the story: God educates his nation (disobedient Israel disciplined). When God judges his own people because of their sins, he may use evil persons or powers. In this situation, however, such evil persons are still subject to the vengeance of God. Sooner or later God's sovereign justice prevails. His kingdom purposes for human history will succeed, not the purposes of evil. Although Assyria has long been destroyed, God's last enemy will not meet its final doom until Jesus' return to earth.

ORIGINAL HISTORICAL SETTING

Author and Date of Writing
Nahum, perhaps around 650 BC

Nahum did not name his father or any king, and he left no personal traces in his prophecy. He named himself as an "Elkoshite," that is, from the town of Elkosh, which is otherwise unknown. If Nahum prophesied soon after the fall of Thebes, the king of Judah was the idolatrous and long-reigning Manasseh, the "Ahab of Judah," who became a vassal of Assyria (2 Chron. 33:11-13). At this point Assyria was at its most arrogant and imperialistic height under Ashurbanipal (669–627). The year 650 would fit the evidence for the completion of Nahum's book, but this is simply a best-guess estimate.

First Audience and Destination
People in Nineveh or perhaps people in Judah

The first hearers of Nahum may have been the Ninevites themselves. Possibly the prophet traveled there to deliver his message, just as Jonah had done for an earlier generation. Ultimately, however, this was a message for God's people. Nahum was preserved by the people of Judah in their canon of Scripture at least partly because it contained a message important to them.

Occasion
Assyria had long terrorized the ancient world. It had conquered Samaria and Thebes and appeared invincible. Nahum did not describe the specific occasion for his prophecy other than that it came as "the vision of Nahum." Like the other prophets, he was specifically aware of the divine origin of his ministry.

ASSYRIAN SUPREMACY IN THE SEVENTH CENTURY

BLACK SEA

SCYTHIANS

CIMMERIANS

Mt. Ararat

Kanish
Togarmah •Malatya

URARTU

KUMMUHU

NAIRI

Lake
Tuz

DIA

Taurus Mountains

KUE (CILICIA) Carchemish• Haran

T. Leylan
Gozan
T. Barsip T. Halaf

Dur-sharrukin
Nineveh Calah

Arbela
Ekallatum

ASSYRIA

Tarsus

Arpad
Aleppo •Calneh
Ebla • Emar
Qarqar

BETH-EDEN
•Tiphsah
Rezeph

Terqa

Asshur

Arrapha

Cyprus

Arvad
Sumur
Byblos

Hamath
Qatna

Tadmor

Euphrates

Dur-kurigalzu

Eshnunna

De

MEDITERRANEAN
SEA

Sidon • Damascus
PHOENICIA ARAM
Tyre • Mt. Hermon
Acco • Hazor
Megiddo • •Ashtaroth
Shechem • •Ramoth-gilead

Sippar
Babylon •Cuthah
Borsippa

*Esarhaddon
rebuilds Babylon*

BABYLONIA

Nippur

Ashdod
Ashkelon
Gaza •Jerusalem
Raphia JUDAH

Rabbah (Amman)

*Manasseh brought in chains
before the Assyrian king*

Uruk

Sais • Tanis Pelusium
Migdol

Syro-
Arabian
Desert

Ur

On (Heliopolis)

Elath
Noph
(Memphis) Ezion-geber

EGYPT Sinai

Mt. Sinai

LEGEND
- ● Modern city
- • City
- ▲ Mountain peak
- ☼ Siege
- ← Campaigns of Esarhaddon (c. 671–669 B.C.)
- ← Campaigns of Ashurbanipal II (c. 667–663 B.C.)
- ▨ Assyrian Empire at its zenith

*Ashurbanipal sacks
Thebes as the Assyrian
Empire reaches its
maximum extent
(Nah. 3:10–13)*

RED
SEA

No-amon
(Thebes)

LITERARY FEATURES

Genre and Literary Style
A brief prophecy written in Hebrew poetry

Nahum is one of three prophetic books whose initial audience was outside of God's people.
(The other two are Obadiah and Jonah, directed against Edom and Nineveh respectively.) H
book "forth tells" the sins of Nineveh and God's wrath against it. Then it "foretells" the con
ing destruction of Nineveh, and indeed the entire Assyrian Empire. A secondary theme is th
restoration of Judah (1:15; 2:2).

The entire book is written in Hebrew poetry. Nahum's style is vivid, with excellent use o
metaphors and word pictures. In English Bibles, Nahum is the seventh of the twelve Mino
Prophets. In the Hebrew canon it belonged to the composite book called "The Twelve." (Se
Genre and Literary Style for **HOSEA** for more information.)

Themes
Judgment on Nineveh, God's wrath against sin

Nahum was the only prophet whose message focused extensively on Nineveh's coming con
demnation. In this way it complements the book of Jonah, in which God's judgment again
Nineveh was averted. Ultimately God will judge all his enemies, and his kingdom will triump
Thus, this book has an ongoing message for God's people. They should never doubt the ser
ousness of his wrath against sin, despite apparent delays in carrying out his justice.

Book Features and Structure

Nahum 1:2-8 is a psalm about God's awesome power. These verses are based on successiv
letters of the Hebrew alphabet, but the acrostic is incomplete. (See **Book Features an
Structure** for **LAMENTATIONS** for information about acrostic poetry.) Of furthe
interest is that this book concludes with a question, as does Jonah, the other prophetic boo
that focuses on Nineveh.

The three chapters of the book are suitable indications of its structure. Chapter 1 focuses o
God's wrath; chapter 2 deals with Nineveh's condemnation; and chapter 3 presents Nineveh
coming destruction.

HABAKKUK

Habakkuk, the seventh-century Israelite prophet to Judah, has given his name to this book as its composer. His name is possibly related either to the verb *embrace* in Hebrew or to an Assyrian plant called the hambakuku.

▶ *Key Text: 2:4*

"Behold, his soul which is lifted up is not upright in him: but the just shall live by his faith."

▶ *Key Term: "Dialogue"*

The book reports a dialogue between the prophet and God. The prophet asked God questions about his ways, and God answered. The book shows one righteous way to bring concerns to God when his ways appear incomprehensible.

▶ *One-Sentence Summary*

When Habakkuk asked God questions about the nature of evil and its punishment, God answered by revealing his righteousness and sovereignty, and the prophet then responded with worship and faith.

Relief from the palace of Sargon II, King of Assyria. The historical context of Habakkuk's prophecy was a conflict between Assyria and Babylon. This relief depicts that conflict. The fragment shows Assyrian soldiers towing a boat laden with munitions along a river during one of Sargon's campaigns against Merodach-baladan, king of Babylon.

GOD'S MESSAGE IN THE BOOK

Purpose

This book preserves the divinely inspired dialogues and prayers of Habakkuk. These originate as a one-on-one conversation between the prophet and God, but they no doubt reflect the kind of questions that many righteous people of Judah living in Habakkuk's time were also asking. The righteous of all eras may ask similar questions. God's people today will benefit from hearing God's replies to Habakkuk's questions: (1) Why does evil seem to go unpunished for so long, and (2) Why does God sometimes reprove the less evil by sending an even greater evil?

Christian Worldview Elements

Habakkuk focuses attention on the worldview categories of *God, sovereignty and providence,* and *ethics and morality.* The book causes readers to consider the attributes of God when their experience appears to deny that he is just. Further, the book addresses the issue of God's care for his people in the presence of great evil. The question of what is moral in international relations, particularly when one nation wars against another, is also in view.

▶ **GOD**
CREATION
▶ **SOVEREIGNTY AND PROVIDENCE**
FAITH AND REASON
REVELATION AND AUTHORITY
HUMANITY
REBELLION AND SIN
COVENANT AND REDEMPTION
COMMUNITY AND CHURCH
DISCIPLESHIP
▶ **ETHICS AND MORALITY**
TIME AND ETERNITY

Teachings about God

The answers God gave the prophet show him as the Revealer of truth. The revelations God made focus on his absolute sovereignty over human history. Habakkuk's own passion was a concern for the glory of God's name to be known among all people: "His glory covered the heavens, and the earth was full of his praise" (3:3).

Teachings about Humanity

Apart from divine revelation, human reasoning will never understand the ways of God. They will always be a mystery. It is fitting for people to ask God for revelation, but they must wait for the divine answers to their questions. When God reveals himself, people are to acknowledge his perfections by worship and praise.

Teachings about Salvation

The Apostle Paul quoted Habakkuk 2:4 ("the just shall live by his faith") twice as evidence of the doctrine of justification by faith in the Old Testament (Rom. 1:17; Gal. 3:11). Steadfast persevering trust in God for deliverance has always been the hallmark of God's people. The final verses of the book, a hymn of faith in the God who saves, includes the remarkable confession, "Yet I will rejoice in the LORD, I will joy in the God of my salvation" (3:18).

214

CHRIST IN HABAKKUK

Habakkuk stood in awe at God's holiness and power. His reaction to the presence of God (3:16) is similar to that of the Apostle John when the risen Christ appeared to him on the Isle of Patmos (Rev. 1:17).

GOD'S STORY

When the Events of This Book Happened
At the time Babylon was becoming the world superpower (around 612–605 BC)

The book appears to belong to a time after Babylon (Chaldea) had risen to power (1:6) but before Babylon had directly attacked Judah. Babylon conquered Assyria in 612, and in 605 they defeated the Egyptians at the battle of Carchemish on the Euphrates River. Later that same year Nebuchadnezzar made his first attack against Jerusalem.

The kings of Judah during this period were Josiah (640–609, killed in battle by the Egyptians); Jehoahaz (ruled three months in 609); and Jehoiakim (609–598), who changed loyalties from Egypt to Babylon. Second Kings 22:1–24:7 and 2 Chronicles 34:1–36:8 describe the rule of these three kings. It is unknown which of these was king when Habakkuk prophesied.

How Habakkuk Fits into God's "Story"

The events of Habakkuk's time belong to "chapter 2" of the story: God educates his nation (disobedient Israel disciplined). God has a plan for his people that cannot be defeated. The essence of that plan is for them to acknowledge his greatness, his goodness, and his glory. These attributes are revealed by his sovereign acts in history. Such events are on his schedule, for "an appointed time," and "it will surely come, it will not tarry" (2:3). Although this book does not highlight the future completion of God's kingdom (as many prophetic books do), it does emphasize God's majesty as the King (see 3:1-6).

ORIGINAL HISTORICAL SETTING

Author and Date of Writing
Habakkuk, perhaps around 610 BC

Habakkuk is unknown apart from this book. He did not name his father or town of origin. Because of what he includes about the international military scene (see ***When the Events of This Book Happened*** above), he almost certainly prophesied near the end of the seventh century. As such, he was a contemporary of Jeremiah and Zephaniah, and probably lived to see his prophecy of the Chaldean conquest of Judah fulfilled (with Jerusalem and the temple burned in 586). The year 610 fits the evidence for the completion of Habakkuk's book—after the fall of Assyria to Babylon but before King Josiah's death or the battle of Carchemish—but this is simply a best-guess estimate.

First Audience and Destination
People in Judah living during Habakkuk's lifetime

The first hearers were the kings and people living in the land of Judah during the years before the Babylonian captivity.

Occasion

Habakkuk did not tell what prompted him to write down his book. He recorded the private dialogue of himself with God and his personal response as a written account for the benefit of the people. Because the last chapter contains liturgical notations (3:1,19), those verses were probably included in worship services at the temple.

► THE RISE OF THE NEO-BABYLONIAN EMPIRE

"The Lord replied, . . . 'I am raising up the Babylonians to be a new power on the world scene'" (Hab. 1:6 NLT).

Assyrians flee to Haran only to be defeated by coalition forces led by Nabopolassar (610 B.C.).

Egyptian forces led by Necho II are defeated by Nebuchadnezzar, son of Nabopolassar (605 B.C.).

Medes and Chaldean coalition destroy Assyrian capital (612 B.C.).

Asshur falls to Cyaxares (614 B.C.).

Nabopolassar takes Babylon (626 B.C.).

Josiah killed in battle with Necho II (609 B.C.).

LEGEND
● Modern city
● City
▲ Mountain peak
⚔ Battle of Carchemish
⚙ Siege
◄— Medes forces
◄— Chaldean forces
◄— Assyrian forces
◄— Egyptian forces
▭ Neo-Babylonian influence

0   100   200   300 Miles
0   100   200   300 Kilometers

LITERARY FEATURES

Genre and Literary Style
Prophetic dialogue, woes, and prayer written in Hebrew poetry

As a prophetic writer, Habakkuk included materials in an unusual format, although he included classic elements of "forth telling" and "foretelling." His "forth telling" included great dec-
larations of God's attributes as well as woes on the wicked (see especially 2:9-17). His "foretelling" predicted both near events (Judah's devastation by Chaldea (fulfilled in 586), as well
as the more remote event of the destruction of Chaldea (fulfilled in 539 by the Persians).

The entire book is written in Hebrew poetry. Habakkuk's style reveals him as one whose
greatest concern was for the honor of God's name (1:12; 3:3). In English Bibles, Habakkuk is
the eighth of the twelve Minor Prophets. In the Hebrew canon it belonged to the composite
book called "The Twelve." (See *Genre and Literary Style* for **HOSEA** for more
information.)

Themes
God's honor, God's sovereignty in the face of evil

The majestic glory of God is evident throughout the book, in particular in Habakkuk's confession that has become a standard in Christian worship: "But the LORD *is* in his holy temple: let
all the earth keep silence before him" (2:20). The supremacy of God in international events is
especially evident in the dialogue section of the book.

Book Features and Structure
The dialogue of Habakkuk with God makes this book noteworthy among the prophetic works
of Scripture. This is seen in the following organizational scheme:

- *Habakkuk's first question:* "Why is evil in Judah not being punished?" (1:1-4).
- *God's first answer:* "God will use Chaldea to punish evil in Judah" (1:5-11).
- *Habakkuk's second question:* "How can God righteously use the more wicked
  (Chaldea) to punish the less wicked (Judah)?" (1:12–2:1).
- *God's second answer:* "Chaldea will also be punished for its evil" (2:2-20).

The book has two major sections. First is the dialogue between the prophet and God (1–2).
Second is the prophet's prayer of faith (3).

ZEPHANIAH

Zephaniah, the seventh-century prophet from Judah, has given his name to this book as its composer. His name means "The LORD Hides" in Hebrew.

▶ *Key Text: 3:17*

"The LORD thy God in the midst of thee is mighty; he will save, he will rejoice over thee with joy; he will rest in his love, he will joy over thee with singing."

▶ *Key Term: "Day of the LORD"*

Zephaniah predicted the future day of the Lord as a time of ruin for Jerusalem. The initial coming of the day of the Lord was manifested by Judah's fall to Babylon; its final fulfillment lies in the future in the context of Christ's return.

▶ *One-Sentence Summary*

Although Zephaniah prophesied coming judgment against the nations, his main message was against Judah, whose sins were so serious that they would go into exile on "the day of the LORD," but later they would be restored to righteousness.

▼ Oil lamp from the late Iron Age or Persian period. "At that time I will search Jerusalem with lamps and punish those who sit contented in their sins" (Zeph. 1:12 NLT).

GOD'S MESSAGE IN THE BOOK

Purpose

This book preserves the divinely inspired prophecies that Zephaniah made during his ministry to Judah about four decades before Jerusalem's fall to Babylon. He argued that the coming "day of the LORD" would involve God's judgment on God's people as well as on the pagan nations. God would later restore a remnant of his people, who would then worship him forever as the King of Israel.

Christian Worldview Elements

Zephaniah focuses on the worldview categories of *rebellion and sin* and *covenant and redemption*. The people of Judah had sinned greatly, particularly the religious and political leaders. God's judgment would ultimately result in the surviving remnant coming to salvation. Zephaniah demonstrates a long-term view of redemption from his own day until the time of restoration.

GOD
CREATION
SOVEREIGNTY AND PROVIDENCE
FAITH AND REASON
REVELATION AND AUTHORITY
HUMANITY
► **REBELLION AND SIN**
► **COVENANT AND REDEMPTION**
COMMUNITY AND CHURCH
DISCIPLESHIP
ETHICS AND MORALITY
TIME AND ETERNITY

Teachings about God

God is righteous and jealous for his people. In the coming "day of the LORD," he will bring about justice on all who have opposed him by living in violence and treachery, including those who claimed to belong to him. Although there is no direct prediction of Christ or the coming of the Holy Spirit, Christians have understood Zephaniah's prediction of the day when "the king of Israel, *even* the LORD, *is* in the midst of thee" (3:15) to refer to Jesus.

Teachings about Humanity

Zephaniah shows the universal tendency toward evil present among humans. All kinds of people—Jerusalemites, Philistines, Moabites, Assyrians, and Ethiopians—will alike be condemned because of their sins against God. Arrogance, oppression, and violence deserve God's judgment, no matter what persons or nations have committed them. "The day of the LORD" will come against them all (see 2:11).

Teachings about Salvation

Because of Zephaniah's emphasis on the day of the Lord, his understanding of salvation focuses on God's subsequent blessing on the righteous remnant of Israel. God's restoration of the covenant people, however, also means that all the nations of the earth will know him: "they may all call upon the name of the LORD, to serve him with one consent" (3:9). See Revelation 21:24-26 for a New Testament expression of this truth.

CHRIST IN ZEPHANIAH

Zephaniah announced that the King of Israel was in their midst (3:15). Jesus was crucified as King of the Jews (Mark 15:26). As Judah did not recognize the presence of the divine king in their circumstances, so many Jewish leaders failed to recognize the presence of God in Jesus Christ.

GOD'S STORY

When the Events of This Book Happened
During the reign of King Josiah (ruled 640–609 BC)

Second Kings 22–23 and 2 Chronicles 34–35 provide the historical narrative for Josiah's reign. In international affairs Josiah saw the shift of world power move from Assyria and Egypt to Babylon. The most significant religious event in Judah was the revival and restoration of temple worship led by Josiah (about 622 BC). Tragically, Josiah's reforms were unable to undo the damage done by his idolatrous grandfather Manasseh. After Josiah's untimely demise, three of his sons and one grandson reigned as the last of the Davidic dynasty in Jerusalem. Within twenty-five years of Josiah's death, the Babylonians completely destroyed the temple and carried the people into exile (586 BC). It is not clear whether Zephaniah prophesied before or after Josiah's reforms.

How Zephaniah Fits into God's "Story"

The events of Zephaniah's time belong to "chapter 2" of the story: God educates his nation (disobedient Israel disciplined). Zephaniah's use of "day of the Lord" language shows that he meant it as a decisive turning point in God's dealings with people. One such turning point for his people was the "day of the Lord" that sent them into Babylonian captivity. But, as New Testament writers came to know, in some ways the day of the Lord will not reach its fullest expression until the days before Christ's return. God's plans to be the King in the midst of his people is a magnificent prophecy that will ultimately be fulfilled in the final expression of God's kingdom. The last two chapters of the Bible describe the complete realization of this promise.

ORIGINAL HISTORICAL SETTING

Author and Date of Writing
Zephaniah, perhaps around 625 BC

Zephaniah was a contemporary of Jeremiah and Habakkuk. He identified himself by a more complete genealogy than any other prophet (1:1) and ministered during the reign of Josiah. He was the great-great-grandson of a certain Hezekiah, probably the famous king. If so, Zephaniah belonged to the royal family. (King Josiah was Hezekiah's great-grandson.) Zephaniah's attacks on the sins of the elite—princes, priests, judges, and false prophets— suggest that he was acquainted with the powerful and that he had true boldness (see 3:3-5). The evils of Judah that he described match the religious corruption rooted out by Josiah's reform. If, as appears likely, Zephaniah preached shortly before 622, he contributed greatly to the reforms of Josiah's rule.

First Audience and Destination
People in Judah living during Zephaniah's lifetime

The first hearers were the kings and people living in Judah some forty years before the Babylonian captivity.

Occasion

The specific occasion for Zephaniah's prophecies is not known. He stated only that "the word of the LORD" came to him (1:1). As noted above, however, his message fits the period of religious and social corruption present during the early rule of Josiah (see 2 Kings 22–23). The revival Josiah instituted marked a genuine return to worship of the Lord. Zephaniah did not tell what prompted the collection of his writings.

Restored gate at the site of the ancient city of Nineveh of Assyria. "And he will stretch out his hand against the north, and destroy Assyria; and will make Nineveh a desolation, and dry like a wilderness" (Zeph. 2:13).

LITERARY FEATURES

Genre and Literary Style
Prophecies written entirely in Hebrew poetry

Zephaniah's prophecies both "forth tell" and "foretell." He includes the three classic element of Hebrew prophecy: (1) call to people to turn from their sins in the face of divine judgment (which in fact happened); (2) predictions of near events (such as the fall of Judah and Jerusalem); and (3) predictions of remote events (such as the restoration of a remnant in righteousness).

The entire book is written in Hebrew poetry. Zephaniah's poetic style is largely dark: the coming day of the Lord will be bitter; the penalties will be sure and severe. On the other hand, there are rays of light when he speaks of the coming time of renewal. In English Bibles Zephaniah is the ninth of the twelve Minor Prophets. In the Hebrew canon it belonged to the composite book called "The Twelve." (See **Genre and Literary Style** for **HOSEA** for more information.)

Themes
Day of the Lord, repentance, judgment, restoration

The "day of the LORD" looms large in Zephaniah (see also Joel). Because of the certainty of this day, people should take heed and repent of their sins. Yet judgment (both on Judah and the nations) appears inevitable. While the theme of restoration is not developed as fully as it is in other prophetic books (such as Isaiah), it is unmistakably and clearly the note on which the book concludes.

Book Features and Structure

One often overlooked biblical theme is that of the happiness of God. Zephaniah noted God' coming pleasure in the full ingathering of his people. Just as these people are urged to "sing" and "shout" to God when they are restored (3:14), so God himself will "rejoice over thee with joy" and "joy over thee with singing" (3:17). Just as God's people find bliss in God, so one source of bliss for God is his people.

The book consists of only 53 verses. They may be organized into three sections: the day of the Lord (1:1–2:3); the judgment of the nations (2:4–3:8); the restoration of the remnant (3:9-20).

HAGGAI

Haggai, the sixth-century prophet who returned to Judah from Babylonian exile, has given his name to this book as its composer. His name means "Festive" in Hebrew.

▶ *Key Text: 1:8*

"Go up to the mountain, and bring wood, and build the house; and I will take pleasure in it, and I will be glorified, saith the LORD."

▶ *Key Term: "Rebuilding"*

The primary focus of this book is rebuilding the Jewish temple in Jerusalem after the return from Babylonian captivity.

▶ *One-Sentence Summary*

When Haggai proclaimed God's command to rebuild the temple, giving God's promises that the glory of the second temple would exceed that of the first temple, the people obeyed with a willing heart.

▼ Stonework showing examples of carpenters with their tools. The LORD called on the people to rebuild the temple (Hag. 1:2-11).

GOD'S MESSAGE IN THE BOOK

Purpose

This book preserves the divinely inspired sermons that Haggai gave during his ministry in the last months of 520 BC. These prophecies were originally for the people of Judah who had recently returned from the Babylonian captivity and were lethargic about their primary duty to reestablish the true worship of God at his temple. Unlike most biblical prophets, Haggai's message was obeyed, and his sermons were kept as a permanent reminder of his ministry. From a broader perspective, the second temple, the Jewish community, and a stable Jerusalem were important circumstances for the coming of Jesus more than five centuries later.

Christian Worldview Elements

Haggai deals particularly with the worldview categories of *covenant and redemption* and *community*. Despite the Babylonian captivity, the returned exiles were still the covenant people. Their return was evidence that God had not forsaken them. As the covenant community, they were called on to worship as a community in the way that God commanded.

GOD
CREATION
SOVEREIGNTY AND PROVIDENCE
FAITH AND REASON
REVELATION AND AUTHORITY
HUMANITY
REBELLION AND SIN
COVENANT AND REDEMPTION
COMMUNITY AND CHURCH
DISCIPLESHIP
ETHICS AND MORALITY
TIME AND ETERNITY

Teachings about God

God desires to be honored by his people (see **Key Text**). Because of this, he has the right to prescribe what pleases him. His concern in the time of Haggai was to be worshipped properly in his temple. Ultimately, the greatness of the rebuilt temple was that it would one day receive "the desire of all nations." Christians have understood this as being fulfilled by Jesus' appearance at this temple, more than five hundred years after Haggai. Further, God's promise to Zerubbabel that he was "as a signet" (2:23) was a promise of the coming Messiah (a direct descendant of Zerubbabel, Matt. 1:12).

Teachings about Humanity

On one hand, the people that Haggai addressed needed to be rebuked. They were under divine curse because of their inactivity concerning the things of God. It was not so much that they were actively evil but that they were passive when they should have been passionate. On the other hand, the book shows that people can be moved to do right things, but even this must be at God's initiative: "And the LORD stirred up . . . the spirit of all the remnant of the people" (1:14).

Teachings about Salvation

The people who returned from exile were cured of the idolatry that took their ancestors into captivity. Haggai revived an emphasis from the era of the Davidic monarchy: the need for a temple as a place for redeemed people to worship. As throughout Old Testament times, personal trust in God was expressed through participation in right sacrifices and through obeying God's law. Thus, the blessings of salvation are promised in this book to those who fully obey the divine commands.

✝ CHRIST IN HAGGAI

Through Haggai the Lord says he will shake the elements of creation and the nations. Then the nations will come to worship at the new temple that God will fill with his glory (2:6-7). Simeon saw in the baby Jesus a light for the Gentile nations and glory for Israel (Luke 2:32).

🕊 GOD'S STORY

When the Events of This Book Happened
Between August and December of 520 BC

The Persians defeated the Chaldean Empire and the city of Babylon in 539, then initiated the policy of allowing exiles of all ethnic groups to go back to their homeland. The first Israelites returned during Cyrus's rule. They rebuilt the altar and laid the foundations for the temple about 536 (Ezra 6:3-5). The work then halted until after Darius the Great came to the throne of Persia (522–486). The prophetic ministry of Haggai is carefully dated in the second year of Darius. Haggai's ministry was successful in spurring the work, but the second temple was not dedicated until 516, exactly seventy years after Solomon's temple was destroyed (2 Chron. 36:21; Ezra 6:15). The walls of Jerusalem were rebuilt much later, in the time of Nehemiah (445).

How Haggai Fits into God's "Story"

Haggai tells part of "chapter 3" of God's story: God keeps a faithful remnant (Messiah's space and time prepared). Although there was no Davidic king, that did not keep the returning exiles from worshipping properly or doing what they were able to do. The second temple was a pale replica of Solomon's temple, but it would be more important. Jesus, the Son of God and Son of David, was presented in this temple and ended his public ministry by teaching there. The book of Haggai shows how one of God's prophets played a key role in bringing this temple into being.

ORIGINAL HISTORICAL SETTING

Author and Date of Writing
Haggai, around 520 BC

Haggai was a contemporary of Zechariah. Hardly anything is known about him. He did not note his lineage or his hometown. Presumably he was one of the exiles from Babylon that returned to Judah in the 530s. He did, however, date precisely the four occasions on which "the word of the LORD came" to him (1:1; 2:1,10,20). In modern equivalents, these dates are (1) August 29, 520; (2) October 17, 520; (3) and (4) December 18, 520. According to Ezra 6:14, Haggai saw the successful conclusion of his ministry in the completion of the temple. Presumably he wrote down his messages as they were given to him, and he compiled them shortly thereafter.

First Audience and Destination
Israelites in Jerusalem after they returned from exile

The original hearers and destination are clearly stated. The first audience was the people of Jerusalem that had returned to exile. In particular Zerubbabel the governor and Joshua the high priest were recipients of some of Haggai's exhortations.

Occasion

Ezra 4–5 describes the opposition that the returning exiles faced when they attempted to rebuild the temple. Opposition, however, became an excuse for inactivity. For more than fifteen years, inertia ruled. God raised up Haggai to rouse the Jews from their doldrums.

 Remains of the throne of Darius the Great (Hag. 1:1).

THE RETURN OF JEWISH EXILES TO JUDAH

First Sheshbazzar, then Zerubbabel led groups of Jewish exiles back to Judah between about 537 and 522 B.C.

Area conquered by Cambyses in 525 B.C.; Egypt frequently rebelled against Persian rule from ca. 500 B.C. onward.

Ezra leads a group of Jews back to Jerusalem. He was appointed minister of religious affairs by Artaxerxes 458 B.C.

Temple rebuilt and dedicated in 520 B.C.

Nehemiah hears of dire conditions in Judah and returns to Jerusalem under royal appointment 444 B.C.

LEGEND
- • City
- ○ City (uncertain location)
- ← Sheshbazzar's and Zerubbabel's route
- ← Ezra's and Nehemiah's route
- ▢ Cyrus's Persian Empire

LITERARY FEATURES

Genre and Literary Style
Prophetic sermons written in Hebrew prose

Although Haggai was clearly a postexilic prophet, his prophecies both "forth tell" and "fore tell" in the classic manner of the Hebrew prophets: (1) call to people to turn from their sin (in this case, the sin of unconcern for the temple) and (2) predictions of future events (such as the glory that would come to the second temple).

The book is written in Hebrew prose, rather than poetry. In English Bibles, Haggai is the tenth of the twelve Minor Prophets. In the Hebrew canon it belonged to the composite book called "The Twelve." (See *Genre and Literary Style* for **HOSEA** for more information.

Themes
Lord of hosts, rebuilding the temple, future blessings

Haggai, Zechariah, and Malachi all emphasize God's name as "LORD of hosts" (see *Book Features and Structure* below). The conviction that he was in charge of all armies logically led to confidence that he would enable the rebuilding of the temple and bring about the blessings that were promised.

Book Features and Structure

The last three books of the Old Testament use the name "LORD of hosts" more than ninety times, although Isaiah and Jeremiah—as well as some of the historical books—also make use of it. The word *hosts* literally means "armies" and can refer to earthly armies, heavenly bodies (such as stars and planets), and angelic armies. The name emphasizes God's supremacy over all things on earth and in heaven. Such a God deserves to be worshiped in a temple of his choosing, and he can enable his worshippers to construct such an edifice, despite any opposition.

The book has only 38 verses, and in the Old Testament only Obadiah is shorter. It is organized around the four divinely given messages that the prophet dated (see *Author and Date of Writing* above).

ZECHARIAH

Zechariah, the sixth-century prophet who returned to Judah from Babylonian exile, has given his name to this book as its composer. His name means "The LORD remembers" in Hebrew.

▶ Key Text: 8:3

"Thus saith the LORD; I am returned unto Zion, and will dwell in the midst of Jerusalem: and Jerusalem shall be called a city of truth; and the mountain of the LORD of hosts the holy mountain."

▶ Key Term: "Jerusalem"

This book focuses on the city of Jerusalem, which still lay in ruins in Zechariah's day. Both the near-term rebuilding of the city and the ultimate, everlasting destiny of Jerusalem as the city in which God delights are in view.

▶ One-Sentence Summary

Through night visions and prophetic oracles, Zechariah predicted the welfare of Jerusalem as God's beloved holy city into which the King would enter riding a donkey, the one also called God's Servant and Branch.

Olive press (Zech. 4).

GOD'S MESSAGE IN THE BOOK

Purpose

This book preserves the divinely inspired prophecies that Zechariah received during his ministry in 520–518 BC (or possibly extending later). These prophecies were originally for the people of Judah who had recently returned from the Babylonian captivity and were uncertain about the future prospects for the city of Jerusalem, once great but still in ruins from the Babylonian invasion. His message was essentially one of encouragement: the greatest days of Jerusalem lay in the glorious future. Because of Zechariah's messianic prophecies that Jesus fulfilled, the greatest glory of Jerusalem was that Jesus blessed the city with his presence.

Christian Worldview Elements

Zechariah draws attention to the worldview categories of *covenant and redemption* and *community*. Despite the Babylonian captivity, the returned exiles were still the covenant people. Their return was evidence that God had not forsaken them. The "glory days" for the covenant community were still in the future, not in the past, which had implications for how they should function together as a community in the present.

GOD
CREATION
SOVEREIGNTY AND PROVIDENCE
FAITH AND REASON
REVELATION AND AUTHORITY
HUMANITY
REBELLION AND SIN
▶ **COVENANT AND REDEMPTION**
▶ **COMMUNITY** AND CHURCH
DISCIPLESHIP
ETHICS AND MORALITY
TIME AND ETERNITY

Teachings about God

Zechariah emphasizes God's mercy—for his name's sake—on his beloved people. For this reason they will one day dwell in security and blessing in Jerusalem forever. God's Spirit is present to enable his servants (4:6). Jesus is predicted in a number of places: his royal entrance into Jerusalem (9:9); his betrayal for thirty silver pieces (11:12); and his role as Shepherd (13:7) and Branch (3:8; 6:12).

Teachings about Humanity

In general, Zechariah looks forward to the time that God's people—having been punished for their sins—will be restored in righteousness. In particular, the book shows what God can accomplish through individuals committed to obedience. These exemplary persons are Zechariah the prophet, Joshua the priest (3:1-10), and Zerubbabel the governor (4:6-10). These men foreshadow the coming of the Messiah, the greatest Prophet, Priest, and King.

Teachings about Salvation

Zechariah draws attention to the future redemption of God's people corporately, as they live safely in the land and he lives among them (chap. 8). This salvation will follow the horrible "day of the LORD" when God will defeat the nations that have come against Jerusalem (chap. 14). All those who share in this salvation will enjoy "holiness unto the LORD of hosts" (14:21).

CHRIST IN ZECHARIAH

The Gospels incorporate more passages from Zechariah than from any other prophet. In Zechariah we see foreshadowed the piercing of Jesus' body (12:10; compare John 19:34,37; Rev. 1:7).

GOD'S STORY

When the Events of This Book Happened
The dated prophecies are 520–518 BC

Zechariah dated several of his prophecies. He began about the same time as Haggai but continued for at least two years longer. The last six chapters possibly come from the time after the temple was completed in 516. See **When the Events of This Book Happened** for **HAGGAI**.

How Zechariah Fits into God's "Story"

Zechariah tells part of "chapter 3" of God's story: God keeps a faithful remnant (Messiah's space and time prepared). This book looks at the kingdom of God from three time frames. The first is the time present to the prophet (God's people living in a ruined Jerusalem, wondering whether they had any future at all). The second is the time of the King's coming to Jerusalem on a donkey (fulfilled by Jesus in his first coming). The third is the ultimate glory of the city (yet to be fulfilled by Jesus at his second coming; see the last two chapters of Revelation). Thus, Zechariah has an extremely broad kingdom focus.

233

ORIGINAL HISTORICAL SETTING

Author and Date of Writing
Zechariah, perhaps around 518 BC

Zechariah was a contemporary of Haggai. The only thing really known about him is that he was the son of Berechiah and grandson of Iddo (1:1). Presumably he was one of the exiles that returned to Judah in the 530s. He dated two of his visions, which enables scholars to integrate his ministry with that of Haggai. His initial call came in October or November 520 (1:1); the eight night visions came on February 15, 519 (1:7); a third message came on December 7, 518. Zechariah almost certainly did not live long enough to see the walls of Jerusalem rebuilt (in 445 BC, some 75 years after his initial call).

Most critical scholars have argued that Zechariah 9–14 were written by a later, unknown prophet, a Deutero-Zechariah, with a different style and perspective. (This is parallel to the argument for a Deutero-Isaiah. See *Author and Date of Writing* for **ISAIAH**.) There are, however, no really strong arguments for denying that the sixth-century prophet wrote the entire book. Presumably he wrote down his messages as they were given to him, and they were compiled shortly thereafter.

First Audience and Destination
Israelites in Jerusalem after they returned from exile

The first audience was the people of Jerusalem that had returned to exile. In particular Zerubbabel the governor and Joshua the high priest received some of Zechariah's messages of encouragement.

Occasion

Zechariah described his prophetic call as simply "the word of the LORD." For more than fifteen years the Jews had been back in Jerusalem, but the city was still in physical disarray. The walls were still ruined, and the people were questioning the future of the city. God raised up Zechariah to encourage these Jews with a vision of Jerusalem's glorious future. He did not tell what prompted the collection of his writings.

The western slope of the Mount of Olives on which Jesus gave his Olivet discourse. "And his feet shall stand in that day upon the mount of Olives, which is before Jerusalem on the east" (Zech. 14:4).

LITERARY FEATURES

Genre and Literary Style
Prophecies, including visions and words from God, written mainly in Hebrew prose but with some poetry

Zechariah's prophecies both "forth tell" and "foretell." The book includes the three classic elements of Hebrew prophecy: (1) call to people to turn from their sins, (2) predictions of near events (such as God's blessing on Zerubbabel), and (3) predictions of remote events (such as the coming of the King to Jerusalem riding a donkey).

Like Ezekiel and Daniel, Zechariah received symbolic visions as a part of his ministry. These included both near and distant prophetic elements. The book is written mainly in good Hebrew prose, rather than poetry. Chapters 9–10 are the main poetic section. In English Bibles, Zechariah is the eleventh of the twelve Minor Prophets. In the Hebrew canon it belonged to the composite book called "The Twelve" (see **Genre and Literary Style** for **HOSEA** for more information.)

Themes
Lord of hosts, Jerusalem, the Servant

Haggai, Zechariah, and Malachi all emphasize God's name as "Lord of hosts" (see **Book Features and Structure** for **HAGGAI**). The Jerusalem theme should be compared with the similar theme of Nehemiah. Zechariah's messianic prophecies, particularly on Jesus as the coming Servant are similar to those in the book of Isaiah.

Book Features and Structure
One feature of predictive prophecy in several biblical books but especially prominent in Zechariah is telescoping. Sometimes near and remote prophecies are so compressed together that it is difficult to tell whether a specific prediction is near or distant. (This is like looking at two mountaintops through a telescope: they appear to be close together, but they are many miles apart.) Thus, Zechariah's prophecies about the future of Jerusalem are often telescoped. They include events all the way from his lifetime to the final glorious days of the city.

The book has two distinct parts. Part 1 (1–8) focuses on Zechariah's night visions and conclude with God's blessings on Jerusalem. Part 2 (9–14) focuses on Zechariah's oracles (sermons) and concludes with God's victory in the final war against Jerusalem.

MALACHI

Malachi, the fifth-century prophet to Judah, has given his name to this book as its composer. His name means "My Messenger" in Hebrew.

▶ *Key Text: 1:11*

"For from the rising of the sun even unto the going down of the same my name shall be great among the Gentiles; and in every place incense shall be offered unto my name, and a pure offering: for my name shall be great among the heathen, saith the LORD of hosts."

▶ *Key Term: "Messenger"*

Malachi, God's messenger, noted that while true priests of God served as his messengers (2:7), God would one day send "my messenger" (3:1, John the Baptist) to prepare the way for "the messenger of the covenant" (3:1, Jesus).

▶ *One-Sentence Summary*

Malachi rebuked God's people for specific violations of the covenant, such as laws concerning sacrifices, divorce, and tithes, but he also prophesied the coming of the Messenger who will set all things right.

▼ Copper-smelting furnace at Timna. The Lord's messenger will be like a refiner's fire (Mal. 3:1-4).

GOD'S MESSAGE IN THE BOOK

Purpose

The book of Malachi preserves the divinely inspired words received by the prophet during h (possibly brief) ministry around 450 or 420 BC. These prophecies were originally for the secor or third generation of people in Judah after the return from the Babylonian captivity. The ter ple was functioning; the city was rebuilt; and people had become perfunctory in their worsh and lifestyles. His message was essentially one of accusation: as God's messenger, he charge them with violations of the covenant and gave specific examples. But he also looked ahead a time of wonderful blessing.

Christian Worldview Elements

Malachi deals particularly with the worldview categories *covenant and redemption* and *ethics and morality*. Those who have been included in God's covenant have a serious obligation to live in obedience to the covenant terms. Those claiming to be God's people cannot tolerate negligent living.

GOD
CREATION
SOVEREIGNTY AND PROVIDENCE
FAITH AND REASON
REVELATION AND AUTHORITY
HUMANITY
REBELLION AND SIN
▶ **COVENANT AND REDEMPTION**
COMMUNITY AND CHURCH
DISCIPLESHIP
▶ **ETHICS AND MORALITY**
TIME AND ETERNITY

Teachings about God

Malachi presents God's immutability (he does not change). For this reason, his promises are enduring. Further, he is one who judges rightly, beginning with his own people. The eternal God, moreove is personal, as frequent use of the pronoun "I" in this book emphasizes. Christ is prophesied as th Messenger who will purify priests and people alike (3:1-5). The Holy Spirit is not mentioned.

Teachings about Humanity

God's people were addressed in this book, yet they were disheartened and disillusioned. (Th promises that earlier prophets had made of a coming golden age seemed empty.) These peop illustrate that in times when God does not appear to be acting on behalf of his people, it is ea for them to become complacent. It is even easy for them to be apathetic about obeying God specific moral commands. This book offers God's cure for such doubtful people.

Teachings about Salvation

Redemption in Malachi has two aspects. First is the notion of the covenant (mentioned six time Salvation comes because God has initiated it in his covenant. Second is the work of the comir Messenger. Malachi predicted that his coming would bring cleansing: "He is like a refiner's fir and like fuller's soap" (3:2). The implications of this prophecy would not be entirely clear un Jesus fulfilled it by his atoning death.

CHRIST IN MALACHI

Malachi describes Christ as the Sun of righteous who brings healing to his people. He so comes as a refiner's fire to purify the sons of Levi so they can make an offering in righteousness.

GOD'S STORY

When the Events of This Book Happened

Shortly before (or after) Nehemiah's governorship, about 450 or 420 BC

The context of this book is the generation after the prophets Haggai and Zechariah. Persia was the superpower of the ancient Near East. The Jerusalem temple was functioning; there was a Persian governor (1:8); Judah was an unimportant backwater. The people had become complacent. Sins that Malachi condemned match those that Nehemiah attacked. The priests were corrupt (Mal. 1:6–2:9; Neh. 13:7-8); the tithe was neglected (Mal. 3:8-10; Neh. 10:37-39); Jewish men had married pagan wives (Mal. 2:11-15; Neh. 10:30; 13:23-27). (See **When the Events of This Book Happened** for **NEHEMIAH**.) Malachi's ministry may have preceded Nehemiah's arrival in Judah, or perhaps he challenged people that had reverted to their old ways after Nehemiah's time.

How Malachi Fits into God's "Story"

Malachi tells part of "chapter 3" of God's story: God keeps a faithful remnant (Messiah's space and time prepared). As the last book of the Old Testament to be written, Malachi gives a discouraging picture of God's people. When the action opens on the New Testament four centuries later, the picture is still bleak for the people as a whole. Malachi, however, prophesied events that would shake up the Jewish world and begin a new way of thinking about God's kingdom. John the Baptist, the messenger who prepared the way for the Lord (Mal. 3:1; Mark 1:2), came announcing the coming of God's kingdom (Matt. 3:2). Then, also in fulfillment of Malachi, Jesus came as the Messenger of the covenant preaching the kingdom (Mark 1:15). Malachi also looks ahead to the final day, when the Lord will burn up wickedness, but God's people will be set free (Mal. 4:1-3; see also the **Key Text**).

ORIGINAL HISTORICAL SETTING

Author and Date of Writing
Malachi, perhaps around 450 or 420 BC

The prophet did not name his parents or the rulers of his day, which makes precise dating his life impossible. Almost nothing is known about him. He was probably born in the land of Judah after the exiles began returning from Babylon in the 530s. Presumably he wrote down his messages as they were given to him, and they were compiled shortly thereafter.

First Audience and Destination
Israelites in Judah after the Babylonian exile

The first audience was the people of Judah of the second or third generation after the return from captivity that had become lethargic in their relationship to God.

Occasion

Malachi described his prophecy as "the burden of the word of the LORD to Israel" (1:1). He did not tell about receiving visions or describe the mechanism by which God spoke to him. Malachi had as strong a sense of being God's mouthpiece as any of the prophets who had preceded him, and he often spoke as the voice of God using the pronoun "I." He did not tell what prompted the collection of his writings.

he Chapel of Elijah on Mount Horeb, commemorating the traditional site to which Elijah ed. "Remember ye the law of Moses my servant, which I commanded unto him in Horeb or all Israel, with the statutes and judgments. Behold, I will send you Elijah the prophet efore the coming of the great and dreadful day of the LORD" (Mal. 4:4-5).

LITERARY FEATURES

Genre and Literary Style
Disputations and prophecies written in Hebrew prose

As a prophetic writer, Malachi included materials in an unusual format (see **Book Features and Structure** below), although he included classic elements of "forth telling" and "fore telling." His "forth telling" emphasized the sins of the people caused by their indifference to God. His "foretelling" focused on distant events (such as the coming of John the Baptist and Jesus).

The entire book is written in Hebrew prose. The prophet used a number of vivid metaphors, however. In English Bibles, Malachi is the last of the twelve Minor Prophets. In the Hebrew canon it belonged to the composite book called "The Twelve." (See **Genre and Literary Style** for **HOSEA** for more information.)

Themes
Lord of hosts, messenger, proper sacrifices, proper marriage, proper giving

Haggai, Zechariah, and Malachi all emphasized God's name as "Lord of hosts." The messenger theme has been noted as the **Key Term**. The specific covenant violations (2:10) had to do with offering unblemished animals in sacrifice, marrying only within the covenant family, and keeping the tithing regulations.

Book Features and Structure
Malachi's most unusual feature was his style of disputation as God's spokesman. He accused the people of doubting God by quoting their own words, sometimes prefaced by "ye say." Examples include the following:

- "Yet ye say, Wherein hast thou loved us?" (1:2)
- "And ye say, Wherein have we despised thy name?" (1:6)
- "Yet ye say, Wherein have we wearied *him*?" (2:17)
- "Yet ye have robbed me. But ye say, Wherein have we robbed thee?" (3:8)

To these questions (and more) the prophet gave God's answer, but sometimes he answered a question with a question (1:2), adding to the adversarial feel of this book.

The book may be organized into two sections. Chapters 1–2 are God's rebuke on the people's present neglect of God. Chapters 3–4 are God's announcement of the coming Messenger and the coming day of judgment (and blessing).

MATTHEW

THE GOSPEL ACCORDING TO MATTHEW

his title has been associated with the first Gospel as long as it has been known. It was named is because its author was believed to be Matthew, the apostle of Jesus.

▶ *Key Text: 16:16,18*

And Simon Peter answered and said, Thou art the Christ, the Son of the living God. . . And I say also unto thee, That thou art Peter, and upon this rock I will build my hurch; and the gates of hell shall not prevail against it."

▶ *Key Term: "Messiah"*

his book shows Jesus' fulfillment of the Scriptures as the promised Messiah more emphatially than any other Gospel.

▶ *One-Sentence Summary*

1 his life, death, and resurrection, ·sus fulfilled the prophecies ›out the Jewish Messiah and ·eated the church.

Church of the Beatitudes (Matt. 5:3-12). ▶

GOD'S MESSAGE IN THE BOOK

Purpose

The original purpose of this Gospel was to provide a written proclamation of the redemptio God brought about through Jesus with an emphasis suitable for Jewish Christians: *Jesus the promised Messiah.* God's people who read and study Matthew today should view with this original purpose in mind.

Christian Worldview Elements

Matthew touches on almost every element involved in developing a Christian worldview. In particular, this Gospel develops the categories of *covenant and redemption, discipleship, ethics and morality,* and *time and eternity.*

GOD
CREATION
SOVEREIGNTY AND PROVIDENCE
FAITH AND REASON
REVELATION AND AUTHORITY
HUMANITY
REBELLION AND SIN
▶**COVENANT AND REDEMPTION**
COMMUNITY AND CHURCH
▶**DISCIPLESHIP**
▶**ETHICS AND MORALITY**
▶**TIME AND ETERNITY**

Teachings about God

The first Gospel shows God in action, taking the initiative in fulfilling the Scriptures about the coming Messiah. It teaches about the Trinity and it contributes greatly to the Christian understanding of the deity of Christ. Jesus' constant reference to him self as the Son of Man plays a key role in understanding Jesus' earthly mission.

Teachings about Humanity

The author documented the sinfulness of humans in stark terms: Both Jews and Romans wer responsible for Jesus' crucifixion. Yet he also showed that humans committed to followir Jesus can accomplish great good. Matthew noted the importance of people putting faith i Jesus; he also showed Jesus' criticism of those with little faith.

Teachings about Salvation

Salvation is presented mainly in terms of belonging to the kingdom of God, which arrived i a fresh way in the person of Jesus (12:28). The death and resurrection of Jesus were the divir means by which God provided salvation. Although Jesus took the message of the kingdo only to Jews during his lifetime, his last act in this Gospel was to commission his followers t go to Gentiles ("all nations") as well (28:18-20).

CHRIST IN MATTHEW

When the wise men came to Jerusalem, they asked, "Where is he that is born King of the Jews? (2:2). "This is Jesus the King of the Jews" (27:37) was placed in writing above Jesus as he was crucified. Matthew presents Jesus as King and Israel's Messiah. More than any Gospel writer, he quotes from the Old Testament to make his case.

GOD'S STORY

When the Events of This Book Happened
During Jesus' earthly life, 6 BC–AD 30

Matthew's Gospel begins with the announcement of Jesus' coming birth, around 6 B.C., and ends with his post-resurrection ministry in the spring of A.D. 30. (See **When the Events of This Book Happened** for **LUKE** for further details about dates.)

How Matthew Fits into God's "Story"

Matthew tells "chapter 4"—the most important chapter—of God's story: God purchases redemption and begins the kingdom of God through Jesus Christ. Jesus' original hearers had no concept of a Messiah with two comings. One of his great concerns was to explain for his followers that the kingdom was not arriving in a single "one-step" manner. Most first-century Jews supposed that the Messiah would usher in the kingdom of God (or "age to come") in an irresistible, visible, dramatic way on the day of the Lord (Dan. 2). Especially in his parables Jesus taught that God's kingdom had truly come, but in a resistible, invisible, gradual way. In Matthew, at Jesus' first coming, only a few wise men acknowledged him as King (2:1-12); at his second coming he will be the King that judges all people (25:31-46).

ORIGINAL HISTORICAL SETTING

Author and Date of Writing
Matthew the apostle, perhaps around AD 55–65

The book is anonymous, but early Christian tradition uniformly affirmed that Matthew composed this Gospel. He was also known as Levi, a tax collector ("publican") whom Jesus called to be an apostle (Matt. 9:9; Mark 2:14). The organization and fondness for numbers in the book point to an author interested in mathematical precision. Many scholars of the past two centuries have denied that Matthew wrote this book, partly because of their belief that the author fabricated many of the details, such as the miracles of Jesus. Such invention is harder to explain if the account was written by an eyewitness to Christ's life. The Christian tradition of authorship by Matthew is surely correct.

Because most scholars believe Matthew used Mark's Gospel as a source, Matthew should be dated in the AD 50s or later. Matthew quoted Jesus' prophecy of the coming destruction of the temple (24:2; fulfilled in AD 70) without mentioning that it had come to pass as Jesus said. This leads many conservative scholars to conclude that Matthew published his Gospel before 70. Others, however, accept the decade of the 70s. Critical scholars uniformly date Matthew after 70, perhaps near the end of the first century. A typical conservative estimate for its composition is the decade from 55 to 65.

First Audience and Destination
Jewish Christians, perhaps living in Antioch of Syria

Matthew did not directly mention his audience, but his interest in showing that Jesus fulfilled the Scriptures points to a Jewish-Christian audience. He began his Gospel with a genealogy that recalls the entire history of the Jewish people, also pointing in this direction. This understanding has generally been held throughout Christian history.

Antioch of Syria is a best-guess deduction. This major Roman city had a significant number of Greek-speaking Jewish Christians involved in carrying out Jesus' missionary commission (Matt. 28:18-20; Acts 11:19; 13:1-3). Further, the first known quotation from this Gospel was made by Ignatius of Antioch around AD 110.

Occasion

Matthew did not explain what prompted him to write. The assessment of many students is that he composed his Gospel largely to help Jewish Christians interpret Jesus as the fulfillment of the Scriptures. Most scholars believe that the author was prompted by reading Mark's Gospel plus a (now lost) record of Jesus' teachings (sometimes called "Q"). There is much to commend the view that Matthew interwove Mark, "Q," his own research, and eyewitness memories into his own careful account.

246

PALESTINE IN THE TIME OF JESUS

- ● City
- ○ City (uncertain location)
- ● Decapolis city
- ○ Decapolis city (uncertain location)
- ★ Administrative capital
- ▲ Mountain peak
- — Major roads
- — Other roads
- First procuratorship
- Territory of Antipas
- Territory of Philip
- Syrian territory

Coponius was named the first prefect and established the administrative capital at Caesarea Maritima

Sidon

ITUREA

Mt. Hermon ▲

PHOENICIA (TYRE)

Litani R.

Tyre

Caesarea-Philippi (Panias)

GAULANITIS

King's

Cadasa (Kedesh)

Gischala (Gush Halav)

Huleh

Ptolemais (Acco)

GALILEE

Capernaum

Bethsaida

BA

Sepphoris

Geba

Mt. Carmel

Jotapata

Sea of Galilee

Gergesa (Kursi)

Gamala

Nazareth

Tiberias

Hippos

Xaloth (Chessulloth)

Mt. Tabor ▲

Yarmuk R.

Abila

A

Dora

Legio (Megiddo)

Jezreel Valley

Gadara

Caesarea Maritima (Strato's Tower) ★

Scythopolis (Beth-shan)

Dion

DECAPO

Ginae (Jenin)

Pella

MEDITERRANEAN SEA

SAMARIA

Aenon

Salim

Gerasa (Jerash)

Apollonia

Sebaste (Samaria)

Mt. Ebal ▲

Neapolis (Shechem)

Mt. Gerizim ▲

Amathus

Antipatris (Aphek)

Yarkon R.

Coreae

Joppa

Alexandrium

Ephraim (Ophrah)

PEREA

Gedor (Gadara)

Lydda

JUDEA

Archelais

Philadel

Jamnia

Azotus (Ashdod)

Emmaus (Nicopolis)

Jericho

Esbus (Heshbon)

Jerusalem

Cypros

Bethany

Mt. Nebo ▲

Medeba

Ascalon (Ashkelon)

Hyrcania

Mesad Hasidim (Qumran)

Betogabris (Beth-guvrin)

Hebron

DEAD SEA

Callirrhoe (Zereth-shahar)

Machaerus

Gaza

En-gedi

highway

IDUMEA

247

LITERARY FEATURES

Genre and Literary Style
A Gospel composed in ordinary Greek

The question, What, exactly, are the Gospels in comparison to other literary genres? has been discussed at length by scholars. The Gospels are more like biographies than any other ancient literary type. Yet they lack many features common to biography (such as regular attention to place and date) and they omit many years of the central character's life. The best suggestion is that the Gospels are a unique literary genre brought into being by the coming of the unique Son of God to the world. As such, the Gospels may be defined as "kerygmatic history." The Greek term *kerygma* meant "proclamation," a reminder that the Gospels proclaim the good news about Jesus in written form—just as the apostles orally proclaimed the good news and called people to commitment to Jesus. The term "history" indicates that the author—like every historian—selected and arranged his material to suit his own purposes.

Matthew wrote in the ordinary (*Koine*) Greek spoken throughout the Roman world of the first century. His style is both more concise and more polished than Mark. It is less sophisticated in vocabulary and precision than Luke. Christian tradition records that Matthew composed material in Hebrew or Aramaic, but the present Gospel bears no marks of being a translated document.

Themes
Jesus as Messiah, the kingdom of God, the church, prophecy

Matthew focuses on Jesus as the Messiah (Christ), the Anointed One. He penned the term "kingdom" more than fifty times, usually in the phrase "kingdom of heaven" or "kingdom of God." Of the four Gospels only Matthew mentions the "church" (16:18; 18:17). The Olivet Discourse (24–25) is the most extensive prophetic portion found in any New Testament book except Revelation.

Book Features and Structure

Matthew loved to quote Scripture, particularly with reference to how the birth and death of Jesus fulfilled prophecy. He is also well-known for presenting the teachings of Jesus in five major discourses. Matthew signaled the end of every discourse with words such as "when Jesus finished saying these things" (see 7:28; 11:1; 13:53; 19:1; 26:1).

Matthew noted a transition to a new aspect of Jesus' ministry by using the words, "from that time Jesus began to" (4:17; 16:21). This observation may be used to organize this Gospel into three sections: (1) introduction to the Messiah (1:1–4:16); (2) development of the Messiah's ministry (4:17–16:20); and (3) completion of the Messiah's ministry (16:21–28:20).

MARK

THE GOSPEL ACCORDING TO MARK

This title has been associated with the second Gospel as long as it has been known. It was named this because its author was believed to be (John) Mark, the first-century Christian associated especially with Peter and Paul.

▶ *Key Text: 10:45*

"For even the Son of man came not to be ministered unto, but to minister, and to give his life a ransom for many."

▶ *Key Term: "Servant"*

Omitting Jesus' birth and reporting relatively few of his teachings, this Gospel emphasizes Jesus' deeds as One who actively served the needs of people.

▶ *One-Sentence Summary*

In his life, death, and resurrection, Jesus did the deeds of the (suffering) Servant of the Lord, notably through his death as a "ransom for many."

▼ Excavated ruins of Capernaum synagogue (Mark 1:21-28).

GOD'S MESSAGE IN THE BOOK

Purpose

The main purpose of this Gospel was to provide a written proclamation of the redemption brought about through Jesus with an emphasis suitable for Gentile Christians: *Jesus is the perfect Servant of the Lord*. God's people who read and study Mark today should view it with its original purpose in mind.

Christian Worldview Elements

Mark deals particularly with the worldview categories of *covenant and redemption* and *discipleship*. The death of Jesus to save sinners is the event to which the entire Gospel drives. Further, the original disciples of Jesus—often slow to learn, yet transformed by Jesus—can be seen as modeling for all generations what following Jesus really means.

GOD
CREATION
SOVEREIGNTY AND PROVIDENCE
FAITH AND REASON
REVELATION AND AUTHORITY
HUMANITY
REBELLION AND SIN
► **COVENANT AND REDEMPTION**
COMMUNITY AND CHURCH
► **DISCIPLESHIP**
ETHICS AND MORALITY
TIME AND ETERNITY

Teachings about God

Jesus emphasized God as "your Father" in this Gospel. He is also the Father of Jesus, and from his opening words Mark declared Jesus to be "the Son of God." The Holy Spirit is present empowering Jesus' ministry and mission. This is seen especially in his triumph over every unholy spirit.

Teachings about Humanity

Jesus encountered both the sick and the sinful in this Gospel. He healed the sick and forgave the sinful. Multitudes (at the feeding of the 5,000 and the triumphal entry) and small groups (the apostles) were transformed by Jesus. Yet other large crowds (at Jesus' trial and crucifixion) and small groups (Jewish religious leaders) utterly rejected him. Mark emphasized that humans could not remain neutral about Jesus. They had to decide either for him or against him.

Teachings about Salvation

A higher percentage of this book is given over to the events of Jesus' suffering and death than any other Bible book. By quoting the three times that Jesus' predicted his death, Mark emphasized the necessity of the cross, that he "must" die (8:31; 9:31; 10:33). At the Last Supper Jesus explained his death was as a substitute: "for many" (14:24).

CHRIST IN MARK

Mark's presentation of Jesus is action packed and fast paced. He emphasizes Jesus' mighty acts and his role as Suffering Servant who calls followers to take up their own cross and follow him.

GOD'S STORY

When the Events of This Book Happened
During Jesus' earthly ministry, AD 26–30

Mark began his account with the preaching of John the Baptist, who came on the scene probably in the year 26. The crucifixion and resurrection occurred in the spring of AD 30. See **When the Events of This Book Happened** for **LUKE**.

How Mark Fits into God's "Story"

Mark tells "chapter 4"—the most important chapter—of God's story: God purchases redemption and begins the kingdom of God through Jesus Christ. As with all the Gospels, Mark prominently featured the kingdom of God in the teachings of Jesus. See **How Matthew Fits into God's Story**.

The traditional site on the Jordan River where Jesus was baptized.

251

ORIGINAL HISTORICAL SETTING

Author and Date of Writing
John Mark, perhaps around AD 50–60

The book is anonymous, but early Christian tradition uniformly asserted that Mark compose this Gospel in conjunction with Peter's memories. He was a secondary figure in Acts. Mar became infamous for deserting Paul and Barnabas on their first missionary journey (Act 12:25; 13:5). He later did mission work with Barnabas and eventually won his way back int Paul's good graces (Col. 4:10; 2 Tim. 4:11). At the time Peter wrote his first letter, perhaps few years after Mark wrote his Gospel, the aged apostle called Mark "my son" (1 Pet. 5:13 Most critical scholars deny that Mark was the author or that he wrote on the basis of Peter recollections, but there are a number of incidental details in the book that support this con clusion. In particular Bible students have noted that Mark's outline is identical to the outlin that Peter used in his preaching (Acts 3:13-15; 10:36-41).

During the past two centuries, a general but not universal consensus has emerged (amon all kinds of scholars, both critical and conservative, Protestant and Roman Catholic) that Mar was the first Gospel written. The reasons focus on Mark's more elementary chronology an style of writing as compared to the other Gospels. In any event, most conservative scholar conclude that Mark published his Gospel before AD 70, prior to the temple's destructio (Mark 13:2). A good estimate for its composition is the decade from 50 to 60, when both Pete and Mark were still alive and certainly had opportunities for collaboration on this project.

First Audience and Destination
Probably Gentile Christians living around Rome

The original hearers and destination are not stated but are believed from tradition. Irenaeus an Clement of Alexandria (both late second century) each identified Rome as the place of origin A number of details in the Gospel support this conclusion, such as the quick, business-like pac with which Jesus is presented, heightened by Mark's frequent use of "immediately." Sever terms with Latin origins also point in this direction.

Occasion

Scholars have long debated the human factors that prompted the composition of this Gospe Frankly this is all a matter of conjecture. Some have suggested that the impetus was the grow ing realization that Jesus' return might be in the distant future. Until then, his followers had need for a written account of the life of their Master. Since Peter was an eyewitness to almo everything recorded in this Gospel, his memories provided Mark with an outstanding historic basis for writing. Another suggestion is that this Gospel was written for Christians facing perse cution, perhaps the Roman persecution instigated by the Emperor Nero in AD 64. Th Christians would thus be encouraged. Since their Master had faced the injustice of religious an political authorities victoriously, they too could triumph no matter what they had to suffer.

GALILEE IN THE TIME OF JESUS

LEGEND

ECONOMY:

- Grapes
- Olives
- Dates
- Figs
- Pottery
- Wheat
- Fishing

- • City
- ★ Territory capital
- ▲ Mountain peak
- ← Travels of Jesus
- —— Roads

Sidon

0   5   10 Miles
0 5 10 Kilometers

Mt. Hermon

T Y R E

Pharpar River

Tyre

Litani River

ULATHA

Caesarea-Philippi

GAULANITIS

MEDITERRANEAN SEA

Cadasa (Kedesh)

Upper Galilee

Lake Huleh

Thella

Gischala (Gush Halav)

Merom

Baca

Seleucia

Jesus moves His ministry to Capernaum

Chorazin

Sogane

Capernaum

Plain of Bethsaida

Beth Kerem Valley

Lower Galilee

Plain of Gennesaret

GALILEE

Bethsaida

Homeland of 3 disciples: Peter, Andrew, and Philip

Ptolemais (Acco)

Gabara

Gennesaret

Jotapata

Magdala

Sea of Galilee

Gergesa (Kursi)

Gamala

Jesus turns water into wine

Cana

Hippos

Sepphoris

Tiberias

Mt. Hebron

Mt. Carmel

Gath-hepher

Jesus preaches in the synagogue and is rejected

Nazareth

Dabaritta

Japha

Sennabris

Yarmuk River

Esdraelon Valley

Mt. Tabor

Dora

Nain

Mt. Moreh

Gadara

DECAPOLIS

Capercotnei

Jesus raised to life a widow's son

SAMARIA

Scythopolis (Beth-shan)

Pella

Jordan River

PEREA

253

LITERARY FEATURES

Genre and Literary Style
A Gospel composed in ordinary Greek

See **Genre and Literary Style** for **MATTHEW** for information about what a "Gospel"
is. Assuming Mark was the first to compose a Gospel, he may be credited as the one who inno-
vated this genre. Mark wrote in ordinary (*Koine*) Greek, in a style characterized by frequent use
of the present tense to describe the action. His vigorous, vivid vocabulary is generally wordier
than Matthew or Luke (when these Gospels are parallel). The style is consistent with someone
who is writing down the memories of another as they are recounted to him.

Themes
Jesus as Servant, the kingdom of God, Jesus' suffering and death, Galilee

The first three of these are so evident as not to require comment. Interestingly, Mark centered
his account of the ministry of Jesus entirely in Galilee, with the exception of his suffering and
death (see 1:14 and 16:7).

Book Features and Structure

One of the most striking features of this Gospel is the Messianic Secret. This refers to the times
that Jesus asked his disciples or someone for whom he worked a miracle to keep the secret
about his identity or what he had done (1:34,44; 3:12; 5:43; 7:36-37; 8:26,30; 9:9). These
reflect Jesus' desire to accomplish his primary mission of dying for sin, which could have been
hindered by people who wanted him to behave as a political deliverer (the Messiah-King) or
as a miracle worker. (Critical scholars view this feature as a fictional device by Mark to explain
why Jesus was not acknowledged as the Messiah during his earthly ministry.)

Another feature that should be mentioned briefly is the manuscript history of the last
twelve verses of this Gospel (16:9-20). Because the earliest and best handwritten copies of
Mark omit these verses, some contemporary interpreters (and translations) have concluded
that they are a later addition to the Gospel.

The **Key Text** (10:45) provides a useful organizational basis for this Gospel. The first section, "Jesus the Servant," shows Jesus in action through the occasion of Peter's confession
(8:30). The second section, "Jesus the Ransom," begins in 8:31 with Jesus' prediction of his
crucifixion and goes to the end of the book.

LUKE

THE GOSPEL ACCORDING TO LUKE

This title has been associated with the third Gospel as long as it has been known. Its author was believed to be Luke, the first-century Christian physician who was a traveling companion of Paul.

▶ *Key Text: 19:10*

"For the Son of man is come to seek and to save that which was lost."

▶ *Key Term: "Savior"*

The saving activity of Jesus, both in his ministry and in his death, is the focus of this book. Because his mission was to save others he did not save himself (23:35).

▶ *One-Sentence Summary*

Jesus not only lived and ministered as the perfect human, but he also died and rose to new life as the Savior for sinners.

▼ Area thought to be where the manger was in which the infant Jesus was placed (Luke 2:7).

GOD'S MESSAGE IN THE BOOK

Purpose

The author explicitly stated his purpose in the preface (1:1-4). He wrote his Gospel to provide an orderly account of the beginnings of Christianity so that the reader will have reliable information about Jesus Christ. Every fair understanding of this Gospel accepts this as a beginning point for understanding.

Christian Worldview Elements

Luke focuses attention on a number of worldview elements. In particular he focuses on *humanity, covenant and redemption,* and *ethics and morality.* Luke's special ability to portray individuals vividly with a few words and his unique presentation of Jesus' teachings contribute to these emphases.

> GOD
> CREATION
> SOVEREIGNTY AND PROVIDENCE
> FAITH AND REASON
> REVELATION AND AUTHORITY
> ▶ **HUMANITY**
> REBELLION AND SIN
> ▶ **COVENANT AND REDEMPTION**
> COMMUNITY AND CHURCH
> DISCIPLESHIP
> ▶ **ETHICS AND MORALITY**
> TIME AND ETERNITY

Teachings about God

In this Gospel, God initiates everything concerning salvation. The glory of God is especially emphasized, from the song of the angels (2:14) to the triumphal entry (19:38). Equally important is the glory of Jesus himself, from the transfiguration (9:32) to his resurrection splendor (24:26). Jesus is, of course, the virgin-born Son of God in this book. The Spirit is active from Jesus' conception to the great power of his ministry (1:35; 4:14). The Spirit is also the gift Jesus promised to his followers (11:13).

Teachings about Humanity

This Gospel focuses on humanity in two ways. First, Jesus is the ideal or perfect Human. Luke shows what a Spirit-filled person, wholly obedient to God, is like. (Note the centurion's confession at Jesus' death: "Certainly this was a righteous man," 23:47.) Second, Luke painted a vivid portrait of a number of individuals Jesus impacted, showing the value of each human life.

Teachings about Salvation

The turning point in this Gospel is 9:51, when "he stedfastly set his face to go to Jerusalem." Jerusalem was the proper place for Jesus to offer himself as a sacrifice. In his own words, "Ought not Christ to have suffered these things, and to enter into his glory?" (24:26). On the night he was betrayed, he taught his disciples that his death was a substitute and that it brought about the new covenant (see Jer. 31:31-34).

CHRIST IN LUKE

Luke writes primarily for Gentiles and focuses on Jesus as offering salvation to Jew and Gentile alike. Luke shows Jesus' compassion for the poor and the oppressed.

GOD'S STORY

When the Events of This Book Happened
During Jesus' earthly life, 7 BC–AD 30

Luke's Gospel begins earlier than either Matthew or Mark, with the announcement of John's birth, around 7 BC. It ends with his ascent to heaven in the spring of AD 30. Jesus was born before Herod the Great died in 4 BC, possibly two or three years earlier. The probable year of Jesus' birth is 6 BC.

The years 30 and 33 are the only years when Pontius Pilate governed Judea that Passover fell on a Friday. Thus, discussion of the year of Jesus' crucifixion centers around these two years. John's ministry began in "the fifteenth year of the reign of Tiberius Caesar" (3:1). This probably refers to the fifteenth year after beginning his authority over the provinces (AD 11), giving a date of AD 25–26 for the beginning of John's ministry. Jesus' ministry from baptism to crucifixion probably lasted about three-and-a-half years (see **When the Events of This Book Happened** for **JOHN**). If so, he was baptized late in A.D. 26 (when he was age 32; see Luke 3:23), and he was crucified on Passover of AD 30 (Friday, April 7, in modern calendar notation).

How Luke Fits into God's "Story"

Luke tells "chapter 4"—the most important chapter—of God's story: God purchases redemption and begins the kingdom of God through Jesus Christ. See **How Matthew Fits into God's Story**.

Garden tomb (Luke 23:53).

ORIGINAL HISTORICAL SETTING

Author and Date of Writing
Luke, perhaps around AD 60–61

The book is anonymous, but early Christian tradition uniformly affirmed that Luke composed this Gospel as well as Acts. See *Author and Date of Writing* for **ACTS** for reasons supporting Luke's authorship of Acts. The dedications to Theophilus, the similar Greek style and vocabulary, and special shared emphases of the books (such as prayer and joy) all point to common authorship.

Luke was a secondary figure in the book of Acts, known not by name but by his use of the pronouns "we" and "us" when he was present to the actions he was describing. Paul named him three times in his letters (Col. 4:14; 2 Tim. 4:11; Philem. 24). He was a Gentile, a medical doctor, and a loyal supporter of Paul. His home city and the nature of his conversion are unknown. Most critical scholars believe that the author of the third Gospel and Acts was someone other than the Luke of Paul's letters or the "we" of Acts.

The date of Luke must be after Mark (which Luke almost certainly used as a source) but before Acts, which was perhaps published around 61–62. If Luke researched his Gospel while Paul was imprisoned in Caesarea, then perhaps he wrote and published from Caesarea (about AD 59) or possibly after he arrived in Rome with Paul after the famous shipwreck (about AD 61). Other scholars have argued that Luke, like all the Gospels, must be dated later, from the AD 70s or 80s.

First Audience and Destination
Theophilus, a Gentile whose residence is unknown

Luke explicitly dedicated this Gospel to Theophilus ("God's friend"), whom he called "most excellent." Mentioned only in the prefaces to Luke and Acts, he appears to have been a Gentile of high social status who had been "instructed" in Christianity but wanted more detailed information about Jesus. Theophilus may have provided financial patronage for Luke, underwriting his research expenses.

Occasion

The needs of Theophilus provided the immediate prompting for Luke's writing. Already "many" had written of Jesus' life, and in his preface Luke said that he used sources, including eyewitnesses. Luke possibly used the two years Paul was in jail in Caesarea (Acts 24:26-27; 27:1) to research the Gospel. He had access to any number of witnesses to Jesus' life, possibly including Jesus' mother (Luke 2:19,51). Most scholars believe that he was also aided by reading Mark's Gospel plus a (now lost) record of Jesus' teachings (sometimes called "Q"). There is much to commend the view that Luke interwove Mark, "Q," and his own research findings into his own careful account.

JESUS' BIRTH AND EARLY CHILDHOOD

LEGEND
- City
- City (uncertain location)
- ▲ Mountain peak
- ← Mary and Joseph's journey
- ← Jesus' journey to Jerusalem
- Territory of Archelaus
- Territory of Antipas

34 E

36 E

Gischala (Gush Halav)
Ptolemais (Acco)
GALILEE
Capernaum
Bethsaida
Sea of Galilee
Mt. Carmel
Sepphoris
Cana
Nazareth
Arbela
Mt. Tabor
Gabriel announces to Mary that she will bear a son
Dora
Mt. Moreh
DECAPOLIS
Caesarea Maritima (Strato's Tower)
SAMARIA
Sebaste (Samaria)
Aenon
Salim
Antipatris (Aphek)
Sychar
PEREA
Joppa
Lebonah
JUDEA
Jesus visits temple in Jerusalem at the age of twelve
Jericho
Azotus (Ashdod)
Jerusalem
Qumran
Medeba
Ascalon (Ashkelon)
Beth-zur
Bethlehem
Hebron
Machaerus
Mary and Joseph return to Palestine under divine guidance
Gaza
IDUMEA
Birth of Jesus (7–6 B.C.)
Raphia
Beersheba
Arad
Masada
Pelusium
Jesus is brought to Jerusalem for sacrificial ceremony
Joseph and his family flee to Egypt because an angel forwarned them of Herod's intent to murder Jesus
NABATEA
Arabah

MEDITERRANEAN SEA

Wilderness Of Shur

Petra

32 N

30 N

0   25   50   75   100 Miles
0   25   50   75   100 Kilometers

34 E

36 E

LITERARY FEATURES

Genre and Literary Style
A Gospel composed in outstanding Koine *Greek*

See *Genre and Literary Style* for **MATTHEW** for information about what a Gospel is. Luke was the most versatile of all the Gospel writers. The preface is classical Greek, and the rest of chapters 1–2 resembles a Hebrew style. The body of the Gospel is in excellent *Koine* Greek. Luke's large vocabulary and careful style mark him as an educated "man of letters." Luke was more self-conscious that he was writing "a history" than the other Gospel writers, as his attention to dating certain events shows.

Themes
Jesus as Savior, universal good news, the poor and outcast, prayer, joy

Luke's portrait of Jesus concentrates on him as the Savior. As such, his birth brought good news to all people, and at his ascension he commissioned his followers to go to all the nations. Luke drew a particularly sympathetic portrait of those on the fringes of society whom Jesus changed: a leper, a sinful woman, Zacchaeus, a widow with only two mites. This Gospel shows Jesus at prayer more than the other Gospels, and it clearly demonstrates the joy that Jesus brought to people.

Book Features and Structure
This is the longest and most inclusive of the Gospels. Luke is known for a number of striking literary features. In the first two chapters he reported four wonderful poems (often set to music). In the middle section he included a number of Jesus' parables found nowhere else (in particular "the prodigal son" and "the good Samaritan"). At the end of his narrative, he reported resurrection appearances found in no other Gospel.

Luke's emphasis on Jerusalem may serve as a structural guideline. First, Jesus' childhood and early ministry (1:1–9:50); second, Jesus' journey toward Jerusalem (9:51–19:27); third, Jesus' ministry and passion in Jerusalem (19:28–24:53).

JOHN

THE GOSPEL ACCORDING TO JOHN

his title has been associated with the fourth Gospel as long as it has been known. It was amed this because its author was believed to be John, the apostle of Jesus.

▶ Key Text: 3:16

"For God so loved the world, that he gave his only begotten Son, that whosoever elieveth in him should not perish, but have everlasting life."

▶ Key Term: "Lord"

rom the opening prologue to the end of the Gospel, Jesus is portrayed as Lord and God, with proportionately greater emphasis on his deity than in the other Gospels.

▶ One-Sentence Summary

sus is the sign-working Son of God who gives eternal life on the basis of his death and esurrection to all who believe in him.

anias' waterfall and river. "If anyone thirsty, he should come to Me and rink! The one who believes in Me, as e Scripture has said, will have reams of living water flow from deep ithin him" (John 7:37b-38 HCSB).

GOD'S MESSAGE IN THE BOOK

Purpose

The author explicitly states his purpose near the end of his book (20:30-31). He wrote his Gospel to provide an account of Jesus' life and the signs he performed so that people will believe in him and experience eternal life. Because the verb *believe* may be translated "continue to believe," his purpose no doubt included building up Jesus' followers as well as converting unbelievers.

Christian Worldview Elements

John deals particularly with the worldview categories of *covenant and redemption, discipleship,* and *time and eternity.* Jesus' death as an "appointment with destiny" is especially emphasized. The importance of believing in Jesus in order to be his disciple and to receive eternal life are pronounced.

GOD
CREATION
SOVEREIGNTY AND PROVIDENCE
FAITH AND REASON
REVELATION AND AUTHORITY
HUMANITY
REBELLION AND SIN
▶ **COVENANT AND REDEMPTION**
COMMUNITY AND CHURCH
▶ **DISCIPLESHIP**
ETHICS AND MORALITY
▶ **TIME AND ETERNITY**

Teachings about God

John emphasized the sovereignty and the love of God in sending Jesus. Jesus perfectly reveals God (1:18). In particular Jesus' astounding proclamations that begin with "I am" are remarkable claims about both his person and work. Jesus' teaching on the Spirit ("the Comforter") is more extensive than in any other Gospel (chaps. 14–16). This Gospel especially reveals the glory and the name of the Father and the Son.

Teachings about Humanity

Humans are sinners in need of a Savior. They are unable to do anything toward their salvation but are wholly dependent on God's initiative through Jesus. Many individuals demonstrate this: Nicodemus, the Samaritan woman, the man born blind.

Teachings about Salvation

This Gospel, more than the others, emphasizes strongly a personal relationship with Jesus that's built on faith in him and his sacrificial death. Faith in Jesus *is* salvation and eternal life. One such text is 10:27-28: "My sheep hear my voice, and I know them, and they follow me. And I give unto them eternal life." John balances between God's sovereign election of some for eternal life (6:44) and the invitation to "whosoever" (3:16).

CHRIST IN JOHN

In John, Jesus is the Logos, the Word of God who was with God and was God. Jesus is God in flesh. Jesus' deity is further amplified in his seven "I am" sayings (I am the bread of life; the light of the world; the door of the sheep; the good shepherd; the resurrection and the life; the way, the truth, and the life; the true vine).

GOD'S STORY

When the Events of This Book Happened
During Jesus' earthly ministry, AD 26–30

Although the prologue goes back to "in the beginning," the narrative of Jesus' life begins with John the Baptist's recognition of Jesus as the Lamb of God and concludes with Jesus' post-resurrection reinstatement of Peter by the Sea of Galilee. See **When the Events of This Book Happened** for **LUKE** for more information on the dates for Jesus' birth and crucifixion.

John's Gospel helps determine the development of Jesus' ministry (from his baptism to his death) by describing Jesus' trips to Jerusalem to participate in various Jewish festivals. The probable dates for these are as follows:

:13—Passover of the first temple cleansing	Spring AD 27
:1—Passover of the healing by the pool	Spring AD 28
:4—Passover just before the feeding of 5,000	Spring AD 29
2:1,12—Passover of the triumphal entry	Spring AD 30

Based on this understanding, Jesus ministered for three years plus the time between his baptism and the first temple cleansing.

How John Fits into God's "Story"

John tells "chapter 4"—the most important chapter—of God's story: God purchases redemption and begins the kingdom of God through Jesus Christ. See **How Matthew Fits into God's Story**.

Door to the Church of the Nativity, the traditional site of Jesus birth. "I am the door. If anyone enters by Me, he will be saved, and will come in and go out and find pasture" (John 10:9 HCSB).

ORIGINAL HISTORICAL SETTING

Author and Date of Writing
John the apostle, possibly around AD 80–90

As with all the Gospels, the book is anonymous. Early Christian tradition uniformly affirmed that John composed this Gospel. He was a fisherman from Galilee, son of Zebedee and brother of James, whom Jesus called to be an apostle (Mark 1:19; 3:17). According to Acts, John and Peter were the prominent leaders of early Christianity.

Many scholars of the past two centuries have denied that John wrote this book, partly because of their belief that the author fabricated many details, such as the miracles and the discourses of Jesus. Such invention is harder to explain if the account was written by an eyewitness of Jesus' life. The author, however, claimed to be an eyewitness (21:24) and referred to himself in the third person as "the disciple whom Jesus loved" (13:23; 19:26; 20:2; 21:7,20). The tradition of authorship by John is undoubtedly correct.

This Gospel was the last to be written, for it assumes knowledge of many events in Jesus' ministry (which are omitted). On the other hand, it offers much new material. The decade of the AD 80s is a good estimate for the composition of this Gospel.

First Audience and Destination
Probably Christians living in Roman Asia

This issue has been vigorously debated by scholars. According to strong and consistent Christian tradition, John lived a long life and ministered in Ephesus, the largest city in the Roman province of Asia. There is no good reason to doubt this original destination. Scholars, however, are divided as to whether the first audience was Greek, Jewish, or simply Christian. Those who see a Greek (non-Christian) audience note, among other things, that John began with emphasizing Jesus as the Logos, "the Word," a concept from Greek philosophy. The Jewish audience view emphasizes that John wanted people to believe Jesus was the Messiah (20:31). The similarities between this book and the letters of John, which were clearly written for believers, probably mean that this Gospel was first intended for the benefit of believers. In God's providence, it has become remarkably effective in impelling unbelievers to embrace Jesus as Lord and Savior.

Occasion

John did not relate the human factors that prompted him to write. It appears evident, however, that he was prompted to give a fuller account of some aspects of Jesus' ministry than the other Gospels related. This may have been prompted by John's advancing age and awareness that he had a unique perspective on Jesus' life to preserve.

THE PASSION WEEK IN JERUSALEM

Begun by Herod Agrippa I
(A.D. 41–44) and
completed later

Josephus' Third North Wall

Golgotha
(Gordon's Calvary)

Josephus' Second North Wall

Bezetha

Fish
Gate

Via Dolorosa

Sheep's Pool
(Pool of
Bethesda)

Antonia
Fortress

Sunday
*Jesus descends from
Bethany and enters
the temple precincts*

Sunday night
*Jesus returns to
Bethany to lodge
with His friends*

To Beth...
(see in...

Tuesday
*Jesus teaches
and disputes
with authorities*

Tyropoeon Valley

Friday morning
9. *Jesus is crucified*

Golgotha
(traditional
location)

Wilson's Arch
(bridge)

Tower's
Pool

Tower of
Hippicus

Monday
*Cleansing of
the temple*

Sheep
Gate

Gethsemane

Thursday night
3. *Jesus is
arrested*

Temple
Mount

Altar

Solomon's Portico
Shushan Gate
Beautiful Gate

Friday morning
8. *Jesus again
before Pilate*

Gennath
Gate
Josephus

Xystus

First N. Wall
Warren's
Gate

Barclay's Gate
Royal Portico

Temple

Huldah
Gates

Pinnacle of
Temple
(traditional
location)

Friday daybreak
5. *Jesus before
the Sanhedrin*

Friday daybreak
6. *Jesus before
Pilate*

Tower of
Phasael

Tower of
Mariamne

Herod
Antipas'
Palace

Valley
Gate

Robinson's
Arch
(stairs)

Thursday evening
2. *Jesus retires to
Gethsemane with
His disciples*

Praetorium
Herod's Palace

**Upper
City**

Theater

Thursday/Friday
4. *Jesus is taken to
the house of Caiaphas
for a preliminary
hearing*

Herod's
Family
Tomb(s)

Escarpment

House of
Caiaphas, the
High Priest

Friday morning
7. *Jesus before
Herod Antipas*

Ophel

Citadel

Gihon Spring

Hezekiah's
Tunnel

Serpent's
Pool

Essene Quarter

**Lower
City**

City of
David

Thursday
1. *Jesus shares the
Passover meal with
His disciples*

Upper Room
(traditional
location)

Siloam

Water
Gate

Essene Gate

Kidron Valley

Hinnom Valley

N

0   1/8   1/4 Mile
0   150   300 Meters

LEGEND

⊐⊏ Gate

▬ Tower

⸽⸽⸽⸽⸽ Wall

⬤ Possible locations
of the Chamber of
Hewn Stone

MOVEMENTS OF JESUS

⬅ Sunday

⬅ Monday

⬅ Thursday/Friday

⬅-- Jesus before the
Sanhedrin

265

LITERARY FEATURES

Genre and Literary Style
A Gospel composed in simple but elegant Koine *Greek*

See *Genre and Literary Style* for **MATTHEW** for information about what a Gospel is. John wrote with a limited vocabulary, joining his sentences with "and." His style lent itself to developing a number of contrasting concepts: love versus hate; light versus dark; life versus death; truth versus falsehood; above versus below.

Themes
Jesus as Lord and God, Jesus' signs, Jesus' "I am" teachings, Jesus' "hour"

John's emphases on Jesus' lordship and deity have already been noted. Yet this Gospel related far fewer of Jesus' miracles than did the others. John selected a limited number because of their sign value in pointing to Jesus' true identity. The "I am" teachings also point to Jesus' identity, in particular because of their connection with the earlier revelation of God as "I Am" (Exod. 3:14). In this Gospel, Jesus calls his appointment with death his "hour" (contrast 2:4; 7:30 with 13:1; 17:1).

Book Features and Structure
John wrote about many incidents missing from the other Gospels. These include a number of miracles (water to wine, the man born blind, Lazarus raised), a number of teachings (the "I am" sayings, the new birth discourse with Nicodemus, the upper room discourse); and other incidents (meeting the Samaritan woman, washing the disciples' feet). John tells nothing of Jesus' birth, baptism, temptation, casting out demons, telling of parables, or institution of the Lord's Supper.

Another feature that should be mentioned briefly is the manuscript history of John 7:53–8:11 (the adulterous woman story). Because the earliest and best handwritten copies of John omit these verses, some contemporary interpreters (and translations) have concluded that they are a later addition to the Gospel.

The organization of the book is straightforward. The main body is sandwiched between a formal prologue (chap.1) and epilogue (chap. 21). The first main section focuses on Jesus' signs and his conflicts with "the Jews" (chaps. 2–12). The second section describes Jesus' "glorification" as he is crucified and accomplishes the purpose for which God sent him into the world (chaps. 13–20).

ACTS

THE ACTS OF THE APOSTLES

This title has always been associated with this book. It refers to the deeds Jesus' apostles did in the thirty or so years following his return to heaven.

▶ *Key Text: 1:8*

"But ye shall receive power, after that the Holy Ghost is come upon you: and ye shall be witnesses unto me both in Jerusalem, and in all Judaea, and in Samaria, and unto the uttermost part of the earth."

▶ *Key Term: "Spirit"*

This book records what the apostles and early Christians accomplished as they were empowered by the Holy Spirit. The author understood that none of this would have been possible apart from the Holy Spirit.

▶ *One-Sentence Summary*

Christianity spread from Jerusalem to Rome and from Jews to Gentiles by the power of the Holy Spirit, working especially through Peter and Paul.

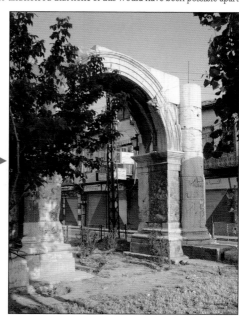

Roman arch at the "Street called Straight," the street where Saul of Tarsus stayed for three days following his conversion on the road to Damascus (Acts 9:1-19).

GOD'S MESSAGE IN THE BOOK

Purpose

The author's purpose was twofold. First, he wrote as a historian, penning "volume 2" of his two-part work. The first part told what Jesus "began both to do and to teach" (Acts 1:1); the second part is a selective record of what Jesus continued to do through his Spirit and his apostles. The second part of his purpose was theological. He showed that Christianity and the church had become the legitimate heir of Israel (and of the Scriptures of Israel). This is seen especially in the biblical quotations in the book, for example "this is that" in Peter's citation of Joel (Acts 2:16-21), James's quotation of Amos (Acts 15:16-17), and Paul's reference to Isaiah (Acts 28:25-28).

Christian Worldview Elements

Acts offers insight into a number of worldview categories. In particular the categories of *sovereignty and providence, community and church,* and *discipleship* are pushed to the forefront. Without the contribution of Acts, there would be little biblical basis for understanding the historical origins of the church as the new people of God.

GOD
CREATION
▶ **SOVEREIGNTY AND PROVIDENCE**
FAITH AND REASON
REVELATION AND AUTHORITY
HUMANITY
REBELLION AND SIN
COVENANT AND REDEMPTION
▶ **COMMUNITY AND CHURCH**
▶ **DISCIPLESHIP**
ETHICS AND MORALITY
TIME AND ETERNITY

Teachings about God

The Father is in particular the Sender of the Holy Spirit. The book shows that from the beginning of Christianity Jesus has been the center of proclamation. His life, death, and resurrection were the essence of the good news. Above all, however, this book reveals the Holy Spirit more extensively than any other book. The age of Christianity is the era in which all that believe receive the gift of the Spirit.

Teachings about Humanity

Particularly by tracing the spread of Christianity from Jews to Samaritans and then to Gentiles, this book shows that all kinds of people are included in salvation. A Pharisee that persecuted Jesus' followers, an African official, a Roman centurion, and a slave girl in Philippi were all touched by the power of Jesus. On the other hand, some leading authorities (both Jewish and Gentile) rejected the proclamation about Jesus.

Teachings about Salvation

Over and over in this book, the basic Christian message is presented: Jesus fulfilled the prophecies of Scripture by his deeds and life; he was crucified; God raised him; the necessary human response is to repent of sins and believe in him; those who do so receive God's good gift of the Spirit. Salvation in Acts focuses on the Spirit's filling believers so that they live holy lives and do God's will.

CHRIST IN ACTS

Jesus, triumphant over death, spends forty days in conversation with his disciples. He then ascends to the Father and sends, ten days later, the Holy Spirit to indwell and empower believers. Acts is an account of what Jesus continued to do through his church in the wisdom and power of the Holy Spirit.

GOD'S STORY

When the Events of This Book Happened
During the church's first decades, AD 30–61

The crucifixion and resurrection of Jesus occurred in AD 30 (see ***When the Events of This Book Happened*** for **LUKE**). The last event recorded is Paul's two-year imprisonment in Rome while he was waiting for his case to come before the emperor. This imprisonment occurred about 60–61. The approximate years of key events in Acts are as follows: AD 33, death of Stephen and conversion of Saul (chaps. 7–8); AD 49, council in Jerusalem concerning circumcision (chap. 15); AD 57, Paul's arrest in Jerusalem on a false charge (chaps. 21–22).

How Acts Fits into God's "Story"

Acts begins "chapter five" of God's story: God spreads the kingdom through the church. It is the exciting record of the spread of God's kingdom during the transition from Israel to the church. The book opens with Jesus' explanation of the kingdom of God (1:3) and closes with Paul's "preaching the kingdom of God" (28:31). Peter discharged the responsibility Jesus entrusted to him in giving him the "keys of the kingdom" (Matt. 16:19). He was the human instrument through whom the Holy Spirit was poured out on three successive ethnic groups: Jews (chap. 2); Samaritans (chap. 8); and Gentiles (chap. 10). The time had come when no longer could sinners express obedient faith (and citizenship in God's kingdom) by animal sacrifices and participation in Israel, as they had during the Old Testament era (Matt. 21:43). Now they expressed faith (and belonging to God's kingdom) by believing in Jesus and participating in the church.

ORIGINAL HISTORICAL SETTING

Author and Date of Writing
Luke, perhaps around AD 61–62

Like the Gospel according to Luke, this book is anonymous. On the other hand, unifor[m] Christian tradition affirms that Luke wrote both. The evidence for Lukan authorship with[in] the book is found in three "We Sections" in which "we" and "us" occurs (16:10-1[7]; 20:5–21:18; 27:1–28:16). At these times the writer was an eyewitness of Paul's minist[ry] (from Troas to Philippi on Paul's first journey, from Philippi to Jerusalem on the third journe[y] and from Caesarea to Rome). By a process of deduction, all the associates of Paul except f[or] Luke can be eliminated. If Luke was the author of the "We Sections," then by extension h[e] wrote the rest of Acts (since the Greek style and vocabulary is noticeably the same). By fu[r]ther extension, Luke must also be the author of the third Gospel. See *Author and Date [of] Writing* for **LUKE** for more information.

Determining the date for Acts depends on what to make of the end of the book. From Ac[ts] 25:11 the primary historical question raised by the book is, What happened to Paul when h[e] appeared before Caesar? Yet Acts does not tell. Many Bible students are persuaded that, in h[is] desire to publish, Luke was unwilling to wait on the outcome of Paul's case. He went ahea[d] with publication at the end of Paul's two-year detention described in 28:30. If this is true, Ac[ts] is to be dated at 61 or 62. Other scholars, particularly those that reject the traditional under[-]standing of authorship, date the book in the 80s. (The influential nineteenth-century radic[al] critic F. C. Baur believed Acts was written in the second century as an imaginative fiction.)

First Audience and Destination
Theophilus, a Gentile whose residence is unknown

Both Luke and Acts were written for Theophilus. See *First Audience and Destination* f[or] **LUKE**.

Occasion

The needs of Theophilus and perhaps his ongoing financial patronage provided the immedia[te] occasion for Acts. If Luke began researching Acts while Paul was detained in Caesarea (se[e] *Occasion* for **LUKE**), then he had direct access to Philip, who was an eyewitness of mo[st] of the events for chapters 1–12 (21:8; 23:33; 24:27). Luke also had direct access to Paul, th[e] central character for chapters 13–28, and was himself an eyewitness of some of the events h[e] recorded.

EXPANSION OF THE EARLY CHURCH IN PALESTINE

LEGEND
- City
- ▲ Mountain peak
- ← Philip's routes
- ← Peter and John's routes
- ◄- Peter's routes

Ptolemais (Acco)
LOWER GALILEE
Capernaum
GAULANITIS
Jotapata
Sea of Galilee
Mt. Carmel
Sepphoris
Esdraelon Valley
Nazareth
▲ Mt. Tabor
Yarmuk R.

4. Peter meets with Cornelius

Caesarea Maritima
SAMARIA
Scythopolis (Beth-shan)
Pella
DECAPOLIS

1. Philip preaches throughout Samaria

4. Philip settles in Caesarea Maritima

Sebaste (Samaria)
Mt. Ebal
Sychar
Neapolis (Shechem)
Mt. Gerizim

3. Peter raises Tabitha (Dorcas) to life

Apollonia
Antipatris (Aphek)
Lebonah

1. Peter and John are sent to investigate claims that Samaritans are receiving the gospel preached by Philip

MEDITERRANEAN SEA

Joppa
Yarkon R.
2. Peter heals Aeneas, a paralytic
Lydda
Gophna
PEREA

Peter and John are arrested

3. Philip preaches in Azotus

Jamnia
Emmaus
Jericho
Mt. Nebo ▲

Azotus (Ashdod)
JUDEA
Bethlehem
Jerusalem
Judean Wilderness
Qumran

Ascalon (Ashkelon)
Betogabris (Beth-guvrin)
Marisa (Mareshah)
Stephen is stoned to death

Anthedon
Neapolis
Hebron
DEAD SEA

2. Philip baptizes an Ethiopian official and explains the words of Isaiah
Gaza

En-gedi

IDUMEA
Masada

Beersheba

NABATEA

N. Besor
Arnon R.

0   10   20 Miles
0   10   20 Kilometers
35 E

271

LITERARY FEATURES

Genre and Literary Style
A historical narrative written in excellent Koine *Greek*

The overall genre of Acts is "historical narrative." In this sense Acts parallels other works from antiquity, especially those also known as "Acts." Luke's work (like his Gospel) was not simply a recounting of facts but a careful theological interpretation. He included summaries of important early Christian speeches, giving samples of a variety of speakers (Peter, Stephen, Paul), audiences (Jewish, Greek, Christian), and circumstances (friendly, hostile). Luke used a large vocabulary and carefully polished Greek style.

Themes
Lordship of Jesus in building the church, activity of the Spirit, Peter and Paul

Jesus, who sent out the apostles, closed doors and opened new ones, always as "Lord of the harvest" sending out people to spread the gospel. The Spirit's work in filling Jesus' followers is a prominent theme. The two central characters are Peter (1–12) and Paul (13–28), entrusted with different responsibilities but equally empowered and equally obedient to their specific commissions from Jesus.

Book Features and Structure

In the Christian canon Acts fills a pivotal role. As "volume 2" of a two-part work, it looks back to the life of Jesus. By virtue of its description of Paul's conversion and ministry, it provides historical context for understanding Paul's letters. Without Acts there would be no firm basis for understanding the origins of Christianity.

The ***Key Text***, Acts 1:8, provides a useful way of organizing the book. The apostles proclaim Jesus in Jerusalem (chaps. 1–7); the apostles proclaim Jesus in Judea and Samaria (chaps. 8–10); the apostles go "unto the uttermost" (chaps. 11–28).

ROMANS

THE EPISTLE TO THE ROMANS

As with all the New Testament letters written by Paul the apostle, this epistle is titled according to its first recipients, in this case the Christians in Rome.

▶ *Key Text: 1:16-17*

"For I am not ashamed of the gospel of Christ: for it is the power of God unto salvation to every one that believeth; to the Jew first, and also to the Greek. For therein is the righteousness of God revealed from faith to faith: as it is written, The just shall live by faith."

▶ *Key Term: "Righteousness"*

The Greek noun translated "righteousness" is *dikaiosune*. It is closely related to the verb *dikaioo*, usually translated "justify." This book is a long theological argument about how unrighteous sinners may receive right standing with God (are justified).

▶ *One-Sentence Summary*

Righteousness with God is given freely (imputed) to all those who have faith in Jesus Christ for salvation according to God's eternal plan.

▼ Circus Maximus in Rome (Rom. 1:15).

GOD'S MESSAGE IN THE BOOK

Purpose

Paul wrote to the Roman Christians in order to give them a substantial resume of his theology. This epistle stands as Paul's theological self-confession. Behind this was his concern to prepare the Roman believers for his intended ministry there and to create interest in the preaching mission to Spain that he planned.

Christian Worldview Elements

As the greatest doctrinal presentation of salvation in the Bible, Romans touches on almost every element of a Christian worldview. Among the most prominent are *God, rebellion and sin, covenant and redemption, community and church,* and *ethics and morality.*

> **GOD**
> CREATION
> SOVEREIGNTY AND PROVIDENCE
> FAITH AND REASON
> REVELATION AND AUTHORITY
> HUMANITY
> **REBELLION AND SIN**
> **COVENANT AND REDEMPTION**
> **COMMUNITY AND CHURCH**
> DISCIPLESHIP
> **ETHICS AND MORALITY**
> TIME AND ETERNITY

Teachings about God

Above all, in Romans God is supreme in all matters of salvation, which serves his glory and the good of his people. He is both "just, and the justifier" (3:26). There is no fuller presentation of the person and work of Christ. The Holy Spirit is the One by whose indwelling believers are enabled to live holy lives (chap. 8).

Teachings about Humanity

There are only two kinds of human beings: sinners who are condemned "in Adam" and believing sinners "in Christ" who are therefore declared righteous. Those who have been justified by faith are expected to live holy personal lives and to live in Christian community with each other by the power of the Spirit.

Teachings about Salvation

Salvation is a complex concept that includes past, present, and future. For individual believers, Christ has saved from the penalty of sin (justification, chaps. 4–5); he is saving from the power of sin (sanctification, chaps. 6–7); and he will save from the presence of sin (glorification, chap. 8). For the community of believers, salvation came first to Israel (chaps. 9–10), and in the present era, it is coming to Gentiles (and some Jews) who make up the church (chap. 11).

CHRIST IN ROMANS

In this letter to the Romans, Paul presents Christ as "a descendent of David according to the flesh and was established as the powerful Son of God by the resurrection from the dead" (1:3-4 HCSB). Through Jesus' death we are reconciled to God and by his life we are saved (5:10).

GOD'S STORY

When the Events of This Book Happened
About AD 57

The historical events recorded in this book concern Paul's personal situation and travel plans. Romans fits the period near the end of Paul's third missionary journey, when he was anticipating traveling to Rome once he had finished accompanying the "love offering" from the Gentile churches to the Jerusalem church.

How Romans Fits into God's "Story"

Romans is part of "chapter 5" of God's story: God spreads the kingdom through the church. It explains how Jesus, the greatest descendant of Abraham and David (who are illustrations in this book), is also the One by whose death sinners may be justified—and so become part of God's kingdom. The "parable of the olive tree" (chap. 11) shows that God's kingdom plan includes both Jews and Gentiles, but especially Gentiles in the present age. The only specific mention of the kingdom in Romans notes its spiritual rather than its material nature (14:17).

"For if you were cut off from your native wild olive, and against nature were grafted into a cultivated olive tree, how much more will these—the natural branches—be grafted into their own olive tree?" Rom. 11:24 HCSB).

275

ORIGINAL HISTORICAL SETTING

Author and Date of Writing
Paul the apostle, about AD 57

This book claims to be written by "Paul, a servant of Jesus Christ." All New Testament scholars accept this claim. He was a devout Pharisee converted to faith in Jesus and called to become apostle to the Gentiles on the famous "Road to Damascus" (Acts 9). Paul's ministry may be divided into three parts:

- The period of personal growth in discipleship, about AD 33–47 (Acts 9–12)
- The period of three missionary journeys, about AD 48–57 (Acts 13–21)
- The period of consolidating the churches, about AD 58–65 (Acts 22–28)

Romans was written near the end of Paul's third missionary journey, which culminated in his arrest in Jerusalem.

First Audience and Destination
Christians worshipping in house churches in Rome

Little is known about how Christianity first arrived in Rome. No biblical evidence supports the tradition that Peter was the first to preach the gospel in Rome. The gospel may have been taken there by Jews from Rome who believed in Jesus on Pentecost (Acts 2:10). It was already present in AD 49, when the Emperor Claudius expelled Jews from the city, among whom were the Christian couple Priscilla and Aquila (Acts 18:2).

By the time Paul wrote Romans, the majority of believers there were probably Gentile. Paul knew a number of Roman Christians by name (chap. 16), and his greeting pattern indicates that they met in house churches scattered throughout the city (16:5; vv. 14 and 15 probably each reflect a house church group).

The city of Rome was a splendid if corrupt monument to centuries of Roman military success. It may have had a million people, half of them slaves. Rome was the economic and political center of the world. Truly all roads led to Rome.

Occasion

Paul had never preached in Rome, and he had long desired this privilege. He had finished his great endeavor of the third missionary journey, the collection for the saints in Jerusalem (see **Occasion** for **2 CORINTHIANS**). He was at this time spending the winter in Corinth (AD 56–57), for the Mediterranean Sea was unsafe for travel for three months (Acts 20:3). Paul's mind was now turning to Rome (where he wanted to preach and to encourage the Roman Christians) and to Spain. With "time on his hands" in Corinth, he penned this letter to the Roman Christians in order to introduce himself and his theology. He was aided by Tertius the scribe (16:22).

PAUL'S VOYAGE TO ROME
Acts 27:1–28:31

Rome

Paul spends two years preaching the gospel as he awaits his appeal to Nero

Taverns
of Applus
Puteoli
Pompeii

ADRIATIC
SEA
Brundisium

ITALIA

Tarentum

TYRRHENIAN
SEA

Messana
Rhegium

Sicily
Syracuse

Minor

Malta

Ship lost in storm

Ship smashes
into reef and
all aboard
swim to shore

MACEDONIA

THRACE

BLACK SEA

Sinope

Amphipolis
Neapolis
Berea
Thessalonica

Byzantium
(Istanbul)

Heraclea

BITHYNIA
AND PONTUS

Ancyra
(Ankara)

GALATIA

Tavium

Parnassus

Larissa

Adramyttium

ASIA

Ancyra

Sebaste

Delphi

Pergamum

Tripolis

CAPPADO

Archelais

Olympia

ACHAIA

Athens

Ephesus

Cirenna

Seleucia

PHRYGIA

Tarsus

CILICIA

Sparta

Cyclades
Islands

Cnidus

Rhodes

LYCIA

PAMPHYLIA

Myra

Change to a
larger grain ship

Phoenix
Cauda
Fair
Havens

Salmone
Lasea

Crete

Cyprus

MEDITERRANEAN SEA

Cyrene

Syrtis Major

CYRENAICA

Alexandria

EGYPT

Memphis

Porcius Festus sends Paul to
Rome to appeal to Caesar

Caesarea Maritima
Antipatris

JUDEA

Sid

Jer

LEGEND

- • City
- Etesian winds
- ← Paul's routes
- —— Appian Way

0   100   200   300 Miles
0   100   200   300 Kilometers

LITERARY FEATURES

Genre and Literary Style
A long, formal epistle written in Koine *Greek*

See *Genre and Literary Style* for **1 THESSALONIANS** for information about the genre "epistle." All four standard parts of a first-century epistle appear in Romans: salutation (1:1-7), thanksgiving (1:8-17), main body (1:18–16:18), farewell (16:19-24). Some scholars designate Romans as a tractate (a formal treatise rather than a pastoral letter). Paul's Greek is careful, and Romans reflects Paul at his most typical writing style.

Themes
Righteousness, law, sin, justification, sanctification

Romans is rightly called "the Mount Everest of Christian theology." The themes listed, of course, are all doctrinal. Because the Reformation of the sixteenth century was driven by recovery of the doctrines of Romans, a few words are in order. There is an ongoing scholarly debate about the precise meaning of "righteousness of God" in Romans. Luther and the Reformers argued for an "objective genitive" view—"rightness with God." (Others before and since have argued for a "subjective genitive" interpretation—God's own personal rightness.) Luther and the Reformers also argued vigorously that justification is imputed (reckoned, a legal action) to sinners as opposed to the Roman Catholic view that it is imparted (infused) to sinners. Since the 1970s Paul's understanding of the law has been an object of intense scrutiny, with some scholars arguing that Paul rejected the Mosaic law as a way of life for Gentiles but not for Jews.

Book Features and Structure

Romans is the longest of Paul's letters, and it has always had "pride of place" in the Pauline collection. It stands as the most comprehensive statement of the gospel in all the Bible. His passion for his subject led him to emotional outbursts, especially the famous, "God forbid!" In developing his argument he often (1) appealed to Scripture, and (2) argued with an imagined opponent (called a "diatribe"), using phrases such as "O man" (2:1; 9:20).

Like so many of Paul's epistles, the body of the letter has two parts. The first section may be called "God's provision of righteousness" (chaps. 1–11); the second may be called "the saint's fruit of righteousness" (chaps. 12–16).

278

1 CORINTHIANS

THE FIRST EPISTLE TO THE CORINTHIANS

This book is so named because it is the first canonical letter that Paul the apostle wrote to the Christians in Corinth.

Key Text: 15:58

"Therefore, my beloved brethren, be ye stedfast, unmoveable, always abounding in the work of the Lord, forasmuch as ye know that your labour is not in vain in the Lord."

Key Term: "Charity" [Love]

Although this letter reflects a church facing many difficult issues, the solution always involves love ("charity" in the KJV; *agape* in Greek). The "Love Chapter" (13) is the best known and most beloved part of the letter.

One-Sentence Summary

The many problems a congregation may have, whether doctrinal or practical, will be resolved as that church submits properly to the lordship of Christ and learns to love one another genuinely.

Looking through a gate into the ancient city of Corinth.

GOD'S MESSAGE IN THE BOOK

Purpose

Paul wrote to the Corinthian Christians in order to address the difficulties they were facing (see **Occasion** below). His desire, of course, was for the church to change where it needed to change and to be encouraged where it was doing the right things.

Christian Worldview Elements

First Corinthians deals particularly with the three worldview categories of *community and church; discipleship;* and *ethics and morality.* No Bible book more fully develops the interrelationship among these three categories.

GOD
CREATION
SOVEREIGNTY AND PROVIDENCE
FAITH AND REASON
REVELATION AND AUTHORITY
HUMANITY
REBELLION AND SIN
COVENANT AND REDEMPTION
► **COMMUNITY AND CHURCH**
► **DISCIPLESHIP**
► **ETHICS AND MORALITY**
TIME AND ETERNITY

Teachings about God

God the Father is the supreme Lord, for whose glory all things are to be done (10:31). The theological centrality of Jesus' bodily resurrection is developed in the sustained argument of the "Resurrection chapter" (15). His lordship over the church means that he has the right to order its life and worship. The Spirit's life-giving presence has brought the church into existence, given each of its members spiritual gifts, and enables its members to live *holy* lives because he is the *Holy* Spirit.

Teachings about Humanity

Humanity in this book is seen mainly within the context of Christian community. Redeemed people have been transformed by Christ, are called and enabled to love one another, and are destined for resurrection. Such persons, however, still struggle with sins such as divisiveness, sexual immorality, and disorder in worship.

Teachings about Salvation

This letter contains what may be the first-composed written summary of the New Testament understanding of redemption: "For I delivered unto you first of all that which I also received, how that Christ died for our sins according to the scriptures" (15:3). Further, this book emphasizes that God saves only those individuals who believe in Christ's death (1:21).

CHRIST IN 1 CORINTHIANS

To a church fascinated by wisdom and power, Paul declares Christ to be both the power (1:18,24) and the wisdom (1:21,24,30) of God.

GOD'S STORY

When the Events of This Book Happened
From AD 50 to 55

Paul reached Corinth in AD 50 as part of his second missionary journey. After preaching in Macedonian cities (Philippi, Thessalonica, and Berea), he traveled south to Athens and then arrived in Corinth (Acts 17–18). He stayed for more than a year in Corinth, capital of Achaia. The date of Paul's ministry in Corinth is fixed by the reference in Acts 18:12 to Gallio as the proconsul (KJV "deputy") of Achaia, known from an inscription to have governed in Corinth in 51–52. Paul wrote 1 Corinthians some five years after he had first preached there (see **Author and Date of Writing** below).

How 1 Corinthians Fits into God's "Story"

First Corinthians is part of "chapter 5" of God's story: God spreads the kingdom through the church. This epistle shows that proclaiming the kingdom of God did not end with Jesus but continued as a major theme of the apostles. In 1 Corinthians, Paul mentioned the kingdom five times (4:20; 6:9-10; 15:24,50). The kingdom is a powerful present reality, yet its glorious future lies after "flesh and blood" have been laid aside at the resurrection. Paul explicitly thought of the kingdom in moral terms. There is no place in the kingdom for those who practice immorality in this life.

ORIGINAL HISTORICAL SETTING

Author and Date of Writing
Paul the apostle, about AD 55

This book claims to be written by "Paul, called to be an apostle of Jesus Christ through the will of God." All New Testament scholars accept this claim. See **Author and Date of Writing** for **ROMANS** for more information about Paul. The apostle wrote this letter around AD 55, probably near the end of his long ministry in Ephesus on his third missionary journey (Acts 19).

First Audience and Destination
Christians in Corinth

Acts 18 describes how Christianity first came to Corinth through Paul's preaching. Silas, Timothy, Priscilla, Aquila, and Apollos also helped establish the church in Corinth. The members had come from both Jewish and pagan backgrounds.

Corinth was a large and splendid commercial city, with Greek roots and a Roman overlay in the first century. Its population was perhaps 500,000. Because of its location at the Corinthian isthmus, it benefited from both land and sea routes. Corinth, rather than Athens, was chosen as the Roman capital of Achaia. Like all large cities of the Roman Empire, Corinth was both very religious (with a number of pagan temples) and very immoral (with the worship of Aphrodite sanctioning religious prostitution).

Occasion

Paul's ministry in Corinth had resulted in a well-established, thriving congregation. He had moved on from there and now was living in Ephesus. Several factors converged to make this letter necessary.

1. Paul had written a (now lost) letter advising the believers not to associate with people claiming to be Christians but living immorally. The church misunderstood Paul's meaning (5:9-11).

2. Paul had received an oral report from "the house of Chloe" that the church had divided into several competing factions (1:11-12).

3. Paul had learned that the church was tolerating open sexual immorality (5:1).

4. Paul had received a "committee" (composed of Stephanas, Fortunatus, and Achaicus) sent by the Corinthians. They brought him more information about the church and had a list of written questions for Paul to respond to (7:1; 16:17).

Paul therefore wrote this letter to respond to this great variety of issues. He apparently used the professional secretarial help of Sosthenes and sent the letter by Timothy (1:1; 4:17).

Mars Hill in Athens, a place where Greek intellectuals gathered for discussions and debate. Paul preached there just before going to Corinth. Later he wrote the Corinthians, "Where is the philosopher? Where is the scholar? Where is the debater of this age? Hasn't God made the world's wisdom foolish?" (1 Cor. 1:20 HCSB).

LITERARY FEATURES

Genre and Literary Style
A long epistle written in Koine *Greek*

See ***Genre and Literary Style*** for **1 THESSALONIANS** for information about the genre "epistle." The four standard parts of a first-century epistle all appear in 1 Corinthians salutation (1:1-3), thanksgiving (1:4-9), main body (1:10–16:18), farewell (16:19-21). Like most of Paul's writings, this is a pastoral letter, driven by the occasion and needs of the recipients, rather than a tractate (a formal treatise). Paul's Greek is careful, and 1 Corinthians reflects the typical Pauline writing style.

Themes
Christian unity, morality, women's roles, spiritual gifts, the resurrection

The variety of themes (and more could be mentioned) is imposed by the occasion of the epistle. Recently the issues of women's roles and spiritual gifts have been of great interest in evangelical Christianity, showing the abiding value of this book. Concerning women, Paul affirmed the value of women who prayed or prophesied in worship (11:2-16) yet limited women's leadership (14:33-38). Concerning spiritual gifts, Paul distinguished between spiritual gifts (sovereignly given by the Spirit to believers at the new birth) and natural talents. (The gift of "tongues" in Corinth was to be strictly regulated, but Paul's basic command was to "forbid not," 14:39.)

Book Features and Structure

The most noteworthy literary feature of this book is Paul's use of the words "now concerning." Most scholars believe that he used this device to move through the list of questions brought to him by the committee (16:17). These items were as follows, with the verse containing "now concerning" indicated: male and female in marriage (7:1), virgins (7:25), food offered to idols (8:1), spiritual gifts (12:1), the collection for the saints in Jerusalem (16:1), Apollos (16:12).

The body of the letter is best seen containing three answers. First, Paul answered the matter of divisions in the church (received orally from Chloe's people), 1–4. Second, Paul dealt with immorality (received in an oral report), 5–6. Third, he answered the church's list of questions (brought in writing by the committee), 7–16.

2 CORINTHIANS

THE SECOND EPISTLE TO THE CORINTHIANS

his book is so named because it is the second canonical letter that Paul the apostle wrote to he Christians in Corinth.

Key Text: 12:9

"And he said unto me, 'My grace is sufficient for thee: for my strength is made perfect n weakness.' Most gladly therefore will I rather glory in my infirmities, that the power f Christ may rest upon me."

Key Term: "Defense"

Of all Paul's letters, this is the most personal—and the most defensive. In it Paul mounted a efense ("apology" in the good sense) of his apostolic authority and ministry.

One-Sentence Summary

rue Christian ministry, though it may have to be efended against false ttacks, is commissioned y Christ and empowered y his Spirit.

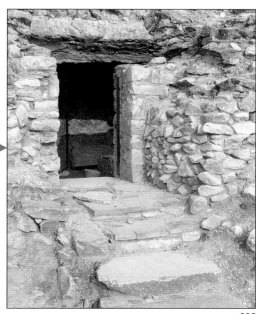

aul was imprisoned
many times (2 Cor. 11:23).
Here is the traditional
rison in Philippi where
aul and Silas were held
ntil God freed them by
means of the earthquake.

285

GOD'S MESSAGE IN THE BOOK

Purpose

Paul wrote to the Corinthian Christians in order to express his relief at the success of his sever letter and the mission of Titus, to ask for money for the poor saints in Jerusalem, and to defen his ministry as an apostle to the minority of unrepentant Corinthians (see **Occasion** below His desire, of course, was to encourage the majority and to lead the minority to change its min

Christian Worldview Elements

Second Corinthians focuses attention on the worldview categories of *revelation and authority, community and church,* and *ethics and morality.* Of all Paul's letters, this one deals the most extensively with the matter of authority as it relates to a local church, an ongoing important issue.

GOD
CREATION
SOVEREIGNTY AND PROVIDENCE
FAITH AND REASON
► **REVELATION AND AUTHORITY**
HUMANITY
REBELLION AND SIN
COVENANT AND REDEMPTION
► **COMMUNITY AND CHURCH**
DISCIPLESHIP
► **ETHICS AND MORALITY**
TIME AND ETERNITY

Teachings about God

God is the Father of Jesus Christ (1:3; 11:31) who sovereignly sent him as the great "unspeakable gift" (9:15). Jesus is the source of all comfort for his people. By his death and resurrection, Jesus is Lord the new creation (5:14-17). The life-giving Spirit has come as the "earnest" or deposit, gua anteeing the believer's future (5:5). "Where the Spirit of the Lord *is*, there *is* liberty" (3:17)

Teachings about Humanity

There were two kinds of people in the Corinthian church: those who submitted to genuin apostolic authority and those who did not. Paul sent blistering criticism on the latter (chap. 10–11). This book contains the most extensive teaching in Scripture about the status redeemed humans between the death of the body and the resurrection. This is referred to the "intermediate state," when persons are "with the Lord" in conscious bliss while waitin for the consummation (5:1-8).

Teachings about Salvation

This letter contains Paul's most extensive discussion on the contrast between the "o covenant" and the "new covenant" (chap. 3). Although salvation was real in the Mosaic er it came with fading glory, for the old covenant was meant to be temporary. The new covena arrived with Jesus Christ, and its glory can never be surpassed. The benefit to the believer the new covenant era is incomparable (3:18).

CHRIST IN 2 CORINTHIANS

Jesus Christ, God's Son, is not an ambiguous, fickle word from God, not "yes and no" but "yes." Conformity to Christ's image is the goal of the Christian life. Christ, working through the Spirit, brings this about.

GOD'S STORY

When the Events of This Book Happened
From AD 50 to 56

See **When the Events of This Book Happened** for **1 CORINTHIANS**. Paul wrote 2 Corinthians some six years after he had first preached there (see **Author and Date of Writing** on next page).

How 2 Corinthians Fits into God's "Story"

Second Corinthians is part of "chapter 5" of God's story: God spreads the kingdom through the church. This book emphasizes the spiritual nature of what God is doing in spreading the kingdom of God. Paul rejected material or merely human resources (such as clever arguments). The Spirit of the Lord was accomplishing everything important. Thus, Paul could boast about his own human weakness and argue that "the weapons of our warfare *are* not carnal, but mighty through God to the pulling down of strong holds" (10:4). Ultimately, in God's kingdom the invisible and eternal will triumph over what is visible and temporary (4:16-18).

▼ The *bema*, or judgment seat, at Corinth. This is probably the place Paul was brought before Gallio the proconsul (Acts 18:12-17).

ORIGINAL HISTORICAL SETTING

Author and Date of Writing
Paul the apostle, about AD 56

This book claims to be written by "Paul, an apostle of Jesus Christ by the will of God." All biblical scholars accept this claim. See **Author and Date of Writing** for **ROMANS** for more information about Paul. The apostle wrote this letter around AD 56, after he had concluded his ministry in Ephesus on his third missionary journey and had arrived in Macedonia (Acts 20:1-2; 2 Cor. 7:5-7).

First Audience and Destination
The Christians in Corinth

See **First Audience and Destination** for **1 CORINTHIANS**.

Occasion
See **Occasion** for **1 CORINTHIANS**. Careful study of 2 Corinthians has resulted in the following understanding of the events that led to its composition.

1. First Corinthians was not well received by the congregation. Timothy evidently returned to Paul in Ephesus with a report that the church was still greatly troubled. This was partly caused by the arrival in Corinth of "false apostles" (11:13-15). (These were evidently Jewish Christians who emphasized sophisticated rhetoric, perhaps also they were Judaizers, asking the Corinthians to live according to Mosaic regulations.)

2. Paul visited Corinth, which he described as sorrowful or with "heaviness" (2:1;13:2-3). Evidently the "false apostles" led the Corinthians to disown Paul.

3. Paul then wrote a (now lost) "severe letter" of stinging rebuke to Corinth from Ephesus. He sent this letter by Titus (2:3-4). Sometime shortly after this, Paul left Ephesus and traveled on, first to Troas and then to Macedonia (2:12-13).

4. Titus finally tracked Paul down in Macedonia with good news. Most of the church had repented and returned to the gospel and accepted Paul's authority (7:5-7).

Paul decided to write the Corinthians one more time, his fourth known letter to them, expressing his relief but still pleading with the unrepentant minority. He apparently used the professional secretarial help of Timothy and sent the letter by Titus (1:1; 8:17).

First-century street in Corinth.

LITERARY FEATURES

Genre and Literary Style
A long epistle written in Koine *Greek*

See **Genre and Literary Style** for **1 THESSALONIANS** for information about the genre "epistle." The standard parts of a first-century epistle appear in Corinthians, except that the thanksgiving is missing: salutation (1:1-2), main body (1:3–13:10), farewell (13:11-14). Like most of Paul's writings, this is a pastoral letter, driven by the occasion and needs of the recipients, rather than a tractate (a formal treatise).

Second Corinthians 2:14–7:4 is often referred to as "The Great Digression" because it could be removed without upsetting the narrative of Paul's travels. (This "digression" presents important doctrinal material found here only in Paul's writings.) Paul's Greek is typical but in this letter given to passionate outbursts and irony.

Themes
Apostolic authority, new covenant, intermediate state, sacrificial giving

The variety of themes is driven by the occasion of the epistle. The first three of these have already been mentioned. The matter of sacrificial giving is the focus of chapters 8–9, the most extensive teaching in the New Testament on Christian stewardship. Paul asked the churches he had founded to send a large, generous offering to the poor believers of Jerusalem. This occupied much of his energy during the last part of his third missionary journey. He mentioned it in his three longest epistles (Rom. 15:28,31; 1 Cor. 16:1-4; 2 Cor. 8–9).

Book Features and Structure
The most noteworthy literary feature of this book is the distinct change in tone and subject matter between chapters 1–9 and 10–13. The first section is generally warm and friendly, while the last section is noticeably harsh. Many critical scholars have concluded that chapters 10–13 were originally the "Severe Letter" Paul wrote after 1 Corinthians but before 2 Corinthians 1–9 (see **Occasion** above). Because no Greek manuscript supports this separation, it is best to affirm the original unity of 2 Corinthians. The differences in tone may be accounted for by judging that Paul wrote the last section to an unrepentant minority of Corinthians.

The body of the letter has three major sections. First, Paul discussed his itinerary as an apostle (including "The Great Digression" on doctrine), 1–7. Second, Paul appealed for generous giving, 8–9. Third, he defended his ministry against the false apostles, 10–13.

GALATIANS

THE EPISTLE TO THE GALATIANS

As with all the New Testament letters written by Paul, this epistle is titled according to its first recipients, in this case Christians in the Roman province of Galatia.

Key Text: 2:16

"Knowing that a man is not justified by the works of the law, but by the faith of Jesus Christ, even we have believed in Jesus Christ, that we might be justified by the faith of Christ, and not by the works of the law: for by the works of the law shall no flesh be justified."

Key Term: "Faith"

"Faith alone" is the heartbeat of this book. Paul's insistence that no human work can contribute to a person's right standing with God makes this book critical for all those who cherish the doctrine of salvation as a gift of God's grace.

One-Sentence Summary

Sinners are justified (and live out a godly life) by trusting in Jesus Christ alone, not by keeping the law or by counting on good works.

Manumission inscriptions at Delphi. What this did for literal slaves, Christ has done for those who were slaves to sin and legalism. "Christ has liberated us into freedom. Therefore stand firm and don't submit again to the yoke of slavery" (Gal. 5:1 HCSB). Galatians is the Christian's manumission document.

GOD'S MESSAGE IN THE BOOK

Purpose

Galatians was written to accomplish three purposes. First, Paul defended his authority as an apostle of Jesus. Second, he argued the doctrinal case for salvation by faith alone. Third, he showed that everyday Christian living is based on freedom from the law in the power of the Holy Spirit

Christian Worldview Elements

Galatians directs attention to the worldview categories of *revelation and authority, covenant and redemption,* and *ethics and morality.* Chapters 1–2 focus on the first category (particularly Paul as an agent of divine revelation). Chapters 3–4 develop the second category. Chapters 5–6 show that Christian ethics are truly founded in the liberty of love.

GOD
CREATION
SOVEREIGNTY AND PROVIDENCE
FAITH AND REASON
▶ **REVELATION AND AUTHORITY**
HUMANITY
REBELLION AND SIN
▶ **COVENANT AND REDEMPTION**
COMMUNITY AND CHURCH
DISCIPLESHIP
▶ **ETHICS AND MORALITY**
TIME AND ETERNITY

Teachings about God

God is the Father of Jesus who brings about all things related to salvation (including setting apostles apart for service, 1:15). Jesus is the Son of God by whose death righteousness is provided (2:21). The Holy Spirit is given to all believers, enabling them to subdue "the flesh" and to grow in Christian character ("the fruit of the Spirit").

Teachings about Humanity

Galatians contrasts two kinds of people in the world. First, there are those under God's curse (3:10). This includes persons who suppose that they can attain salvation by doing good works. They are doomed to live according to the evil works of the flesh and will not be part of God's kingdom. Second, there are those who, by God's grace, have been set free from the curse by faith in Christ who bore the curse by his death (3:13). Such persons live according to the Spirit's power and will "reap life everlasting" (6:8).

Teachings about Salvation

Galatians stands as Paul's passionate testimony that salvation is a gift of God's grace. It is unearned and undeserved and must be received by faith alone. Paul is careful not to turn faith into a work, for he argues that "faith came" (3:23-25) to those who were helpless slaves (see also Eph. 2:8; Phil. 1:29). This view of salvation so strongly gripped the apostle that if someone offered a different doctrine, "let him be accursed" (1:8).

CHRIST IN GALATIANS

Christ became a curse for us so that he could redeem us from the curse of the law (3:13). Believers are crucified with Christ and yet they live. Christ himself becomes their very life (2:19-20).

GOD'S STORY

When the Events of This Book Happened
From AD 47 to 49 (or from AD 50 to 55)

Two ways of understanding the events in Galatians have been presented. Scholars of all kinds (conservative, critical, Protestant, Catholic) have supported each view.

The South Galatian View. Paul established churches in cities of southern Galatia (Iconium, Lystra, and Derbe), about AD 47 on his first missionary journey (Acts 14). In his epistle to them, he described two visits to Jerusalem:

- Gal. 1:18-19 = Acts 9:26-30 (3 years after conversion)
- Gal. 2:1-10 = Acts 11:29-30 (14 years after conversion = famine relief)

After these two trips to Jerusalem, Paul began his missionary journeys and established the churches in Galatia.

The North Galatian View. Paul established churches in cities of northern Galatia (not mentioned in Acts, but see Acts 18:23), about AD 50 on his second missionary journey. The Jerusalem visits he noted in his letter are understood differently than above:

- Gal. 1:18-19 = Acts 9:26-30 (3 years after conversion)
- Gal. 2:1-10 = Acts 15:6-29 (14 years after first visit = Jerusalem Council)

Only after the Jerusalem Council (and after his first missionary journey to southern Galatia) did Paul establish the churches that he was now writing.

How Galatians Fits into God's "Story"

Galatians is part of "chapter 5" of God's story: God spreads the kingdom through the church. Faith, not ethnic background or keeping the laws of Moses, determines citizenship in the kingdom. Believers in Jesus Christ now constitute "the Israel of God" (6:16). The only reference to the kingdom emphasizes its spiritual and moral character: "they which do such [evil] things shall not inherit the kingdom of God" (5:21).

ORIGINAL HISTORICAL SETTING

Author and Date of Writing
Paul the apostle, about AD 49 (or about 52–55)

The book claims to be written by Paul and no one doubts that he wrote this letter. See **Author and Date of Writing** for **ROMANS** for more information about Paul's life.

The date of writing depends on whether the North or the South Galatian View is true. The South Galatian View seems preferable because (1) Acts specifically mentions Paul's preaching only in southern Galatia; (2) the alternate view asserts that Paul deliberately (misleadingly?) omitted referring to his Jerusalem visit of Acts 11:29-30; and (3) the vehemence of the epistle makes better sense if it preceded the Jerusalem Council.

First Audience and Destination
Christians living in the Roman province of Galatia

These Christians came mainly from a Gentile background. They had been believers in Christ for a few years at most. Galatia was a large Roman province snaking from north to south (in the center of modern Turkey). *Galatians* was originally an ethnic term for the original settlers of the northern part of the region who had migrated from Gaul. The Romans had extended the original Galatian region southward to become a large province whose capital was Ancyra in the north.

Occasion
After Paul left the Galatian churches, troublemakers had come there proclaiming a different version of the gospel (1:6-9; 5:7-12). They criticized Paul as a self-appointed apostle who did not truly reflect the message of Jesus. These agitators evidently wanted Christianity to be a sect within current Judaism. Gentiles, they said, had to become Jews (accepting circumcision and living according to Mosaic laws, for example dietary rules) before they could be saved and be a part of God's people. These false teachers are called "Judaizers," based on the verb translated "to live as do the Jews" in Galatians 2:14.

Paul understood Christianity as a different religion than the Judaism of the first century (although it was the fulfillment of the pure Israelite religion of the Old Testament era). He reacted violently against the Judaizers by penning this letter (5:12). If Paul wrote at the earlier date, he probably composed from Antioch of Syria, his "home base," and Galatians is his earliest letter (written between his first and second missionary journeys). If he wrote to churches in northern Galatia, he probably composed from Corinth or Ephesus (during the second or third missionary journeys).

PAUL'S CONVERSION AND EARLY MINISTRY
Galatians 1:11-24

COMMAGENE

Taurus Mountains

Cilician Gates

CILICIA

Tarsus

Issus

Amanus Mts.

Syrian Gates

6. Paul and Barnabas establish a strong church where believers were first called Christians

Seleucia Tracheotis

Seleucia Pieria

Antioch

Aleppo

Euphrates R.

7. Paul and Barnabas travel to Jerusalem with aid for famine

SYRIA

Salamis

Hamath

Emesa

8. Paul and Barnabas return to Antioch

Cyprus

Paphos

Palmyra (Tadmor)

Tripolis

Byblos

Orontes R.

3. Paul baptized and preaches about his newfound faith

MEDITERRANEAN SEA

Litani R.

Sidon

Mt. Hermon

COELE-SYRIA

Damascus

2. Paul has a vision of Jesus and converts

5. Paul returns to his hometown of Tarsus

Tyre

PHOENICIA

Caesarea-Philippi

Ptolemais (Acco)

Capernaum

Canatha (Kenath)

Tiberias

Gamala

Mt. Hauran

4. Paul flees to Arabia then returns to Jerusalem

Caesarea Maritima

Scythopolis

Bostra

Antipatris

Pella

Joppa

Philadelphia (Amman)

JUDEA

Jabbok R.

LEGEND

- ● City
- ▲ Mountain peak
- ⤛ Pass

Azotus (Ashdod)

Jericho

Gaza

Jerusalem

Raphia

IDUMEA

DEAD SEA

N

← Paul sent to Damascus

•••← Paul spends time in Arabia

← Paul returns to Jerusalem

← Paul flees from Hellenists

1. Paul sanctioned to arrest followers in Damascus

Arabah

NABATEA

← Paul and Barnabas travel to Antioch

← Paul and Barnabas sent to Jerusalem

← Paul and Barnabas return to Antioch

▭ Kingdom of Agrippa I

LITERARY FEATURES

Genre and Literary Style
An epistle written in Koine *Greek*

See ***Genre and Literary Style*** for **1 THESSALONIANS** for information about the genre "epistle." The standard parts of a first-century epistle appear, except that the thanksgiving is missing: salutation (1:1-5), main body (1:6–6:15), farewell (6:16-18). This is a pastoral letter, driven by the occasion and needs of the recipients, rather than a tractate (a formal treatise). Paul's Greek is at its most passionate in this letter.

Themes
Grace, faith, justification, freedom, fruit of the Spirit

Justification by grace alone through faith alone became the rallying cry of the Reformation. Galatians has been called "Luther's Book" because of these themes. Because of its emphasis on freedom from law, the Christian life, Galatians has also been called "the Charter of Christian Liberty." By the power of the Spirit, Christians produce a harvest of righteous character, without which there is no evidence of eternal life.

Book Features and Structure
Contrasting concepts are more prominent here than in any other Pauline letter. The most evident of these are divine revelation versus human insight, grace versus law, justification versus condemnation, Jerusalem versus Mount Sinai, sonship versus slavery, the fruit of the Spirit versus the works of the flesh, and liberty versus bondage.

The structure of the book is threefold, corresponding to the three parts of Paul's purpose for writing (see **Purpose** above). The first two chapters are personal; the middle two chapters are doctrinal; and the last two chapters are practical.

EPHESIANS

THE EPISTLE TO THE EPHESIANS

As with all New Testament letters written by Paul the apostle, this epistle is titled according to its first recipients, in this case Christians in the city of Ephesus.

Key Text: 3:10-11

"To the intent that now unto the principalities and powers in heavenly places might be known by the church the manifold wisdom of God, according to the eternal purpose which he purposed in Christ Jesus our Lord."

Key Term: "Unity"

Ephesians focuses on the unity between Christ the head of the church and the church as the body of Christ, as well as the unity between Jew and Gentile in God's greatest masterpiece, the church.

One-Sentence Summary

In God's eternal plan, God's great masterpiece the church has now been manifested, in which Christ is united with all the redeemed whether Jew or Gentile, transforming relationships in this life and leading to a glorious future.

Theater at Ephesus.

GOD'S MESSAGE IN THE BOOK

Purpose

Paul wrote to the Christians in and around Ephesus into order to develop fully in writing his magnificent understanding of the doctrine of the church and to instruct believers about the importance of holy conduct, particularly in Christian family relationships. Ephesians presents the church as the focal point of displaying God's glory forever (3:21).

Christian Worldview Elements

Ephesians directs attention to the worldview elements of *sovereignty and providence, revelation and authority, community and church,* and *time and eternity.* God's sovereign eternal plan for the church, once a "mystery" but now revealed, is the heart of this book. This plan, conceived in the eternal past, is being developed in the present age and will endure into the eternal future.

GOD
CREATION
▶ **SOVEREIGNTY AND PROVIDENCE**
FAITH AND REASON
▶ **REVELATION AND AUTHORITY**
HUMANITY
REBELLION AND SIN
COVENANT AND REDEMPTION
▶ **COMMUNITY AND CHURCH**
DISCIPLESHIP
ETHICS AND MORALITY
▶ **TIME AND ETERNITY**

Teachings about God

Ephesians is filled with texts that contribute to a fully orbed doctrine of the Trinity. God the Father is the One whose eternal plan for the church has now been revealed. Jesus the Son is the exalted Head of the body, the church, and for whose glory the church exists. The church is a house or temple in which God's Spirit lives, yet the Spirit fills each believer individually.

Teachings about Humanity

Ephesians shows the dreadful condition of all who are still in their natural condition: "dead in trespasses and sins" (2:1). Paul summarizes this as "having no hope, and without God" (2:12). The alternate group includes those whom God has changed and who are in a supernatural state: made alive together with Christ (2:5). Old distinctions between Jew and Gentile used to count for something, but now in the church they no longer apply.

Teachings about Salvation

The best known and most loved New Testament summary of the gospel is Ephesians 2:8-9, with its emphasis on grace and faith. Ephesians also notes God's delight in electing persons to salvation. The language of predestination to eternal life is pronounced (1:5,11), as is Paul's notion that "Christ also loved the church, and gave himself for it" (5:25). (The long-standing theological dispute about divine election, predestination, is a matter of discerning the basis of God's choice. All students who take the Bible seriously affirm divine predestination; the debate is simply over its basis.)

CHRIST IN EPHESIANS

Christ, through his death, brought peace between God and man and between Jew and Gentile. He is the cornerstone and head of the church, which is his body.

GOD'S STORY

When the Events of This Book Happened
From AD 53 to 61

Paul first proclaimed Christ in Ephesus on his third missionary journey, arriving there about AD 53 (Acts 19). He wrote this letter to the church at a time that he was imprisoned (Eph. 6:20). Christian tradition is surely correct in affirming that Paul wrote from Rome while he was waiting for his appeal to come before the Emperor, as Acts 28 describes. Paul's two-year detention in Rome was about AD 60–61.

How Ephesians Fits into God's "Story"

Ephesians is part of "chapter 5" of God's story: God spreads the kingdom through the church. Ephesians shows that there are really only two opposing kingdoms in the universe. The devil is "the prince of the power of the air" (2:2), the ruler of a kingdom of sin and death. God's kingdom is diametrically opposed: "For this ye know, that no whoremonger, nor unclean person, nor covetous man, who is an idolater, hath any inheritance in the kingdom of Christ and of God" (5:5). The church (the body of Christ) is the expression of the kingdom in which God receives everlasting glory (3:21).

ORIGINAL HISTORICAL SETTING

Author and Date of Writing
Paul, about AD 61

The letter claims to be written by "Paul, an apostle of Jesus Christ by the will of God." For the last two centuries, critical scholars have argued that Paul was not the author. The arguments against Pauline authorship of Ephesians include the following. (1) The Greek style and vocabulary are different from the undisputed Pauline letters. (2) The doctrine of the church is too advanced for Paul's time. (3) The parallels between Ephesians and Colossians open the possibility that a sincere admirer of Paul used Colossians as a source for writing a letter in his own (later) day, claiming Paul's name to lend his work greater authority. Each of these points may be refuted. The letter's self-claim and the unbroken Christian tradition of Pauline authorship should be accepted.

Assuming that Paul is the author, he wrote from Roman imprisonment as described at the end of Acts, around AD 60–61. Those who reject Pauline authorship date the letter toward the end of the first century.

First Audience and Destination
Christians living in (and around) the city of Ephesus

The gospel came to Ephesus on Paul's third missionary journey. He stayed longer in Ephesus than he did in any other city (Acts 19:10). Paul's Ephesian work was the most visibly successful of all the places of his ministry. The church included both Jews and Gentiles. Because the words "in Ephesus" are missing from Ephesians 1:1 in some of the earliest and best manuscripts, many believe that this was originally a circular letter, intended for several cities (as was Galatians). This would account for Paul's lack of referring to individuals and his note that he had only heard of the readers' faith (1:15).

Ephesus was the most important city in the Roman province of Asia and may have had a population of 600,000. Like Corinth, Ephesus was a great commercial center and port city. Although a number of governmental activities were in Ephesus, the official capital was Pergamum. It was very religious (especially with the famous temple to Diana [or Artemis], one of the "Seven Wonders of the World") and very immoral.

Occasion

Paul had ample opportunity to think over the full implications of Christianity and the church during his Roman imprisonment. He had evidently just written the Colossians (to deal with the Colossian heresy; see *Occasion* for **COLOSSIANS**). He concluded that the doctrinal message of that letter was worth expanding and distributing to a wider audience. Thus he composed this letter and had it sent with the help of Tychicus (6:21) to Ephesus (and perhaps to other nearby churches; compare Rev. 1:11).

THE THIRD MISSIONARY JOURNEY OF PAUL

BLACK SEA

Amastris
Pontus-Mts.
Pompeiopolis
Heraclea
Amisus
ONIA
THRACE
Philippi • Neapolis • Porsule
Perinthus
Byzantium (Istanbul)
Amphipolis
Apollonia
Doriscus
Chalcedon
BITHYNIA
AND PONTUS
Hadrienopolis
Amaseia
Thessalonica
Samothrace
MARMARA SEA
ssa
Lemnos
Troas
MYSIA
Ancyra
(Ankara)
GALATIA
Tavium
Parnassus
Caesarea
(Mazaca)
Assos
Adramyttium
ASIA
Anatolian
Plateau
Sebaste
Paul restores life
to young Eutychus
Pergamum
Lesbos
Thyatira
LYCAONIA
Archelais
CAPPADOCIA
Mitylene
ACHAI
Corinth
Euboea
AEGEAN
SEA
Chios
Smyrna
LYDIA
Sardis
Philadelphia
Antioch in
Pisidia
Iconium
Paul revisits the
churches of Galatia
Paul revisits the
troubled church
at Corinth
Ephesus
Tripolis
Laodicea
PHRYGIA
Seleucia
CILICIA
nchreae
idaurus
Athens
Paul establishes
churches and writes
1 and 2 Corinthians
Samos
Priene
Aphrodisias
Colossae
PISIDIA
Cremna
Lystra
Derbe
Tarsus
Cilician Gates
Issus
Sounion
Miletus
CARIA
PAMPHYLIA
Taurus Mountains
Sparta
Patmos
Halicarnassus
Cos
Cnidus
LYCIA
Attalia • Perga
Seleucia
Tracheotis
An
Cyclades
Islands
Rhodes
Xanthus
Patara
Seleucia Pieria
Rhodes
Paul resumes his
missionary travels
Hama
Crete
Paphos
Cyprus
Salamis
Fair Havens
Tripolis
Byblos

LEGEND
- • City
- ■ Site of the Seven Churches of Asia
- ▲ Mountain peak
- — Roads
- ⋈ Pass
- ← Paul's routes

Sidon
MEDITERRANEAN
SEA
Tyre
Cyrene
Ptolemais (Acco)
AICA
Caesarea Maritima
Antipatris
Jerusalem
Gaza • JUDEA
Alexandria
EGYPT
Pelusium
Qattara
Depression
Memphis
Nile R.

LITERARY FEATURES

Genre and Literary Style
An epistle written in Koine *Greek*

See **Genre and Literary Style** for **1 THESSALONIANS** for information about th genre "epistle." All four standard parts of a first-century epistle appear in Ephesians: salutatio (1:1-2), thanksgiving (1:3-23), main body (2:1–6:20), farewell (6:20-24). Some scholars de ignate Ephesians as a "tractate" (a formal treatise rather than a pastoral letter). Paul's Greek at its most composed and dispassionate in this letter.

Themes
Grace, heavenly places, mystery

Romans has been called the king of Paul's epistles, but Ephesians is the queen. "Grace (Greek, *charis*) permeates the letter from first to last (1:2; 6:24). In fact, each of the thirtee letters bearing Paul's name have the word *grace* at the beginning and end, like bookends. Th term *heavenly places* is found here only in the New Testament (1:3,20; 2:6; 3:10; 6:12). I may have been a Pauline coinage for this book. "Mystery" does not mean something obscur or hard to understand but a divine truth previously hidden, now made known by God's agen of revelation.

Book Features and Structure

Paul's style is deliberative and reflective, in tone the "coolest" of his letters (in contrast t Galatians and 2 Corinthians, the "hottest"). His vocabulary and style are noticeably differen He also wrote sentences that are notorious in their length and complexity. In the original, 1:3-1 is a single sentence of 202 Greek words, followed immediately by 1:15-23, a single sentenc of 169 Greek words.

The structure of the book is twofold, displaying Paul's typical outline. The first three chap ters are doctrinal, describing the heavenly position of the church; the last three chapters ar practical, describing the earthly condition of the church.

PHILIPPIANS

THE EPISTLE TO THE PHILIPPIANS

s with all New Testament letters written by Paul the apostle, this epistle is titled according
o its first recipients, in this case Christians in the city of Philippi.

Key Text: 3:10

"That I may know him, and the power of his resurrection, and the fellowship of his
ufferings, being made conformable unto his death."

Key Term: "Joy"

Forms of the noun *joy* and the verb *rejoice* occur sixteen times in this short letter. Philippians
s the biblical book that most extensively defines and describes joy.

One-Sentence Summary

Knowing Jesus Christ is much more joyful and important than anything else because God has
exalted Jesus, the crucified servant, with the name above every name.

Agora at Philippi.

GOD'S MESSAGE IN THE BOOK

Purpose

Paul wrote to the Philippians to thank them for the financial gift they had sent through Epaphroditus. He further wanted to report on Epaphroditus and to tell about Timothy's probable visit to them. As an added bonus Paul wanted to give them some important doctrinal teaching about Christ (and knowing him) as well as to offer practical advice on living the Christian life vigorously and joyfully.

Christian Worldview Elements

Philippians directs attention to the worldview elements of *covenant and redemption, community and church,* and *discipleship.* Redemption as a personal relationship with God through knowing Jesus Christ is prominent in this book. So also is the concept of a local church as a worshipping and witnessing community.

GOD
CREATION
SOVEREIGNTY AND PROVIDENCE
FAITH AND REASON
REVELATION AND AUTHORITY
HUMANITY
REBELLION AND SIN
► **COVENANT AND REDEMPTION**
► **COMMUNITY AND CHURCH**
► **DISCIPLESHIP**
ETHICS AND MORALITY
TIME AND ETERNITY

Teachings about God

For his glory God the Father has both exalted Jesus Christ and called a people to know him, whom he tenderly cares for. Jesus, by very nature God, humbled himself by death on a cross but thereby has been exalted with the greatest name. The Spirit of God enables all true worship and provides help for God's people.

Teachings about Humanity

In Philippians there are two essential categories of human beings: enemies of the cross of Christ and those who know him (3:18-20). The former are destined for destruction, the latter for resurrection. Among those who know him, however, some proclaim him purely, but others do so from false motives (1:15-18).

Teachings about Salvation

Salvation is presented from the viewpoint of knowing Christ. Knowing Christ, more than just the remedy for sins, is a valuable treasure for which everything else in life is to be happily cast aside. This applies not only to whatever good things one was and did before, but it also means that his followers will joyfully suffer (as he did). They will ultimately share in his resurrection

CHRIST IN PHILIPPIANS

Christ, who existed in the form of God, emptied himself of his privileges as God and became a human being and a slave. After this, God exalted him and gave him the name that is above every name. At the name of Jesus, all creatures will bow and confess him as Lord.

GOD'S STORY

When the Events of This Book Happened
From AD 49 to 61

Paul first preached in Philippi on his second missionary journey, arriving there about AD 49 (Acts 16). He wrote this letter to the church while he was imprisoned (Phil. 1:13-17). According to Christian tradition he wrote from his two-year imprisonment in Rome while he was waiting to appear before the emperor (Acts 28, about AD 60–61).

How Philippians Fits into God's "Story"

Philippians is part of "chapter 5" of God's story: God spreads the kingdom through the church. Although the terms *king* and *kingdom* are missing, the letter is filled with (future-oriented) kingdom concepts. First is the "day of Christ," clearly equivalent to the Old Testament "day of the Lord," that time when Paul and the Philippians will stand before him, complete at last (1:6,10; 2:16). Second is the glorious time when Christ's lordship is universally acknowledged (2:11).

ORIGINAL HISTORICAL SETTING

Author and Date of Writing
Paul, about AD 61

The letter claims to be written by Paul, and all biblical students accept this testimony. Se *Author and Date of Writing* for **ROMANS** for more information about Paul's life Some scholars have argued that all or part of Philippians 3 was written at a different time fror the main letter, but no Greek manuscript evidence supports this. It is much better to accep that Philippians was first written in the form it now appears.

According to tradition, Philippians is one of the four prison epistles written from Rome. I the twentieth century some scholars argued that the many travels implied in the letter mak better sense if Paul wrote from Ephesus a few years earlier. They have conjectured an othe wise unknown imprisonment (not mentioned in Acts or anywhere in Paul's letters) during h third missionary journey, around 55–56. While this theory remains possible, it is an argumer based on silence, and the traditional view that Philippians was written from Rome abow 60–61 appears much more likely.

First Audience and Destination
Christians living in the city of Philippi

The gospel came to Philippi on Paul's second missionary journey. This was the first church Pa planted after his Macedonian vision (Acts 16:9). Because Luke was an eyewitness of th founding of this church (as the use of *we* in Acts 16 indicates), a great deal is known abou the individuals that made up the original core of the congregation, such as Lydia and the ci jailer. Paul did not stay in Philippi very long, but Luke himself probably stayed behind as th church's spiritual leader (the use of *we* stops after Acts 16:17). By reading Acts and Philippian carefully, one discovers that Paul had visited the church at least twice since its beginning ar that it was a true source of joy for him.

Philippi was an important commercial city in the province of Macedonia. (The capital wa Thessalonica.) The city had a privileged status as a colony of Rome, so its citizens were co sidered citizens of Rome (note Paul's emphasis on heavenly citizenship in 3:20-21). Accordir to Acts there were evidently not enough Jews in the city to support a synagogue, so the ci and the church were primarily Gentile. Like other cities of its day, Philippi was very religiou and very immoral.

Occasion

While Paul was imprisoned in Rome, the Philippian church had sent him a financial gift, perhaps to assist with his living expenses or his legal fees, through Epaphroditus, one of their leaders, (4:10-20). While Epaphroditus was with Paul, he had gone through a near-fatal illness. The Philippians had received word of this, and Paul had learned that they were gravely concerned about Epaphroditus. At last, however, Epaphroditus had recovered, and Paul was ready to send him home (2:25-29). He took this occasion, therefore, to write the Philippians a thank-you letter in which he complimented Epaphroditus and brought them up-to-date on his own ministry. The doctrinal and practical emphases in the letter are probably a response to information brought by Epaphroditus. Thus, Paul composed this letter (probably with Timothy's help, whom he also wanted to send to Philippi at a later time, 1:1; 2:19-24) and sent it to Philippi with Epaphroditus.

THE SECOND MISSIONARY JOURNEY OF PAUL

LITERARY FEATURES

Genre and Literary Style
An epistle written in Koine *Greek*

See *Genre and Literary Style* for **1 THESSALONIANS** for information about the genre "epistle." All four standard parts of a first-century epistle appear in Philippians: salutation (1:1-2), thanksgiving (1:3-11), main body (1:12–4:20), farewell (4:21-23). This is a pastoral letter, driven by the occasion and needs of the recipients, rather than a tractate (a formal treatise). Paul's Greek is at its most typical in this letter.

Themes
Righteousness, humility, gratitude, Christ's exaltation and lordship

In Philippians (as in Romans) righteousness is a gift of grace to believers, and it is to bear fruit in the believer's life (1:11; 3:9). The humility of Christ is the pattern for believers to follow in this life. Since this included suffering in Jesus' life, it may well include suffering in the believer. Paul's gratitude for the Philippians' gift is another theme where a pattern to follow is evident. There is no finer biblical presentation of the lordship of Jesus Christ (2:9-11).

Book Features and Structure

Most biblical students agree that Philippians 2:6-11 is a hymn about Christ that Paul was quoting, probably something that he himself had composed earlier. A number of poetic features appear here. This is a six-stanza hymn in which stanzas 1–3 (vv. 6-8) focus on the humiliation of Jesus and stanzas 4–6 (vv. 9-11) focus on his exaltation. This hymn is the most concentrated New Testament passage to combine the doctrines of the person (identity—who he is) and the work (actions—what he did) of Christ.

The structure of the book is looser than is usual for Paul. Chapter 1 is personal; chapter 2 teaches humility; chapter 3 deals with true righteousness; chapter 4 contains Paul's thank-you note.

COLOSSIANS

THE EPISTLE TO THE COLOSSIANS

As with all New Testament letters written by Paul the apostle, this epistle is titled according to its first recipients, in this case Christians in the town of Colosse.

Key Text: 1:18

"And he is the head of the body, the church: who is the beginning, the firstborn from the dead; that in all things he might have the preeminence."

Key Term: "Preeminence"

Colossians declares the supremacy of Christ in all things, whether of creation or redemption. This teaching was the cure to a deadly heresy facing early believers.

One-Sentence Summary

Jesus Christ is supreme Lord of the universe and Head of the church, and therefore he is the only One through whom forgiveness is possible, making legal obligations or philosophical studies irrelevant in matters of salvation.

A view of the Lycus River Valley where Colosse, Laodicea, and Hierapolis were located.

GOD'S MESSAGE IN THE BOOK

Purpose

Paul wrote the Colossian Christians to combat a dangerous teaching, known only through his criticism of it in this letter (see **Occasion** below). Although he condemned this heresy, his main approach was to exalt the person of Jesus Christ and to urge the Colossians to give up anything that denied Jesus his preeminent position as Lord.

Christian Worldview Elements

Colossians focuses on the worldview categories of *God, revelation and authority,* and *covenant and redemption.* No Bible book more explicitly teaches that Jesus is fully God. Paul was self-consciously an agent of divine revelation in this book. Jesus' unique-ness and the exclusiveness of Christianity as the only way to salvation are also prominent elements.

▶ **GOD**
CREATION
SOVEREIGNTY AND PROVIDENCE
FAITH AND REASON
▶ **REVELATION AND AUTHORITY**
HUMANITY
REBELLION AND SIN
▶ **COVENANT AND REDEMPTION**
COMMUNITY AND CHURCH
DISCIPLESHIP
ETHICS AND MORALITY
TIME AND ETERNITY

Teachings about God

God is the Father of Jesus, and his fullness is in his Son (1:19; 2:9). Jesus is especially the "firstborn" (1:15,18). Colossians 1:15-18 is the most elevated passage in Paul's letters presenting the identity of Christ. When Jesus returns, his people will appear with him in glory (3:4). The Spirit is mentioned only once (1:8), as the source of love.

Teachings about Humanity

Because Colossians was first written to stop false teachings, it shows just how easy it is for people to be led astray from truth, particularly in matters of eternal destiny. In every age powerful enemies of truth oppose genuine understanding of God and the human condition. Apart from Christ, all are "dead in . . . sins" (2:13). Christ brings new life and transformation of relationships, particularly within the home (3:18–4:1).

Teachings about Salvation

Any understanding of salvation which is "Jesus plus" is defective. Good works, keeping Jewish law, accepting certain philosophical principles, and other positive human accomplishment cannot add anything to what Jesus has already achieved. Therefore salvation is a matter of being rightly related to him by faith and refusing to trust anything else, no matter how valuable. Christ allows nothing to rival him in redeeming sinners.

☉ *CHRIST IN COLOSSIANS*

Christ is Creator of all things, whether visible or invisible. He is the One who holds all creation together. The fullness of God lived in him and through Christ's death God reconciled everything to himself.

☉ GOD'S STORY

When the Events of This Book Happened
From about AD 53 to 61

Paul had never been in Colosse. The gospel had evidently gone there from Ephesus, where Paul lived during his third missionary journey, arriving about AD 53 (Acts 19). He wrote while he was imprisoned (4:3,18). Christian tradition is surely correct in affirming that Paul wrote from Rome during the two years that he was waiting for his appeal to come before Nero (about AD 60–61), as Acts 28 describes.

How Colossians Fits into God's "Story"

Colossians is part of "chapter 5" of God's story: God spreads the kingdom through the church. Colossians shows that two kingdoms are in conflict. On one hand is the domain of darkness, into which all humans are born. On the other hand, there is "the kingdom of his dear Son" into which God's people have been transferred (1:13). This kingdom is a present reality, for which Paul and all other Christian ministers are working (4:11). Paul's use of the "firstborn" language is parallel messianic prophecy: "Also I will make him my firstborn, higher than the kings of the earth" (Ps. 89:27).

ORIGINAL HISTORICAL SETTING

Author and Date of Writing
Paul the apostle, about AD 61

The letter claims to be written by Paul the apostle. For the past two centuries some (but not all) critical scholars have denied that Paul wrote this letter. They have argued that Colossians reflects the issues of a later time than Paul and was written by an unknown later Christian who used Paul's name to bolster his own authority. The basic arguments are (1) that the false teaching attacked is Gnosticism, which did not become a destructive influence until the end of the first century and (2) that the Christology is too highly developed for Paul. However, in response (1) there is no proof that the Colossian heresy was directly related to Gnosticism, and (2) the Christology is no more exalted than Philippians 2:9-11, which is clearly Pauline. The letter's self-claim and the unbroken Christian tradition of Pauline authorship should be accepted.

Paul wrote from Roman imprisonment as described at the end of Acts, around AD 60–61. Those who reject Pauline authorship date it toward the end of the first century.

First Audience and Destination
Christians living in the town of Colosse

Christianity came to Colosse through the ministry of Epaphras (1:7). He evidently brought the gospel while Paul was in Ephesus on his third missionary journey. Paul had only "heard" of the Colossians (1:4,9). The false teaching mixed Jewish and Greek elements (see **Book Features and Structure** below), suggesting that the believers were probably from both Jewish and Gentile backgrounds.

Colosse was an unimportant town in the province of Asia in the Lycus River Valley, about a hundred miles inland (east) from Ephesus. Its better known sister cities were Hierapolis and Laodicea (2:1; 4:13-16).

Occasion

While Paul was imprisoned in Rome, Epaphras had visited him and brought news about the churches in the Lycus River Valley (4:12). Paul had learned from him about the presence of false teachers in the Colossian congregation that were threatening the survival of the church. He therefore wrote this letter, evidently with the secretarial assistance of Timothy, using Tychicus as the letter carrier.

This is one of four letters, called the prison epistles, written while Paul was waiting to appear before the emperor. Careful reading shows the following relationships:

- Colossians and Philemon were both sent to Colosse (Col. 1:1; 4:17; Philem. 2).
- Colossians and Ephesians were carried by Tychicus (Col. 4:7; Eph. 6:21).
- Ephesians reflects a theological development of Colossians.

All three of these were probably written not long after Paul arrived in Rome; and all three were perhaps carried together by Tychicus, who was also accompanying Onesimus (see *Occasion* for **PHILEMON**). Philippians was likely the last of the four to be written because Paul was expecting to be released soon (Phil. 1:19).

Tel Colossae near the modern town of Honaz, Turkey.

LITERARY FEATURES

Genre and Literary Style
An epistle written in Koine *Greek*

See *Genre and Literary Style* for **1 THESSALONIANS** for information about the genre "epistle." The standard parts of a first-century epistle appear: salutation (1:1-2), thanksgiving (1:3-8), main body (1:9–4:6), farewell (4:7-18). This is a pastoral letter, driven by the occasion and needs of the recipients, rather than a tractate (a formal treatise). This letter was written in Paul's typical style.

Themes
Firstborn, fullness, freedom

Jesus Christ is the "firstborn" over all creation (1:15) as well as "firstborn" from the dead (1:18) showing that he is supreme over creation and supreme over the church. He is, furthermore, the "fullness" of the godhead (1:19; 2:9). Because of Christ's death, Christians are free from human regulations (2:13-23).

Book Features and Structure

The nature of the Colossian heresy must be inferred by Paul's attacks. The essential falsehood was that Jesus was a created being, someone less than God and more than human. There was a certain emphasis on Jewish elements: (1) legal restrictions concerning circumcision, diet, and holy days, 2:11-17; 3:11; (2) veneration of angels, 2:18. There were also Greek elements: (1) self-denial, 2:21-23; (2) adherence to philosophy and human wisdom, 2:4,8; (3) emphasis on secret knowledge, 2:18. The Colossians were "under the spell" of a syncretistic blend of Jewish and Hellenistic elements that Paul recognized as a serious threat to the survival of true Christianity.

The book follows Paul's classic pattern. The first two chapters are doctrinal (Christ as the head of the church). The last two are practical (holy Christian living).

1 THESSALONIANS

THE FIRST EPISTLE TO THE THESSALONIANS

This book is so named because it is the first canonical letter that Paul the apostle wrote to the Christians in Thessalonica.

Key Text: 4:16-17

"For the Lord himself shall descend from heaven with a shout, with the voice of the archangel, and with the trump of God: and the dead in Christ shall rise first: Then we which are alive and remain shall be caught up together with them in the clouds, to meet the Lord in the air: and so shall we ever be with the Lord."

Key Term: "Coming"

This book mentions the return of Christ in every chapter. The Greek noun *parousia*, here rendered "coming," can also be translated "arrival" or "presence."

One-Sentence Summary

Whatever difficulties and sufferings believers experience in this life, the coming of Christ is the true hope of the Christian.

Triumphal arch of Roman Emperor Galerius in Thessalonica.

GOD'S MESSAGE IN THE BOOK

Purpose

Paul wrote this letter mainly to correct a deficiency in the Thessalonians' understanding of the coming of Christ and related events. He also wanted to encourage these new converts in basic doctrine and to inspire them to make progress in holy living.

Christian Worldview Elements

First Thessalonians focuses attention especially on the worldview categories of *community and church, ethics*, and *time and eternity*. This is the only Bible book explicitly teaching that believers alive at the coming of Christ will be "caught up" to meet him.

GOD
CREATION
SOVEREIGNTY AND PROVIDENCE
FAITH AND REASON
REVELATION AND AUTHORITY
HUMANITY
REBELLION AND SIN
COVENANT AND REDEMPTION
► **COMMUNITY AND CHURCH**
DISCIPLESHIP
► **ETHICS** AND MORALITY
► **TIME AND ETERNITY**

Teachings about God

God is the Father who actively works to bring about salvation. He is presently working holiness into his children. Jesus died and rose again at his first coming, and he will return in glory at his second coming. The Spirit, the active agent by whom God makes the gospel alive, is God's gift enabling his people to have great joy (1:5-6; 4:8).

Teachings about Humanity

There are only two kinds of people: those who have received the word of God and those who have rejected it (2:13-16). The destiny of the one group is the experience of the wrath of God leading to their destruction. The destiny of the other group is to be with the Lord forever. This latter group is called on to live a holy life that pleases God.

Teachings about Salvation

The basis of salvation is Jesus' death and resurrection (4:14; 5:10). The letter summarizes salvation as past, present, and future in this way: "Ye turned to God from idols to serve the living and true God; and to wait for his Son from heaven, whom he raised from the dead, *even* Jesus, which delivered us from the wrath to come" (1:9-10).

CHRIST IN 1 THESSALONIANS

Christ is a source of comfort because he is coming again. At his coming those who have died in him will rise first. Then believers who are living will be caught up to join those who have died and be together with him.

GOD'S STORY

When the Events of This Book Happened
About AD 50

After preaching in Philippi, Paul went next to Thessalonica (Acts 17). He reached the Thessalonians about AD 50 as part of his second missionary journey during a time when he was moving quickly, establishing churches in rapid succession. A short time later he arrived in Corinth and stayed there more than a year (Acts 18). He wrote this letter from Corinth, probably within a few months of preaching to the Thessalonians.

How 1 Thessalonians Fits into God's "Story"

First Thessalonians is part of "chapter 5" of God's story: God spreads the kingdom through the church. When Paul first preached in Thessalonica, his opponents caused trouble because he proclaimed "that there is another king, one Jesus" (Acts 17:7). Jesus' kingdom was understood as a rival to the kingdom of Caesar, yet Jesus' kingdom was not a political-military enterprise. In this letter Paul emphasized the moral and spiritual nature of those who belong to King Jesus (2:12). The vocabulary Paul used to describe Jesus' return was the same as that describing a great king's arrival (*parousia*) at one of his cities.

ORIGINAL HISTORICAL SETTING

Author and Date of Writing
Paul the apostle, about AD 50

All New Testament scholars accept the claim of the letter to be written by Paul. See **Author and Date of Writing** for **ROMANS** for more information about Paul. The apostle wrote this letter around AD 50 from Corinth (see **Occasion** below).

First Audience and Destination
Christians in Thessalonica

Acts 17:1-8 describes how Christianity first came to Thessalonica through Paul's preaching. Silas and Timothy had helped him. The believers had come from both Jewish and pagan backgrounds. Paul was forced by persecution to leave Thessalonica early, possibly staying there only three weeks. These new believers had enthusiastically embraced the gospel but were not taught in the way of the Lord.

Thessalonica was the capital of Macedonia and numbered perhaps 200,000 in the first century. It was a seaport and commercial center lying at the intersection of the Egnatian Way and the road leading north toward the Danube River. Like other Roman cities it was both religious and immoral.

Occasion

After Paul fled Macedonia, Timothy and Silas finally caught up with him in Athens. Paul was so concerned to learn about the spiritual state of the Thessalonians that he dispatched Timothy to them (1 Thess. 3:1-5). Timothy stayed there for a time, strengthening and encouraging these new believers. At last Timothy caught up with Paul a second time, this time in Corinth (Acts 18:5; 1 Thess. 3:6).

Timothy's report was essentially positive. The congregation was thriving and growing in virtue, although they were enduring persecution of some kind. Paul's ministry there, however, had emphasized that Christ's coming could be very soon. Thus the Thessalonians were unprepared when some of their members had died (4:13). Had those who died missed the kingdom? Would they see the King? Paul found it important to expand his teaching on "eschatology" (end times) and to clarify their confusion. He penned this letter perhaps within months of first preaching in Thessalonica.

Attic funerary stele showing a mother and child. "Although we could have been a burden as Christ's apostles, instead we were gentle among you, as a nursing mother nurtures her own children" (1 Thess. 2:7 HCSB).

LITERARY FEATURES

Genre and Literary Style
An epistle written in Koine *Greek*

Unlike the Gospels, which were a new literary genre inspired by Christianity, epistles were a well-known first-century literary form. First Thessalonians is one of the earliest of Paul's letters to survive, although Galatians may be earlier. This is the earliest Pauline epistle that contains all four standard elements of an epistle, of which many secular examples have been discovered.

- *Salutation* (1:1). The form is "from sender to recipient: greetings." Paul always identified himself as the author and named the recipient. In place of the conventional word *greetings* Paul always used "grace and peace."
- *Thanksgiving* (1:2-3). This was a prayer directed to God on behalf of the readers. The secular examples invoked a variety of deities, depending on which god was served.
- *Body* (1:4–5:22). This obviously was the main point of the letter. Paul typically wrote a doctrinal argument followed by a shorter practical application.
- *Farewell* (5:23-28). The writer gave greetings and otherwise concluded the document. Paul always used the word "grace" (Greek, *charis*) in his farewell.

Like most of Paul's writings, this is a pastoral letter, driven by the occasion and needs of the recipients, rather than a tractate (a formal treatise). First Thessalonians represents Paul's typical careful use of the Greek language.

Themes
Return of Christ, "the rapture," importance of holiness

Because Paul was writing in response to the needs of the congregation, their own concerns became the themes of the epistle. The doctrinal concern with right eschatology (beliefs about the end times) is balanced with Paul's practical concern with right living (holiness in light of Christ's return).

Book Features and Structure

This is the only Bible book that explicitly mentions that Christians who are alive at Christ's coming will be changed to resurrection life and rise to meet him in the air without dying (4:16-17). This doctrine is often called the rapture, based on the Latin term for "caught up." For the past two centuries evangelical believers have had a lively debate concerning the relationship of the rapture to the second coming. Equally devout and Bible-believing scholars have disagreed. What is clear is (1) that Jesus will visibly, bodily return, (2) those who are already dead in Christ will one day be raised, and (3) Christians alive at Christ's *parousia* will be "raptured" without dying.

This epistle is not organized by doctrinal material followed by practical advice. Instead, Paul moves back and forth. On the other hand, only practical material follows the transitional word *therefore* at 5:6.

2 THESSALONIANS

THE SECOND EPISTLE TO THE THESSALONIANS

This book is so named because it is the second canonical letter that Paul the apostle wrote to the Christians in Thessalonica.

Key Text: 2:15

"Therefore, brethren, stand fast, and hold the traditions which ye have been taught, whether by word, or our epistle."

Key Term: "Stand"

This book was written to believers who had been shaken by false teaching concerning the end times. The apostle's advice to "stand fast" applies no matter what doctrinal or practical challenge believers face.

One-Sentence Summary

Whatever difficulties believers face, they should stand firm and continue living useful lives, since Christ's return may be in the distant future.

Roman soldier. "Therefore, brothers, stand firm and hold to the traditions you were taught, either by our message or by our letter" (2 Thess. 2:15 HCSB).

GOD'S MESSAGE IN THE BOOK

Purpose

Paul wrote this letter mainly to correct a new deficiency in the Thessalonians' understanding of the coming of Christ and related events (see **Purpose** for **1 THESSALONIANS**). He also wanted to correct the problem brought about because some had stopped working (in light of their belief that the day of the Lord had come).

Christian Worldview Elements

Second Thessalonians, like its sister letter, focuses attention especially on the worldview categories of *community and church*, *ethics*, and *time and eternity*.

GOD
CREATION
SOVEREIGNTY AND PROVIDENCE
FAITH AND REASON
REVELATION AND AUTHORITY
HUMANITY
REBELLION AND SIN
COVENANT AND REDEMPTION
▶ **COMMUNITY AND CHURCH**
DISCIPLESHIP
▶ **ETHICS** AND MORALITY
▶ **TIME AND ETERNITY**

Teachings about God

God's supremacy in all things, particularly concerning salvation and the consummation of the world, is taught in this letter. His justice is especially taught in the way he will ultimately punish all evildoers. Jesus' coming is taught in this book, and he will easily overcome "the man of sin," that is, "the son of perdition" (2:3) as a display of his glory on "the day of the Lord." The Holy Spirit, mentioned only at 2:13, sanctifies (makes holy) those God has chosen to save.

Teachings about Humanity

This letter shows two sharply opposed groups of humanity. On one hand are those who know God and have come to obey the gospel. On the other hand are all others, "Who shall be punished with everlasting destruction from the presence of the Lord" (1:9).

Teachings about Salvation

In 2 Thessalonians, salvation is seen from the future perspective of deliverance from judgment and destruction on the day of the Lord. In the end, those who perish do so "because they received not the love of the truth, that they might be saved" (2:10).

CHRIST IN 2 THESSALONIANS

Christ came the first time as a baby. His second coming will be different. He will come with his powerful angels who will punish God's enemies, those who refuse peace with God made possible by the death of Christ.

GOD'S STORY

When the Events of This Book Happened

About AD 50 to 51

See *When the Events of This Book Happened* for **1 THESSALONIANS**. Second Thessalonians was probably written only a few months after the first epistle.

How 2 Thessalonians Fits into God's "Story"

Second Thessalonians is part of "chapter 5" of God's story: God spreads the kingdom through the church. Paul emphasized the spiritual nature of the kingdom of God in this letter. He urged the Thessalonians to "be counted worthy of the kingdom of God, for which ye also suffer" (1:5). The portrait of Christ's return in a blaze of glory and wrath against his enemies is one of the most kingly portraits of Jesus in all the epistles (2:8-12).

The Via Egnatia, which passes through Thessalonica, was a Roman road that ran from Byzantium in the east to the western coast of Italy.

ORIGINAL HISTORICAL SETTING

Author and Date of Writing
Paul the apostle, about AD 50

The letter claims to be written by Paul the apostle. For the past two centuries some (but not all) critical scholars have rejected that Paul wrote this letter. They have argued that the eschatology (end times doctrine) of this letter contradicts the eschatology of 1 Thessalonians. This letter was therefore written by an unknown later Christian who used Paul's name to bolster his own authority. The basic argument is that in 2 Thessalonians, Christ's coming appears to be distant, and a number of signs must precede it. Yet in the first epistle, his return appears to be imminent and without warning. Clearly the letters have differing emphases, but they are not incompatible. Down through the centuries Christians have held that the day of the Lord may come at any time (imminence), but that it is not necessarily immediate. The letter's self claim and the unbroken Christian tradition of Pauline authorship should be accepted.

Paul wrote from Corinth just a few months after he wrote 1 Thessalonians. Those who reject Pauline authorship date the letter toward the end of the first century.

First Audience and Destination
Christians in Thessalonica

See *First Audience and Destination* for **1 THESSALONIANS**.

Occasion

After Paul sent 1 Thessalonians, the church had received a further report that the "day of the Lord"—the end times—had come. The return of Christ was immediate. This had come as ? from Paul himself (2:2). The church was thrown into turmoil, and many of the members had quit their jobs and were waiting for the second coming. Paul therefore had to write them again to correct the doctrinal error and to urge them to settle down and get back to work.

The highway near Thessalonica (modern Salonica) going toward Athens.

LITERARY FEATURES

Genre and Literary Style
An epistle written in Koine *Greek*

See **Genre and Literary Style** for **1 THESSALONIANS** for information about the genre *epistle*. The standard parts of a first-century epistle appear: salutation (1:1-2), thanksgiving (1:3-11), main body (2:1–3:15), farewell (3:16-18). This is a pastoral letter, driven by the occasion and needs of the recipients, rather than a tractate (a formal treatise). It was written in Paul's typical style.

Themes
Return of Christ, "day of the Lord," rejection of idleness

In this letter Paul developed the "day of the Lord" theme that was already well established in the Old Testament prophets. (See **JOEL** and **ZEPHANIAH**.) The "day of the Lord" is now seen to be the time associated with Christ's return, when he will destroy God's enemies and bring God's people to glory. Paul's rejection of idleness is summarized in this instruction, "If any would not work, neither should he eat" (3:10).

Book Features and Structure
The literary tone of 2 Thessalonians is noticeably cooler than for the first epistle. In the first letter he was warm with enthusiasm about their progress in the gospel and offered calm advice about congregational order in a series of staccato-like instructions (1 Thess. 5:12-22). In the second letter he was gravely concerned about the spiritual state of the Thessalonians and offered them a sharp rebuke about maintaining congregational order (2 Thess. 3:6-15).

This epistle follows Paul's usual pattern of doctrinal material followed by practical. The doctrinal focus (on the day of the Lord) ends at 3:14; the practical advice begins at 3:15 (the **Key Text)** and goes to the end of the book.

1 TIMOTHY

THE FIRST EPISTLE TO TIMOTHY

This book is so named because it is the first canonical letter that Paul the apostle wrote to Timothy.

Key Text: 6:11

"But thou, O man of God, flee these things; and follow after righteousness, godliness, faith, love, patience, meekness."

Key Term: "Godliness"

Godliness (Greek, *eusebeia*) is the virtue that sums up all others. Timothy's many ministry challenges would succeed only if he proceeded from godly character.

One-Sentence Summary

Whatever challenges Christian leaders face in life and ministry, they are to make progress in godliness and help maintain order in congregational life.

Arab farmer plowing his rocky field. Paul told Timothy that elders who are good leaders are worthy of ample compensation. He quoted Deuteronomy 25:4: "You must not muzzle an ox that is threshing grain" (1 Tim. 5:18 HCSB).

GOD'S MESSAGE IN THE BOOK

Purpose

Paul wrote his dear friend Timothy to accomplish a number of objectives. First, he wished to encourage Timothy in his Christian growth. Second, he offered advice about being a better Christian leader. Third, he offered instructions about church organization, particularly congregational officers.

Christian Worldview Elements

First Timothy deals with the worldview categories of *community and church, discipleship,* and *ethics and morality.* This book, more fully than any other, instructs about organizing church life.

GOD
CREATION
SOVEREIGNTY AND PROVIDENCE
FAITH AND REASON
REVELATION AND AUTHORITY
HUMANITY
REBELLION AND SIN
COVENANT AND REDEMPTION
▶**COMMUNITY AND CHURCH**
▶**DISCIPLESHIP**
▶**ETHICS AND MORALITY**
TIME AND ETERNITY

Teachings about God

This epistle contains the classic biblical summary of God's attributes: "the King eternal, immortal, invisible, the only wise God" (1:17). He is also "the blessed and only Potentate, the King of kings, and Lord of lords" (6:15). Jesus is the only Mediator between God and mankind (2:5). The Holy Spirit's person is clearly affirmed (3:16; 4:1).

Teachings about Humanity

As one of the six New Testament letters first written to a single individual (1 and 2 Timothy, Titus, Philemon, 2 and 3 John), this book shows the importance of what one person can be and do. The individuals addressed in these books (Timothy, Titus, Philemon, "the elect lady," and Gaius) were all redeemed sinners working for the kingdom of God in one way or another. They all benefited from the advice and encouragement offered by the letter they received. These persons stand as examples of living out one's life for the glory of God and in the hope of eternal life.

Teachings about Salvation

Salvation in this letter, as everywhere in Paul's writings, focuses on Jesus Christ. Paul summarized his understanding by reminding Timothy of "the mystery of godliness," evidently an early Christian hymn or poem: "God was manifest in the flesh, justified in the Spirit, seen of angels, preached unto the Gentiles, believed on in the world, received up into glory" (3:16).

CHRIST IN 1 TIMOTHY

Christ's purpose for coming into the world is to save sinners. Paul says Christ took him as a worst case scenario. He argues that if Christ can save Paul, he can save anyone.

GOD'S STORY

When the Events of This Book Happened
About AD 62–63

After Paul was released from the Roman imprisonment described in Acts 28, he engaged in further travel. One stop was Ephesus, where he ministered for a time before traveling on to Macedonia (1:3). From Macedonia Paul wrote to Timothy, whom he had asked to stay in Ephesus. The dates for these events are only approximate.

How 1 Timothy Fits into God's "Story"

First Timothy is part of "chapter 5" of God's story: God spreads the kingdom through the church. Although the term *kingdom* does not appear in this letter, God is twice called "King" (1:17; 6:15). While this language is more common in the Old Testament than the New, it is still appropriate in the era of the new covenant. God is not only the King as Sovereign of the universe, he is the King of the people of God, whom he has called to know and worship him.

Bust of Nero, the Roman emperor AD 54–68 during whose reign both Paul and Peter were martyred. Paul instructed Timothy, "I urge that petitions, prayers, intercessions, and thanksgivings be made for everyone, for kings and all those who are in authority, so that we may lead a tranquil and quiet life in all godliness and dignity" (1 Tim. 2:1-2 HCSB).

ORIGINAL HISTORICAL SETTING

Author and Date of Writing
Paul the apostle, about AD 63

The book claims explicitly to be written by "Paul, an apostle of Jesus Christ" (1:1). Until about two centuries ago, all Bible students affirmed this belief. With the rise of critical approaches to Scripture, nonconservative scholars have adopted the position that an unknown admirer of Paul wrote 1 Timothy (as well as 2 Timothy and Titus). Opinions vary whether these letters contain any genuine Pauline fragments. The chief objection is historical. The travels mentioned in these three epistles do not fit into the framework provided by Acts. If Paul indeed perished at the end of Acts, he could not be the author of these books. It is also held that the congregational form encouraged in these letters (with bishops and deacons officially recognized) is too advanced for Paul's day. The Greek style is also noticeably different from that of the undisputed Pauline letters.

These objections may be satisfactorily answered. (1) It is by no means certain that Paul died at the end of the Acts 28 imprisonment. In fact, the evidence from Philippians 1:25 is that Paul expected to be released. (2) Little is actually known about the congregational form of the Pauline churches. Bishops and deacons certainly functioned in Philippi years before 1 Timothy was written (Phil. 1:1). (3) The difference in Greek style does not prove anything, for the Greek of 1 and 2 Timothy and Titus is more like the Greek of the undisputed Pauline letters than any other part of the Bible. The letter's self-claim and the unbroken Christian tradition of Pauline authorship should be accepted.

Paul wrote after he was released from the Roman imprisonment described at the end of Acts, around AD 63. Those who reject Pauline authorship date the letter toward the end of the first century.

First Audience and Destination
Timothy, Paul's dearest friend, who was in Ephesus

Timothy had the task of being an apostolic representative. He was from Lystra (in modern Turkey). His father was Gentile, but his mother Eunice was a Jewish Christian (Acts 16:1; 2 Tim. 1:5). Timothy had probably come to the gospel through Paul during his first visit to Lystra (1 Tim. 1:2). Timothy joined Paul on his second missionary journey, helping Paul in Macedonia and Achaia (Acts 17–18). He traveled with Paul later on and was with him during his Roman imprisonment (Phil. 1:1; Col. 1:1).

After Paul's release, he assigned Timothy the responsibility of helping the church of Ephesus with its difficulties. Paul's comments about Timothy in Philippians 2:19-24 and his statements in 1 and 2 Timothy show Paul's affection for his loyal associate. Paul later asked Timothy to rejoin him (2 Tim. 4:9,21), and Hebrews 13:23 indicates that Timothy was later imprisoned. (For information about Ephesus, see *First Audience and Destination* for **EPHESIANS**.)

Occasion

Paul had left Timothy in Ephesus when he found that false teaching had upset the stability of the church there. The exact nature of this teaching is impossible to determine, but it included both Jewish speculative elements ("fables and endless genealogies," 1:4) as well as Greek philosophical elements ("profane *and* vain babblings, and oppositions of science falsely so called," 6:20). Timothy had to deal with false teachers as well as organize the church along good lines. Thus, from somewhere in Macedonia, Paul wrote to encourage Timothy and to remind him of his responsibilities.

Library of Celsus at Ephesus. Paul had urged Timothy to remain in Ephesus and correct certain teachings that were diverting the church from the gospel (1 Tim. 1:3).

LITERARY FEATURES

Genre and Literary Style
An epistle written in Koine *Greek*

See **Genre and Literary Style** for **1 THESSALONIANS** for information about the genre *epistle*. The standard parts of a first-century epistle appear in 1 Timothy, except that the thanksgiving is missing: salutation (1:1-2), main body (1:3–6:19), farewell (6:20-21). This letter and 2 Timothy and Titus share certain vocabulary and style elements that make these three books distinctive. So clearly do they belong together that they are often considered as a unit, the pastoral epistles.

Themes
Sound doctrine, bishops and deacons, widows

Sound doctrine is crucial as the cure for false teaching. This is the only New Testament book that gives qualifications for both the primary spiritual officers of a congregation (bishops = elders) and the secondary officers (deacons = helpers). Paul also instructed Timothy about widows, including women officially qualified to serve (5:9-13, compare with 3:8-13).

Book Features and Structure

See **Book Features and Structure** for **2 TIMOTHY** for information about the "Faithful Sayings" in the Pastoral Epistles.

The letter moves through a variety of topics. In general chapters 1–5 focus on Timothy's public responsibilities in the life of the congregation, while chapter 6 focuses on Timothy's private spiritual character as a "man of God."

2 TIMOTHY

THE SECOND EPISTLE TO TIMOTHY

This book is so named because it is the second canonical letter that Paul the apostle wrote to Timothy.

► Key Text: 2:2

"And the things that thou hast heard of me among many witnesses, the same commit thou to faithful men, who shall be able to teach others also."

► Key Term: "Committed"

Timothy was to commit (entrust) the treasure of the gospel that had been committed to him to those who would faithfully transmit it to the next generation, just as he had committed his eternal destiny to the One who would keep it for "that day" (1:12).

► One-Sentence Summary

Christian leaders are to be unashamed of the gospel and to carry on faithfully with the message about Christ entrusted to them.

Lighted lamp in reconstructed Jewish house. "I remind you to keep ablaze the gift of God that is in you through the laying on of my hands" (2 Tim. 1:6 HCSB).

GOD'S MESSAGE IN THE BOOK

Purpose

Paul wrote this letter as his last will and testament. He wished to remind Timothy of what mattered most to him in case he did not survive his imprisonment until Timothy arrived. He also urged Timothy (and Mark) to come to him in haste in order to be with him in his last days.

Christian Worldview Elements

Second Timothy deals particularly with the worldview categories of *revelation and authority* and *time and eternity*. This book especially sees God's revelation as a "deposit" which should not be tampered with but passed on faithfully. As Paul's last writing, it shows how an aged saint can live in the light of death's approach.

GOD
CREATION
SOVEREIGNTY AND PROVIDENCE
FAITH AND REASON
▶**REVELATION AND AUTHORITY**
HUMANITY
REBELLION AND SIN
COVENANT AND REDEMPTION
COMMUNITY AND CHURCH
DISCIPLESHIP
ETHICS AND MORALITY
▶**TIME AND ETERNITY**

Teachings about God

God is the powerful Father who has graciously gifted his servants for ministry. Scripture is itself "God-breathed" (KJV, "by inspiration of God," 3:16). Jesus is both God and man: "Remember Jesus Christ, raised from the dead, descended from David." (2:8). The Holy Spirit is the powerful presence of God indwelling believers and enabling them to continue their ministry (1:14).

Teachings about Humanity

See *Teachings about Humanity* for **1 TIMOTHY**.

Teachings about Salvation

Salvation is both sovereignly determined by God and the divine gift to all who believe. Paul summarized the evangelistic aspect of his ministry with a statement combining both emphases: "Therefore I endure all things for the elect's sakes, that they may also obtain the salvation which is in Christ Jesus with eternal glory" (2:10).

CHRIST IN 2 TIMOTHY

God's saving grace through Christ was not an afterthought, a response to unforeseen developments in the world. It was planned before time. Christ has abolished death and brought life and immortality through His death and resurrection.

GOD'S STORY

When the Events of This Book Happened
About AD 63–66

Paul had traveled to a number of places after he was released from the Roman imprisonment of Acts 28. He had written 1 Timothy and Titus during this time of liberty. Now, however, he had been rearrested and was facing his last imprisonment. From his Roman cell Paul wrote to Timothy, whom he had asked to come to him, possibly from Ephesus. The dates for these events are only approximate.

How 2 Timothy Fits into God's "Story"

Second Timothy is part of "chapter 5" of God's story: God spreads the kingdom through the church. Because Paul was at the end of his life, he thought of the kingdom of God as a present heavenly reality, a destination at which he was about to arrive (4:18). Even so, he looked forward to the future glorious form of the kingdom that would be revealed in connection with Jesus' "appearing" on earth again (4:1). Thus at the end of his life, kingdom thinking was still prominent in Paul's theological framework.

ORIGINAL HISTORICAL SETTING

Author and Date of Writing
Paul the apostle, about AD 66

See *Author and Date of Writing* for **1 TIMOTHY** for information about objection to Pauline authorship. Assuming that Paul is the author, he wrote from his final Roman imprisonment, around AD 66. Those who reject Pauline authorship date the letter toward the end of the first century.

First Audience and Destination
Timothy, Paul's dearest friend, possibly in Ephesus

See *First Audience and Destination* for **1 TIMOTHY**. There is no definite indication in this letter concerning Timothy's location. Many students think it likely that he was still serving the Lord in Ephesus (1 Tim. 1:3).

Occasion
Paul had been rearrested in an unknown place and was back in Rome. The Roman government's official hostility to Christianity (which arose after the great fire of Rome in AD 64 when Nero decided to make Christians his scapegoats) was probably the context for Paul's final imprisonment. Paul was evidently in an imperial prison. He was not even given the benefit of adequate clothing against the cold and damp (4:13).

Paul was virtually alone. Only Luke had access to him; others had abandoned him or been sent out in ministry (4:10-12). Paul had been through a preliminary hearing that persuaded him that he would soon be executed (4:16). He therefore wanted company before he died and twice begged Timothy to come (4:9,21). He also wanted his books, his coat, and the fellowship of Mark (4:12-13). It is not known whether Timothy arrived in Rome in time to say good-bye to his beloved mentor face-to-face.

Forum and Temple of Augustus in Rome. Paul's last imprisonment and execution were in Rome.

LITERARY FEATURES

Genre and Literary Style
An epistle written in Koine Greek

See **Genre and Literary Style** for **1 THESSALONIANS** for information about the genre *epistle*. The standard parts of a first-century epistle appear in 2 Timothy: salutation (1:1-2), thanksgiving (1:3-7), main body (1:8–4:18), farewell (4:19-22). This letter, like 1 Timothy and Titus, has certain vocabulary and style elements that make these three books distinctive. They so clearly belong together that they are often considered as a unit, the Pastoral Epistles.

Themes
Divine election, inspiration of Scripture, being unashamed, sound doctrine

The first two of these has already been noted. The need for courage in the gospel is noted repeatedly: Paul and Onesiphorus were not ashamed (1:12,16; 2:15). Timothy and all God-approved workmen must also be unashamed of Christ (1:8; 2:15). Sound doctrine is crucial as the cure for false teaching. Sound doctrine is prominent in this letter as it is in all the Pastoral Epistles.

Book Features and Structure

Scattered throughout 1 and 2 Timothy and Titus are five faithful sayings, none of which is cited elsewhere. These were almost certainly confessions used publicly in worship. (The first and third of these add the words, "and worthy of all acceptation," which was perhaps a congregational oral unison response to the words, "This is a faithful saying," the leader's call to recitation.)

- "Christ Jesus came into the world to save sinners," 1 Timothy 1:15.
- "If a man desire the office of a bishop, he desireth a good work," 1 Timothy 3:1.
- "Godliness is profitable unto all things, having promise of the life that now is, and of that which is to come," 1 Timothy 4:8. (Possibly 4:10 is the "Faithful Saying.")
- "For if we be dead with *him*, we shall also live with *him*: If we suffer, we shall also reign with *him*: if we deny *him*, he also will deny us: If we believe not, *yet* he abideth faithful: he cannot deny himself," 2 Timothy 2:11-13.
- "Not by works of righteousness which we have done, but according to his mercy he saved us, by the washing of regeneration, and renewing of the Holy Ghost; which he shed on us abundantly through Jesus Christ our Saviour; that being justified by his grace, we should be made heirs according to the hope of eternal life," Titus 3:5-7.

The letter is organized into two main sections. Through 4:5, the general subject is being committed to ministry; from 4:6 to the end of the letter is Paul's personal farewell, the most poignant and personal words to come from the apostle.

TITUS

THE EPISTLE TO TITUS

This book is so named as the letter that Paul the apostle wrote to Titus.

▶ *Key Text: 2:1*

"But speak thou the things which become sound doctrine."

▶ *Key Term: "Doctrine"*

This book emphasizes that sound doctrine is the necessary foundation for everything worthwhile in the life of a congregation or an individual.

▶ *One-Sentence Summary*

Whatever challenges they face in life and ministry, Christian leaders are to maintain order in the congregation, but only according to sound doctrine.

▼ Porpoise mural in the Knosos palace on Crete, the place where Titus ministered.

GOD'S MESSAGE IN THE BOOK

Purpose

Paul wrote his friend in ministry Titus to accomplish a number of objectives. First, he wished to encourage Titus in his Christian growth. Second, he offered instructions about church organization, particularly congregational officers and various age groups. Finally, he wanted Titus to come to Nicopolis to spend the winter with him.

Christian Worldview Elements

Titus focuses on the worldview categories of *community and church, discipleship,* and *ethics and morality.* This book especially shows the necessary relationship between sound doctrine and sound behavior.

GOD
CREATION
SOVEREIGNTY AND PROVIDENCE
FAITH AND REASON
REVELATION AND AUTHORITY
HUMANITY
REBELLION AND SIN
COVENANT AND REDEMPTION
▶**COMMUNITY AND CHURCH**
▶**DISCIPLESHIP**
▶**ETHICS AND MORALITY**
TIME AND ETERNITY

Teachings about God

Three times in this short letter the phrase "God our Saviour" is used (1:3; 2:10; 3:4). The phrase "Christ Jesus our Saviour" appears twice (1:4; 3:6). These two are combined remarkably in the expression, "the great God and our Saviour Jesus Christ" (2:13), one of the strongest statements of the deity of Christ in Scripture. The only direct reference to the Spirit concerns his role in the regeneration of sinners (3:5).

Teachings about Humanity

See **Teachings about Humanity** for **1 TIMOTHY**.

Teachings about Salvation

In his first coming Jesus died to "redeem us from all iniquity, and purify unto himself a peculiar people" (2:14). These people long for the day of full salvation at his return, the "blessed hope" (2:13) of his appearing. The vocabulary of salvation in this letter includes justification by grace (3:7), regeneration (3:5), and eternal life (3:7).

CHRIST IN TITUS

Christ came to redeem human beings from lawlessness, to create a special people, eager to do good works now and to look forward to Christ's appearing a second time.

GOD'S STORY

When the Events of This Book Happened
About AD 62–63

After Paul was released from the Roman imprisonment described in Acts 28, he engaged in further travel. One place he stopped was Crete, where he ministered for a time (1:5). From an unknown location Paul wrote to Titus, whom he had asked to continue on in Crete. The dates for these events are only approximate.

How Titus Fits into God's "Story"

Titus is part of "chapter 5" of God's story: God spreads the kingdom through the church. Although the term *kingdom* does not appear in this letter, the concept is evident. Local congregations of believers in Jesus Christ are little "kingdom outposts," waiting for the time that their King will appear gloriously (2:13). For this reason, it is important for local churches to be organized properly and to maintain sound doctrine.

Paul stopped in Crete on his ship voyage to Rome. Some scholars believe Paul was released after his first imprisonment at Rome. During the time between his first and second imprisonment, he returned to Crete with Titus. In his letter to Titus, Paul wrote, "The reason I left you in Crete was to set right what was left undone" (Titus 1:5).

ORIGINAL HISTORICAL SETTING

Author and Date of Writing
Paul the apostle, about AD 63

See **Author and Date of Writing** for **1 TIMOTHY** for information about critical objections to Pauline authorship. Assuming that Paul is the author, he wrote after he was released from the Roman imprisonment described at the end of Acts, around AD 63. Those who reject Pauline authorship date the letter toward the end of the first century.

First Audience and Destination
Titus, Paul's trusted friend, who was on Crete

Titus had the task of being an apostolic representative. One of Paul's early converts (1:4), he was a Gentile, evidently from Antioch of Syria. Paul took Titus with him to Jerusalem to discuss the nature of the gospel (Gal. 2:1-3). Titus was so vibrant a disciple that the Jerusalem leaders were persuaded that Paul's law-free gospel was acceptable (Gal. 2:3-5). Titus was with Paul in Ephesus on his third missionary journey and was Paul's ambassador to the troubled church in Corinth, carrying both the "severe letter" and 2 Corinthians (see **Occasion** for **2 CORINTHIANS**).

After Paul was released from his Roman imprisonment, he assigned Titus the responsibility of helping the churches on the island of Crete with their doctrinal and organizational difficulties. After this letter was written, Paul sent him to Dalmatia (2 Tim. 4:10). Titus proved to be a courageous and strong leader.

Crete is one of the largest islands in the Mediterranean Sea, lying directly south of the Aegean Sea. It is about 160 miles across, with a long history of civilization. In the Old Testament it was called Caphtor, and the Philistine people probably migrated from there to southern Palestine. Paul's shipwreck adventure occurred after the captain of the ship he was on declined to spend the winter in Crete (Acts 27). Life in Crete was distressing because of the lying and laziness of the people (1:12).

Occasion

It is not known when the gospel first came to Crete. Paul had left Titus there when he discovered that false teaching had upset the stability of the churches there. The exact nature of this teaching is impossible to determine, but it was probably similar to the error facing the Ephesian church about the same time (see **Occasion** for **1 TIMOTHY**). Both the false teaching and the Cretan character made Titus's task a big one. From an undisclosed location, possibly Macedonia or Ephesus, Paul wrote this letter to encourage Titus and to remind him of the responsibilities he faced on Crete.

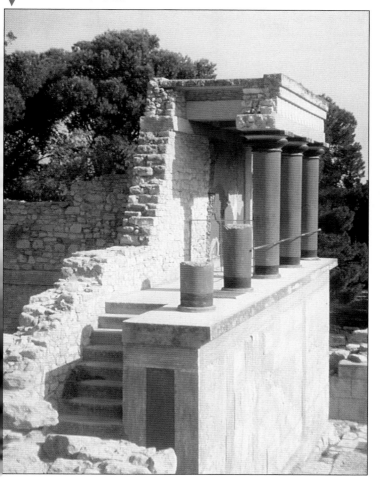

▼ Palace of Minos on Crete.

LITERARY FEATURES

Genre and Literary Style
An epistle written in Koine *Greek*

See ***Genre and Literary Style*** for **1 THESSALONIANS** for information about the genre *epistle*. The standard parts of a first-century epistle appear in Titus, except that the thanksgiving is missing: salutation (1:1-4), main body (1:5–3:14), farewell (3:15). This letter and 1 and 2 Timothy share certain vocabulary and style elements that make these three books distinctive. So clearly do they belong together that they are often considered as a unit, "the pastoral epistles."

Themes
Sound doctrine, elders, proper conduct for each age and gender

Sound doctrine is crucial as the cure for false teaching. This letter gives the qualifications for elders (also called bishops), but not for other church officers (see 1 Tim. 3). The term *elder* (Greek, *presbyteros*) refers to the maturity and respect—the character qualities—that church leaders must have and was probably derived from the model of the Jewish synagogues. The term *bishop* (Greek, *episkopos*) is better translated "overseer" and refers to the ministry responsibilities entrusted to church leaders. This term was probably taken from Hellenistic (Greek) cultural patterns. Titus 2:1-9 catalogs appropriate relationships within the congregation.

Book Features and Structure
See ***Book Features and Structure*** for **2 TIMOTHY** for information about the "faithful sayings" in the pastoral epistles.

The letter has three brief chapters and only 46 verses. Chapter 1 deals with church organization; chapter 2 gives advice to various groups in the church; chapter 3 is essentially a reminder of what sound doctrine includes.

PHILEMON

THE EPISTLE TO PHILEMON

This book is so named as the letter that Paul the apostle wrote to Philemon.

▶ *Key Text: verse 16*

"Not now as a servant, but above a servant, a brother beloved, specially to me, but how much more unto thee, both in the flesh, and in the Lord?"

▶ *Key Term: "Brother"*

When master and slave are both Christian, they are brothers, and therefore essentially equal. If Christian brotherhood extends this far, then it covers all relationships among the people of God.

▶ *One-Sentence Summary*

Everyone who has repented of sin and come to Christ should be welcomed as a brother (or sister), treated gently, and forgiven by other believers.

Figure of slave seeking refuge at an altar. Onesimus, Philemon's slave found refuge and freedom in Christ through the ministry of Paul.

GOD'S MESSAGE IN THE BOOK

Purpose

Paul wrote his friend Philemon to urge gentle treatment and forgiveness of a runaway slave, Onesimus. Some scholars believe that Paul's words in verse 21, "knowing that thou wilt also do more than I say," are a strong hint for Philemon to set Onesimus free. Paul also asked Philemon for hospitality when he visited.

Christian Worldview Elements

Philemon deals particularly with the worldview categories of *covenant and redemption* and *ethics and morality*. This book focuses on the ethical responsibilities among redeemed individuals in the covenant community.

GOD
CREATION
SOVEREIGNTY AND PROVIDENCE
FAITH AND REASON
REVELATION AND AUTHORITY
HUMANITY
REBELLION AND SIN
▶ **COVENANT AND REDEMPTION**
COMMUNITY AND CHURCH
DISCIPLESHIP
▶ **ETHICS AND MORALITY**
TIME AND ETERNITY

Teachings about God

In this epistle God the Father is the source of grace and peace and the one to whom Christians pray (vv. 3-4). Jesus is the center of faith, on whose account Paul was in prison (vv. 5,9). The Holy Spirit is not specifically mentioned.

Teachings about Humanity

Philemon addresses slavery, an ethical problem that has vexed human life—and Christianity—for centuries. The book does not attack the institution of slavery as a sin, which could not have gained a hearing in the first century. Instead, it teaches that in Christ both master and slave are to consider each other as brothers. When the concept of the basic equality of all who are in Christ prevails, slavery will not endure as an institution. This truth has demonstrated its power in many cultures.

Teachings about Salvation

Salvation is seen through the perspective of two individuals, the master (Philemon) and the slave (Onesimus). Philemon was indebted to the apostle because Paul had brought the message of salvation to him (v. 19). Onesimus is a classic example of transformation because of the message of salvation: "In time past [he] was to thee unprofitable, but now profitable to thee and to me" (v. 11).

CHRIST IN PHILEMON

Christ's grace is offered to master and slave alike. In Christ, master and slave become brothers.

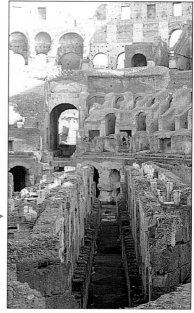 **GOD'S STORY**

When the Events of This Book Happened
From about AD 53 to 61

Philemon had come to Christ through Paul, evidently while Paul was in Ephesus on his third missionary journey. He had arrived there about AD 53 (Acts 19). Paul wrote at a time that he was imprisoned (vv. 10,13). This was the time he was in Rome for two years waiting to appear before Nero (about AD 60–61), as Acts 28 describes.

How Philemon Fits into God's "Story"

Philemon is part of "chapter 5" of God's story: God spreads the kingdom through the church. Although the term *kingdom* does not appear in this letter, its message is kingdom centered. All citizens of God's kingdom are brothers and sisters, and therefore they are under obligation to relate to one another with love and gentleness (see Matt. 5:1-10 for the character qualities of kingdom citizens).

Interior of Colosseum in Rome. Onesimus fled Colosse and came to Rome where he met Paul and was led to faith in Christ.

347

ORIGINAL HISTORICAL SETTING

Author and Date of Writing
Paul the apostle, about AD 61

This book claims to be written by Paul (v. 1). All scholars accept this claim. See *Author and Date of Writing* for **ROMANS** for more information about Paul. The apostle wrote from Roman imprisonment as described at the end of Acts, around AD 60–61.

First Audience and Destination
Philemon, Paul's dear friend, who was in Colosse

Philemon was a wealthy Christian from Colosse with a wife, Apphia, and son, Archippus (Col. 4:17; Philem. 2). Paul had led Philemon to faith in Christ, and they had worked together for the cause of Christ in ways not known (Philem. 1,19). At the time Paul wrote Philemon, he was the host for one of the house churches of Colosse (Philem. 1). For information about Colosse, see *First Audience and Destination* for **COLOSSIANS**.

Occasion

Onesimus, one of Philemon's slaves, had evidently stolen money from his master and then run away to Rome (v. 18). Somehow Onesimus had made his way to the house where Paul was under arrest, and he had been converted to Christ. His life had been transformed, and he had become a useful helper to Paul.

Paul, however, concluded that it was right for Onesimus to return to his master, even though Philemon had every legal right to deal with Onesimus harshly. Severe floggings were common punishments when runaway slaves were caught. Paul therefore wrote this letter to urge Philemon to forgive Onesimus and to treat him gently (vv. 17-18). Paul also alerted Philemon of his plans to visit him whenever he was released (v. 22). Philemon is one of the four prison epistles. See *Occasion* for **COLOSSIANS**.

According to Colossians 4:7-9, Onesimus traveled to Colosse under the protection of Tychicus at the same time that Tychicus was carrying the letter to the Colossians. Thus, when Tychicus traveled from Rome to Colosse, he was responsible for delivering two epistles to congregations (Ephesians and Colossians) as well as returning one slave (Onesimus), who probably hand-delivered the letter to Philemon.

ASIA MINOR

Philemon, a citizen of Colosse, may have come to Christ when Paul held discussions in the lecture hall of Tyrannus at Ephesus over a two-year period. Luke says, "All the inhabitants of the province of Asia, both Jews and Greeks, heard the word of the Lord" (Acts19:10 HCSB). The church at Colosse met in the home of Philemon.

LITERARY FEATURES

Genre and Literary Style
A brief epistle written in Koine *Greek*

See **Genre and Literary Style** for **1 THESSALONIANS** for information about the genre *epistle*. This letter has all four standard parts of a first-century epistle: salutation (vv. 1-3), thanksgiving (vv. 4-7), main body (vv. 8-22), farewell (vv. 23-25). The Greek of this letter is typical for Paul.

Themes
Love, forgiveness

Paul's emphasis on love (Greek, *agape*) as the motive for all relationships among Christians is striking (vv. 5,7,9). Interestingly, Paul's appeal for Philemon to forgive Onesimus's wrongs did not necessarily mean that he was to forget about his financial loss. Paul pledged that he would personally pay back what Onesimus had taken (v. 18).

Book Features and Structure

This is the shortest of all Paul's letters by far, at only 25 verses. It is the classic example of a personal communication, which, under the guidance of God's Spirit, has a place in the canon of Scripture as an inspired and abiding word from God to his people.

The body of the letter has two sections. First is Paul's request for Onesimus (through v. 21). Second is Paul's request for hospitality when he next visits Colosse.

HEBREWS

THE EPISTLE TO THE HEBREWS

This title is based on the belief that the first recipients were Hebrew (or Jewish) believers in Jesus as the Messiah.

▶ *Key Text: 1:1-3*

"God, who at sundry times and in divers manners spake in time past unto the fathers by the prophets, hath in these last days spoken unto us by his Son, whom he hath appointed heir of all things, by whom also he made the worlds; who being the brightness of his glory, and the express image of his person, and upholding all things by the word of his power, when he had by himself purged our sins, sat down on the right hand of the Majesty on high."

▶ *Key Term: "Better"*

This book repeatedly makes the case that Christ and Christianity is better or superior to the old way of the old covenant. The word *better* (Greek, *kreitton* or *kreisson*) appears twelve times.

▶ *One-Sentence Summary*

Jesus Christ, who is better than the angels, Moses, Joshua, and the Hebrew high priests, made a better sacrifice and established a better covenant, ensuring that the old way is obsolete and that faith is the better way to live.

Step-trench cut into the tel of Old Testament Jericho to uncover the many levels of destruction. "By faith the walls of Jericho fell down after being encircled for seven days" (Heb. 11:30 HCSB).

GOD'S MESSAGE IN THE BOOK

Purpose

Hebrews was written to wean Jewish believers in Jesus from depending on the law of Moses or the old covenant, represented by the Old Testament, as the final rule for life. In order to do this the author emphasized the superiority of Jesus Christ both in his person and in his work. The author also showed that the essential weakness of the old covenant was its "planned obsolescence" in God's purposes.

Christian Worldview Elements

Hebrews deals particularly with the worldview categories of *revelation and authority, covenant and redemption,* and *community and church.* No Bible book more fully teaches the superiority of Christ's person and work over all of God's previous dealings with humanity.

GOD
CREATION
SOVEREIGNTY AND PROVIDENCE
FAITH AND REASON
▶ **REVELATION AND AUTHORITY**
HUMANITY
REBELLION AND SIN
▶ **COVENANT AND REDEMPTION**
▶ **COMMUNITY AND CHURCH**
DISCIPLESHIP
ETHICS AND MORALITY
TIME AND ETERNITY

Teachings about God

God is the Father of Jesus Christ. He is wholly other and is to be approached with reverence and fear, "For our God *is* a consuming fire" (12:29). The superiority of Jesus to all possible rivals is the theme of the entire book. The full deity and complete humanity of Jesus is explicitly taught. The Holy Spirit in Hebrews is both the one who speaks in Scripture (3:7; 10:15) and the one alive among believers in the present age (6:4; 10:29).

Teachings about Humanity

Many prominent Old Testament persons are mentioned in Hebrews, and the "roll call of faith" in chapter 11 is an impressive reminder of what believing humans can do. The emphasis in Hebrews, however, is that Jesus has the glory and honor of being humanity at its best. In Psalm 8 God declared "man" as the crown of creation; Hebrews 2 declares that this "man" is none other than Jesus Christ.

Teachings about Salvation

Jesus is a better high priest than the high priests of the old covenant. Further, Jesus' death was a superior sacrifice to any that had been made before, "For it *is* not possible that the blood of bulls and of goats should take away sins" (10:4). At the same time, however, Hebrews affirms that the human response to God's redemptive actions, faith, has always and forever been the single way that pleases God. This Bible book, more clearly than any other, shows the permanence of the new covenant state of affairs and the impermanence of the old covenant.

CHRIST IN HEBREWS

Christ is both God's agent of creation and the one for whom the universe is created. He is superior to angels, Moses, the priesthood, the old covenant, and the Levitical sacrificial system. Christ is both the source of our faith and the one who brings it to perfection. He is the same yesterday, today, and forever.

GOD'S STORY

When the Events of This Book Happened
Probably in the late AD 60s

The historical background is probably the persecution of Christians in Rome after the great fire of AD 64. The only contemporary events mentioned in the book are the persecutions the recipients have experienced and a few notices at the end of the book. These cannot be dated precisely, but late AD 60s seems to fit.

How Hebrews Fits into God's "Story"

Hebrews is part of "chapter 5" of God's story: God spreads the kingdom through the church. Language about the kingdom of God does not dominate this book, but it is striking when it exists. Jesus the Son of God is the King of God's everlasting kingdom (1:8; 7:1-2). The recipients are told about their future eternal state in explicit kingdom language: "Wherefore we receiving a kingdom which cannot be moved, let us have grace, whereby we may serve God acceptably with reverence and godly fear" (12:28).

ORIGINAL HISTORICAL SETTING

Author and Date of Writing
Unknown, perhaps around AD 66

The secret of this book's authorship is one of the longest ongoing challenges for Bible students. In fact, scholarship has hardly advanced further today than Origen of the third century, who said that God alone knew who wrote the epistle. In the earliest centuries Barnabas and Luke were mentioned as possible authors; in the Reformation era, Luther made the brilliant suggestion that Apollos may have been the author. From the fifth to the sixteenth centuries, Paul was believed to be the author, and many handwritten Greek manuscripts added Paul's name to the title, as did many translations.

The consensus of contemporary scholarship is that Paul could not have been the author. The strongest argument is historical: the author put himself in second generation Christianity, distancing himself from eyewitnesses. In the eyes of many Bible students, it is impossible that the one who wrote Hebrews 2:3-4 could also have written Galatians 1:11-12, Paul's vehement claim that he was an eyewitness.

The author was an expert in Scripture, quoting extensively from the Greek translation (the Septuagint). He was almost certainly Jewish, with an outstanding ability in Greek composition. Although knowing his name would be interesting, it would add little to the interpretation of the book's message. The date of composition may be around AD 66, almost certainly before the destruction of Jerusalem (AD 70).

First Audience and Destination
Jewish believers, perhaps in Rome

As the title suggests, the letter was first "to the Hebrews." A number of features point in this direction, particularly the detailed arguments about the sacrificial system and the priesthood of the Old Testament. They were, however, now Christians. The greeting of 13:24 was sent from persons with the author to their fellow Italians "back home." This and the first citation of the epistle, by Clement of Rome about AD 96, suggests that the original recipients were Christians in Italy, perhaps Rome itself.

Occasion

The precise occasion has been debated because interpreters are limited to the data provided by the epistle, which is not entirely clear. These Jewish believers had been persecuted for their new religion (10:32-39). They were now, however, considering giving up Christianity and returning to Judaism, which was legally recognized, unlike Christianity. Hebrews 10:25 may refer to some who had already withdrawn from meeting with the mixed-race congregation. The author, who knew their situation well, composed this letter about the superiority of Christ and Christianity and the danger of turning away to something that was clearly inferior.

A training track at Olympia. The author of Hebrews uses athletic imagery in exhorting fellow Christians to "lay aside every weight and the sin that so easily ensnares us, and run with endurance the race that lies before us, keeping our eyes on Jesus" (Heb. 12:1-2 HCSB).

LITERARY FEATURES

Genre and Literary Style
A long, formal epistle written in excellent Koine Greek

Some scholars designate Hebrews as a tractate (a formal treatise rather than a pastoral letter). Two of the usual features of an epistle (salutation and thanksgiving) are missing, although there is a body (1:1–13:17) and a farewell (13:18-25). In addition, it has a number of sermon-like features. It begins with a rhetorical statement of its thesis (1:1-3) and develops step-by-step arguments. The farewell shows that in its present form it was sent as a letter. The style of argument has parallels to the figurative interpretations made by Philo, the Jewish scholar of Alexandria. The Greek of Hebrews is outstanding, with a large vocabulary and excellent style, suggesting that the author was highly educated. The style is more like that of Luke and Acts than any other New Testament book.

Themes
Superiority of Christ, the new covenant, Christ's priesthood, warnings

The author shows the superiority of Christ in a number of ways: he is better than angels (invisible and powerful spirit beings), than Moses (the great law-giver), than Joshua (the great land-giver), and than Aaron (the high priest). The new covenant Christ made is better because God designed it, unlike the Mosaic covenant, to last forever.

Book Features and Structure

Hebrews is memorable for its serious warning passages (2:1-4; 3:7-19; 4:11-13; 10:19-31; 12:25-29). These should be understood as applying to all who profess Christ (but may not "possess" him). The plea is to prove the genuineness of faith by refusing the pressure to defect. The structure of Hebrews revolves around three main points. First, Christ is superior in his person (1–7). Second, Christ is superior in his sacrificial work (8–10). Third, faith is the better way (10–13).

JAMES

THE EPISTLE OF JAMES

This letter is titled according to its author, James, who was probably the half brother of Jesus.

▶ *Key Text: 2:26*

"For as the body without the spirit is dead, so faith without works is dead also."

▶ *Key Term: "Works"*

This book focuses on the importance of good works as the evidence of genuine faith. As such, it perfectly complements Galatians.

▶ *One-Sentence Summary*

True faith must be lived out in everyday life by good deeds, especially in the face of trials or persecution, and such good works demonstrate the presence of faith and justification before God.

The turbulent waters of the Mediterranean Sea as seen from Caesarea Maritima. James urged his readers to be people of faith and not doubt. "For the doubter is like the surging sea, driven and tossed by the wind" (James 1:6 HCSB).

GOD'S MESSAGE IN THE BOOK

Purpose

James was originally composed to let (Jewish) believers in Jesus know the importance of having a practical, living, everyday faith. For James, practical faith equaled good works, and those who professed faith yet had no good works could not presume that they were truly God's people. James also wrote to give good advice about what to do in the presence of temptations, trials, and persecution.

Christian Worldview Elements

James focuses on the worldview categories of *community and church* and *ethics and morality*. This book teaches the importance of good works as the inevitable and essential fruit of salvation.

GOD
CREATION
SOVEREIGNTY AND PROVIDENCE
FAITH AND REASON
REVELATION AND AUTHORITY
HUMANITY
REBELLION AND SIN
COVENANT AND REDEMPTION
► COMMUNITY AND CHURCH
DISCIPLESHIP
► ETHICS AND MORALITY
TIME AND ETERNITY

Teachings about God

God is good and the Father of his redeemed children. James often calls him "the Lord," evidently parallel to the Old Testament usage of "the LORD" (Yahweh), in particular calling him "the Lord of sabaoth" (meaning "hosts," 5:4). Jesus is mentioned only twice (1:1; 2:1), which contributes to the distinctive Old Testament feel to this book. The Spirit is not referred to (but 4:5 may be an exception, as in the New American Standard Bible).

Teachings about Humanity

James had a realistic, some would say pessimistic, view of the effects of sin in human life. The rich oppress the poor; temptation is a constant danger; all persons are possessed of an evil tongue. Even believers can be called "adulterers and adulteresses" (4:4) for being too friendly with the evil world, like the people of Israel who "went a-whoring after other gods" (Judg. 2:17; 8:33). The advice James offered was to submit to God's sovereign goodness, to seek to live a life of true religion, and to do good deeds.

Teachings about Salvation

God saves through the action of "the engrafted word" (1:21), bringing the response of faith. While Paul emphasized that faith alone saves, James emphasized that saving faith is never alone. For Paul, justification is a legal declaration of righteousness before God (see **ROMANS**). James, however, used justification in the sense of being righteous before people. Thus he can say, "Ye see then how that by works a man is justified, and not by faith only" (2:24). Good works are open to observation by others; faith is not; therefore good works make faith visible. Good works are never the root (cause) of salvation, but they are always the fruit (result) of salvation.

CHRIST IN JAMES

Salvation made James a slave of his half brother Jesus, the resurrected Lord (1:1). Jesus the Lord shares God's unique glory (2:1). Looking forward to his return will be a source of patience with the trials and tests of life.

GOD'S STORY

When the Events of This Book Happened
Probably in the AD 40s

The only events mentioned in the book are the persecutions the recipients have experienced. These cannot be dated precisely, but the decade of the AD 40s seems to fit.

How James Fits into God's "Story"

James is part of "chapter 5" of God's story: God spreads the kingdom through the church. The kingdom of God is mentioned only once in this book. This instance is consistent with the letter's overall teaching that God's values and the wicked world's values oppose each other. Those who are rich in this world are likely to miss the kingdom; those who are poor in this world will be "heirs of the kingdom" (2:5). This is strikingly like the teaching of Jesus in the Gospels (Luke 6:20).

ORIGINAL HISTORICAL SETTING

Author and Date of Writing
James, perhaps around AD 45

The author identified himself as "James, a servant of God and of the Lord Jesus Christ" (1:1). James is the English translation of the Hebrew name *Jacob* when it appears in the New Testament, *Yakobos* in Greek. There were several Jameses in the New Testament, including two apostles (Matt. 10:2-3). This letter was almost certainly written by the James who rose to prominence in the church of Jerusalem (Acts 12:17; 15:13; 21:18). This was "James the Lord's brother" (Gal. 1:19; 2:9). The son of Mary and Joseph, James had not believed that Jesus his older half brother was the Messiah until after the resurrection, when Jesus appeared to him (Matt. 13:55; John 7:5; 1 Cor. 15:7).

James was an effective leader as Acts and this letter shows. He apparently rose to leadership in the Jerusalem church sometime around the time that Peter left Jerusalem, about AD 44 (see Acts 12, esp. v. 17). The tenor of his letter is such that it must predate the Jerusalem Council of AD 49 that opened Christianity officially and fully to Gentiles (Acts 15). Thus, the epistle is likely to be dated between 44 and 49, with the year 45 being a reasonable estimate, perhaps composed in Jerusalem. James was probably the first New Testament book written.

According to the Jewish historian Josephus, James was martyred in AD 62. Christian tradition indicates that he was thrown from the pinnacle of the temple.

First Audience and Destination
Jewish believers living somewhere outside Palestine

This letter was written to Jewish followers of Jesus. Their meeting place was called a "synagogue" in the original (2:2), and they were led by "elders" (5:14). They were part of "the twelve tribes which are scattered abroad" (1:1), meaning Jews living outside Palestine. They lived in an unknown city of the Roman Empire where they spoke Greek. No reference is made to Gentiles.

Occasion

No one knows how James came to know about these believers. They had been victims of harassment of some kind and were being taken advantage of by their rich neighbors (1:2; 2:6). He wrote these discouraged disciples to encourage them not to lose heart. They also needed to know that the elements of true religion taught both in the Old Testament and by Jesus—giving, praying, fasting, living a holy life, and caring for widows, orphans, and the poor—were still part of the royal law of love that they were to live by (Matt. 6:1-18; James 1:27; 2:8).

Bronze mirror. "If anyone is a hearer of the word and not a doer, he is like a man looking at his own face in a mirror; for he looks at himself, goes away, and right away forgets what kind of man he was" (James 1:23-24 HCSB).

LITERARY FEATURES

Genre and Literary Style
An epistle written in Koine Greek

James is the first of seven general epistles in the New Testament, all of which are titled according to their author. Two of the usual features of an epistle (thanksgiving and farewell) are missing, although there are a salutation (1:1) and a body (1:2–5:20). James is a pastoral letter, driven by the occasion and needs of the recipients, rather than a tractate (a formal treatise). Many scholars have noted the parallels in style between Proverbs and James. Many practical truths are presented, but they are only loosely connected by the general theme of everyday Christian living. The Greek style is considered above average for the books of the New Testament.

Themes
Faith and works, trials and temptations, rich and poor, the tongue, patience

These themes are all developed to encourage believers disheartened by their circumstances. All these themes deal with living successfully in this life, being aware that everything happens according to God's providence (4:15). Thus doctrinal truths are presented only when they help the reader understand how they relate to living effectively in everyday life.

Book Features and Structure

James is noted not only for its similarity to Proverbs but also for its similarity to the Sermon on the Mount. (It is at least possible that James heard his brother Jesus give this sermon, even though he was not yet a follower.) The following points of connection are noteworthy:

- The poor to be rich in faith and inherit the kingdom, James 2:5; Matthew 5:3
- Contrasting plant pairs, such as grapes versus thorns, James 3:10-12; Matthew 7:15-20
- Blessing promised to peacemakers, James 3:18; Matthew 5:9
- The ease with which earthly riches are corrupted, James 5:2-3; Matthew 6:19-20
- Swearing prohibited ("let your yea be yea"), James 5:12; Matthew 5:33-37

The structure of James is very loose. Each chapter may be characterized by a key term, however: (1) trials, (2) works, (3) tongue, (4) wisdom, (5) patience.

1 PETER

THE FIRST EPISTLE OF PETER

Titled according to its author, this is the first canonical letter by Simon Peter, the apostle of
Jesus.

 ### Key Text: 4:13

*"But rejoice, inasmuch as ye are partakers of Christ's sufferings; that, when his glory
shall be revealed, ye may be glad also with exceeding joy."*

Key Term: "Hope"

This epistle emphasizes hope for suffering believers. Hope (Greek, *elpis*) means "future certainty" rather than a vague expectation of some future occurrence.

One-Sentence Summary

As Christians grow in understanding their privileges in salvation, their blessings of election,
and the theology of suffering, they will live in holiness and humility, waiting for their great
future hope of sharing Christ's glory.

Statue of lion. Peter likened the devil to
"a roaring lion, looking for anyone he
can devour" (1 Pet. 5:8).

GOD'S MESSAGE IN THE BOOK

Purpose

First Peter was written to encourage suffering Christians to live in light of the future. The apostle wanted to give a number of doctrinal insights and also provided many practical instructions such as how to submit to those in authority. This book contains the most extensive New Testament development of a "theology of suffering," and it echoes the teaching of Job that God's glory is served when suffering is permitted.

Christian Worldview Elements

This book directs attention to the worldview categories of *sovereignty and providence, covenant and redemption,* and *ethics and morality.* No Bible book more clearly teaches the relationship between suffering and salvation.

> GOD
> CREATION
> ▶ **SOVEREIGNTY AND PROVIDENCE**
> FAITH AND REASON
> REVELATION AND AUTHORITY
> HUMANITY
> REBELLION AND SIN
> ▶ **COVENANT AND REDEMPTION**
> COMMUNITY AND CHURCH
> DISCIPLESHIP
> ▶ **ETHICS AND MORALITY**
> TIME AND ETERNITY

Teachings about God

This book notes many attributes of God, from his fore-knowledge (1:2) to his grace (5:12). The glory of God is the goal of all things (4:11). Jesus' suffering and death for sinners is highly emphasized, as is his resurrection and return in glory. The Holy Spirit, who inspired the prophets of old, has now been sent to God's people (1:11; 4:14). First Peter 1:2 is an important text for understanding the Trinity.

Teachings about Humanity

First Peter dignifies all classes of human life by showing that living by the gospel makes a great difference in relationships. Christians submit both to government and to masters to the glory of God. In the Christian family, husbands and wives have a mutual responsibility to respect each other. In the congregation, spiritual leaders ("elders," 5:1) lead their flocks by being humble servants, creating a context of mutual submission.

Teachings about Salvation

Salvation in this book is past, present, and future. The past aspect involves God's sovereign election as well as Jesus' suffering and death to purchase salvation (2:9; 3:18). The present aspect involves the regeneration and the ongoing faith of God's people (1:3,21; 5:9). At Christ's return, those "who are kept by the power of God through faith" will receive the "salvation ready to be revealed in the last time" (1:5).

CHRIST IN 1 PETER

The Spirit of Christ was present in the Hebrew prophets pointing them to the sufferings of Christ and the glory that followed his sufferings. Christ is like a lamb without defect or blemish. His precious blood redeems believers from their futile ways. Believers can expect to suffer as he suffered and anticipate the joy of his coming in glory.

GOD'S STORY

When the Events of This Book Happened
Probably in the AD 60s

The only contemporary events the book mentions are the persecutions the recipients have experienced. These cannot be dated precisely, but the decade of the AD 60s seems to fit.

How 1 Peter Fits into God's "Story"

First Peter is part of "chapter 5" of God's story: God spreads the kingdom through the church. The kingdom of God is not directly mentioned. Yet what had been said in Scripture about Israel as God's people is now fulfilled by God's new people: "But ye *are* a chosen generation, a royal priesthood, an holy nation, a peculiar people; that ye should show forth the praises of him who hath called you" (2:9). Israel was the chosen people (Isa. 44:1), so now are Christians; Israel was the royal priesthood (Isa. 61:6), so now are Christians; Israel was a holy nation (Deut. 28:9), so now are Christians; Israel was a peculiar (special) treasure to God (Deut. 14:2), so now are Christians. God's kingdom plan for Israel to praise him (Isa. 43:21) is now fulfilled by his new people, the church.

ORIGINAL HISTORICAL SETTING

Author and Date of Writing
Simon Peter the apostle, perhaps around AD 64

The author called himself "Peter, an apostle of Jesus Christ" (1:1). He was the son of Jonah (or John), the brother of Andrew, and a Galilean fisherman by trade when Jesus called him to become an apostle. His birth name, Simeon (often shortened to Simon), was transformed by Jesus to "Rock" ("Peter" in Greek; "Cephas" in Aramaic).

Peter's role as one of the three most prominent apostles (along with James and John) is well known from the Gospels. Peter rose to become the most visible leader of Christianity in Jerusalem. According to Paul, Peter was the apostle to Jews (Gal. 2:8). Peter's contribution to the New Testament was two epistles and probably collaboration with John Mark in producing the second Gospel. In this letter Peter mentioned that he was in Rome (called "Babylon," as in Revelation) and that Mark was with him (5:13). According to tradition, he was later crucified in Rome during the last years of Nero.

For the past two centuries, many critical scholars have argued that Peter could not be the author of this epistle, primarily for two reasons. First, the excellent Greek of this letter is thought to be beyond what a Galilean fisherman could produce (Acts 4:13). Second, the persecutions are thought to belong to a later era than Nero's. These objections may be satisfactorily answered. First, the Greek style is probably due to the help of Silvanas (Silas), which Peter acknowledged (5:12). Second, the suffering of the believers could just as easily have occurred in Nero's time as in a later era. There is no persuasive reason to deny that Simon Peter wrote this epistle.

First Audience and Destination
Believers living in Roman provinces of Asia Minor

This letter was addressed "to the strangers scattered throughout Pontus, Galatia, Cappadocia, Asia, and Bithynia" (1:1). These five Roman provinces make up roughly the northern half of modern Turkey. The order is probably the route the letter carrier followed. Evidence within the letter suggests that these believers were primarily Gentile (and therefore pagan, 1:18) in background, although there was probably also a Jewish minority (accounting for the frequent Old Testament references).

Occasion

Peter knew a great deal about what these believers had gone through, but he did not tell his source of information. They had been victims of serious persecution and unjust suffering, something Peter called a "fiery trial" (4:12). This in all likelihood was the first official Roman persecution of Christians, instigated by Nero after the great fire in Rome of AD 64. These disciples needed to be encouraged not to lose heart. He wanted to remind them of a number of important doctrinal truths (about God and salvation) as well as to help them see that suffering within the plan of God serves his glory. Thus, Peter wrote this letter with the help of Silvanus (Silas).

A shepherd with his sheep. "For you were like sheep going astray, but you have now returned to the shepherd and guardian of your souls" (1 Pet. 2:25 HCSB).

LITERARY FEATURES

Genre and Literary Style
An epistle written in Koine Greek

First Peter is the second of seven general epistles in the New Testament, all of which are titled according to their author. All four of the usual features of an epistle are present: salutation (1:1-2), thanksgiving (1:3-5), body (1:6–5:11), farewell (5:12-14). Some scholars designate 1 Peter as a tractate (a formal treatise rather than a pastoral letter), particularly since it originated as a circular letter intended for several churches. The Greek style is excellent, on a par with Luke, Acts, and Hebrews.

Themes
Hope, suffering, holiness, humility, submission

The first of these themes is oriented to the future, and it drives the rest. When believers are absolutely certain that there is a glorious future ahead, they can endure whatever negative experiences they must face in the present. Suffering becomes a privilege; holiness means becoming like God; practiciing humility and submission in relationships models living according to Jesus' example, "that ye should follow his steps" (2:21).

Book Features and Structure

This epistle is noted for careful composition and many Old Testament quotations. Rather than give one extensive doctrinal presentation followed by application (such as Paul often did), Peter goes back and forth between doctrinal and practical teachings.

The following structure is based on this doctrinal-practical alteration. *Doctrinal teaching:* 1:1-12, privileges of salvation; 2:4-10, blessings of election; 3:13–4:19, theology of suffering. *Practical teaching:* 1:13–2:3, holiness; 2:11–3:12, submission; 5:1-14, humility.

2 PETER

THE SECOND EPISTLE OF PETER

Titled according to its author, this is the second canonical letter by Simon Peter, the apostle of Jesus.

▶ *Key Text: 1:12*

"Wherefore I will not be negligent to put you always in remembrance of these things, though ye know them, and be established in the present truth."

▶ *Key Term: "Return"*

This epistle shows the importance of holding firmly to the truth in the face of false teachings, particularly the truth that Jesus will visibly, bodily, and gloriously return and bring about the consummation of all things.

▶ *One-Sentence Summary*

As Christians grow in understanding, they will be safeguarded from false teachers, especially those who deny the return of Christ and the end of the world as it now exists.

The triangular-shaped Hittite postern (tunnel) at Hattusas in Asia Minor, which leads within the walls of the city. View is looking into the postern uphill toward the light at the top that is within the ancient defense walls. "So we have the prophetic word strongly confirmed. You will do well to pay attention to it, as to a lamp shining in a dismal place, until the day dawns and the morning star rises in your hearts" (2 Pet. 1:19 HCSB).

GOD'S MESSAGE IN THE BOOK

Purpose

Second Peter was written to warn Christians that were facing the coming of false teachers. The apostle wanted to arm them with true knowledge as opposed to the heresy that was threatening them (2:1). The false teaching that Peter particularly attacked concerned whether Christ's return and the end of the world would really happen.

Christian Worldview Elements

Second Peter focuses attention on the worldview categories of *revelation and authority* and *ethics and morality*. This book especially shows the nature of truth as revealed by God (rather than merely discovered by people) and that this view of truth has a bearing on behavior.

GOD
CREATION
SOVEREIGNTY AND PROVIDENCE
FAITH AND REASON
▶ **REVELATION AND AUTHORITY**
HUMANITY
REBELLION AND SIN
COVENANT AND REDEMPTION
COMMUNITY AND CHURCH
DISCIPLESHIP
▶ **ETHICS AND MORALITY**
TIME AND ETERNITY

Teachings about God

God is the Father of Jesus, and he glorified his Son (1:17). He is the judge of all beings, human and superhuman (2:4). This is the only Bible book that uses the full title "our Lord and Saviour Jesus Christ" (1:11; 2:20; 3:18), a magnificent confession by one who knew him face-to-face during his earthly life. The single reference to the Holy Spirit mentions his role in the inspiration of Scripture (1:21).

Teachings about Humanity

Second Peter shows the great evil of those who are enslaved by error and sin: "as natural brute beasts, made to be taken and destroyed, speak evil of the things that they understand not; and shall utterly perish in their own corruption" (2:12). On the other hand, redeemed humanity can grow in every virtue (1:5-8).

Teachings about Salvation

This book provides an important definition of heresy as "denying the Lord that bought them" (1:12). In other words, a heresy is a serious error about the person or work of Christ, in particular a denial that his death involved the purchase of salvation. There is little that the letter develops about Christ's work, but God's people are described as those "that have obtained like precious faith" with the apostle (1:1). The future dimension of salvation will be revealed on "the day of the Lord" and the coming of "new heavens and a new earth, wherein dwelleth righteousness" (3:10,13).

CHRIST IN 2 PETER

Christ came to live, die, and rise again in space and time. This is not some myth cleverly made up by men. Peter says that he was an eyewitness of Christ's glory on the mount of transfiguration when he, James, and John heard the voice of the Father say, "This is My beloved Son. I take delight in Him!" (2 Pet. 1:17 HCSB).

GOD'S STORY

When the Events of This Book Happened
Probably in the AD 60s

The only contemporary events the book mentions are the coming of false teachers. These cannot be dated precisely, but the decade of the AD 60s seems to fit.

How 2 Peter Fits into God's "Story"

Second Peter is part of "chapter 5" of God's story: God spreads the kingdom through the church. The kingdom of God is directly mentioned in this epistle as the glorious goal of God's chosen people: "Wherefore the rather, brethren, give diligence to make your calling and election sure: for if ye do these things, ye shall never fall: For so an entrance shall be ministered unto you abundantly into the everlasting kingdom of our Lord and Saviour Jesus Christ" (1:10-11).

ORIGINAL HISTORICAL SETTING

Author and Date of Writing
Simon Peter the apostle, perhaps around AD 67

The author named himself "Simon Peter," and after hesitation on the part of a few, this book was accepted as apostolic in the fourth century. See **Author and Date of Writing** for **1 PETER**. For the past two centuries, however, almost all critical scholars have denied that Peter could be the author of this epistle. Both the style and content of this letter are noticeably different from 1 Peter. The difference in style, however, may be accounted for by the loss of Silas's secretarial assistance (1 Pet. 5:12), and the difference in content may surely be attributed to the differing occasions of the two letters. Another argument has been based on the reference to Paul's epistles (3:15-16), which supposedly refer to a time after Paul's letters have been collected, which in turn must be after Peter's lifetime. Yet this reference only means that Peter knew some of Paul's letters.

There is no persuasive reason to deny that Simon Peter wrote this epistle. The date of 6? is a best guess, determined by noting the strong tradition that Peter died during the last part of Nero's reign (ruled AD 54–68).

First Audience and Destination
Believers living in an unknown location

The recipients were not specified geographically. Peter knew these people well enough to call them "beloved" and to have written them a previous letter (3:1). There is no way to know whether these were the same believers addressed in his first epistle.

Occasion

Peter was aware of his own approaching death (1:14). He may already have been imprisoned in Rome, but he did not allude to this. He had become aware that these Christian friends were facing the threat of false teachers who were denying the saving work of Christ. Along with this went a skepticism about the historical facts surrounding the first coming of Jesus. Others were denying the second coming of Christ. As an eyewitness to Christ's life (1:16), perhaps one of the few left alive, Peter determined to write this letter before he died to affirm the reality of the first and second coming of Jesus and to "stir up your pure minds by way of remembrance" (3:1).

Site of Sodom and Gomorrah. Peter reminds his readers of God's judgment on Sodom and Gomorrah (2 Pet. 2:4-6). The cities of Sodom and Gomorrah as well as the other three cities of the plain destroyed by fire (Gen. 19:23-29) may have been located in this region.

LITERARY FEATURES

Genre and Literary Style
An epistle written in Koine *Greek*

Second Peter is the third of seven general epistles in the New Testament, all of which are titled according to their author. One of the usual features of an epistle (thanksgiving) is missing, although there is a salutation (1:1-2), a body (1:3–3:18a), and a farewell (in this letter, a brief doxology, 3:18b). Second Peter is a pastoral letter, driven by the occasion and needs of the recipients, rather than a tractate (a formal treatise). The Greek style is awkward but more like 1 Peter than any other part of the Scriptures.

Themes
Election, false teachers, "day of the Lord"

The letter strongly emphasizes divine predestination in salvation. The material on false teachers should be compared with Jude. The teaching on the "day of the Lord" is in the last chapter. This theme was also developed by Paul (1 Cor. 5:5; 2 Cor. 1:14; 1 Thess. 5:2; 2 Thess. 2:2). It appears to be the same as the "day of God" (2 Pet. 3:12; Rev. 16:14) and the "day of Christ" (Phil. 1:6,10; 2:16). See **JOEL** and **ZEPHANIAH** for this theme in the Old Testament.

Book Features and Structure

This epistle, especially chapter 2, is noted for its similarity to Jude, and most Bible students agree that there is a literary relationship between the two epistles. See **Book Features and Structure** for **JUDE**. Peter developed his letter around three main topics: truth (chap. 1), false teachers (chap. 2), and the return of Christ (chap. 3).

1 JOHN

THE FIRST EPISTLE OF JOHN

Titled according to its author, this is the first canonical letter by John, the apostle of Jesus.

▶ *Key Text: 1:3*

"That which we have seen and heard declare we unto you, that ye also may have fellowship with us: and truly our fellowship is with the Father, and with his Son Jesus Christ."

▶ *Key Term: "Fellowship"*

Fellowship (Greek, *koinonia*) is partnership with Jesus and partnership with other believers in Jesus. The best preventive against false doctrine is true fellowship.

▶ *One-Sentence Summary*

Christians have fellowship with Christ, who is God incarnate, through walking in the light and through living in love, and as a result they are secure in the eternal life that Christ has given them.

▼ Ruins at the Temple of Artemis at Ephesus. This letter likely was addressed to believers in Ephesus.

GOD'S MESSAGE IN THE BOOK

Purpose

First John was written mainly to combat the false doctrines of denying either the incarnation of Jesus Christ (that he came with real humanity and a truly physical body) or the messiahship of Jesus (that he is the Christ). These heresies led to certain false behaviors, in particular a denial of the seriousness of sin. John wrote not only to correct these dangers but to give positive encouragement about true beliefs and true Christian behavior, centered around fellowship with Jesus Christ.

Christian Worldview Elements

This book directs attention to the worldview categories of *faith and reason, covenant and redemption,* and *ethics and morality.* Reality is not just what the senses or reasons indicate but what can be known through faith. First John especially focuses on believing in Jesus' true identity and the reality of eternal life.

GOD
CREATION
SOVEREIGNTY AND PROVIDENCE
▶ **FAITH AND REASON**
REVELATION AND AUTHORITY
HUMANITY
REBELLION AND SIN
▶ **COVENANT AND REDEMPTION**
COMMUNITY AND CHURCH
DISCIPLESHIP
▶ **ETHICS AND MORALITY**
TIME AND ETERNITY

Teachings about God

God is seen especially in his relationship to Jesus Christ. Thus, he is "the Father." Jesus Christ is, in perfect complement, "the Son" (1:3). He is as well "the Christ" (2:22) who came "in the flesh" (4:2-3). The Holy Spirit has been given to believers (3:24; 4:13), and he enables believers to recognize and reject every false spirit (4:1-6).

Teachings about Humanity

First John recognizes only two categories of human beings: those who believe in Jesus Christ and all others (who belong to the spirit of the antichrist). Believers confess when they sin, but their lives are not characterized by sin (1:7-9; 5:16-18). They live in fellowship with God and with one another. Those who continue to live in sin are giving evidence that they have never known God (3:6).

Teachings about Salvation

One of the great texts about salvation is 1 John 2:2: "And he is the propitiation for our sins: and not for ours only, but also for the sins of the whole world." The term "propitiation" refers to removal of divine wrath because of sin, as also in Romans 3:25. Christ's death propitiated God's wrath not only for "our sins," referring to the people to whom John was writing, but includes persons from all ethnic, economic, and social groups (Gal. 3:28; Rev. 7:9-10). The benefits of Christ's death come only to those who believe (5:13).

CHRIST IN 1 JOHN

Jesus is the Word of life who has come to earth and has been seen, heard, and touched. He reveals to us who God is and what God has done for our salvation. He came to make it possible for us to have fellowship with the Father (1:3) and to have fellowship with other believers (1:7). That fellowship is possible because Christ's blood cleanses us and takes away the sin that separates us from God (1:7).

 GOD'S STORY

When the Events of This Book Happened
Probably in the AD 80s

The only contemporary events the book mentions are the teachings of the heretics. These cannot be dated precisely, but the decade of the AD 80s seems to fit.

How 1 John Fits into God's "Story"

First John is part of "chapter 5" of God's story: God spreads the kingdom through the church. The kingdom of God is not directly mentioned. However, Jesus is referred to as "Christ" ten times. Two of these references explicitly use "Christ" as a title rather than a name, calling on the readers to acknowledge him as "the Christ" that is, the Messiah promised by the prophets of Scripture (2:22; 5:1). As the Christ, Jesus is the Anointed One, King over the kingdom of God. Only those who believe Jesus is the Christ receive eternal life, mentioned six times in the letter (1:2; 2:25; 3:15; 5:11,13,20).

▼ Great Theater of Ephesus.

ORIGINAL HISTORICAL SETTING

Author and Date of Writing
John the apostle, possibly around AD 80–90

This letter is actually anonymous, but the style and approach are so much like the fourth Gospel that the epistle and the Gospel are generally acknowledged to be written by the same person. Thus, the rejection of John's authorship of the fourth Gospel by critical scholars also applies to this epistle. Christian tradition, however, has uniformly asserted that this author was John the apostle, which certainly fits the claim that the writer personally saw Jesus (1:1-4). See **Author and Date of Writing** for **JOHN** for more information. Most scholars believe that this epistle was written somewhat after the Gospel, but it is impossible to be certain. The decade of the AD 80s is a good estimate.

First Audience and Destination
Probably Christians living in Roman Asia

This letter was written to Christians (2:12-14,19; 3:1; 5:13). It makes the best sense if it is seen as addressed to the same believers, living in and around Ephesus, who had earlier received the fourth Gospel. See **First Audience and Destination** for **JOHN** for a discussion.

Occasion

John was intimately acquainted with these believers, whom he repeatedly called "little children." He had become aware of dangerous false teachings that threatened these believers. The foundational error appears to be the belief that "matter is sinful." If this is true then (1) Jesus could not have had a material body or else he was necessarily sinful, and (2) human beings are sinful because they have material bodies (rather than because of their sinful deeds or sinful nature), which in turn leads to errors about the relationship of believers to sin. Such dualism (spirit = good; matter = evil) later developed into Gnosticism, a heresy that challenged Christianity in the second and third centuries. John did not say how he became aware of this teaching. He penned his letter, however, as the response of an aged, beloved apostle to Christians in desperate need of his advice.

Ancient olive press. Extracted olive oil was used in a variety of ways in the ancient world. One of the uses was religious. Both persons and objects being dedicated to God's service were anointed with oil. In many places, this oil symbolizes the Holy Spirit. John writes, "But you have an anointing from the Holy Spirit" (1 John 2:20 HCSB).

LITERARY FEATURES

Genre and Literary Style
An epistle written in Koine Greek

First John is the fourth of seven general epistles in the New Testament, all of which are titled according to their author. This epistle does not have the customary features of an epistle, such as salutation, thanksgiving, or farewell. For this reason, some scholars designate 1 John as a tractate (a formal treatise rather than a pastoral letter). As with the Fourth Gospel, John wrote with a limited vocabulary and a simple style. Also, as with the Gospel, his style lent itself to developing contrasting concepts: love versus hate; light versus dark; life versus death.

Themes
The incarnation of Christ, the messiahship of Jesus, living in light and love

The first two of these themes are doctrinal: what Christians must believe. The last theme is behavioral: how Christians are to live. John taught that true believers cannot continue to live a sinful lifestyle but must live in God's moral light and his holy love. The epistle does not teach "sinless perfection," as the King James Version of 3:9 and 5:18 may appear, but rather that whoever is born of God does not continually practice sin.

Book Features and Structure

The only biblical references by name to the "antichrist" are found in his epistle (and its close companion, 2 John); see 1 John 2:18,22; 4:3; 2 John 7. What is striking in John's teaching is that not only will there come a future antichrist, but that there are already many antichrists present. The essence of the "antichrist spirit" is to deny the essential character of Jesus as God incarnate, the Messiah. Thus, John was more concerned about his readers firmly identifying and rejecting the antichrist spirit active in their own day than in their identifying the future (end-time) antichrist.

The letter is noted for its rambling style, which is reflective of an old saint of God with much wisdom to pass along. This, however, makes it almost impossible to generate a clear outline for the letter. In general, chapters 1–2 focus on walking in the light, while chapters 3–5 focus on living in love.

2 JOHN

THE SECOND EPISTLE OF JOHN

Titled according to its author, this is the second canonical letter by John, the apostle of Jesus.

▶ *Key Text: verse 8*

"Look to yourselves, that we lose not those things which we have wrought, but that we receive a full reward."

▶ *Key Term: "Faithful"*

Although the word *faithful* does not appear, this letter is in essence an encouragement to remain faithful to the truth of the gospel in the face of deceivers.

▶ *One-Sentence Summary*

Those who are faithful to the "doctrine of Christ" know the Father and the Son and will one day be fully rewarded.

▼ Baptismal at Church of St. John at Ephesus.

GOD'S MESSAGE IN THE BOOK

Purpose

Second John was written to combat the same false doctrines that were written about in 1 John. In the first letter the teachings were to be applied to a congregational setting; in the second letter they were applied to a personal family setting.

Christian Worldview Elements

This book directs attention to the worldview categories of *discipleship* and *ethics and morality*. John rejoiced about the children of a Christian woman continuing in Christian discipleship ("walking in truth"), and he strongly urged living according to the love command.

GOD
CREATION
SOVEREIGNTY AND PROVIDENCE
FAITH AND REASON
REVELATION AND AUTHORITY
HUMANITY
REBELLION AND SIN
COVENANT AND REDEMPTION
COMMUNITY AND CHURCH
► DISCIPLESHIP
► ETHICS AND MORALITY
TIME AND ETERNITY

Teachings about God

God is the Father of Jesus and is the one who has issued commands that his children are to live by. Jesus is the Messiah, the Son of the Father, who came "in the flesh." The Holy Spirit is not mentioned.

Teachings about Humanity

This book shows (negatively) that many deceivers and antichrists are out to oppose God's people. It also shows (positively) the great good that one Christian ("the elect lady") can accomplish. See also **Teachings about Humanity** for **1 TIMOTHY**.

Teachings about Salvation

The only teaching directly related to salvation is the crucial importance of the incarnation of the Son of God. Those who deny this doctrine are cut off from salvation (v. 7). Redeemed people "walk in" or "abide in" love and truth as a way of living.

CHRIST IN 2 JOHN

John's key concern in this letter is to affirm that Christ has come in the flesh. John warns his readers not to go beyond this teaching about Christ and not to associate with people who modify this teaching.

GOD'S STORY

When the Events of This Book Happened
Probably in the AD 80s

The only contemporary events the book mentions are the teachings of the heretics. These cannot be dated precisely, but the decade of the AD 80s seems to fit.

How 2 John Fits into God's "Story"

Second John is part of "chapter 5" of God's story: God spreads the kingdom through the church. The kingdom of God is not directly mentioned. However, Jesus is referred to as Christ (Messiah) three times, who is opposed by the antichrist (v. 7). This implies the concept of the kingdom of God set in opposition to all other kingdoms, developed elsewhere in Scripture.

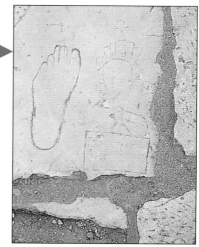

While 1 John was to be applied in a congregational setting, 2 John was addressed to a family setting. Christianity grew in spite of being surrounded by a culture that was governed by values contrary to those articulated in the gospel. Here is a carved paving stone in ancient Ephesus which is probably an advertisement for a house of prostitution.

ORIGINAL HISTORICAL SETTING

Author and Date of Writing
John the apostle, possibly around AD 80–90

This letter claims to be written by "the elder," who is otherwise unnamed. Some have specu-
lated that he was an unknown Christian leader, but the style and content are so much like
1 John that these letters are acknowledged to be written by the same person. Christian
tradition has uniformly asserted that this author was John the apostle. See ***Author and Date
of Writing*** for **JOHN** for more information. Most scholars believe that this epistle was
written somewhat after the Gospel, but it is impossible to be certain. The decade of the AD
80s is a good estimate for the composition of this letter.

First Audience and Destination
An unnamed Christian lady, probably living somewhere in Roman Asia

The letter was written to "the elect lady and her children." She is otherwise unknown, but she
had taught her children to follow the gospel. Since John seems to have known her well ("lady,"
v. 5), she was evidently someone he had met during his ministry, which was centered in
Ephesus. Some have suggested that the congregation addressed generally in 1 John was meeting in the home of "the elect lady." While 2 John certainly fits this reconstruction, there is not
enough data to confirm it.

   Some scholars have proposed that "the elect lady" is a figurative expression to refer to a particular congregation. This does not seem likely since this letter is so evidently parallel to 3 John,
which was written to a named individual.

Occasion

John knew this lady well. He was prompted to write because he had recently become aware
of the excellent Christian reputation of her children (v. 4). They had apparently related to him
facts about a heresy they had faced, identical to the false doctrine facing the recipients of his
first epistle. (See ***Occasion*** for **1 JOHN**.) He penned this letter as a personal note to advise
his friend about the heresy and to urge her to continue in Christian love.

A part of the Roman Harbor Baths and Gymnasium complex excavated at Ephesus.

LITERARY FEATURES

Genre and Literary Style
A brief epistle written in Koine *Greek*

Second John is the fifth of seven general epistles in the New Testament, all of which are titled according to their author. One of the usual features of an epistle (thanksgiving) is missing. There is a salutation (vv. 1-3), a body (vv. 4-11), and a farewell (vv. 12-13). This is a pastoral letter, driven by the occasion and needs of the recipient, rather than a tractate (a formal treatise). The Greek style is identical to that of 1 John.

Themes
The incarnation of Christ; living in truth

As is universal in Scripture, truth in doctrine and truth in living go hand in hand. This little note shows that those who deny Christ's incarnation cannot possibly live faithful lives.

Book Features and Structure

This is the second shortest book in the New Testament, weighing in with only 244 words and 13 verses in the original. (The shortest is 3 John with 219 words and 13 verses.) The body of the letter has two sections. First is John's positive exhortation to walk in Christ's commandments (through v. 6). Second is John's warning about deceivers (from v. 7 to the end).

3 JOHN

THE THIRD EPISTLE OF JOHN

Titled according to its author, this is the third canonical letter by John, the apostle of Jesus.

▶ *Key Text: verse 8*

"We therefore ought to receive such, that we might be fellowhelpers to the truth."

▶ *Key Term: "Truth"*

The word *truth* (Greek, *aletheia*) is used five times. Christians are called on to be committed to "the truth"—and to show hospitality to Christian leaders involved in ministering the truth.

▶ *One-Sentence Summary*

Christians are to recognize and to work for the truth of the gospel, and one way they do this is to show hospitality to Christian ministers that are hard at work.

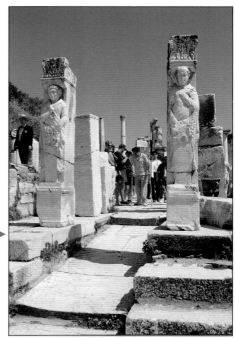

Herakles Gate in Ephesus, the city from which John likely wrote 3 John.

GOD'S MESSAGE IN THE BOOK

Purpose

Third John was written mainly to advise Gaius about his responsibility to receive warmly a group of traveling ministers. Gaius was also warned to beware of a troublemaker (Diotrephes) and to welcome a newcomer (Demetrius).

Christian Worldview Elements

This book directs attention to the worldview categories of *community and church* and *discipleship*. It provides the last picture in the epistles about congregational life and how believers ought to live.

GOD
CREATION
SOVEREIGNTY AND PROVIDENCE
FAITH AND REASON
REVELATION AND AUTHORITY
HUMANITY
REBELLION AND SIN
COVENANT AND REDEMPTION
▶ **COMMUNITY AND CHURCH**
▶ **DISCIPLESHIP**
ETHICS AND MORALITY
TIME AND ETERNITY

Teachings about God

God is mentioned three times (vv. 6,11) as the source of good, not evil, who expects his people to live worthy of him. The essence of God's glory is summarized by calling him "the name." He is not called Father (in contrast to the first two epistles of John). This is the only New Testament book that does not directly mention Jesus Christ, and the Holy Spirit is not referenced.

Teachings about Humanity

This letter is full of contrasts. On one hand, there are several shining examples of what people committed to the truth can accomplish (Gaius, Demetrius, John himself, the traveling ministers). On the other hand, Diotrephes is a negative example of someone who obstructs the truth. See also **Teachings about Humanity** for **1 TIMOTHY**.

Teachings about Salvation

Teaching about salvation is found indirectly by John's constant use of "the truth" (vv. 1,3,4,8,12). "The truth" is evidently his paraphrase for "the gospel of Jesus Christ," thought of in broad terms. This truth is nowhere defined, but its importance is evident.

⳩ CHRIST IN 3 JOHN

John describes a man named Diotrephes who had to be first in everything. This man is the opposite of Christ who humbled himself, became a slave, and suffered an ignominious death. John then urges his readers not to imitate evil but imitate good. Christ is the supreme example of goodness.

GOD'S STORY

When the Events of This Book Happened
Probably in the AD 80s

The contemporary events the book mentions are the travels of the Christian ministers and the activities of certain individuals. These cannot be dated precisely, but the decade of the AD 80s seems to fit.

How 3 John Fits into God's "Story"

Third John is part of "chapter 5" of God's story: God spreads the kingdom through the church. The kingdom of God is not directly mentioned. However, "church" (Greek, *ekklesia*) appears three times (vv. 6,9,10), the only direct references to church in John's letters. Since in the present age local congregations of Christians are manifestations of God's kingdom, the health of churches is of direct concern to the growth of the kingdom.

ORIGINAL HISTORICAL SETTING

Author and Date of Writing
John the apostle, possibly around AD 80–90

See **Author and Date of Writing** for **2 JOHN**.

First Audience and Destination
Gaius, a Christian living in Roman Asia

Gaius is known only through this letter. He was a fine Christian that John loved and knew well ("beloved," v. 5). He probably had leadership responsibility in the congregation that John mentioned in his letter. Where he lived is not known, but it was probably near Ephesus, the place where John lived during his last years.

Occasion
The occasion for this letter is entirely different than the occasion for 1 and 2 John. John had received a report from traveling Christian ministers, who had evidently gone out with his blessing (vv. 3,7). They had told him about Gaius's good ministry and his hospitality to them (v. 5). Yet they reported that Gaius had a question about whether giving such a warm welcome was actually the right thing to do.

Thus, John wrote his friend a short note. In it he commended the practice of showing hospitality for the sake of the gospel. Along the way, he warned about the troublemaker Diotrephes, who had rejected the traveling ministers (vv. 9-10). He also endorsed Demetrius, who was perhaps the letter carrier (v. 12).

The Temple of Hadrian at Ephesus.

LITERARY FEATURES

Genre and Literary Style
A brief epistle written in Koine *Greek*

Third John is the sixth of seven general epistles in the New Testament, all of which are titled according to their author. This letter has all four standard parts of a first-century epistle: salutation (v. 1), thanksgiving (in this letter, a brief petition, v. 2), main body (vv. 3-12), farewell (vv. 13-14). Third John is a pastoral letter, driven by the occasion and needs of the recipient, rather than a tractate (a formal treatise). The Greek style is identical to that of 1 John.

Themes
Welcoming those with the truth, rejecting those without the truth

Since the definition of truth is assumed in this book, its themes are mainly practical. On one hand, ministers of truth are to be recognized and helped whenever possible. On the other hand, those who hinder the truth, especially in a local church, are to be noted and rejected.

Book Features and Structure

This is the shortest book in the New Testament with 219 words in Greek and 13 verses. It is important for the incidental way in which John gave information about his sense of responsibility as an apostle. After more than fifty years of ministry, he was still in the business of giving pastoral care (v. 5) and good advice (v. 12). Even more important was his deliberate awareness that any letter he wrote should be considered authoritative (vv. 9-10). This concept became significant in the second through the fourth centuries when the New Testament canon was being discussed and developed.

The body of the letter has two sections. First is John's positive exhortation to welcome those with the truth (through v. 8). Second is John's warning to those who hinder truth (from v. 9 to the end).

JUDE

THE EPISTLE OF JUDE

This letter is titled according to its author, Jude, who was probably the half brother of Jesus.

 ### Key Text: verse 3

"Beloved, when I gave all diligence to write unto you of the common salvation, it was needful for me to write unto you, and exhort you that ye should earnestly contend for the faith which was once delivered unto the saints."

Key Term: "Contend"

This letter is a reminder that Christians are soldiers in a spiritual warfare. They must "contend" or continue the fight to maintain the truth of the gospel.

One-Sentence Summary

Christians must defend the faith against false teachings and false teachers, and at the same time they must build up their own faith in Christ.

Bab Edh Dhra, believed by many archaeologists to be ancient Sodom and Gomorrah, which "serve as an example by undergoing the punishment of eternal fire" (Jude 7 HCSB).

GOD'S MESSAGE IN THE BOOK

Purpose

Jude was written to condemn false teachers who were trying to persuade Christians that they were free to sin since they had been forgiven and were under God's grace. Jude wanted his readers to oppose this teaching with the truth about God's grace.

Christian Worldview Elements

This book focuses on the worldview categories of *revelation and authority* and *ethics and morality*. It especially emphasizes that God's revealed truth should not be meddled with or changed.

GOD
CREATION
SOVEREIGNTY AND PROVIDENCE
FAITH AND REASON
▶**REVELATION AND AUTHORITY**
HUMANITY
REBELLION AND SIN
COVENANT AND REDEMPTION
COMMUNITY AND CHURCH
DISCIPLESHIP
▶**ETHICS AND MORALITY**
TIME AND ETERNITY

Teachings about God

God is referred to as Father, Savior, and Lord (vv. 1,5,9,25). The grace of God is the attribute that comes to the fore in this book (v. 4). Jesus is also called Lord, and he is the one who keeps his people and brings them to eternal life (vv. 1,21,25). The Spirit, never given to those who reject the truth, enables the prayers of the saints (vv. 19-20).

Teachings about Humanity

Jude shows the great evil of those who are enslaved by falsehood: "raging waves of the sea, foaming out their own shame; wandering stars, to whom is reserved the blackness of darkness for ever" (v. 13). On the other hand, redeemed humanity looks forward to everlasting joy: "Now unto him that is able to keep you from falling, and to present you faultless before the presence of his glory with exceeding joy" (v. 24).

Teachings about Salvation

Jude had intended to write about the "common salvation" of believers, but he wrote instead about false teachers (v. 3). He refers to God as "Saviour" (v. 25). Verse 24 makes clear that salvation is God's doing from start to finish (see also v. 1).

CHRIST IN JUDE

Jude looks to the day when Jesus will reward his followers. He looks from the present perspective, talking about believers being kept for Jesus (v. 1). He knows eternal life is based on Jesus' mercy (v. 21).

GOD'S STORY

When the Events of This Book Happened
Probably in the AD 60s

The only contemporary events the book mentions are the coming of false teachers. These cannot be dated precisely, but the decade of the AD 60s seems to fit.

How Jude Fits into God's "Story"

Jude is part of "chapter 5" of God's story: God spreads the kingdom through the church. The kingdom of God is not directly mentioned. Yet Jude shows great awareness of the history of God's kingdom through time by mentioning a number of men (and angels) involved in God's kingdom activities from ancient times: Enoch, Moses, Michael. He also mentions those opposed to God's kingdom: Cain, Balaam, Korah, and the devil. These references show that there have been opposing camps, from the beginning until Jude's time, and on until God's glory is fully manifested.

View of the Jordan Valley from the top of Mount Nebo, the vicinity of Moses' death. No human knows where Moses died and was buried. Jude alludes to Moses' death: "Yet Michael the archangel, when he was disputing with the Devil in a debate about Moses' body, did not dare bring an abusive condemnation against him but said, 'The Lord rebuke you!'"(Jude 9 HCSB).

ORIGINAL HISTORICAL SETTING

Author and Date of Writing
Jude, perhaps in the AD 60s

The author was "Jude, the servant of Jesus Christ, and brother of James" (v. 1). Jude is the English translation of the Hebrew name *Judah*. (The name *Judas* is identical, *Youdas* in Greek, but most English translators reserve "Judas" for Jesus' betrayer because of the negative connotations of that name.) There were several Judes in the New Testament, but the only one who was James's brother was also the brother of Jesus (Matt. 13:15). He was the son of Mary and Joseph, and, like all Jesus' brothers, had not believed in Jesus until after the resurrection (Acts 1:14). Little is known about him as a Christian leader beyond his authorship of this letter. The decade of the AD 60s fits because of the connection of this epistle with 2 Peter (see **Occasion** below).

First Audience and Destination
Believers living in an unknown location

This letter contains no specific information that permits identification of the first audience. They were Christians that Jude knew well ("beloved," v. 3) and wanted to warn. His quotation of Jewish sources suggests that the recipients were Jewish, but beyond that nothing can be determined.

Occasion

Jude had intended to write on one subject but changed his mind when he learned about dangerous false teachers. They had already infiltrated the congregation, and Jude heaped condemnation on them (v. 13). Their problem was that they were "turning the grace of our God into lasciviousness" (v. 4). This evidently referred to a libertine understanding that God's grace entitles believers to do whatever they want morally without reference to God's commandments. The false teachers were motivated by their own sensual lust and desire for financial gain (v. 16). Thus, Jude wrote this letter of warning. Not only did he attack falsehood; he encouraged these believers to stay true to the faith and to reach out compassionately to those who were tempted to compromise with the false teachers (vv. 20-22).

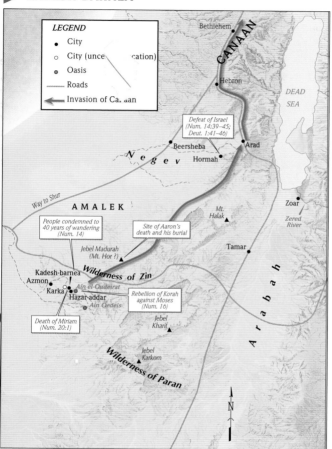

LEGEND
- City
- ○ City (unce... ...cation)
- ● Oasis
- — Roads
- ← Invasion of Canaan

Bethlehem

CANAAN

Hebron

DEAD SEA

Defeat of Israel
(Num. 14:39–45;
Deut. 1:41–46)

Arad

Beersheba

Hormah

N e g e v

Way to Shur

AMALEK

Zoar

Zered River

Mt. Halak ▲

People condemned to
40 years of wandering
(Num. 14)

Site of Aaron's
death and his burial

Tamar

Jebel Madurah
(Mt. Hor ?) ▲

Kadesh-barnea

Azmon

Karka

Wilderness of Zin

Ain el-Qudeirat

Hazar-addar

Ain Qedeis

Rebellion of Korah
against Moses
(Num. 16)

A r a b a h

Death of Miriam
(Num. 20:1)

Jebel Kharif ▲

Jebel Karkom ▲

Wilderness of Paran

N

"The Lord, having first of all saved a people out of Egypt, later destroyed those who did not believe" (Jude 5). Jude's warning points to the wilderness wanderings in the region of Kadesh-barnea where the Hebrews stayed for most of the thirty-eight years after leaving Mount Sinai and before entering the promised land.

LITERARY FEATURES

Genre and Literary Style
An epistle written in Koine Greek

Jude is the last of seven general epistles in the New Testament, all of which are titled according to their author. One of the usual features of an epistle (thanksgiving) is missing, although there is a salutation (vv. 1-2), a body (vv. 3-23), and a farewell (in this letter, a doxology, vv. 24-25). Jude is a pastoral letter, driven by the occasion and needs of the recipients, rather than a tractate (a formal treatise). The Greek style is awkward and is hard to read. (The repetition of the word *ungodly* in v. 15 is an example of the stylistic difficulty.)

Jude quoted noncanonical Jewish sources to back up his arguments, both The Assumption of Moses (v. 9) and 1 Enoch (vv. 14-15). He did not call them Scripture or imply that they were inspired. Rather, he used them as sources of information. The Apostle Paul sometimes used noncanonical sources as well (Acts 17:28; 1 Cor. 15:33; Titus 1:12; 2 Tim. 3:8).

Themes
Contending for the faith, identifying and rejecting what is ungodly

The two themes are complementary. To do one is necessarily to do the other. Forms of the concept ungodliness (Greek, *asebeia*) are used five times (vv. 15,18). This is the opposite of godliness (Greek, *eusebeia*), the **Key Term** for **1 TIMOTHY**.

Book Features and Structure

There is a striking parallel between this letter and 2 Peter 2, both in content and order of presentation. The following may be cited:

- Sinning angels now held captive by God, 2 Peter 2:4; Jude 6
- Divine destruction of Sodom and Gomorrah, 2 Peter 2:6; Jude 7
- False teachers who slander heavenly beings, 2 Peter 2:10; Jude 8
- Balaam as a false prophet, 2 Peter 2:15; Jude 11
- False teachers destined for blackest darkness, 2 Peter 2:17; Jude 13

It is impossible to determine whether Peter used Jude as a source, Jude borrowed from Peter or whether both adapted a common (but now lost) source. Most scholars accept the first alternative, because it seems more likely that a longer letter (2 Peter) would incorporate much of a shorter letter (Jude). (The literary relationship between 2 Peter and Jude is parallel to the literary relationship between Matthew, Mark, and Luke.)

The body of this epistle has two sections. First is Jude's warning about false teachers (through v. 16). Second is Jude's encouragement to pursue the truth (from v. 17 to the end).

REVELATION

THE APOCALYPSE

The first word in the Greek text of this book is *apoakalypsis*, which means "revelation" or "unveiling." Although some English Bibles title it "The Revelation of John," the work is manifestly a revelation to John by Jesus Christ.

▶ *Key Text: 1:7*

"Behold, he cometh with clouds; and every eye shall see him, and they also which pierced him: and all kindreds of the earth shall wail because of him. Even so, Amen."

▶ *Key Term: "Prophecy"*

This book self-consciously calls itself a prophecy at both its beginning and its end (1:3; 22:18-19). It is the only New Testament book that is essentially prophetic.

▶ *One-Sentence Summary*

Jesus the Lord of history will return to earth, destroy all evil and all opposition to him, and bring the kingdom of God to its glorious culmination.

Overview of Patmos, the island in the Mediterranean Sea where John received the Revelation of Jesus Christ.

GOD'S MESSAGE IN THE BOOK

Purpose

This prophetic book originally intended to teach that faithfulness to Jesus ultimately triumphs over all the evils of this world and that Jesus will return to earth as King and Lamb-Bridegroom. God's people who read and study Revelation today should view it with this original purpose in mind.

Christian Worldview Elements

Revelation deals particularly with the worldview categories of *rebellion and sin, ethics and morality,* and *time and eternity.* No Bible book more fully teaches how God is moving time, history, and all creation to the goal he has determined.

GOD
CREATION
SOVEREIGNTY AND PROVIDENCE
FAITH AND REASON
REVELATION AND AUTHORITY
HUMANITY
▶ **REBELLION AND SIN**
COVENANT AND REDEMPTION
COMMUNITY AND CHURCH
DISCIPLESHIP
▶ **ETHICS AND MORALITY**
▶ **TIME AND ETERNITY**

Teachings about God

Revelation teaches the supremacy and glory of God in all things. God is the primary mover who will bring about the return of Christ and the end of the world. The righteous wrath of a holy God is fully displayed in Revelation. The book teaches about the Trinity and contributes greatly to an understanding of the deity of Christ.

Teachings about Humanity

Revelation shows the sinfulness of humans in stark terms. There are only two kinds of people in Revelation: those who follow the Lamb (and bear his special mark) and those who follow the beast (and bear his mark). Those who follow the Lamb are given unimaginably great blessings, but they are a minority. The majority that follows evil is destined for eternal damnation.

Teachings about Salvation

Salvation from sin in Revelation is presented mainly in terms of something God purchased through the death of the Lamb (the first coming of Christ). Those who are saved oppose evil "by the blood of the Lamb, and by the word of their testimony; and they loved not their lives unto the death" (12:11). Final salvation after the resurrection is presented mainly in terms of "the holy city, new Jerusalem" (21:2).

CHRIST IN REVELATION

Christ is the Alpha and the Omega, the first and the last, the one who was coming, is coming, and will come. When he appeared to John on Patmos, the sight was so overwhelming, John fell at his feet like a dead man. Jesus told him not to be afraid but to write down the things he would show him, the things that will take place.

GOD'S STORY

When the Events of This Book Happened
From creation to consummation, but particularly the time of the consummation

Revelation zigzags through time. Although some chronological sequences seem reasonably clear, the visions of the book were not meant to form a seamless story. Revelation includes events from the very beginning (12:4; 17:8) to the first century AD (chaps. 2–3) to the new heavens and new earth (chaps. 21–22). In general, the events through chapter 6 focus on the period up to the "great tribulation," while the things described beginning with chapter 7 seem to belong to the end-time scenario.

How Revelation Fits into God's "Story"

Revelation tells "chapter 6"—the last chapter—of God's story: God consummates redemption and confirms his eternal kingdom. The kingdom theme can hardly be missed. Christ is the victorious King wearing many diadems. He comes and judges the world's people at the end. One of the great announcements in Revelation, near the center of the book is, "The kingdoms of this world are become *the kingdoms* of our Lord, and of his Christ; and he shall reign for ever and ever" (11:15). Revelation shows how the plan of God to bless all nations through the covenant he began with Abraham (Gen. 12) will reach final fulfillment. The kingdom of God inaugurated with Jesus' first coming will be consummated at his second coming.

ORIGINAL HISTORICAL SETTING

Author and Date of Writing
The Apostle John, around AD 95

The book was written by John. He had great authority, even from his place of banishment, the tiny island of Patmos some thirty-five miles out in the Aegean Sea. Most (but not all) early Christian references to the authorship of Revelation affirmed that this was Jesus' apostle of that name. See **Author and Date of Writing** for **JOHN** for more information. Tradition records that John had a long and successful ministry in and around the city of Ephesus during his later life. Some scholars believe the author of Revelation was some other (unknown) John. There is no good reason, however, to deny that the author was indeed the apostle—also the composer of the Fourth Gospel and three epistles.

Revelation originated during a time of Roman persecution of Christians. Some have suggested the last days of the Emperor Nero (ruled AD 54–68) as the time of composition. The severity of the persecution (as well as the spiritual decline of the churches in Revelation 2–3) suggests a later date to most scholars. The last years of Domitian (ruled AD 81–96) are a more likely date for the origin of this book. If this is so, Revelation was the last book of the New Testament to be written.

First Audience and Destination
Persecuted Christians living in seven cities in the Roman province of Asia

The recipients and destination of Revelation were not John's choice. He was following divine orders. This is explicit in Revelation 1:10-11: "I was in the Spirit on the Lord's day, and heard behind me a great voice, as of a trumpet, Saying, I am Alpha and Omega, the first and the last: and, What thou seest, write in a book, and send it unto the seven churches which are in Asia; unto Ephesus, and unto Smyrna, and unto Pergamos, and unto Thyatira, and unto Sardis, and unto Philadelphia, and unto Laodicea." The list follows the order the letter carrier traveled after arriving on the mainland from Patmos.

Occasion

John explained what prompted him to write. While he was exiled on Patmos, the exalted Lord appeared to him and gave him visions that he was instructed to write down. The recipients were Christians living through vicious persecution. All Bible books are inspired by God, but this one, more than any other, bears a sense of divine dictation.

CHURCHES OF THE REVELATION

Chalcedon
Nicomedia
MARMARA SEA
Samothrace
Imbros
Dardanelles
Cyzicus
BITHYNIA AND PONTUS
Nicaea
Abydos
Prusa
Troas
MYSIA
Dorylaeum
Assos
Adramyttium
Lesbos
Mitylene
Cotiaeum
A S I A
Nacoleia
Pergamum
Ancyra
Appia
Thyatira
Hermus R.
Temenothyrae/
Flaviopolis
Chios
Sebaste
Smyrna
Sardis
Philadelphia
LYDIA
Tripolis
PHRYGIA
Apamea
Ephesus
Hierapolis
Samos
Tralles
Laodicea
Samos
Magnesia
Maeander R.
PISIDIA
Ikaria
Trogyllium
Alabanda
Colossae
Miletus
Heraclea
Aphrodisias
Patmos
CARIA
Cibyra

John writes Revelation encouraging Christians to remain faithful.

Halicarnassus
Idyma
PAMPHYLIA
Cos
Cos
Perga
Cnidus
LYCIA
Rhodes
Rhodes
Xanthus
Patara
Myra

MEDITERRANEAN SEA

LEGEND
- • City
- 🏛 Cities of the Seven Churches
- — Major road

28 E   30 E

403

LITERARY FEATURES

Genre and Literary Style
A prophecy composed in Koine *Greek*

Some students of Revelation have classed Revelation as apocalyptic literature. This kind of writing, then popular among Jews, had a number of features: (1) the claim to originate from God through a mediating being, (2) the use of symbolic creatures and actions, (3) conflict between this evil age and the coming age. However, Revelation lacks certain other apocalyptic features: (1) claim to be written by a famous Old Testament character, (2) extensive angelic interpretation, (3) belief that the Messiah was still future.

Revelation is better seen as a prophecy, a message to God's people exhorting them to remain faithful to him. Unlike the apocalyptic literature, Revelation contains serious calls for God's people to repent of sin. Like Isaiah and Jeremiah, it predicts both near and remote future events. The apocalyptic elements are secondary to the book's prophetic message.

The Greek style of Revelation is simple. It is more like the Greek of the fourth Gospel and the three epistles of John than any other part of the New Testament. The book has a number of grammatical peculiarities that make its Greek unusual in places. This may be accounted for by either (1) the author's loss (or change) of a secretary or (2) the author's eagerness to write down his experiences, causing him to write in haste.

Themes
Christ as slaughtered Lamb and conquering King, the second coming, God's sovereignty in history, God's wrath against sin, followers of Jesus overcoming

Revelation's portraits of Jesus show him as a slaughtered Lamb, yet occupying heaven's throne. Further, he is the conquering King who will judge all the world. Christ's return is portrayed in glorious but highly symbolic language. God is clearly in charge of everything that happens, even though he allows evil to have temporary triumphs. Ultimately his wrath against sin is fully poured out. In the face of this, followers of the Lamb are challenged to be faithful overcomers.

Book Features and Structure

Revelation is filled with references to the Old Testament, but John rarely if ever quoted directly. Most of the book is a prophecy, but there are a number of other literary elements. The prologue and epilogue are similar to the New Testament epistles. The seven short letters to individual churches (chaps. 2–3) are clearly epistle-like. Several of the chants or songs are poetry, sometimes like the great poetry of the Old Testament.

Revelation is organized into four great visions, of which the second is the longest. The beginning of each vision is announced with the words "in the Spirit" (1:10; 4:2; 17:3; 21:10), which mean, "I had a new vision brought about by the Spirit."